MANUSCRIPTS
OF THE GREEK BIBLE

MANUSCRIPTS OF THE GREEK BIBLE

An Introduction to Greek Palaeography

BY

BRUCE M. METZGER

George L. Collord Professor of
New Testament Language and Literature
Princeton Theological Seminary

NEW YORK OXFORD
OXFORD UNIVERSITY PRESS

1981

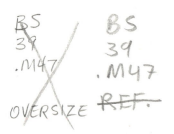

Library of Congress Cataloging in Publication Data

Metzger, Bruce Manning.
Manuscripts of the Greek Bible.

Bibliography: pp. 141–143.
Includes indexes.
1. Bible—Manuscripts, Greek. 2. Palaeography, Greek. 3. Greek language, Biblical. 4. Bible—Manuscripts, Greek—Facsimiles. I. Title.
BS39.M47 220.4′8 80–26205
ISBN 0–19–502924–0

Printing (last digit): 9 8 7 6 5 4 3 2 1

Printed in the United States of America

Preface

THIS book is intended primarily for students of the Greek Bible. Its scope includes manuscripts not only of the Greek New Testament but also of the Greek Old Testament. The latter, though often neglected today, was the Scriptures of the early Christians, and was quoted habitually by Paul and other apostolic writers.

Besides students of the Bible, however, anyone concerned with the Greek classics and their transmission down the centuries will also find something of interest in the following pages. In fact, the importance and utility of palaeography can be appreciated by all who read any literary work from antiquity. Printed books as we know them today have existed for a little over five hundred years, but the writing and publishing of literary works in the Western world began at least twenty-five hundred years ago. The study of palaeography enables us to span the centuries prior to Gutenberg, and makes the literary treasures of antiquity available to the present generation.

Palaeography is of concern also to the historian of art. In every age of the world's history, and to a great extent in some ages, there have been those who took pride in their handwriting and cultivated it to a high degree of excellence. Care given to calligraphy and to the illumination of manuscripts has resulted in the production of deluxe editions fit for the libraries of kings and nobles. Literary works were illustrated with exquisite miniatures, painted in the margins or on separate folios with lovely colors that even after centuries still dazzle the eye. These frequently depict scenes of the Bible, recording both the interest of the passage and the piety of the artist.

Likewise, in terms of practical usefulness for textual criticism, the present volume aims to acquaint the beginner in palaeography with the habits of scribes and the difficulties they faced in copying manuscripts. Such information will enable one to understand and appreciate the reasons for the emergence of variant readings in manuscripts of the Greek Bible.

To this end the Plates in the second part of the book present and illustrate forms of Greek script from the second century B.C. to the fifteenth century A.D. Each of the forty-five manuscripts represented is interesting or important from the view point of palaeography and/or textual criticism of the Greek Bible. Here one will find, to take three or four examples, reproductions of a fragment of Deuteronomy in Greek that contains the sacred name of God (the Tetragrammaton) written in Hebrew letters (Plate 3), a leaf from a copy of the Gospel of Matthew in which

PREFACE

Pilate asks whether he should release *Jesus* Barabbas or Jesus who is called the Christ (Plate 25), a page of Luke's Gospel in which the second petition of the Lord's Prayer is replaced with 'Thy holy Spirit come upon us and cleanse us' (Plate 37), and the earliest manuscript that contains the extra verse in chapter 8 of the Book of Acts (Plate 22). There is also the occasional wry comment or indignant expostulation written in the margin of a manuscript (Plates 28 and 13). Nor have representations been forgotten that provide examples of lectionaries, musical neumes, bilingual texts, and illustrations of Scriptural scenes (for example, Potiphar's wife attempting to seduce Joseph, Plate 20, or the literalistic interpretation of metaphorical language in the Psalms, Plate 27).

Gratitude is expressed to all who have assisted in the production of this volume. It was Henry St. J. Hart, Dean and Tutor at Queens' College, Cambridge, who, more than a decade ago, wrote me suggesting that I should consider putting together an album of life-size facsimiles of New Testament Greek manuscripts. I am particularly indebted to Professor Eric G. Turner of the University of London for reading part one of the book and for making a variety of helpful comments and corrections. With characteristic generosity he also gave me the benefit of his wide palaeographical expertise when more than once I discussed with him certain specimens of Greek hands depicted in part two. Professor Demetrios J. Constantelos of Stockton State College kindly answered my questions concerning Byzantine liturgical manuscripts. Stephen S. Wilburn of the New York office of the Oxford University Press has maintained from the beginning an unfailing interest in the writing and publication of the volume.

The plates have been obtained from a variety of sources. By far the largest number are reproduced from the microfilms assembled over the years by the International Greek New Testament Project and now housed in the archives of the Ancient Biblical Manuscript Center at Claremont, California. Besides the convenience of consultation, the microfilms also offered the opportunity to choose a particular page that provides features of palaeographic and/or textual interest. Other reproductions, particularly of manuscripts of the Greek Old Testament, were made from collections of specimen folios of such manuscripts and, occasionally, from plates in facsimile editions of individual manuscripts. I am grateful to John Joseph Lolla, Jr., for his expertise in handling all such photographic details, and to Michael W. Holmes for assistance in correcting proofs and for compiling the palaeographical index. Figure 2 in the text is reproduced with permission from David Diringer's *The Alphabet* (Hutchinson, London), and Figures 1 and 3 to 8 from B. A. van Groningen's *Short Manual of Greek Palaeography* (A. W. Sijthoff, Leiden). Finally, thanks are due to the several libraries that provided the remaining photographs and that granted permission to reproduce them in this volume.

BRUCE M. METZGER

Contents

PART ONE: GREEK PALAEOGRAPHY

I. Definition and Summary of Research — *page* 3
- §1. DEFINITION — 3
- §2. THE BEGINNINGS OF PALAEOGRAPHY — 3
- §3. MODERN TOOLS FOR PALAEOGRAPHIC RESEARCH — 4

II. The Greek Alphabet — 6
- §4. THE ORIGINS OF THE GREEK ALPHABET — 6
- §5. GREEK NUMERALS — 7
- §6. OFFSHOOTS OF THE GREEK ALPHABET — 10

III. The Pronunciation of Greek — 11
- §7. THE SOUNDS OF GREEK LETTERS — 11
- §8. ACCENT, ORAL AND WRITTEN — 12

IV. The Making of Ancient Books — 14
- §9. THE MATERIALS OF ANCIENT BOOKS — 14
- §10. THE FORMAT OF ANCIENT BOOKS — 15
- §11. PEN, INK, AND OTHER WRITING MATERIALS — 17
- §12. PALIMPSESTS — 18

V. The Transcribing of Greek Manuscripts — 20
- §13. SCRIBES AND THEIR WORK — 20
- §14. STYLES OF GREEK HANDWRITING — 22
- §15. UNCIAL HANDWRITING — 24
- §16. MINUSCULE HANDWRITING — 25
- §17. ABBREVIATIONS AND SYMBOLS — 29
- §18. *Scriptio continua* — 31
- §19. PUNCTUATION — 31

VI. Special Features of Biblical Manuscripts — 33
- §20. THE TETRAGRAMMATON — 33
- §21. *Nomina Sacra* — 36
- §22. HEXAPLARIC SIGNS — 38
- §23. STICHOMETRY AND COLOMETRY — 38
- §24. SUPERSCRIPTIONS AND SUBSCRIPTIONS — 40
- §25. CHAPTER DIVISIONS AND HEADINGS — 40
- §26. THE EUSEBIAN CANON TABLES — 42
- §27. THE EUTHALIAN APPARATUS — 43
- §28. HYPOTHESES — 43
- §29. LECTIONARY EQUIPMENT — 44
- §30. NEUMES — 44
- §31. MINIATURES — 44
- §32. GLOSSES, LEXICA, ONOMASTICA, AND COMMENTARIES — 46

APPENDICES
- I. How to Estimate the Date of a Greek Manuscript — 49
- II. How to Collate a Greek Manuscript — 52
- III. Statistics Relating to the Manuscripts of the Greek New Testament — 54

CONTENTS

PART TWO: PLATES AND DESCRIPTIONS *page* 57
(*For a List of the Plates, see below*)

BIBLIOGRAPHY 141

INDEXES
I. Scripture Passages Shown in the Plates 145
II. Manuscripts Arranged According to their Sigla 145
III. Manuscripts Arranged According to their Present Location 146
IV. Palaeographical Index 147

List of Figures

FIG. 1. Semitic and Greek alphabets *page* 8
FIG. 2. Development of the Greek alphabet 23
FIG. 3. Usual combinations of minuscule letters 27
FIG. 4. Forms of letters in minuscule codices 27
FIG. 5. Combinations of letters in later minuscule codices 27
FIG. 6. Combinations of uncial letters 30
FIG. 7. Combination and superposition of letters 30
FIG. 8. Various abbreviations 30
FIG. 9. The Tetragrammaton in archaic Hebrew letters 34

List of Plates

1. Rahlfs 957. Manchester, John Rylands Library, P. Ryl. 458. *page* 61
2. Rahfls 803. Jerusalem, Palestine Archeological Museum, 7Q1 LXX Ex. 61
3. Rahlfs 848. Cairo, University Library, P. Fouad Inv. 266. 61
4. Gregory–Aland $\mathfrak{p}^{52}$. Manchester, John Rylands Library, P. Ryl. 457. 63
5. Rahlfs 814. New Haven, Yale University, Beinecke Library, P. Yale 1. 63
6. Gregory–Aland $\mathfrak{p}^{46}$. Ann Arbor, University of Michigan, Inv. 6238. 65
7. Gregory–Aland $\mathfrak{p}^{66}$. Cologny-Geneva, Bibliotheca Bodmeriana, Pap. 2. 67
8. Gregory–Aland 0212. New Haven, Yale University, Beinecke Library, Dura Parch. 24. 67
9. Gregory–Aland $\mathfrak{p}^{75}$. Cologny-Geneva, Bibliotheca Bodmeriana, Pap. XIV. 69
10. Rahfls 967. Princeton, University Library, Scheide Pap. 1. 71
11. Rahlfs 962. Dublin, Chester Beatty Library, Pap. V. 73
12. Gregory–Aland 0169. Princeton, Theological Seminary Library, Pap. 5. 73
13. Gregory–Aland B (Codex Vaticanus). Rome, Biblioteca Vaticana, Gr. 1209. 75
14. Gregory–Aland ℵ (Codex Sinaiticus). London, British Library, Add. 43725. 79
15. Rahlfs G (Codex Colberto-Sarravianus). Leiden, University Library, Voss. Gr. Q8. 81
16. Gregory–Aland W (Codex Washingtonianus). Washington, Freer Gallery of Art, cod. 06.274. 83
17. Rahlfs W. Washington, Freer Gallery of Art, cod. Wash. I. 85
18. Gregory–Aland A (Codex Alexandrinus). London, British Library, Royal, I.D.v–viii. 87
19. Gregory–Aland D (Codex Bezae). Cambridge, University Library, Nn.2.41. 90, 91
20. Rahlfs L (Vienna Genesis). Vienna, Nationalbibliothek, Theol. Gr. 31. 93
21. Rahlfs Q (Codex Marchalianus). Rome, Biblioteca Vaticana, Gr. 2125. 95
22. Gregory–Aland E (Codex Laudianus). Oxford, Bodleian Library, Laud. 35. 97
23. Gregory–Aland 047. Princeton, University Library, Garrett ms. 1. 99
24. Gregory–Aland Ψ. Mount Athos, Laura ms. 172 (B′52). 99
25. Gregory–Aland Θ (Koridethi Codex). Tiflis, Inst. Rukop. Gr. 28. 100
26. Gregory–Aland 461 (Uspensky Gospels). Leningrad, State Public Library, Gr. 219. 103
27. Rahlfs 1101 (Khludov Psalter). Moscow, Historical Museum, cod. 129. 103
28. Gregory–Aland G (Codex Boernerianus). Dresden, Sächsische Landesbibliothek, A 145b. 105
29. Gregory–Aland 892. Lodnon, British Library, Add. 33277. 107
30. Rahlfs 1098. Milan, Biblioteca Ambrosiana, O 39 Sup. 109
31. Gregory–Aland S. Rome, Biblioteca Vaticana, Gr. 354. 110
32. Gregory–Aland 1739. Mount Athos, Laura ms. 184 (B′64). 113

CONTENTS

33. Gregory–Aland *l*562. Rome, Biblioteca Vaticana, Gr. 2138. *page* 115
34. Prophetologion. Jerusalem, Greek Patriarchal Library, Saba 247. 117
35. Gregory–Aland 623. Rome, Biblioteca Vaticana, Gr. 1650. 119
36. Gregory–Aland 124. Vienna, Nationalbibliothek, Theol. Gr. 188. 121
37. Gregory–Aland 700. London, British Library, Egerton 2610. 123
38. Gregory–Aland *l*303. Princeton, Theological Seminary Library, 11.21.1900. 125
39. Gregory–Aland *l*809. Sinai, Monastery of St. Catherine, Gr. 286. 127
40. Gregory–Aland 165. Rome, Biblioteca Vaticana, Barb. Gr. 541. 129
41. Gregory–Aland 1922. Florence, Biblioteca Laurenziana, ms. Plut. X. 19. 131
42. Gregory–Aland 2060. Rome, Biblioteca Vaticana, Gr. 542. 133
43. Gregory–Aland 223. Ann Arbor, University of Michigan, ms. 35. 135
44. Gregory–Aland 1022. Baltimore, Walters Art Gallery, ms. 533. 137
45. Gregory–Aland 69. Leicester, Town Museum, Muniment Room, Cod. $\frac{6D32}{1}$ 139

PART ONE

Greek Palaeography

I

Definition and Summary of Research

§1. DEFINITION

PALAEOGRAPHY (παλαιὰ + γραφή) is the science that studies ancient writing, preserved on papyrus, parchment, or paper, occasionally on potsherds, wood, or waxed tablets. Epigraphy deals with ancient inscriptions on durable objects, such as stone, bone, or metal, while numismatics is confined to coins and medals. The distinctions are less superficial than it may seem, for the forms of letters were determined in part by the nature and the size of the material that received them.

Greek palaeography has three aims: first, developing the practical ability of reading and dating the manuscripts; second, tracing the history of Greek handwriting, including not only the form and style of letters, but also such matters as punctuation, abbreviations, and the like; and third, analyzing the layout of the written page and the make-up of ancient book forms (codicology).

§2. THE BEGINNINGS OF PALAEOGRAPHY

PRIOR to the seventeenth century palaeography as a systematic study had not yet come into existence.[1] Confronted with variant readings in ancient manuscripts scholars were content to make *ad hoc* judgments concerning the relative age of documents. The development of palaeography as a discrete discipline had its origin in reaction to charges made in 1675 by the Bollandist scholar Daniel Papebroch denying the authenticity of certain documents constituting the credentials of several Benedictine monasteries. The learned Benedictine monks at St. Maur took up the challenge by founding the science of palaeography. The first treatise to deal with the classification of Latin manuscripts according to their age in the light of handwriting and other internal evidence was the monumental work of the Maurist Jean Mabillon (1632–1707), entitled *De Re Diplomatica* (Paris, 1681; 2 vols., Naples, 1789).

The first scholar who studied Greek palaeography in a systematic way was another Benedictine, Bernard de Montfaucon (1655–1741). Besides producing in fifteen folio volumes a vast work on Greek and Roman antiquities, Montfaucon laid the foundation for the study of Greek manuscripts in his *Palaeographia Graeca, sive de ortu et progressu literarum Graecarum* . . . (Paris, 1708). In this splendid work,

[1] Cf. P. Lehmann, 'Einteilung und Datierung nach Jahrhunderten,' in *Erforschung des Mittelalters*, i (Stuttgart, 1941; reprinted 1959), pp. 114–29; S. Rizzo, *Il lessico filologico degli umanisti* (Rome, 1973), pp. 114–68; Patricia Easterling, 'Before Palaeography: Notes on Early Descriptions and Datings of Greek Manuscripts,' *Studia Codicologica*, ed. by Kurt Treu (Texte und Untersuchungen, cxxiv; Berlin, 1977), pp. 178–87.

still useful on account of the amount of material brought together, 'not only was a new discipline created, but, as it seems, was also perfected.'[2]

During the rest of the eighteenth century and the first part of the nineteenth century no significant advance was made in Greek palaeography.[3] In 1811 Frid. Jas. Bast issued at Leipzig his 'Commentario palaeographica,' bound as an Appendix at the close of Gottfried H. Schaefer's edition of the works of Gregorius Corinthius.[4] Here Bast discusses the forms of individual Greek letters, various compendia, letters designating numerals, and similar matters.

Among nineteenth-century scholars who gave attention to manuscript studies, the most productive by far was Constantine von Tischendorf (1815–1874). Besides undertaking repeated journeys to the Near East in search of Greek manuscripts, Tischendorf worked untiringly in editing the Septuagint, the New Testament (in eight editions), and the text of many apocryphal books. His knowledge of Greek uncial writing was unparalleled, being based upon an examination of some three hundred specimens.

§3. MODERN TOOLS FOR PALAEOGRAPHIC RESEARCH

BEGINNING about the middle of the nineteenth century international scholarship started to give serious attention to the discipline of palaeography and the publication of manuscripts in facsimile reproduction. During the twentieth century, with the development of improved techniques of photography, microfilms of manuscripts have made it virtually unnecessary to travel to far-away libraries in order to consult the documents themselves. Indexes, catalogues, and check-lists are now available to assist the study of all aspects of ancient manuscripts, the most comprehensive being the two volumes entitled *The Palaeography Collection in the University of London Library* (Boston, 1968). Volume 1 is an Author Catalogue, containing an estimated 10,800 cards; volume 2 is a Subject Catalogue, with an estimated 13,100 cards.

The manuscript treasures of the libraries in the Monastery of St. Catherine on Mt. Sinai (founded A.D. 527),[5] in the Greek and Armenian Patriarchates in Jerusalem,[6] and in the monasteries on Mount Athos[7] are now available on 35 mm. negative film at the Library of Congress, Washington, D.C., from which copies

[2] So Viktor Gardthausen evaluates the work, in his *Griechische Palaeographie;* i, *Das Buchwesen im Altertum und im byzantinischen Mittelalter*, 2nd ed. (Leipzig, 1911), p. 7.

[3] A convenient summary of Montfaucon's *magnum opus* was issued under the title *Epitome Graecae palaeographiae*, auctore D. Gregorio Placentinio [Piacentini] (Rome, 1735; reprinted, Milan, 1970).

[4] Being pp. 701–861 of Schaefer's volume.

[5] *Checklist of Manuscripts in St. Catherine's Monastery, Mount Sinai.* Microfilmed for the Library of Congress, 1950. Prepared under the direction of Kenneth W. Clark (Washington, 1952). See also K. W. Clark, 'The Microfilming Projects at Mount Sinai and Jerusalem,' *The Library of Congress Quarterly Journal of Current Acquisitions*, viii, no. 3 (May 1951), pp. 6–12.

[6] *Checklist of Manuscripts in the Libraries of the Greek and Armenian Patriarchates in Jerusalem.* Microfilmed for the Library of Congress, 1949–50. Prepared under the direction of Kenneth W. Clark (Washington, 1953).

[7] *A Descriptive Checklist of Selected Manuscripts in the Monasteries of Mount Athos.* Microfilmed for the Library of Congress and the International Greek New Testament Project, 1952–53. . . . Compiled under the general direction of Ernest W. Saunders (Washington, 1957). Cf. also Ernest W. Saunders, 'Operation Microfilm at Mt. Athos,' *Biblical Archaeologist*, xviii (1955), pp. 22–41.

may be obtained. Besides consulting the checklists of each of these collections, one should not overlook other, smaller collections which are listed in John L. Sharpe's 'Checklist of Collections of Biblical and Related Manuscripts on Microfilm in the United States and Canada.'[8]

What has been described as the most important research tool to be developed in the past fifty years for Greek studies based on manuscripts is the late Marcel Richard's *Répertoire des bibliothèques et des catalogues de manuscrits grecs*, 2nd ed. (Paris, 1958), with *Supplément* I (1958–1963) (Paris, 1964). This provides the titles of some 900 catalogues describing 55,000 Greek manuscripts belonging to 820 libraries or owners, in 415 locations where the manuscripts are at present deposited.[9]

Historical and critical surveys of published research on manuscripts are helpful in obtaining a general overview of the field. Notable among several such bibliographical aids are the surveys in *Bursians Jahresbericht über die Fortschritte der klassischen Altertumswissenschaft*, the most recent being Wilhelm Weinberger's 'Bericht über Paläographie und Handschriftenkunde' in vol. 236 (1932), pp. 85–113. Still more useful for the study of Greek palaeography are the summaries and evaluations prepared by Gérard Garitte, 'Manuscrits grecs, 1940–1950,' in *Scriptorium*, vi (1952), pp. 114–46, and 'Manuscrits grecs, 1950–1955,' ibid., xii (1958), pp. 118–48; and by Jean Irigoin, 'Les manuscrits grecs, 1931–1960,' in *Lustrum*, vii (1962 [1963]), pp. 1–93, 332–5. Garitte lists and comments on 552 items published during the ten-year period and 680 items for the five-year period; Irigoin's comments are somewhat fuller on nearly 350 items published during the thirty-year period.

So far as the Greek manuscripts in the Vatican Library are concerned, a bibliographical tool of considerable usefulness is the wide-ranging volume compiled by Paul Canart and Vittorio Peri entitled, *Sussidi bibliografici per i manoscritti greci della Biblioteca Vaticana* (Studi e testi, 261; Vatican City, 1970), xv+709 pp. This work provides an index to studies of, monographs on, and references to individual Greek manuscripts in the Vatican collections.

For details concerning the papyri of the Greek Bible, including extensive bibliographies, one may consult with profit Kurt Aland's *Repertorium der griechischen christlichen Papyri*; i, *Biblische Papyri* (Berlin and New York, 1976). Broader in scope, but less detailed for each item, is Joseph van Haelst's *Catalogue des Papyrus littéraires juifs et chrétiens* (Paris, 1976), which, besides Biblical papyri, includes patristic texts, liturgical and private prayers, magical texts, and Latin texts.[10]

[8] *Scriptorium*, xxv (1971), pp. 97–109. Sharpe's list may now be supplemented with Paul Canart, 'Les inventaires spécialisés de manuscrits grecs,' *Scriptorium*, xxiv (1970), pp. 112–16.

[9] For plans to put the information contained in Richard's *Répertoire* into a computer data-bank at the University of Toronto, see W. M. Hayes in *Studia codicologica*, ed. by Kurt Treu (Texte und Untersuchungen, cxxiv; Berlin, 1977), pp. 231–35.

[10] For a detailed review of both Aland's and van Haelst's volumes, with rather extensive corrections for both, see T. C. Skeat, *Journal of Theological Studies*, n.s. xxix (1978), pp. 175–86.

II

The Greek Alphabet

§4. THE ORIGINS OF THE GREEK ALPHABET

Down to about the end of the fifth century B.C., there was no common alphabet recognized by all Greek city-states, but each had its own local variety.[11] Although certain elements were common to all, there were differences as to form, significance, and order of letters. Eventually the Ionic alphabet of twenty-four letters came to supplant the epichoric alphabets. At Athens, where twenty-one letters were commonly used, it was decreed in 403 B.C. that in the future all public acts should be inscribed in Ionic characters. Within a very few years all the other city-states that used non-Ionic alphabets followed the lead of Athens.

According to a widespread tradition, the invention of the Greek alphabet is ascribed to Cadmus, the son of Agenor king of Phoenicia. The semi-legendary account tells how Cadmus, in the fourteenth century B.C., settled in Boeotia, bringing with him an alphabet that comprised sixteen letters.[12] In support of the essential truth of this tradition one can point to (*a*) the fact that the name Cadmus is undoubtedly derived from a common Semitic root which means 'an Easterner' (cf. Hebrew קֶדֶם), and (*b*) the testimony of Herodotus (*Hist.* v.58 and 59), who calls the letters of the Greek alphabet 'Cadmean letters' (Καδμήϊα γράμματα) and 'Phoenician letters' (Φοινικήϊα γράμματα).

Quite apart from such considerations, however, further support is found in the circumstance that (*c*) the names of many of the Greek letters are pure Semitic words,[13] and (*d*) the letters stand in the sequence of the Northwest Semitic alpha-

[11] See L. H. Jeffery, *The Local Scripts of Archaic Greece; A Study of the Origins of the Greek Alphabet and its Development from the Eighth to the Fifth Centuries B.C.* (Oxford, 1961); Benedict Einarson, 'Notes on the Development of the Greek Alphabet,' *Classical Philology*, lxii (1967), pp. 1–24, with 'Corrigenda and Addenda,' pp. 262 f.; *Das Alphabet. Entstehung und Entwicklung der griechischen Schrift*, ed. by Gerhard Pfohl (Darmstadt, 1968); and Joseph Naveh, 'The Greek Alphabet, New Evidence,' *Biblical Archaeologist*, xliii (1980), pp. 22–25.

[12] Concerning Cadmus and the origins of the Greek alphabet, see Rudolf Pfeiffer, *History of Classical Scholarship, from the Beginning to the End of the Hellenistic Age* (Oxford, 1968), pp. 19–24, and Ruth Blanche Edwards, 'Greek Legends and the Mycenaean Age, with Special Reference to Oriental Elements in the Legend of Kadmos,' unpublished Ph.D. dissertation, University of Cambridge, 1968, esp. pp. 218–24. A revised version of Dr. Edwards's research is to be published through A. M. Hakkert under the title, *Kadmos the Phoenician: A Study in Greek Legends and the Mycenaean Age.*

[13] The names currently used of other Greek letters arose at a later date, and are of Greek derivation. The ancient name of *epsilon* was εἶ, but when the sound of the diphthong αι could no longer be distinguished from that of ε, schoolmasters found it necessary to designate ε by the epithet ψιλόν ('simple'). Similarly the ancient name of *upsilon* was ὖ, but when the sound of ου could no longer be distinguished from it, schoolmasters again made use of the same epithet. Furthermore, the name ὦ μέγα, in distinction from ὂ μικρόν, is of relatively recent origin; the earliest firm reference cited by Liddell-Scott-Jones (the work *Partitiones*, attributed to Ælius Herodianus, is spurious and of unknown date) is the *Canones* drawn up by the grammarian Theognostus in the ninth century; cf. Klaus Alpers, *Theognostos* Περὶ ὀρθογραφίας. *Überlieferung, Quellen und Text der Kanones 1–84* (Diss., Heidelberg, 1964), p. 91, lines 25 f. One is therefore not greatly surprised that in

bet. The names[14] that are nearly or entirely identical include ἄλφα = *aleph*, βῆτα = *beth*, θῆτα = *teth*, ἰῶτα = *yod*, κάππα = *kaph*, λάμ(β)δα = *lamed*; μῦ = *mem*, νῦ = *nun*, πεῖ (later πῖ) = *pe*, ταῦ = *tau*.

Semites wrote (and still write) from right to left. This was also the direction in which at an early stage Greeks used to write—as stated by Pausanius (v.25.9, ἐπὶ τὰ λαιὰ ἐκ δεξιῶν) and as corroborated in several very ancient Greek inscriptions. Subsequently there followed a transition period, that of writing in the βουστροφηδόν style ('turning as the ox [ploughs]'), in which the first line is right to left, the second left to right, and so on, alternating.[15] By the beginning of the fifth century B.C. the left to right style had become customary, and it is rare to find a βουστροφηδόν inscription after 500 B.C.

A change in the direction of writing at the same time altered the form of the letters: written from left to right they reproduce the original form as seen in a mirror. Even a cursory comparison of the forms of the several alphabets in Fig. 1 (see p. 8) shows that in many cases the shapes and values of the letters are remarkably similar.

In ancient times the Greek alphabet had three other letters, which eventually fell out of common use. (1) The letter ϝ, called *waw* or *digamma* (i.e. 'double gamma,' from its shape), stood after ϵ and corresponded to the Hebrew letter ו (*w*). (2) The letter ϙ or ϟ, *koppa*, stood after π and corresponded to the Hebrew letter ק (emphatic *q*). In the course of time, because spoken Greek did not require such sounds, *waw* and *koppa* were discarded as letters, the former by the eighth century B.C., and the latter by the sixth century B.C. Both continued to be employed, however, along with (3) the letter ϡ *sampi*, as numerals, *waw* then often having the alternative form ϛ.

§5. GREEK NUMERALS

THE letters of the Greek alphabet, supplemented with the three supernumerary letters, were used since at least the third century B.C. as numerals.[16] The first nine

Rev. 1:8, 11; 21:6; and 22:13 Ἐγώ εἰμι τὸ ἄλφα καὶ τὸ ὦ is read by all of the approximately 250 manuscripts of that book except two of very recent date (Gregory–Aland 1775, A.D. 1847, and 2077, A.D. 1685), which read ὠμέγα. In the late fourth-century poem entitled 'De litteris monosyllabis Graecis ac Latinis' (no. xiii in Ausonius's *Technopaegnion*), the meter indicates that ϵ, υ, and ω are each pronounced as monosyllables; cf. A. E. Gordon, *The Letter Names of the Latin Alphabet* (Berkeley, 1973), pp. 22 f., and (for *omega*) Eberhard Nestle in *Philologus*, lxx (1911), pp. 155 f.

[14] The names of Semitic letters are formed in accord with the acrophonic principle: every sound was represented by the picture-symbol of a particular word which had that sound as an initial characteristic (whether syllable or letter). Thus, the word *aleph* means an ox, and the original drawing of an ox (i.e. an ox's head) is later modified to ⊀ (see Fig. 1, cols. 1 and 2). *Beth* means house, drawn ⊏⊐ , thence formalized into 9 and ultimatedly turned round and closed into our B. *Mem* means water, and the representation of its ripple 〰 can still be seen in all symbols for M, including our own. Cf. P. Kyle McCarter, Jr., *The Antiquity of the Greek Alphabet and the Early Phoenician Scripts* (Harvard Semitic Monographs, ix; Missoula, 1975), and G. R. Driver, *Semitic Writing from Pictograph to Alphabet*, newly rev. ed. by S. A. Hopkins (London, 1976), especially pp. 171–9 and 266–9.

[15] On *boustrophēdon* writing see Ernst Zinn, 'Schlangenschrift,' *Archäologischer Anzeiger* (Beiblatt zum Jahrbuch des Deutschen Archäologischen Instituts, lxv-lxvi [1950–51]), cols. 1–36; reprinted by Gerhard Pfohl, op. cit. (footnote 11 above), pp. 293–320.

[16] On the earliest uses of alphabetic numerals in Greek, see Lloyd W. Daly, *Contributions to a History of Alphabetization in Antiquity and the Middle Ages* (Brussels, 1967), pp. 11 f., with further references. For a general discussion, see W. F. Richardson, 'The Greek Number System,' *Prudentia*, ix (1977), pp. 15–26.

1
2
3
4
5
6
aleph
beth
gimel
daleth
he
waw
zayin
heth
teth
yod
kaph
lamed
mem
nun
samekh
'ayin
pe
sadhe
qoph
resh
shin
tau

FIGURE 1. Semitic and Greek alphabets

Col. 1 gives the Semitic names; col. 2, the characters written in the inscription of Mesha, king of Moab (±850 B.C.); col. 3, the usual (square) Hebrew characters; col. 4, old Greek letters, mainly from the isle of Thera, written from right to left; col. 5, the same, written from left to right; col. 6, the normal Attic characters.

letters of the alphabet stood for the digits, the obsolete *digamma* being retained for 6, and the remaining letters for tens and hundreds, the obsolete *koppa* being retained for 90, and the obsolete *sampi* for 900.

Written with a tick or a horizontal line above the letter to indicate that it is to be taken as a numeral, the letters of the alphabet have the following values:

α′ = 1	ξ′ = 60
β′ = 2	ο′ = 70
γ′ = 3	π′ = 80
δ′ = 4	ϙ′ or ϟ′ = 90
ε′ = 5	ρ′ = 100
ϝ′ or ϛ′ = 6	σ′ = 200
ζ′ = 7	τ′ = 300
η′ = 8	υ′ = 400
θ′ = 9	φ′ = 500
ι′ = 10	χ′ = 600
κ′ = 20	ψ′ = 700
λ′ = 30	ω′ = 800
μ′ = 40	ϡ′ = 900
ν′ = 50	͵α = 1000
	etc.

Because the letters of a Greek word can also carry a numerical value, it is possible to assign a number to any proper name by adding together the numerical equivalents of the several letters. Thus, according to Rev. 13:18 the number of the beast is 666; that is, 666 is the total of the numerical values of the letters comprising the name of the beast.

By employing this system, called gematria, both orthodox and heretical Christians were able to 'prove' the most astounding statements. For example, the author of the second-century *Epistle of Barnabas* uses gematria to show that Jesus Christ is in the Book of Genesis. Referring to the narrative about Abraham, who took 318 men with him in an attempt to rescue his nephew Lot from the clutches of King Chedorlaomer and the other kings of the plain (Gen. 14:14), the author declares (in 9.8) that this number is equivalent to 300 and to 18—and we must acknowledge that he is correct thus far. Then he 'discovers' that 300 is represented by T, which reminds him of the cross with its outstretched cross-bar, and that 18 is equivalent to ιη, the first two letters of the Greek name Ἰησοῦς (see Plate 5). *Ergo*, hidden in the first book of the Old Testament one finds a representation of Jesus on the cross! Many a Church Father, including even St. Augustine, was intrigued by this edifying tidbit, not considering that in the days of Abraham the Greek alphabet was not yet in existence.

§6. OFFSHOOTS OF THE GREEK ALPHABET

THE Greek alphabet occupies a unique place in the history of writing. On the one hand, it transformed the consonantal Semitic script into a modern alphabet, and gave it symmetry and art. On the other hand, its subsequent influence on non-Greek peoples, chiefly through early translations of the Scriptures, has been immense. The Coptic alphabet, used by Christians in Egypt since the second century, consists of thirty-one letters, twenty-four borrowed from the Greek uncial script and seven taken over from a more cursive variety of the demotic script to express sounds not existing in Greek. In the fourth century Bishop Ulfilas created for his Gothic translation of the Bible an alphabet of twenty-seven letters, some nineteen or twenty being taken over from uncial Greek script. In the fifth century St. Mesrop, with the help of a Greek hermit and calligrapher, Rufanos of Samosata, produced the Armenian alphabet of thirty-six letters, several of which show Greek influence. In the ninth century Sts. Cyril and Methodius, in order to translate the Bible into Old Church Slavonic, devised the Glagolitic alphabet of forty letters, taking as a model for many of them the increasingly flamboyant Greek minuscule script of his day. Soon afterward another Slavic alphabet came into being, the Cyrillic, containing forty-three characters, of which twenty-four are derived from Greek uncial script. It is used today by the Bulgarians, the Serbs, the Ukrainians, and the Russians. Thus, the Greek alphabet, having exerted also an indirect influence upon the Etruscan and the Latin alphabets, became the progenitor of almost all European alphabets.

III

The Pronunciation of Greek

§7. THE SOUNDS OF GREEK LETTERS

THE Greek language has had an unbroken literary history from Homer to the present day. During this span of nearly three millennia, many changes have taken place, not least in pronunciation. Modern Greek has lost, besides pitch accent and vowel variety, a number of the inflectional forms of the ancient language, but is still not far removed from it. It is divided into Romaic, or the common speech (δημοτική), and Neo-Hellenic or *katharevousa* (καθαρεύουσα), which seeks to preserve ancient forms and idioms. Although Demosthenes or Plato, for example, could probably have read and understood fairly well a book published in Neo-Hellenic, the pronunciation of it as well as of the modern spoken vernacular differs almost totally from that of ancient Greek.

The question may be raised just how scholars can determine the approximate pronunciation of classical Greek. The answer is that several kinds of evidence provide a certain amount of information bearing upon this matter.[17]

(1) There are occasional statements concerning pronunciation made by ancient authors, particularly grammarians.

(2) Plays on words may serve to show similar pronunciation. For example, Macrobius tells us that the Emperor Augustus, having learned that Herod the Great had arranged for the murder of more than one of his sons, coined the pun, 'It is better to be Herod's pig (ὗν) than his son (υἱόν)' (*Saturnalia* ii.4.11).

(3) The sounds made by animals are sometimes reported in ancient Greek authors. For example, in some fragments of Attic comedy the bleating of sheep is represented by βῆ βῆ (which was certainly not pronounced *vee vee* as in modern Greek).

(4) Representations of Greek proper names in other languages, particularly in bilingual glossaries, provide considerable assistance.

(5) Comparative Indo-European linguistics enables scholars to trace kinship among related words. For example, the verb οἶδα ('I have seen,' hence 'I know') was at one time pronounced with the initial letter *waw* (ϝοῖδα), as is shown by the similar sounding words in Latin (*video*), Gothic (*witan*), German (*wissen*), and Anglo-Saxon (*witan*; compare English 'to wit').

[17] Cf. Edgar H. Sturtevant, *The Pronunciation of Greek and Latin*, 2nd ed. (Philadelphia, 1940; reprinted, Groningen, 1968); W. B. Stanford, *The Sound of Greek; Studies in the Greek Theory and Practice of Euphony* (Sather Lectures, 1966; Berkeley, 1967) [with accompanying phonograph recording]; W. S. Allen, 'Varia onomatopoetica,' *Lingua*, xxi (1968), pp. 1–11; and idem, *Vox Graeca; A Guide to the Pronunciation of Classical Greek*, 2nd ed. (Cambridge, 1974).

(6) Metrical patterns in non-Attic poetry reveal the retention of traditional pronunciation of certain words even after the spelling had been modified. According to Allen, in Homer an original ϝ accounts in some 2,300 cases for absence of elision as well as for other so-called irregularities of meter.[18]

§8. ACCENT, ORAL AND WRITTEN

It is generally acknowledged that in classical Greek accent was basically one of pitch ('tonal accent') rather than one of stress ('dynamic accent'). It is thought that the difference between the pitch of the syllable bearing the accent and that of syllables which did not was approximately a musical fifth, say C to G or do to sol. (The absolute level of the voice's pitch was not, of course, fixed and would vary with changing moods and from person to person.)

According to tradition it was Aristophanes of Byzantium (*c.* 257–180 B.C.), successor to Eratosthenes as head of the Alexandrian Library, who devised the several accent and breathing marks in order to help increasing numbers of foreigners learn how to pronounce Greek. He used the acute mark, called ὀξύς ('sharp, acute'), to denote a rise in pitch, and the grave mark, called βαρύς ('heavy, grave'), to denote a fall in pitch. The circumflex denoted a rise followed by a fall in pitch.

The change from a tonal to a stress accent in Greek cannot be precisely dated. It seems clear that it had taken place by the latter part of the second century A.D., when Clement of Alexandria composed hymns in meters based on stress accentuation. How much earlier the change had occurred and how pervasive it was we do not know.[19]

The rough (⊢) and the smooth (⊣) breathing marks (πνεύματα) at first represented the left and the right half of the letter H, which in the Old Attic alphabet indicated aspiration. Before long they became respectively ˪ and ˩ and eventually (in the eleventh century) these forms became the rounded ʽ and ʼ familiar to us today. Only occasionally are marks of breathing found in the more ancient manuscripts, and then it is generally the rough breathing that is indicated (see Plates 9 and 11). In modern Greek the rough breathing, though written, is disregarded in pronunciation.

When Greek was written for native Greek readers, or for those who were well acquainted with the language, accent and breathing marks were not normally used (any more than we indicate the accent when writing ordinary English). In papyri and the earlier uncial manuscripts marks of this sort are rare and sporadic. By about the seventh century scribes tend to introduce accent and breathing marks in greater numbers, and by the ninth century they are universally used in uncial and minuscule manuscripts. Double accent marks (acute or grave) are sometimes used to distinguish the particles μέν and δέ (see Plate 33).[20] Double dots

[18] Allen, *Vox Graeca*, p. 46; cf. also p. 48.

[19] Cf. C. M. Knight, 'The Change from the Ancient to the Modern Greek Accent,' *Journal of Philology* (Cambridge), xxxv (1919–20), pp. 51–71.

[20] For double accents, see pp. 482–4 in the comprehensive discussion of Moritz Reil, 'Zur Akzentuation griechischer Handschriften,' *Byzantinische Zeitschrift*, xix (1910), pp. 476–529.

(the diaeresis) are frequently employed to help the reader pick out ι or υ (see Plates 4, 7, and 9).

In the course of the development of koine Greek several vowels and diphthongs came to be pronounced alike.[21] Eventually in the early Byzantine period (as also in modern Greek) the vowels η, ι, and υ and the diphthongs ει, οι, and υι were all pronounced like long e in English (the substitution of one of these vowels or diphthongs for another is called itacism). Likewise, ο and ω, as well as αι and ε (see Plate 5), were not sharply distinguished in pronunciation. As a consequence, scribes were liable to make mistakes in the spelling of words that now were pronounced alike. Thus, ἡμῶν // ὑμῶν (1 John 1:4), ἔχομεν // ἔχωμεν (Rom. 5:1), ἔρχεσθαι // ἔρχεσθε (Luke 14:17), and νῖκος // νεῖκος (1 Cor. 15:54) have been confused by scribes who wrote one word while intending to write the other.

In classical Greek the use of the *nu*-moveable (ν ἐφελκυστικόν) in order to avoid hiatus and elision was restricted to certain grammatical categories (words ending in –σι; to the third person singular in –ε; and to ἐστί). In later Greek the use of *nu*-moveable was much extended by scribes, who introduced it at very many places contrary to the rule that it should be used only before a vowel or pause.

[21] Besides occasional references in grammars of New Testament Greek, see A. H. Foster, 'The Pronunciation of Greek in New Testament Times,' *Anglican Theological Review*, v (1922–23), pp. 108–15.

IV

The Making of Ancient Books

§9. THE MATERIALS OF ANCIENT BOOKS

THE materials most widely used for making books in Graeco-Roman antiquity were papyrus and parchment. Of the two, papyrus was by far the more highly regarded. 'Civilization—or at the very least, human history—depends on the use of papyrus,' remarked the Roman antiquarian Pliny the Elder describing the method of manufacture of this writing material.[22] In his day no fewer than nine varieties in size and grade of papyrus sheets were available in the marketplace.

Papyrus is an aquatic plant of the sedge family that grew abundantly in the shallow waters of the Nile in the vicinity of the delta. When mature the plant, which resembles a stalk of corn (maize), was harvested and the stem cut into sections twelve to fifteen inches in length. Each of these was split open lengthwise and the core of pith removed. After the pith was sliced into thin strips, these tape-like pieces were placed side by side on a flat surface, and another layer placed crosswise on top. The two layers were then pressed firmly together until they formed one fabric—a fabric which, though sometimes so brittle now that it can be crumbled into powder, once had a strength equal to that of good, hand-made paper.[23]

Somewhat more durable as writing material was parchment.[24] This was made from the skins of sheep, calves, goats, antelopes, and other animals. The younger the animal, the finer was the quality of skin. Vellum was the finest quality of extra-thin parchment, sometimes obtained from animals not yet born. After the hair had been removed by scraping, the skins were washed, smoothed with pumice, and dressed with chalk. Before the parchment sheet was used for writing, the horizontal lines as well as the vertical margins were marked by scoring the surface

[22] 'Cum chartae usu maxime humanitas vitae constet, certe memoria,' *Natural History*, xiii, 21 (68); cf. also Karl Dziatzko, *Untersuchungen über ausgewählte Kapitel des antiken Buchwesens; mit Text, Übersetzung und Erklärung von Plinius*, Nat. Hist. xiii, §68–69 (Leipzig, 1900); Alfred Lucas, *Ancient Egyptian Materials and Industries*, 4th ed. (London, 1962), pp. 137–40; Ian V. O'Casey, *The Nature and Making of Papyrus* (Barkston Ash, Yorkshire, 1973); and Naphtali Lewis, *Papyrus in Classical Antiquity* (Oxford, 1974).

[23] On the relatively great durability of papyrus, see T. C. Skeat, 'Early Christian Book-Production,' *The Cambridge History of the Bible*, vol. 2, *The West from the Fathers to the Reformation*, ed. G. W. H. Lampe (Cambridge, 1969), pp. 59 f.

[24] The word 'parchment' is derived from the name Pergamum, a city of Asia Minor (cf. Rev. 2:19). Pliny the Elder (*Nat. Hist.* XIII.xxi.68–xxvii.83) tells us that rivalry between King Ptolemy of Egypt and King Eumenes of Pergamum in enlarging their respective libraries prompted the former to put an embargo on the export of papyrus, whereupon the Pergamenes 'discovered' parchment. Actually, however, parchment had been used as writing material long before the altercation reported by Pliny. Cf. Karl Lüthi, *Das Pergament. Seine Geschichte, seine Anwendung* (Bern, 1938); R. R. Johnson, 'Ancient and Medieval Accounts of the "Invention" of Parchment,' *California Studies in Classical Antiquity*, iii (1970), pp. 115–22; Ronald Reed, *Ancient Skins, Parchments, and Leathers* (Studies in Archaeological Sciences; London and New York, 1972); and idem, *The Nature and Making of Parchment* (Leeds, 1975).

with a blunt-pointed instrument drawn along a rule. It was sufficient to draw the lines on one side of the sheet (usually the flesh-side), since they were visible also on the other side. In many manuscripts these guide lines can still be noticed, as also the pinpricks that the scribe made first in order to guide him in ruling the parchment. Different schools of scribes employed different procedures of ruling, and occasionally it is possible for the modern scholar to identify the place of origin of a given manuscript by comparing its ruling pattern (as it is called) with those in other manuscripts whose place of origin is known.[25]

Vellum intended for deluxe volumes, perhaps as presentation copies to royalty, would be dyed a deep purple and written with gold and/or silver ink (see Plate 20). Ordinary books were written with black or brown ink (§11) and sometimes had decorative headings and initial letters[26] colored with blue or yellow or (most often) red ink—whence the word 'rubric,' from *ruber*, the Latin word for 'red.'

The advantages of parchment over papyrus for the making of books seem obvious to us today. It was somewhat tougher and more durable than papyrus, which deteriorates faster in a damp climate. Moreover, parchment leaves could receive writing without difficulty on both sides, whereas the vertical direction of the fibers on the verso side of a sheet of papyrus may have made that side less satisfactory than the recto as a writing surface. Finally, parchment had an advantage over papyrus in that it could be manufactured anywhere.

On the other hand, parchment also had its disadvantages. For one thing, the edges of parchment leaves are liable to become puckered and uneven. Furthermore, according to the observation of Galen,[27] the famous Greek physician of the second century A.D., parchment, which is shiny, strains the eyes of the reader more than does papyrus, which does not reflect so much light.

During the Middle Ages the Arabs learned the technique of making paper from rags. Although less strong than parchment or vellum, paper was more supple and cheaper. By the twelfth and thirteenth centuries paper manuscripts became more and more numerous.

§10. THE FORMAT OF ANCIENT BOOKS

THERE were two main forms of books in antiquity. The older form was the roll. This was made by fastening sheets of parchment or papyrus together side by side, and then winding the long strip around a dowel of wood, bone, or metal, thus producing a volume (a word derived from the Latin *volumen*, meaning 'something

[25] Kirsopp and Silva Lake identify 175 ruling patterns in their *Dated Greek Minuscule Manuscripts to the Year 1200 A.D.* (Monumenta Palaeographica Vetera, First Series, Parts I–x; Boston, 1934–1939); this number is increased to 800 patterns in J. Leroy, *Les Types de réglure des manuscrits grecs* (Paris, 1976). Cf. also Leroy, 'La description codicologique des manuscrits grecs de parchemin,' in *La paléographie grecque et byzantine* (Paris, 1977), pp. 27–44.

[26] For decorated letters see C. Franc-Sgourdéou, 'Les initials historiées dans les manuscrits byzantines aux XIe–XIIe s.,' *Byzantinoslavica*, xxviii (1967), pp. 336–54, and especially Carl Nordenfalk, *Die spätantiken Zierbuchstaben*, 2 vols. (Stockholm, 1970).

For examples of decorated initials in the present volume, see Plates 33 and 40.

[27] *Opera*, iii, p. 776, and xviii, p. 630 (ed. C. G. Kühn).

rolled up'). The writing was placed in columns, each about 2½ to 3½ inches wide, running at right angles to the length of the writing surface. Usually only one side of the writing surface was utilized.

The maximum average length of such a roll was about thirty-five feet;[28] anything longer became excessively unwieldy to handle. Ancient authors therefore would divide a lengthy literary work into several 'books,' each of which could be accommodated in one roll.

The other common form of books in antiquity was the codex, or 'leaf-book.' This was made from either parchment or papyrus in a format resembling modern books. A certain number of sheets,[29] double the width of the page desired, were stacked on top of one another and folded down the middle. It is obvious that a given number of sheets will produce twice the number of leaves and four times the number of pages. The system of four sheets/eight leaves/sixteen pages eventually became the standard format, and from the Latin word *quaternio*, meaning 'a set of four,' was derived the English word 'quire'—which has come to be used (against its etymology) for a gathering, whatever the number of sheets.

At first, most codices were made in single-quire format.[30] The disadvantages of such a format are obvious. Besides being pudgy and somewhat clumsy to use, a single-quire codex tends to break at the spine. Furthermore, if the book is to have an even appearance when it is closed, it must be trimmed along the fore-edge, and this results in the pages at the middle of the book being narrower than those on the outside. For these reasons scribes eventually found it to be more advantageous to assemble a number of smaller quires and to stitch them together at the back.

There was an art connected with the manufacture of such codices. Since the hair-side of parchment is slightly yellower in color than the flesh-side, the aesthetically-minded scribe was careful to place the sheets in such a way that wherever the codex was opened the flesh-side of one sheet would face the flesh-side of another sheet, and the hair-side face hair-side. Similarly, in making a papyrus codex careful scribes would assemble sheets of papyrus in such a sequence that the direction of the fibers of any two pages facing each other would run either horizontally or vertically.[31]

[28] So F. G. Kenyon, 'Book Division in Greek and Latin Literature,' *William Warner Bishop, A Tribute*, ed. by Harry M. Lydenberg and Andrew Keogh (New Haven, 1941), pp. 63–75; esp. p. 68.

[29] The sheets for a papyrus codex were usually obtained by cutting them to a given size from a long roll of papyrus writing material, the roll having been previously manufactured by gluing together sheets of a standard size (*kollemata*). Today the joins (*kolleseis*) from the roll of material are sometimes visible in the pages of a codex. See James M. Robinson's detailed discussion, 'On the Codicology of the Nag Hammadi Codices,' *Les textes de Nag Hammadi . . .*, ed. by Jacques-É. Ménard (Leiden, 1975), pp. 15–31; idem, 'The Manufacture of the Nag Hammadi Codices,' *Essays on the Nag Hammadi Texts in Honour of Pahor Labib*, ed. by Martin Krause (Leiden, 1975), pp. 170–90; and idem, 'The Future of Papyrus Codicology,' *The Future of Coptic Studies*, ed. by Robert McL. Wilson (Leiden, 1979), pp. 23–70, esp. 23–27.

[30] For a list of single-quire codices, see Eric G. Turner, *The Typology of the Early Codex* (Philadelphia, 1977), pp. 58–60.

[31] On recto and verso in manuscripts, see E. G. Turner, *The Terms Recto and Verso; the Anatomy of the Papyrus Roll* (Actes du XVe Congrès International de Papyrologie, Première Partie; Papyrologica Bruxellensia, 16; Brussels, 1978).

It is obvious that the advantages of the codex form of book greatly outweigh those of the scroll. The Church soon found that economy of production (since both sides of the page were used) as well as ease when consulting passages (no need to unroll the more cumbersome scroll) made it advantageous to adopt the codex rather than the scroll for its sacred books. It may be, also, that the desire to differentiate the external appearance of the Christian Bible from that of Jewish scrolls of the synagogue was a contributing factor in the adoption of the codex format.[32]

In the present volume Plates 1, 2, and 3 show fragments from rolls; the fragment in Plate 8 may be from a roll; all the other Plates reproduce pages, or portions of pages, from codices.

§II. PEN, INK, AND OTHER WRITING MATERIALS

FROM time immemorial the Greeks wrote on parchment and papyrus with a reed (κάλαμος or δόναξ), sometimes also with a tiny brush. When the stalk of the reed had been thoroughly dried, one end of it was sharpened to a point and slit into two equal parts. We first hear of the quill pen in the fifth or sixth century A.D., but no doubt it was in use before that.

The ink (μέλαν) used by Greek scribes for writing on papyrus was a carbon-base ink, black in color, made from soot, gum, and water. Since this kind of ink did not stick well to parchment, another kind was devised. One recipe for this second kind used nut-galls (oak-galls). These were pulverized and then water was poured over the powder. Sulfate of iron was afterward added to it, as well as gum arabic. By the fourth century after Christ this type of ink tended to supersede carbon-based ink even for writing on papyrus. Nut-gall ink in the course of time takes on a rusty-brown color. The chemical changes it undergoes may, in fact, liberate minute quantities of sulphuric acid that can eat through the writing material (see Plate 20).

Other colors of ink were also used. Titles, first lines of chapters, and even whole manuscripts were sometimes written with red ink. This was made from minerals, either cinnabar (κιννάβαρις) or minium (μίλτος). Purple ink (πορφύρα) was made of a liquid secreted by two kinds of gastropods, the murex and the purpura.

The writing on some vellum manuscripts is in silver and/or gold letters. The vellum of these codices is often purple, but sometimes it is white. Such *editions de luxe* were costly and valuable, and they were usually intended for great dignitaries of church and state. Purple manuscripts that have survived include uncial copies of the Gospels dating from the sixth century (Gregory–Aland O, N, Σ, Φ, and 080)

[32] See Peter Katz, 'The Early Christians' Use of Codices instead of Rolls,' *Journal of Theological Studies*, xliv (1945), pp. 63–5. For a different view see Saul Lieberman, *Hellenism in Jewish Palestine* (New York, 1950), Appendix on 'Jewish and Christian Codices,' pp. 203–8, and for a list and discussion of nearly one hundred pre-Constantinian Biblical papyri, see E. A. Judge and S. R. Pickering, 'Biblical Papyri prior to Constantine: Some Cultural Implications of their Physical Form,' *Prudentia*, x (1978), pp. 1–13, especially pp. 5 ff.

and the ninth century (*l*36), and minuscule copies from the ninth and tenth centuries (565 and 1143 respectively). In a remarkable copy of the Gospels dating from the fourteenth century, which once belonged to the Medicis (Gregory–Aland 16), the general run of the narrative is written in vermillion; the words of Jesus and angels are crimson and occasionally in gold; the words quoted from the Old Testament and those spoken by the disciples are blue; and, finally, the words of the Pharisees, Judas Iscariot, and the devil are black.

Besides pen and ink, other implements used by ancient and mediaeval scribes included a ruler or straightedge (*κανών*) and a stylus (*γραφίς*) or a thin lead disk (*κυκλομόλιβδος*) for drawing lines on the parchment; a pair of compasses (*διαβήτης*, *καρκίνοι*) for keeping the lines equidistant from each other; a sponge (*σπόγγος*) for making erasures and for wiping off the point of the pen; a piece of pumice stone (*κίσηρις*) for smoothing the nib of the pen as well as roughnesses on the papyrus or parchment; a penknife (*γλύφανος* or *σμίλη*) to sharpen the pen; and an inkstand (*μελανοδόκον* or *μελανοδοχεῖον*) to hold the ink.

§12. PALIMPSESTS

SOMETIMES the parchment of a manuscript was used a second (or even a third) time. Particularly during a period of economic recession, when the cost of writing materials increased, an older, worn-out volume would be used again. The original writing was scraped and washed off, the surface re-smoothed, and the new literary material written on the salvaged pages. Such a manuscript is called a palimpsest, which means 'rescraped' (from *πάλιν* and *ψάω*). Several processes have been used in the attempt to read the almost totally obliterated underwriting. In the nineteenth century certain chemical reagents (such as ammonium hydrosulphide) were employed to bring out traces of the ink remaining in the parchment. The twentieth century has seen the use of the ultra-violet lamp and, still more recently, the vidicon camera, which acquires an image of very, very faint writing in digital form, records it on magnetic tape, and then reproduces it by an electro-optical process.[33]

One of the half-dozen or so most important parchment manuscripts containing portions of the Old and New Testaments in Greek is such a palimpsest. Its name is codex Ephraemi rescriptus, dating from the fifth century.[34] In the twelfth century it was erased and many of the sheets rewritten with the text of a Greek translation of thirty-eight treatises or sermons by St. Ephraem, a Syrian Church Father of the fourth century. (This is not the only instance when sermons have

[33] For a description of the last-mentioned process, see John F. Benton, Alan R. Gillespie, and James M. Soha, 'Digital Image-Processing Applied to the Photography of Manuscripts, with Examples Drawn from the Pincus MS of Arnald of Villanova,' *Scriptorium*, xxxiii (1979), pp. 40–55.

[34] The under-writing was deciphered and edited by Tischendorf (Leipzig, 1843) before the invention of the ultra-violet lamp. For a list of additions and corrections gained by the use of such a lamp, see Robert W. Lyon, 'A Re-Examination of Codex Ephraemi Rescriptus,' *New Testament Studies*, v (1958–59), pp. 260–72. J. Harold Greenlee has given attention to the under-writing of nine other fragmentary New Testament manuscripts (namely 0103, 0104, 0132, 0134, 0135, 0209, 0245, 0246, and 0247); see his *Nine Uncial Palimpsests of the Greek New Testament* (Studies and Documents, vol. xxxix; Salt Lake City, 1968).

covered over the Scripture text!) Sometimes the under-writing of palimpsests was not thoroughly expunged, and in these cases, particularly when it happens to stand between the columns of the upper writing, one can decipher it without undue difficulty (see Fig. 9 and Plate 30).

The palimpsesting of manuscripts came to be prohibited by the Church. Among the canons passed by the Trullan Synod (A.D. 592) for the Quinisext Ecumenical Council, the 68th canon forbids the sale of old manuscripts of the Scriptures to *βιβλιοκάπηλοι* ('book dealers'), or *μυρεψοί* ('perfumers'), or to any person whatever.

V

The Transcribing of Greek Manuscripts

§13. SCRIBES AND THEIR WORK

PRIOR to the invention of printing with movable type in the middle of the fifteenth century, each copy of every piece of literature was produced by hand—a long and painstaking task, fraught with possibilities of introducing accidental changes into the text. Books were expensive, for it would take many weeks or even months to finish a handwritten copy of a literary treatise of considerable length.

Something of the drudgery of copying can be appreciated from the colophons, or notes, that scribes not infrequently appended at the close of their handiwork. A typical example, found in many non-Biblical manuscripts, expresses relief: 'As travellers rejoice to see their home country, so also is the end of a book to those who toil [in writing].' Other manuscripts close with an expression of gratitude: 'The end of the book—thanks be to God!' A traditional colophon that occurs in more than one manuscript of the ancient classics describes the physiological effects of copying: 'Writing bows one's back, thrusts the ribs into one's stomach, and fosters a general debility of the body.' In an Armenian manuscript of the Gospels a scribal note complains that a heavy snow-storm was raging outside, and that the scribe's ink froze, his hand became numb, and the pen fell from his fingers.

Along with such colophons reflecting the difficulties and drudgery of copying manuscripts, there are others that express the scribe's feeling of satisfaction at having created an immortal work. A frequently occurring colophon is the couplet:

ἡ μὲν χεὶρ ἡ γράψασα σήπεται τάφῳ·
γραφὴ δὲ μένει εἰς χρόνους πληρεστάτους.

('The hand that wrote [this] moulders in a tomb, but what is written abides across the years [lit. to fullest times]').[35]

Christian scribes, for the most part monks under the supervision of a prior (ἡγούμενος), often make reference to their unworthiness, describing themselves with such derogatory epithets as 'least,' 'the very least,' 'poor,' 'wretched,' 'thrice wretched,' 'unprofitable,' 'the most clumsy of all men,' 'a sinner,' 'a sinner of all sinners,' 'the greatest of sinners,' and the like.[36] Not infrequently the scribe will add a prayer to God or Christ to have mercy upon him (see Plates 26, 32, 39, and 43).

[35] Cf. Gérard Garitte, 'Sur une formule des colophons de manuscrits grecs,' *Collectanea Vaticana in honorem Anselmi M. Card. Albareda*, i (Vatican City, 1962), pp. 369–91, who lists fifty-one examples of the colophon. Supplements to Garitte's list were made by St. Y. Rudberg, *Scriptorium*, xx (1966), pp. 66 f.; K. Treu (who added 52 items), ibid., xxiv (1970), pp. 56–64; and J. Koder, ibid., xxviii (1974), p. 295.

[36] For other epithets of depreciation, see C. Wendel, 'Die ταπεινότης des griechischen Schreibermönches,' *Byzantinische Zeitschrift*, xliii (1950), pp. 259–66.

Two modes of producing manuscripts were in common use in antiquity. According to one procedure, an individual would procure writing material and make a new copy, word by word and letter by letter, from an exemplar of the literary work desired. It was inevitable (as anyone can see who tries to copy by hand an extensive document) that accidental changes would be introduced into the text as it was transmitted by successive generations of copyists.

The accuracy of the new copy would, of course, depend upon the degree of the scribe's familiarity with the language and content of the manuscript being transcribed, as well as upon the care exercised in performing the task. In the early years of the Christian Church, marked by rapid expansion and consequent increased demand by individuals and by congregations for copies of the Scriptures, the speedy multiplication of copies, even by non-professional scribes, sometimes took precedence over strict accuracy of detail. But even for the best trained and most conscientious scribe, the likelihood of error was compounded by certain features of ancient writing. In uncial Greek script certain letters resemble other letters, and if the exemplar was worn and the condition of the ink poor, one can understand that a scribe might easily confuse the letters ε, θ, ο, and c. Such confusion, in fact, accounts for the variant readings *ὅς* and *θεός* (oc and $\overline{\text{θc}}$; see §21) in 1 Tim. 3:16. In 2 Pet. 2:13 the variant readings ΑΠΑΤΑΙC and ΑΓΑΠΑΙC are palaeographically very similar. If λ is written too close to another λ, the two can be mistaken for ᴍ—which accounts for the variant readings *ἅμα* and *ἀλλά* in Rom. 6:5. The question whether Justus, mentioned in Acts 18:7, was surnamed Titius or Titus depends on whether one reads ΤΙΤΙΟΥΙΟΥCΤΟΥ or ΤΙΤΟΥΙΟΥCΤΟΥ. The collocation of letters is made still more confusing by the presence of ΟΝΟΜΑΤΙ immediately preceding the name.

Another possible source of error would confront the scribe when two adjacent or nearly adjacent lines of writing in the exemplar happened to end with the same word or sequence of letters. In such circumstances the scribe, in looking back to the exemplar, might inadvertently omit the intervening line or lines. (In technical language, such an error arises from parablepsis, occasioned by homoeoteleuton, or the 'similar ending' of lines.) In 1 John 2:23 the Textus Receptus, following the later manuscripts, lacks the words *ὁ ὁμολογῶν τὸν υἱὸν καὶ τὸν πατέρα ἔχει*—an error that arose when the eye of the scribe mistakenly passed from the words *τὸν πατέρα ἔχει* in the first half of the verse to the same three words at the close of the verse.

The other mode of producing books was that followed at a scriptorium. Here a lector (*ἀναγνώστης*) would read aloud, slowly and distinctly, from the exemplar while several scribes seated about him would write, producing simultaneously as many new copies as there were scribes at work.[37] Although it increased produc-

[37] Cf. T. C. Skeat, 'The Use of Dictation in Ancient Book-Production,' *Proceedings of the British Academy*, xlii (1956), pp. 196 ff.

During the Middle Ages scribes would write while seated at a desk or table; in antiquity, on the other hand, it appears that they wrote either while seated and holding the writing material on their knee or lap or sometimes while standing and holding a writing tablet in their hand. For discussions see B. M. Metzger, 'When Did Scribes Begin to Use Writing Desks?' *Historical and Literary Studies, Pagan, Jewish, and Christian* (Leiden and Grand Rapids, 1968), pp. 123–37, and

tivity, dictation also multiplied the types of errors that could creep into a text. A particular source of trouble arose from the circumstance that certain vowels came to be pronounced alike. For example, as was mentioned earlier (§8), in the course of time the pronunciation of the Greek pronouns of the first and second persons plural became indistinguishable. Consequently, in the New Testament it is sometimes difficult or impossible to decide on the basis of divergent evidence in the manuscripts which form was originally intended by the author.

On the whole, however, many such errors in transcription would be caught by the *διορθωτής* ('corrector') of the scriptorium, who inspected for accuracy the finished work of individual scribes. The corrector's work in a manuscript is usually revealed by different handwriting, different ink, and the 'secondary' placing of his work in relation to the principal handwriting. Deletions may be indicated by enclosing a passage in round brackets; by cancelling a letter or letters by means of a stroke drawn through them; by placing a dot ('expunging dot') above, or below, or to either side; or by a combination of these methods (see Plates 7, 33, and 37).

§14. STYLES OF GREEK HANDWRITING

BASICALLY there were two kinds of Greek handwriting and several kinds of letters. The book-hand was the more elegant and formal script, customarily employed for literary works; the cursive-hand was the everyday script, ordinarily used for nonliterary documents such as letters, accounts, petitions, deeds, receipts, and the like. The variety of cursive hands was well-nigh infinite; the nonliterary papyri testify to this in a most eloquent way.[38]

According to the terminology used by many (though not all[39]) palaeographers, there were four kinds of Greek letters—capitals, uncials, cursives, and minuscules (see Fig. 2). Capitals, characterized by angularity and straight lines, are used in inscriptions, being cut or engraved on some hard substance, such as stone or metal. Each letter is made separate and distinct from every other letter. Uncials are a modification of capitals, in which curves are freely introduced as being more readily inscribed with a pen on parchment or papyrus. For example, ΣE in capitals is written cϵ in uncials. Both capitals and uncials are written as though bounded between two horizontal lines that determine the height and the size of the letters, with only one or two projecting above or below. This 'bilinear' quality is particularly noticeable in the calligraphic production of Bibles, in which scribes maintained an extraordinary evenness of script from the first page to the last.

G. M. Parássoglou, 'Δεξιὰ χεὶρ καὶ γόνυ. Some Thoughts on the Positions of the Ancient Greeks and Romans When Writing on Papyrus Rolls,' *Scrittura e civiltà*, iii (1979), pp. 5–21.

38 Referring to Latin hands, E. A. Lowe aptly remarks, 'Cursive script is to calligraphy what dialect is to literary diction' ('Handwriting,' in *The Legacy of the Middle Ages*, ed. by C. G. Crump and E. F. Jacob [Oxford, 1938], p. 205).

39 Among present-day palaeographers who do not accept the traditional terminology are Guglielmo Cavallo, who uses 'majuscules' for the category usually called 'uncials,' and E. G. Turner, who restricts the use of 'uncial' to Latin palaeography (in accord with the explicit testimony of Jerome; cf. his *Praef. in Lib. Iob*, Migne, *Patrologia Latina*, xxviii, col. 1142) and uses the term 'capital' for all ancient Greek handwriting in which 'each letter is made by itself, for itself, and stands alone, i.e. is unligatured' (letter dated 22 November 1978).

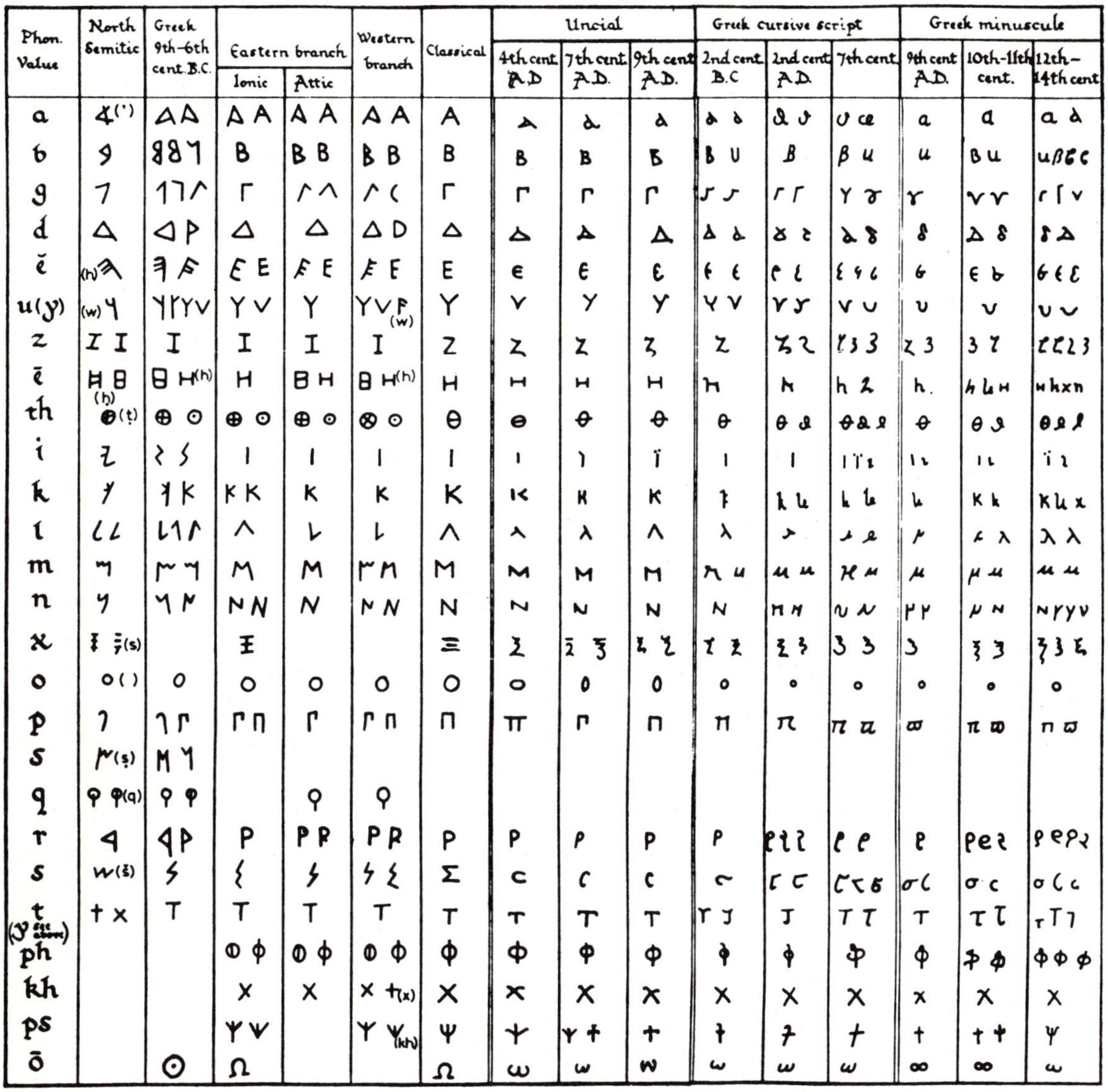

Phon. Value
North Semitic
Greek 9th–6th cent. B.C.
Eastern branch
Ionic
Attic
Western branch
Classical
Uncial
4th cent. A.D.
7th cent. A.D.
9th cent. A.D.
Greek cursive script
2nd cent. B.C.
2nd cent. A.D.
7th cent.
Greek minuscule
9th cent. A.D.
10th–11th cent.
12th–14th cent.
a
b
g
d
ĕ
u(y)
z
ē
th
i
k
l
m
n
x
o
p
s
q
r
s
t
ph
kh
ps
ō

Figure 2. Development of the Greek alphabet

For daily use this way of writing took too much time, and at an early date cursive writing developed from the uncial and continued to be used concurrently with it. Besides being more convenient, cursive letters were often simplified as well as combined when the scribe would join two or more together without lifting the pen (ligature). At the beginning of the ninth century a special form of the cursive was developed which came almost immediately into widespread use for the production of books, supplanting uncial hands (see §16).

It must be borne in mind that most of the books of the New Testament were originally not intended for publication, and others were meant for only a limited circle of readers. It is understandable, therefore, that the original of, say, one of the New Testament Epistles would have been written in a cursive form of script, quite different in appearance from the earliest known copies of that Epistle which are extant today.

§15. UNCIAL HANDWRITING

FROM the fourth century B.C. till the eighth or ninth century A.D. the book-hand changed very slowly and often harked back to earlier styles. During a given period more than one style of book-hand was in use, and the transition from one style to a new one always lasted at least one generation (see p. 50).

What Schubart called *Zierstil*, or 'decorated style' with serifs and roundels,[40] developed in the second and first centuries B.C. (see Plate 2); it continues to turn up in succeeding centuries at least as late as the third century A.D.[41]

The style of writing called Biblical Uncial or Biblical Majuscule—though its use is by no means confined to copies of the Bible—takes its name from its resemblance to the stately hands of the great Biblical codices, Vaticanus, Sinaiticus, and Alexandrinus (Plates 13, 14, and 18). Of all styles of ancient handwriting this one attained the greatest fixity of form. The *upsilon* regularly and the *rho* often extend below the line.

From about the fifth century A.D. the vertical strokes of writing became thicker and in ρ, υ, φ, and ψ longer, while the horizontal or sloping strokes of Γ, Δ, ε, Ζ, Κ, Π, C, and Τ often acquired heavy dots or serifs at their ends. The mute iota is seldom written; when it does occur, it is, of course, written adscript.

[40] Wilhelm Schubart, *Griechische Palaeographie* (Munich, 1925; reprinted, 1966), pp. 22 and 97 ff. Turner, however, questions whether the presence of serifs and decorative roundels without further discrimination is adequate to characterize a style (E. G. Turner, *Greek Manuscripts of the Ancient World* [Oxford and Princeton, 1971], p. 25). For a description of various kinds of decorative appendages, see André Bataille, *Pour une terminologie en paléographie grecque* (Paris, 1954), pp. 39–40.

[41] The extended currency of this style of handwriting for several centuries B.C. and A.D. casts doubt on O'Callaghan's attempt to date certain Greek papyrus fragments from Qumran Cave VII to about A.D. 50. See José O'Callaghan's '¿Papiros neotestamentarios en la cueva 7 de Qumrân?' *Biblica*, liii (1972), pp. 91–100 (English trans. by Wm. L. Holladay, Supplement to *Journal of Biblical Literature*, xcii, no. 2 [June, 1972]), followed by several other articles and a book entitled *Los papiros griegos de la cueva 7 de Qumrân* (Madrid, 1974). Furthermore, O'Callaghan's identification of the contents of the fragments as New Testament has found little or no support (see p. 62 below, note 1). His views have been carried to quite unjustifiable conclusions by David Estrada and William White, Jr., *The First New Testament* (Nashville, 1978).

The sixth and seventh centuries saw the development of a hand commonly called the Coptic Uncial[42]—though Gardthausen[43] objected to the nomenclature. Characteristic of this hand are formal rounded letters of large size, and *omega* often has an elongated central shaft.

As time went on, the style of uncial writing began to deteriorate. It lost the grace of the earlier specimens; sometimes it was written with a marked slope to the right, and sometimes the strokes were heavy and cumbersome. The circular letters ϵ, θ, ο, c became oval, and often were laterally compressed, thus appearing narrow in proportion to their height (see Plate 31). Breathing and accent marks, at first only sporadically employed, came to be used more regularly in the ninth century and thereafter (see §8).

In its final development in the tenth and eleventh centuries, uncial writing reverted from the slanting to the upright position but lost none of its exaggerated and pictorial quality. In this form it is known as Slavonic Uncial (since the Slavs took most of their alphabet from it) and was reserved chiefly for liturgical books.

§16. MINUSCULE HANDWRITING

THE uncial hand had a long and distinguished history, which extended over a period of about 1500 years. It was superseded for the writing of books by a special form of cursive letters developed at the close of the eighth or beginning of the ninth century. This minuscule script was a small book-hand that could be written more rapidly as well as more compactly, thus saving both time and parchment. The credit for initiating this reform in Greek handwriting has been commonly attributed to the scholarly monks at the monastery of the Studion at Constantinople,[44] but more recently it has been argued that the perfecting of the minuscule script for book production was the work of humanistic scholars who were involved in the revival of Greek culture at Constantinople during the second epoch of iconoclasm (A.D. 814–42).[45]

This modified form of the current cursive hand became popular among scribes throughout the Greek world almost at once, though some liturgical books continued for a few centuries to be written in the more stately uncial hand. Thus, Greek manuscripts generally fall into two rather well-defined groups, the earlier being written in uncials and the later in minuscules. The minuscule manuscripts

[42] For a list of sixty-one examples (including twenty-nine Biblical texts) of manuscripts that are written in the Coptic uncial, see Jean Irigoin, 'Onciale grecque de type copte,' *Jahrbuch der österreichischen byzantinischen Gesellschaft*, viii (1959), pp. 29–51. For other examples of Coptic uncial, see Turner, *Greek Manuscripts*, p. 126, addenda to no. 47.

[43] Op. cit. (footnote 2 above), ii, pp. 249 f.

[44] T. W. Allen, 'The Origin of the Greek Minuscule Hand,' *Journal of Hellenic Studies*, xl (1920), pp. 1 ff. For the rules drawn up by the Abbot Theodore to guide monks at the Studion in Constantinople while they copied manuscripts, see Migne, *Patrologia Graeca*, ic, cols. 1733–1758, esp. 1739 f.; cf. also Eugène Marin, *De Studio coenobio Constantinopolitano* (Paris, 1897), and Alice Gardner, *Theodore of Studium; His Life and Times* (London, 1905).

[45] So Bertrand Hemmerdinger, *Essai sur l'histoire du texte de Thucydide* (Paris, 1955), pp. 33–39.

of the New Testament outnumber the uncial manuscripts by about eight to one.[46]

The earliest dated minuscule Greek manuscript known today was written A.D. 835, probably in Constantinople, and contains the four Gospels (see Plate 26). The script is by no means novel or experimental in character. The letters are regular and well-formed, and there can be little doubt that this type of handwriting was in use for some time before A.D. 835—perhaps for more than half a century. However, no examples of minuscule writing that can be plausibly ascribed to this period have been preserved—or at least identified.

Unlike uncial hands, in minuscule script the letters are often combined according to certain rules. Most letters may be connected on both sides; several, however, may be joined only on one side. Thus, ζ, ι, ν, ξ, ο, ρ, φ, and ω may be joined only to the preceding letter, and ϵ, η, κ, and σ only with the following. (See Fig. 3; it should be mentioned that these differences refer only to the pure minuscule forms and do not take into account an occasional chance connection of letters.) It goes without saying that a letter, which may itself be connected, is never linked to a letter that admits of no connecting. That is the reason that υ stands unconnected in the word *οὐκ*, though in sequences it may by nature be linked on both sides. The spaces, therefore, in this kind of writing are often the result of the nature of the letters, and are not a means of separating the words in order to make reading easier. At the same time, however, one can notice over the centuries a tendency among scribes more and more frequently to separate words within a line.

It has been customary to classify minuscule manuscripts into three or four periods. According to Thompson,[47] followed by van Groningen[48] and (essentially) by Hatch,[49] they fall into the following four classes:

(I) *Codices Vetustissimi*—those written in the ninth century and in the first half of the tenth;

(II) *Codices Vetusti*—those that date from the middle of the tenth to the middle of the thirteenth century;

(III) *Codices Recentiores*—those that were copied sometime between the middle of the thirteenth to the middle of the fifteenth century;

(IV) *Codices Novelli*—those which were produced after the invention of printing with moveable type (*c.* 1456).

[46] For statistics concerning the several categories of Greek manuscripts of the New Testament, as well as information as to their location, see Appendix III, pp. 54 ff. below.

As for the Greek Old Testament, according to information kindly supplied by Prof. Robert Hanhart, Director of the Göttingen Septuaginta Project (letter dated 24 February 1979), the number of all known manuscripts of the LXX is about 2050 (excluding lectionary texts and commentary-manuscripts, which cannot always be clearly differentiated from catena-manuscripts), of which about 1745 are listed in Alfred Rahlfs, *Verzeichnis der griechischen Handschriften des Alten Testaments* (Göttingen, 1914). In this index all manuscripts—uncials, minuscules, and papyri—are included in a single numerical sequence, which has several gaps to allow for additions.

[47] *An Introduction to Greek and Latin Palaeography* (Oxford, 1912), p. 220.

[48] *Short Manual of Greek Palaeography*, 3rd ed. (Leiden, 1963), p. 34.

[49] In *Facsimiles and Descriptions of Minuscule Manuscripts of the New Testament* (Cambridge, Massachusetts, 1951), p. 20, Hatch adopts the fourfold classification but divides the second and third periods at the year 1200.

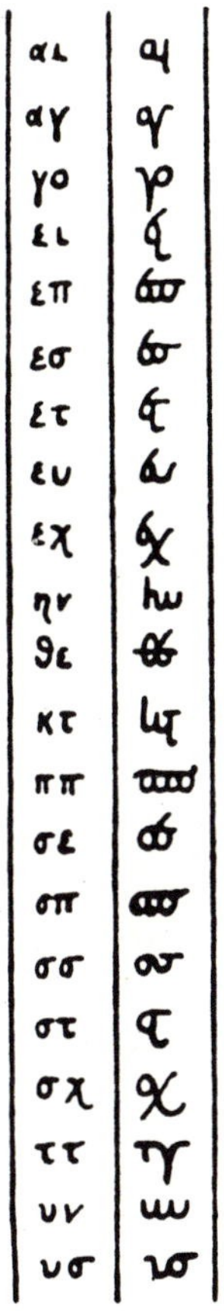

FIGURE 3.

Usual combinations of minuscule letters.

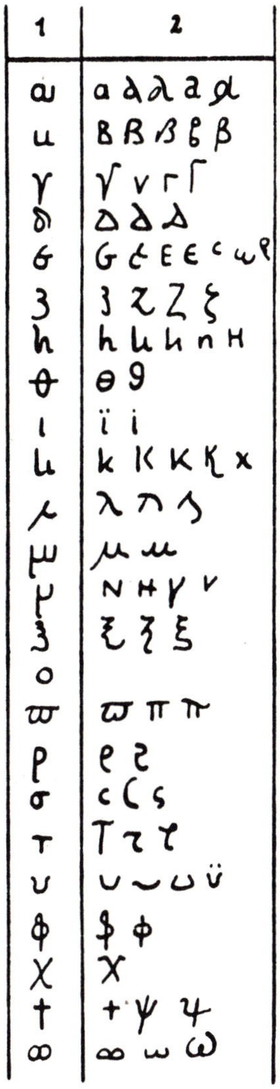

FIGURE 4.

Forms of letters in minuscule codices. Col. 1 gives the pure forms, used in the vetustissimi codices; col. 2, altered minuscules, in cursive and uncial forms.

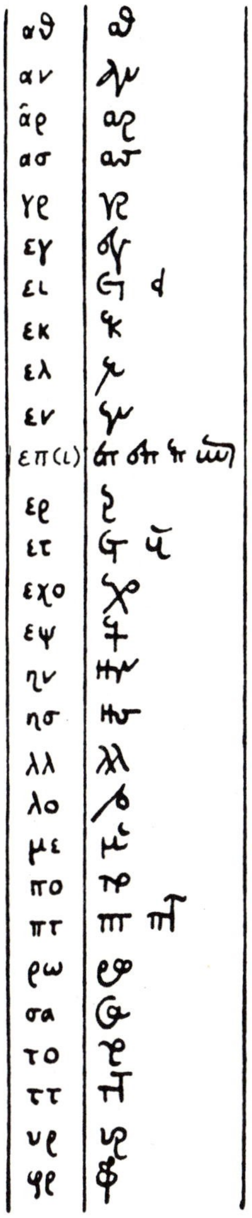

FIGURE 5.

Combinations of letters used in later minuscule codices.

During the first period well-nigh all minuscule manuscripts excel in the extraordinary regularity and care with which they are written. The letters stand upright, sometimes inclining a little to the left, and are practically identical in height (see Fig. 4). Only square breathing marks are used, and the silent iota in the so-called improper diphthongs is (when represented at all) written adscript. Only occasionally do scribes combine two or more letters into what are called ligatures.

The second period is characterized by an increased variety of handwriting, some varieties slanting to the right. The letters are generally pendant from the line; the breathing marks are sometimes square, sometimes rounded. Iota adscript occurs, especially in the first half of the period, and iota subscript is found in codices of the twelfth century. Uncial forms of letters, which seem to have been consciously avoided in the early part of the first period, begin to find their way back in greater numbers, and new ligatures are devised (see Fig. 5). Several distinctive types of hands were developed in this and in the following period, to which palaeographers have given names in accord with their characteristic features (such as 'Perlschrift,' 'Fettaugenmode' (!), 'minuscule bouletée,' 'en as de pique').[50]

The third period also displays much diversity of handwriting. In some cases the writing is neat and regular in appearance, and in others it is irregular and more or less difficult to read. A turn for the worse seems to have come after A.D. 1204, the date of the fourth crusade, when the Latins captured Constantinople. Scribes are capricious in the use of diverse forms of the same letter. They frequently use uncial forms of the letters ϒ, λ, ϵ, ʜ, θ, ɴ, and ϲ, though minuscule forms also occur. Furthermore, in both cases often a tall and a short variety will be used, with several special shapes when entering into ligatures—many of which are themselves new. The iota adscript is very rare. As the result of rapid copying (chiefly of non-Biblical texts) accents and abbreviations are sometimes linked directly with the letters themselves; for example, the acute accent is merely a stroke starting from the vowel and pointed upward, while breathing and accent are composite. Scribes often make quasi-abbreviations by writing some letters above others (see §17). In all this it is difficult to trace any logical development, as each scribe seems to have his own peculiar usage, sometimes founded upon an ancient model, sometimes quite eclectic.

The fourth period begins with the invention of printing with movable type. This is generally reckoned to be A.D. 1456, though the first dated book printed completely in Greek, namely Constantine Lascaris's *Erotemata* (a Greek grammar),

[50] Cf. Herbert Hunger, 'Die Perlschrift, eine Stilrichtung der griechischen Buchschrift des 11. Jahrhunderts,' *Studien zur griechischen Paläographie* (Vienna, 1954), pp. 22–32; idem, 'Die sogenannte Fettaugen-Mode in griechischen Handschriften des 13. und 14. Jahrhunderts,' *Byzantinischen Forschungen*, iv (1972), pp. 105–13 (both reprinted in Hunger, *Byzantinistische Grundlagsforschung: Gesammelte Aufsätze* [London, 1973]); idem, 'Archaisierende Minuskel und Gebrauchschrift zur Blütezeit der Fettaugenmode,' *La paléographie grecque et byzantine, Paris 21–25 Octobre 1974* (Colloques internationaux du Centre National de la Recherche scientifique, no. 559; Paris, 1977), pp. 283–90; Jean Irigoin, 'Une écriture du Xe siècle: la minuscule bouletée,' ibid., pp. 191–99; Paul Canart, 'Le problème du style d'écriture dit "en as de pique" dans les manuscrits italo-grecs,' *Atti del 4° congresso storico-calabrese* (Naples, 1969), pp. 53–69. For the 'Zierstil' in uncial script, see footnote 40 above.

was published at Milan 30 January 1476 by Dionysius Paravesinus.[51] The wide interest of Italian humanists in the works of classical authors, as well as the desire to form large libraries, encouraged the continued copying of manuscripts to supplement the work of printers.[52] Scholars, as a rule, had private collections of manuscripts, some of them written in their own handwriting. With the general exception of Biblical and liturgical manuscripts, the copies are written mostly in a very cursive form of minuscule, with many abbreviations and ligatures.

The forms of letters found in minuscule codices of this period were imitated by the early printers with astonishing fidelity, including diversity of forms of the same letter.[53] In fact, instead of twenty-four characters for the letters of the alphabet, fonts of Greek type contained as many as two hundred sorts.[54] It was not until the nineteenth century that the ligatures ȣ (*ου*) and ϛ (*στ*) were abandoned. Our distinction between *σ* and *ς* is all that remains of alternative forms; in other cases either the cursive or the uncial has prevailed.

§17. ABBREVIATIONS AND SYMBOLS

OVER the centuries scribes devised various methods of saving space and time while writing Greek.[55] Most copies of the Scriptures make some pretense to calligraphy and therefore the number of abbreviations is kept to a minimum; nevertheless a certain number sometimes found their way into such copies. There are several ways of abbreviating Greek: superposition of letters, combination, suspension, contraction, and the use of conventional signs and symbols.

(1) Superposition, as the word itself indicates, means the placing of letters above other letters rather than next to each other. This generally takes place at the end of a word and at the end of a line. When final *nu* occurs in this position, it is written as a horizontal stroke above the preceding letter (see Plates 7, 9, 10, 13, 14, 15).

[51] See Richard P. Breadon, 'The First Book Printed in Greek,' *Bulletin of the New York Public Library*, li (1947), pp. 586–92. Cf. also Robert Proctor, *The Printing of Greek in the Fifteenth Century* (Oxford, 1900), p. 52, and Deno J. Geanakopolos, *Greek Scholars in Venice, Studies in the Dissemination of Greek Learning from Byzantium to Western Europe* (Cambridge, Massachusetts, 1962), index *s.v.* 'Lascaris, Constantine.'

[52] In 1492, more than a third of a century after Gutenberg's invention of printing with movable type, Johannes Trithemius wrote a treatise entitled *De laude scriptorum* ('In Praise of Scribes') in which he argues that printing does not render copying by hand superfluous, that not all books are as yet printed, and that those in print are neither easily accessible nor inexpensive. The Latin text is edited with an Introduction by Klaus Arnold, and translated into English by Roland Behrendt (Coronado Press, Lawrence, Kansas, 1974). For specimens of Greek manuscripts written in the fifteenth and sixteenth centuries, see Dieter Harlfinger, 'Zu griechischen Kopisten und Schriftstilen des 15. und 16. Jahrhunderts,' *La paléographie grecque et byzantine* (footnote 50 above), pp. 327–62, and idem, *Specimina griechischer Kopisten der Renaissance* (Berlin, 1974), and on Trithemius, see Elizabeth L. Eisenstein, *The Printing Press as an Agent of Change*, i (Cambridge, 1979), pp. 14–5, 94–5, and 385.

[53] Cf. Victor Scholderer, *Greek Printing Types 1465–1927* (London, 1927). For a list of ligatures used in early Greek printed books, see William Wallace, 'An Index of Greek Ligatures and Contractions,' *Journal of Hellenic Studies*, xliii (1923), pp. 183–93, and W. H. Ingram, 'The Ligatures of Early Printed Greek,' *Greek, Roman and Byzantine Studies*, vii (1966), pp. 371–89.

[54] The type used in Lascaris's *Erotemata* contained 55 capitals and 161 lower-case sorts, besides stops, etc. Cf. Robert Proctor, *The Printing of Greek in the Fifteenth Century* (Oxford, 1900), pp. 56 ff.

[55] For lists of Greek abbreviations, see Al. N. Oikonomides, *Abbreviations in Greek Inscriptions, Papyri, Manuscripts, and Early Printed Books* (Chicago, 1974). This volume contains photolithographically reproduced lists originally drawn up by Avi-Yonah, Kenyon, Allen, and Ostermann and Giegengack.

(2) Combination of letters is achieved either by having one or more strokes in common (see Fig. 6, and Plates 15 and 20), or by writing them in or across each other (see Fig. 7).

FIGURE 6. Combinations of uncial letters.

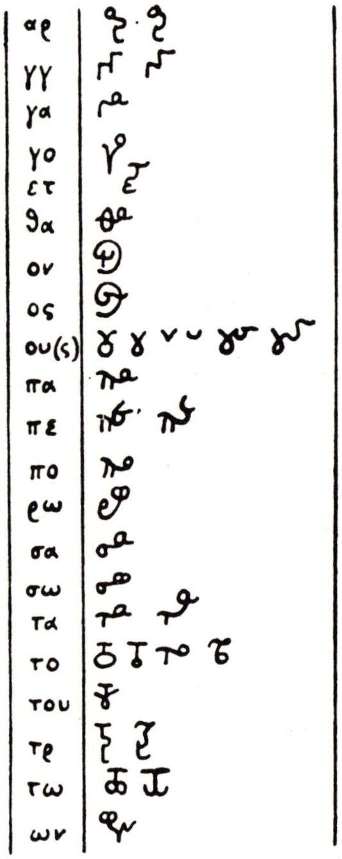

FIGURE 7.

Combination and superposition of letters.

FIGURE 8.

Various abbreviations.

(3) Suspension means the omission of the end of a word. Frequently occurring examples are $\overset{\chi}{\alpha\rho}$ (for ἀρχή) and $\overset{\hat{\epsilon}}{\tau}$ (for τέλος) in Gospel manuscripts adapted for lectionary usage (see Plates 17, 23, 24, 31, and 32). *Kaí*-compendium is in two forms, ϗ (see Plates 7, 15, and 20) and Ϛ (see Plates 33 and 36).

(4) Contraction involves the omission of one or more letters in the central part of the word (see §21).

(5) Conventional signs and symbols indicate corrections (see end of §13), or editorial apparatus (see §22). Other marks, adapted from Greek shorthand,[56] can signify a syllable or a word. They are often, though not exclusively, used at the end of words (see Fig. 8). For the staurogram and the *chi-rho* monogram, see Plates 17 and 35.

§18. *Scriptio continua*

It will be noticed on even the most casual inspection that most Greek manuscripts are written without separation between words and sentences. This kind of writing, called *scriptio continua*, is easiest to read when one is reading aloud, syllable by syllable.[57] Occasionally the grouping of syllables into words is ambiguous. For example, in Rom. 7:14 *οἴδαμεν* may be divided into *οἶδα μέν*, and in 1 Tim. 3:16 the words *ὁμολογουμένως μέγα ἐστίν* may be taken as *ὁμολογοῦμεν ὡς μέγα ἐστίν*. In Lev. 5:4 uncial manuscripts read ΗΨΥΧΗΗΑΝΟΜΟϹΗΔΙΑϹΤΕΛΛΟΥϹΑ, which in some editions of the Septuagint (Tischendorf; Swete) is read *ἡ ψυχὴ ἡ ἄνομος ἡ διαστέλλουσα*, whereas the same letters (in accord with the Hebrew) can be read *ἡ ψυχὴ ἣ ἂν ὁμόσῃ διαστέλλουσα* (Rahlfs).

It must not be thought, however, that such ambiguities occur frequently. In Greek it is the rule, with very few exceptions, that native Greek words can terminate only in a vowel (or diphthong) or in one of three consonants, *ν*, *ρ*, and *ς*. In order to indicate word-division at the close of a non-Greek name, scribes would sometimes use a mark shaped like a grave accent (for example λωτ` in Plate 5) or like a smooth breathing mark (for example ΓΑΛΓΑΛ' in Plate 17).

When it was necessary to divide a word at the end of a line, scribes were usually careful to observe the following rules: (*a*) all consonants go with the following vowel and begin the next line, except that λ, *μ*, *ν*, and *ρ* are joined to the preceding vowel when there is a following consonant; (*b*) double consonants are separated; and (*c*) compound words are generally divided into their component parts.

§19. PUNCTUATION

Marks of punctuation occur only sporadically or not at all in the most ancient manuscripts. According to tradition the invention of a system of punctuation, like

[56] Cf. H. J. M. Milne, *Greek Shorthand Manuals, Syllabary and Commentary, edited from Papyri* (Oxford, 1934), and the discussion (with bibliography) by B. M. Metzger, 'Stenography and Church History,' *Twentieth Century Encyclopedia of Religious Knowledge*, i (Grand Rapids, 1955), pp. 1060 f. Origen, so Eusebius informs us, 'dictated to more than seven shorthand-writers, who relieved each other at fixed times, and he employed as many copyists, as well as girls skilled in calligraphy—for all of whom Ambrose provided the necessary resources without stint' (*Eccl. Hist.* VI.xxiii.2).

[57] For discussions of evidence from antiquity (including Acts 8:30) that as a rule a person, even when alone, would customarily read aloud, see the literature mentioned in Metzger, *The Text of the New Testament*, p. 13, n. 3, supplemented by B. M. W. Knox, 'Silent Reading in Antiquity,' *Greek, Roman, and Byzantine Studies*, ix (1968), pp. 421–36.

the breathing and accent marks mentioned above (§8), is commonly ascribed to Aristophanes of Byzantium. This involved the use of a single point with certain values in certain positions (*θέσεις*). The high point (*στιγμὴ τελεία*) is the strongest, equivalent to a full stop; the point on the line (*ὑποστιγμή*) and the point in a middle position (*στίγμη μέση*) were used with different values by different scribes. The middle point eventually disappeared, and about the ninth century the comma was introduced. The interrogation mark (;) first appears about the eighth or ninth century.

The development of the custom of dividing a text into paragraphs can be traced from stage to stage. In the Chester Beatty–Schiede Ezekiel papyrus (first half of the third century), if a paragraph finished within a line, the scribe left a space about the width of an average letter before beginning the next letter. Likewise the first letter of the next line was drawn out a little into the left-hand margin, and usually written slightly larger than the average. If a paragraph finished at the end of a line, this emphasis of the first letter of the next line was sufficient to mark the paragraph division (see Plate 10). By the middle of the fourth century the three scribes of codex Sinaiticus indicated a new paragraph by placing the first letter so that it extended slightly into the left-hand margin; the preceding line may or may not be full (see Plate 14). In the latter case scribe D usually equalized the line with one or more filling marks (the *diplé*, >). By the fifth century the scribe of codex Alexandrinus used an enlarged letter conspicuously placed in the left-hand margin (see Plate 18). In later centuries scribes, disliking partially filled lines at the right-hand margin, would fill out the line with the opening words of the new paragraph, enlarging whatever letter happened to stand first in the following line (see Plates 36 and 37).

In minuscule script it became more or less common practice to mark the conclusion of a paragraph or chapter with a more emphatic sign, such as two or more dots with or without a horizontal dash. (For the use of the lozenge, see Plate 33.)

Although the exegete can learn something concerning the history of the interpretation of a passage by considering the punctuation of a passage in the manuscripts, neither the editor nor the translator need, of course, feel bound to adopt the punctuation preferred by scribes.[58]

[58] See the discussion by C. Lattey and F. C. Burkitt, 'The Punctuation of New Testament Manuscripts,' *Journal of Theological Studies*, xxix (1927–28), pp. 396–98. Cf. also B. M. Metzger, 'The Punctuation of Rom. 9:5,' *Christ and Spirit in the New Testament*, ed. by B. Lindars and S. S. Smalley (Cambridge, 1973), pp. 95–112; reprinted in Metzger, *New Testament Studies, Philological, Versional, and Patristic* (Leiden, 1980), pp. 57–74.

For a brief discussion of punctuation used by ancient classical Greek writers, see Rudolf Pfeiffer, *History of Classical Scholarship from the Beginning to the End of the Hellenistic Age* (Oxford, 1968), pp. 179 ff. and 269.

VI

Special Features of Biblical Manuscripts

In addition to palaeographical and codicological features that manuscripts of the Greek Bible share with other ancient documents, the former contain certain special features. Most of these are intended, in one way or another, to serve as 'helps for the reader.'

§20. THE TETRAGRAMMATON

The Tetragrammaton, or Tetragram, is a term denoting the mystic and ineffable name of God, written in Hebrew Bibles as יהוה, that is YHWH, Yahweh with the vowels omitted. It was, and still is, considered irreverent to pronounce the Name; hence, when reading the Hebrew Scriptures it became customary to substitute the word Adonai, 'Lord' (literally, 'my lords'). When the vowel points were added to the Hebrew consonantal text, the vowels of Adonai were accordingly given to the Tetragrammaton.

When writing the sacred name, devout scribes at Qumran would sometimes use palaeo-Hebrew script for the four letters, while writing the rest of the Scripture text in ordinary Hebrew (Aramaic) characters.[59] At a later date the Tetragrammaton was occasionally written in letters of gold, though Tannaitic sages condemned such a practice.[60]

So great was the desire to preserve intact the sacred name of God that Hellenistic Jews, when translating the Hebrew Bible into Greek, copied the actual letters of the Tetragrammaton in the midst of the Greek text. Several kinds of such representation have survived,[61] of which the following may be mentioned.

(*a*) The oldest known manuscript of the Septuagint that presents the Tetra-

[59] According to Harmut Stegemann ('Religionsgeschichtliche Erwägungen zu den Gottesbezeichnungen in den Qumrantexten,' *Qumrân: Sa piété, sa théologie et son milieu*, ed. by M. Delcor et al. [Bibliotheca Ephemeridum theologicarum Lovaniensium, xlvi; Paris et Leuven, 1978], pp. 195–218), Dead Sea scrolls that exhibit the Tetragrammaton in archaic Hebrew letters are: Biblical texts without commentary (2QEx^{b} = 2Q *3*; 3QThreni = 3Q *3*), Pesharim (4QpIs^{a} = 4Q *161*; 1QpMicah = 1Q *14*; 1QpHab; 1QpZeph = 1Q *15*; 4QpPs^{a} = 4Q *171*), and apocryphal Psalms (1QPs^{b} = 1Q *11*; 11QPs^{a}); scrolls that exhibit normal square Hebrew letters for the Tetragrammaton are: Biblical texts without commentary (4QDt^{q}, ed. P. W. Skehan in *BASOR*, 136, 1954, pp. 12–15; 4QDt^{n}, ed. F. M. Cross in *SWDS*, 20, pp. 31 f.), Pesharim (4QpIs^{b} = 4Q *162*; 4QpIs^{c} = 4Q *163*; 4QpNah = 4Q *169*; 4QpZeph = 4Q *170*; 4QpPs^{b} = 4Q *173*), and apocryphal Psalms (4QPs^{f}; 11QPs^{b}; 11QPsAp^{a}). See also J. P. Siegal, 'The Employment of Palaeo-Hebrew Characters for the Divine Names at Qumram in the Light of Tannaitic Sources,' *Hebrew Union College Annual*, xlii (1971), pp. 159–72, and Patrick W. Skehan, 'The Divine Name at Qumran, in the Masada Scroll, and in the Septuagint,' *Bulletin of the International Organization for Septuagint and Cognate Studies*, no. 13 (Fall, 1980), pp. 14–44, esp. 28 ff.

[60] Babylonian Talmud, *Shabbath* 103b. For a discussion of the reasons for such a prohibition, see J. P. Siegel, 'The Alexandrians in Jerusalem and their Torah Scroll with Gold Tetragrammata,' *Israel Exploration Quarterly*, xxii (1972), pp. 39–43.

[61] Besides those cited here, G. Mercati discusses instances of deformed Tetragrammata in the 'Post Scriptum' to his 'Sulla scrittura del tetragramma nelle antiche versioni greche del Vecchio Testamento,' *Biblica*, xxii (1941), pp. 365 f.

grammaton is a very fragmentary papyrus roll of Deuteronomy (P. Fouad Inv. 266), dating from the first century B.C. The more than one hundred surviving fragments of the Greek text of chapters 17–33 preserve thirty-one instances of יהוה written in square Hebrew letters[62] (for three such fragments, see Plate 3). Fragmentary remains of Origen's Hexapla (see §22), copied during the ninth or tenth century, also use the square letters for the divine Name (see Plate 30).

(*b*) Fragments of a roll of the Twelve Prophets in Greek, found in a cave (Naḥal Ḥever) near Engedi in the Judean Desert, dating, it is thought, from about 50 B.C.—A.D. 50, contain instances of the Tetragrammaton in palaeo-Hebrew letters.[63] The same kind of archaic script is also employed in palimpsest fragments from the fifth or sixth century preserving portions of Aquila's Greek version of the Old Testament (see Fig. 9).[64]

(*c*) A modification of the palaeo-Hebrew letters occurs in a papyrus fragment of Genesis (P.Oxy. 1007), dating from the latter part of the third century A.D. Here the scribe abbreviated the Tetragrammaton by doubling the initial *yod*,[65] written in the shape of a z with a horizontal line through the middle, and carried unbroken through both characters (ƶƶ). The same form of *yod* is found on Jewish coins of the second century B.C. This compendium (without the horizontal stroke) exactly corresponds with that employed in Hebrew manuscripts of a later period (י״י).

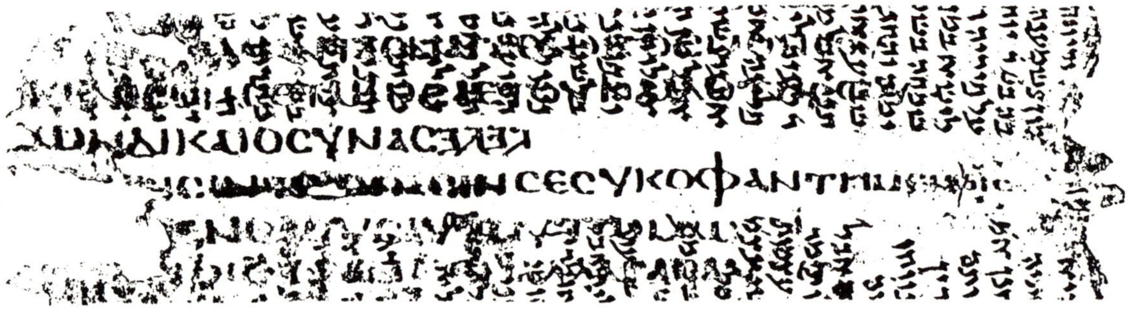

FIGURE 9. The Tetragrammaton in archaic Hebrew letters

A portion from the center-fold of a palimpsest fragment dated to the fifth or sixth century. The under-writing preserves Psalm 103:6 in Aquila's Greek version, with the Tetragrammaton in archaic Hebrew letters; the upper-writing is from the Jerusalem Talmud. Actual size, reproduced from Plate viii in C. Taylor's edition (see footnote 64 below).

ποι]ων δικαιοσυνας 𐤉𐤄𐤅𐤄
και κ]ρισιν τοις πασιν σεσυκοφαντημενοις

[62] In addition to the literature cited in the bibliography for Plate 3, see Flavio Bedodi, 'I "nomina sacra" nei papiri greci veterotestamentari precristiani,' *Studia papyrologica*, xiii (1974), pp. 89–103, esp. 98 ff.

[63] Cf. D. Barthélemy, *Les devanciers d'Aquila: Premier publication intégrale du texte des fragments du Dodécapropheton* (Leiden, 1963). As is the case with manuscripts from Qumran, the scribe does not clearly distinguish the shape of *yod* from that of *waw*.

[64] Edited by F. C. Burkitt, *Fragments of the Book of Kings according to the Translation of Aquila. . . .* (Cambridge, 1879), and by C[harles] Taylor, *Hebrew-Greek Cairo Genizah Palimpsests from the Taylor-Schechter Collection . . .* (Cambridge, 1900).

[65] A. S. Hunt, *The Oxyrhynchus Papyri*, vii (London, 1910), pp. 1–3 (#1007). (It was intended to provide in the present volume a photographic reproduction of the verso of the fragment, which contains the abbreviation of the Tetragrammaton, but unfortunately that side of the papyrus is so dirty and the writing so faint that even a photograph under infra-red light turned out to be unsatisfactory.)

Besides employing Hebrew letters to write the Tetragrammaton in Greek texts, in other cases scribes have used Greek letters in order to represent the ineffable Name of God. The following are instances of such usage.

(*d*) From Cave IV at Qumran comes a papyrus fragment of Leviticus in the Greek Septuagint that presents the divine Name phonetically in the form ιαω.[66] Later the word Ἰαώ was adopted by Gnostics[67] and by those who drew up magical formulae and amulets.[68]

(*e*) In a few Hexaplaric manuscripts (e.g. Q, 86, 88, 234^{mg}, 264) the Greek letters πιπι are used to represent roughly the shape of the square Hebrew letters of the Tetragrammaton (see Plate 21).[69]

The question may be raised what the practice would have been in Hellenistic synagogues (such as those that the Apostle Paul visited) when the reader of the Scripture lesson came upon the Hebrew Tetragrammaton in the Greek text before him. One may answer with a fair degree of confidence that, like any reader of the Hebrew Old Testament, he either would say Adonai ('Lord'), or, in keeping with the Greek context, would use *κύριος*.[70] A tell-tale hint of the latter practice, as Burkitt points out,[71] is provided in the Aquila fragments; where there was no room to write the Hebrew characters, 'instead of *οἴκῳ* יהוה we find *οἴκῳ* *κ̅υ̅* [for *κυρίου*].' Likewise Origen, in commenting on Psalm 2:2, says expressly that among Greeks Adonai is pronounced *κύριος*.[72] It was inevitable, however, that by the time of Jerome, ignorant readers, imagining the Tetragrammaton to be a Greek word, actually pronounced it 'Pipi'![73]

[66] For a brief description of the fragment (prior to its full publication), see P. W. Skehan, 'The Qumran Manuscripts and Textual Criticism,' *Vetus Testamentum, Supplement*, iv (1957), p. 157; reprinted, with minor alterations, in *Qumran in the History of the Biblical Text*, ed. by F. M. Cross and S. Talmon (Cambridge, Massachusetts, 1975), p. 271. In codex Marchalianus (Plate 21) *ιαω* occurs in two marginal annotations attached to Ezek. 1:2 and 11:1 (pp. 509 and 588). Perhaps the word was pronounced *yahó*.

[67] For references, see G. W. H. Lampe, ed., *A Patristic Greek Lexicon, s.v.*

[68] See the index in Karl Preisendanz, *Papyri Graeci Magici*, iii (Leipzig and Berlin, 1941), pp. 223 f.

[69] Ceriani suggested that it may have been Origen or Eusebius who substituted the Greek letters for the Semitic form (*Monumenta sacra et profana*, ii, pp. 106 ff.); cf. also J. F. Schleusner, *Novus Thesaurus . . . Veteris Testamenti, s.v. πιπι*; Hatch-Redpath, *Concordance*, p. 1135, and *Supplement*, p. 126.

[70] If the Apostle Paul followed a copy of the Septuagint with the Tetragrammaton written in Hebrew letters, he would no doubt have substituted *κύριος* (or perhaps occasionally *θεός*) when dictating an epistle to be sent to predominately Gentile congregations. No New Testament manuscript contains the Tetragrammaton in Old Testament quotations (or anywhere else, it need scarcely be added). For further discussion, see George Howard, 'The Tetragram and the New Testament,' *Journal of Biblical Literature*, xcvi (1977), pp. 63–83, and, on a more popular level, idem, 'The Name of God in the New Testament,' *Biblical Archaeology Review*, iv, 1 (1978), pp. 12–14, 56.

[71] Burkitt, op. cit. (footnote 64 above), p. 15, par. 4.

[72] *οὐκ ἀγνοητέον δὲ περὶ τοῦ ἐκφωνουμένου παρὰ μὲν Ἕλλησι τῇ "Κύριος" προσηγορίᾳ παρὰ δὲ Ἑβραίοις τῇ* "'Αδωναΐ," *Sel. in Psalmos*, Ps. 2.2 (Migne *PG*, xii, col. 1104A).

[73] In his discussion of the ten names of God, Jerome says that the ninth name 'is a tetragrammaton, which the Jews consider *ἀνεκφώνητον*, that is ineffable, and which is written with these letters: Iod, He, Vau, He; which, certain ignorant ones, because of the similarity of the characters, when they would find them in Greek books, were accustomed to pronounce Pipi' (*Epist.* 25, *Ad Marcellam*, ed. Hilberg, p. 219). In the following century Evagrius mentions the tradition that on the sacred breastplate of the High Priest was inscribed the name IIIIII (see Paul de Lagarde, *Onomastica sacra*, i [Göttingen, 1870], pp. 205 f.).

It may be added that in the Syriac translation of the Septuagint made by Bp. Paul of Tella (A.D. 616–617), the Hebrew name of God is represented by ܦܝܦܝ (*pypy*). This usage is discussed in a Scholion ot Jacob of Edessa (A.D. 675); see A. M. Ceriani, *Monumenta sacra et profana*, ii, fasc. 4 (Milan, 1863), pp. 106–12; Eberhard Nestle, *Zeitschrift für die Deutschen morganländischen Gesellschaft*, xxxii (1878), pp. 465–508 (also pp. 735 f. and xxxiii [1879]; pp. 297 ff.), and Bernard Pick, 'Shem Hammephorash' in John McClintock and James Strong, *Cyclopædia of Biblical, Theological and Ecclesiastical Literature*, ix, pp. 652 f.

§21. *Nomina Sacra*

During the first centuries of the Church, Christian scribes developed a system of contractions for certain sacred words. These *nomina sacra*, as the Latin palaeographer Ludwig Traube called them,[74] eventually came to include fifteen such terms. Some were contracted by writing only the first and the last letters (θεός, κύριος, Ἰησοῦς, Χριστός, and υἱός); others, by writing only the first two and the last letters (πνεῦμα, Δαυίδ, σταυρός, and μήτηρ) or the first and last two letters (πατήρ, Ἰσραήλ, and σωτήρ); still others, by writing the first and last syllables (ἄνθρωπος, Ἱερουσαλήμ, and οὐρανός). In order to draw the reader's attention to the presence of a *nomen sacrum*, the scribe would place a horizontal line above the contraction. In the developed Byzantine usage the fifteen *nomina sacra* in their nominative and genitive forms are as follows:

θεός	θ̅ς̅	θ̅υ̅
κύριος	κ̅ς̅	κ̅υ̅
Ἰησοῦς	ι̅ς̅	ι̅υ̅
Χριστός	χ̅ς̅	χ̅υ̅
υἱός	υ̅ς̅	υ̅υ̅
πνεῦμα	π̅ν̅α̅	π̅ν̅ς̅
Δαυείδ	δ̅α̅δ̅	
σταυρός	σ̅τ̅ς̅	σ̅τ̅υ̅
μήτηρ	μ̅η̅ρ̅	μ̅ρ̅ς̅
πατήρ	π̅η̅ρ̅	π̅ρ̅ς̅
Ἰσραήλ	ι̅η̅λ̅	
σωτήρ	σ̅η̅ρ̅	σ̅ρ̅ς̅
ἄνθρωπος	α̅ν̅ο̅ς̅	α̅ν̅ο̅υ̅
Ἱερουσαλήμ	ι̅λ̅η̅μ̅	
οὐρανός	ο̅υ̅ν̅ο̅ς̅	ο̅υ̅ν̅ο̅υ̅

Scholars differ in accounting for the origin and development of the system of *nomina sacra*. According to Traube,[75] their origin is to be found in the need among Hellenistic Jews for devising a Greek equivalent for the Hebrew Tetragrammaton.

Others have sought to explain the *nomina sacra* as reflecting certain usages in secular texts. Rudberg[76] and Nachmanson,[77] for example, drew attention to the

[74] *Nomina Sacra: Versuch einer Geschichte der christlichen Kürzung* (Munich, 1907). This standard work is now supplemented by the additional data collected by A. H. R. E. Paap, *Nomina Sacra in the Greek Papyri of the First Five Centuries A.D.: the Sources and Some Deductions* (Leiden, 1959); José O'Callaghan, '*Nomina sacra*' *in Papyris Graecis saeculi III neotestamentariis* (Analecta Biblica, 46; Rome, 1970); idem, ' "Nominum sacrorum" elenchus in Graecis Novi Testamenti papyris a saeculo IV usque ad VIII,' *Studia papyrologica*, x (1971), pp. 99–122; idem, 'Consideraciones sobre los "nomina sacra" del Nuevo Testamento (del siglo IV al VIII),' *Akten des XIII. Internationalen Papyrologenkongresses*, Marburg/Lahn, 1971 (Münchener Beiträge zur Papyrusforschung und antiken Rechtsgeschichte, 66. Heft; Munich, 1974), pp. 315–320; Flavio Bedodi, 'I "nomina sacra" nei papiri greci veterotestamentari precristiani,' *Studia papyrologica*, xiii (1974), pp. 89–103; and C. H. Roberts, *Manuscript, Society and Belief in Early Christian Egypt* (London, 1979), pp. 26–48.

[75] Op. cit., pp. 31 f.

[76] Gunnar Rudberg, 'Zur paläographischen Kontraktion,' *Eranos*, x (1910), pp. 71–100; idem, 'Verschleifung und Kontraktion,' *Eranos*, xiii (1913), pp. 156–61; cf. also idem, *Neutestamentlicher Text und Nomina sacra* (Skrifter utgifna af Kungl. Humanistiska Vetenskaps-Samfundet; Uppsala, 1915); idem, 'De nominibus sacris adnotatiunculae,' *Eranos*, xxxiii (1933), pp. 147–51.

[77] Ernst Nachmanson, 'Die schriftliche Kontraktion

contractions that sometimes occur in pre-Christian ostraca and inscriptions in representing proper names, titles of rulers, names of months, numerals, and certain formulae.

Paap,[78] rejecting Traube's view of a Jewish origin for the *nomina sacra*, attributes their origin to Jewish Christians, because 'for them the Greek word for "God" had exactly the same value as the tetragrammaton and for that reason was entitled to a distinction in its written forms'; thus, $\overline{\theta\varsigma}$ comes to be used for *θεός*.

On the other hand, Schuyler Brown argues that it was *κύριος* and not *θεός* which was used to represent the Tetragrammaton. Because *κύριος* then became a title common to both God and Jesus, it was altogether natural, he thinks, that 'the initial contraction of *κύριος* was rapidly extended in one direction to *θεός* and in the other direction to Ἰησοῦς and Χριστός.'[79] The extension of usage came about because

> Christian scribes wished to give graphic expression to the theological equation already present in the earliest apostolic preaching, in which *κύριος*, the name of the God of Israel, was used as a title for Jesus Christ. In other words, the four nouns which are universally accorded special treatment in the early papyri of the New Testament are not simply *nomina sacra* but rather *nomina divina*.[80]

Roberts, who supposes that the use of *nomina sacra* originated among Christians at Jerusalem, designates them as 'the embryonic creed of the first Church.'[81]

In subsequent generations the system of contraction was extended to a variety of other words that carried deep theological connotations. For several centuries a certain amount of experimentation took place, involving such eccentricities as $\overline{\pi\rho o\phi\alpha\varsigma}$ and $\overline{\epsilon\pi\rho o\phi\sigma\epsilon\nu}$ and $\overline{\eta\sigma\alpha\varsigma}$ in the second-century British Museum Gospel.[82] As late as the second half of the fourth century the scribe responsible for a fragment of 1 Corinthians twice wrote *κόσμου* in the form $\overline{\kappa\mu o\upsilon}$.[83] These, and other similar 'sports,'[84] failed to establish themselves in general practice, and eventually conventional usage among Christian scribes throughout the Greek-speaking world fixed upon the fifteen *nomina sacra*,[85] mentioned earlier, as deserving special treatment.[86]

auf den griechischen Inschriften,' *Eranos*, x (1910), pp. 100–41.

[78] Op. cit. (footnote 74 above), p. 124.

[79] 'Concerning the Origin of the *Nomina sacra*,' *Studia papyrologica*, ix (1970), p. 18.

[80] Ibid., p. 19.

[81] C. H. Roberts, op. cit. (footnote 74 above), p. 46.

[82] H. I. Bell and T. C. Skeat, *Fragments of an Unknown Gospel and Other Early Christian Papyri* (London, 1935), p. 4. Cf. also Roberts's discussion of these and other eccentric *nomina sacra*, op. cit., pp. 39 and 83 f.

[83] *Oxyrhynchus Papyrus* 1008 ($\mathfrak{p}^{15}$).

[84] For instances of other words sporadically contracted in manuscripts, see Kurt Aland, *Repertorium der griechischen christlichen Papyri*, i (Berlin and New York, 1976), pp. 420–28.

[85] The question why it was these fifteen names, and only these, that came to be so regarded has not been answered satisfactorily. In any case, however, the standardization of usage indicates 'a degree of organization, of conscious planning, and uniformity of practice among the Christian communities which we have hitherto had little reason to suspect' (T. C. Skeat, op. cit. [footnote 23 above], p. 73).

[86] Occasionally an unwary scribe, misinterpreting several letters as a *nomen sacrum*, transcribed them erroneously; for example, *ὄνοι* ('asses') in Aristotle's *History of Animals* has been transcribed as ἄνθρωποι. See D'Arcy W. Thompson, '*ὄνος: ἄνθρωπος*,' *Classical Quarterly*, xxxix (1945), pp. 54–55, and F. W. Walbank, 'Men and Donkeys,' *Classical Quarterly*, xxxix (1945), p. 122. For other examples of such confusion, see I. C. Vollgraff, *Studia palaeographica* (Leiden, 1871), pp. 69–77; Gérard Garitte, '"Terra mitium": Nomina sacra et fautes de copie,' *Scriptorium*, v (1951), pp. 104–5; and H. Sählin, 'Zum Verständnis von drei Stellen des Markus Evangeliums,' *Biblica*, xxxiii (1952), pp. 53–66.

§22. HEXAPLARIC SIGNS

ORIGEN's monumental edition of the Old Testament, the massive, 10,000-page Hexapla (see Plate 30), set forth six transcriptions of the entire Old Testament in parallel columns, namely (1) the Hebrew text, (2) its transliteration into Greek letters, (3) the extremely literalistic Greek translation made in the first half of the second century A.D. by Aquila, a Jewish proselyte; (4) the freer Greek translation made in the latter part of the second century A.D. by Symmachus, an Ebionite Christian; (5) the Septuagint translation (LXX) made in the third and second centuries B.C.; and (6) the free revision of the Septuagint made in the second century A.D. by Theodotion, variously described as a Jewish proselyte (so Irenaeus), an Ebionite Christian (so Jerome), or a follower of Marcion (so Epiphanius). Besides these four Greek translations, in certain sections of the Old Testament Origen included the text of three other Greek versions, thus providing in these sections a total of nine columns. According to Eusebius (*Hist. Eccl.* VI.16) one of these anonymous versions was discovered during the reign of Caracalla (A.D. 211–217) buried in an earthenware jar at Jerico.[87]

Employing the critical signs invented by Aristarchus and other scholars at the famed Alexandrian library, Origen marked the text of the Septuagint to show its exact relation to the Hebrew. All words and paragraphs in the Septuagint which were not represented in the Hebrew he marked with an obelus (—); all lacunae in the Greek, on the other hand, were filled in from one of the other translations (mostly from Theodotion) and marked with an asterisk (*). Two points (:) indicate the end of each textual change (see Plate 15). If something had been wrongly translated in the Septuagint, the correct rendering was inserted either by itself or behind the one marked with an obelus.

This work, on which Origen spent more than fifteen years of unremitting labor, was of such gigantic dimension that it probably was never copied in its entirety. According to Eusebius, Jerome, and other Fathers, however, the last four columns also existed in a separate form known as the Tetrapla. The fifth column (the LXX) was frequently copied and circulated on its own (see Plate 21), though scribes unfortunately tended to disregard the asterisks and obeli.[88]

§23. STICHOMETRY AND COLOMETRY

FROM ancient times the average hexameter line of writing (*στίχος*), comprising sixteen syllables of about thirty-six letters, was taken as a standard of measure for

[87] For modern debate concerning the identity of these three anonymous versions (called the Quinta, the Sexta, and the Septima), see Sidney Jellicoe, *The Septuagint and Modern Study* (Oxford, 1968), pp. 118–23, and Hermann-Josef Venetz, *Die Quinta des Psalteriums; ein Beitrag zur Septuaginta- und Hexaplaforschung* (Hildesheim, 1974). On the discovery of manuscripts in antiquity, see Colin H. Roberts, *Buried Books in Antiquity* . . . A Public Lecture delivered at the Library Association on 25 October 1962 (Arundell Esdaile Memorial Lecture, 1962; [London,] 1963).

[88] The most extensive collection of Hexaplaric materials is in Frederick Field, *Origenis Hexaplorum quae supersunt . . . fragmenta*, 2 vols. (Oxford, 1867–75; reprinted, Hildesheim, 1964). The most important addition to Field's collection is the recently published palimpsest in the Ambrosian Library at Milan (see Plate 30). For bibliography on the Hexapla, see S. P.

literary works.[89] The number of *στίχοι* served (*a*) to show the length of a treatise or book, (*b*) to provide a standard for payment to the scribe and the pricing of the book, (*c*) to guard against later interpolations and excisions, and (*d*) to permit, through the notation in the margin of the *στίχοι* by fifties, the general location of citations.

Manuscripts of both the Old Testament[90] and the New Testament[91] occasionally provide stichometric information—though in some cases the figures given for the same book vary widely. The earliest Biblical manuscript that contains such notation is the Chester Beatty Papyrus of the Pauline Epistles ($\mathfrak{p}^{46}$). At the end of the Epistle to the Romans, the scribe indicates 1000 stichoi (see Plate 6); at the end of Hebrews (which in this manuscript follows Romans), 700; Ephesians, 316; Galatians, 375; and Philippians, 225 (or 222). The numbers for the other *στίχοι* have not survived or are illegible.

In the Gospels, according to Lake, 'the most ordinary system [of stichometry] gives 2600 stichoi for Matthew, 1600 for Mark, 2800 for Luke, and 2300 for John; but these are probably corruptions of 2560, 1616, 2750, 2024 respectively, which are found in several MSS., and imply the presence of xvi.9–20 in Mark, and the omission of vii.53–viii.11 in John.'[92]

Another stichometric reckoning, called *ῥήματα*, is found in the Ferrar group of Gospel manuscripts. Rendel Harris,[93] followed by Scrivener,[94] thought that they represent a retranslation of a Syriac stichometry; Lake,[95] however, regarded the theory as implausible in view of the fact that all the Ferrar manuscripts appear to be of Calabrian origin.

Colometry[96] is the division of a text into *κῶλα* and *κόμματα*, that is, sense-lines of clauses and phrases so as to assist the reader to make the correct inflection and the proper pauses. It was applied to the Septuagint Greek text of the poetical books of the Old Testament.[97] One of the earliest examples of a portion of the Septuagint arranged in cola is the second- (or third-) century A.D. Bodleian fragment of the Psalms.[98]

Brock, C. T. Fritsch, and S. Jellicoe, *A Classified Bibliography of the Septuagint* (Leiden, 1973), pp. 87 ff.

[89] See J. Rendel Harris, 'Stichometry,' *American Journal of Philology*, iv (1883), pp. 133–57 and 309–31 (reprinted, with additions, *Stichometry* [London, 1893]), and Kurt Ohly, *Stichometrische Untersuchungen* (Berlin, 1928).

[90] See William Sanday, *Studia Biblica et Ecclesiastica*, iii (Oxford, 1891), pp. 266 ff., and H. B. Swete, *An Introduction to the Old Testament in Greek*, rev. by R. R. Ottley (Cambridge, 1914; reprinted, New York, 1968), pp. 348–50.

[91] See J. M. A. Scholz, *Novum Testamentum Graece*, i (Leipzig, 1830), pp. xxviii ff.

[92] Kirsopp Lake, *The Text of the New Testament*, 6th ed., rev. by Silva New (London, 1929), p. 61.

[93] *On the Origin of the Ferrar Group* (London, 1894), pp. 7–10.

[94] F. H. A. Scrivener, *A Plain Introduction to the Criticism of the New Testament*, 4th ed., i (London, 1894), pp. 381–3.

[95] Op. cit., p. 61.

[96] Cf. Albert Debrunner, 'Grundsätzliches über Kolometrie im Neuen Testament,' *Theologische Blätter*, v (1926), pp. 231–3; Roland Schütz, 'Die Bedeutung der Kolometrie für das Neue Testament,' *Zeitschrift für die neutestamentliche Wissenschaft*, xxi (1922), pp. 161–84; James A. Kleist, 'Colometry and the New Testament,' *Classical Bulletin*, iv (1928), pp. 26 f.; and Paul Gächter, 'Codex D and Codex Λ,' *Journal of Theological Studies*, xxxv (1934), pp. 248–66.

[97] In codex Vaticanus (B) and codex Sinaiticus (א) of the fourth century seven books are copied colometrically, namely Psalms, Proverbs, Ecclesiastes, the Song of Songs, Job, Wisdom of Solomon, and Ecclesiasticus.

[98] Edited by J. W. B. Barns and G. D. Kilpatrick, *Proceedings of the British Academy*, xliii (1957), pp. 227 f.

Similarly all the books of the New Testament, except the Book of Revelation, were sometimes written in sense-lines. The oldest New Testament manuscript with the text arranged colometrically is codex Bezae (D; see Plate 19). It is not known when or by whom the colometric arrangement of the text was introduced into the Gospels, but the Acts and the Epistles were divided into sense-lines by a scholar named Euthalius (or Evagrius), who lived, it is thought, in the fourth century (see §27).

§24. SUPERSCRIPTIONS AND SUBSCRIPTIONS

In the oldest manuscripts of the Greek Bible the titles of the several books tend to be short and simple; for example, *Γένεσις*, *Κατὰ Μαθθαῖον*, *Ἀποκάλυψις Ἰωάννου*. In later copies these titles became longer and more complex; for example, *ἡ βίβλος τῶν γενέσεων* (Rahlfs 129), *τὸ κατὰ Ματθαῖον ἅγιον εὐαγγέλιον* (Gregory–Aland 209 and many others), and, eventually, *ἡ ἀποκάλυψις τοῦ πανενδόξου εὐαγγελιστοῦ, ἐπιστηθίου φίλου, παρθένου, ἠγαπημένου τῷ Χριστῷ, Ἰωάννου τοῦ θεολόγου υἱοῦ Σαλώμης καὶ Ζεβεδαίου, θετοῦ δὲ υἱοῦ τῆς θεοτόκου Μαρίας, καὶ υἱοῦ βροντῆς* ('The Revelation of the all-glorious Evangelist, bosom friend [of Jesus], virgin, beloved to Christ, John the theologian, son of Salome and Zebadee, but adopted son of Mary the Mother of God, and Son of Thunder'; Gregory–Aland 1775, written A.D. 1847).

The subscriptions (*ὑπογραφαί*), appended to the end of the books, were originally (like the titles) brief and simple. In the course of time these too became more elaborate, and often included traditional information (or misinformation!) regarding the place at which the book was written, and sometimes the name of the amanuensis.[99] It is probable that the subscriptions attached to the Pauline Epistles (and retained in the King James Version) are the work of Euthalius (see §27). Six of these subscriptions are false or improbable; that is, they are either absolutely contradicted by the contents of the Epistle (1 Cor., Gal., 1 Tim.) or are difficult to be reconciled with them (1 and 2 Thess., Titus).[100]

§25. CHAPTER DIVISIONS AND HEADINGS

In order to assist readers, at an early period the books of the Greek Bible were divided into chapters. In Septuagint manuscripts the variety of such systems of division—which, according to Swete, 'seem to be nearly as numerous as the capitulated copies of the LXX'[101]—suggests that they were drawn up independently by a number of different scribes or editors.

In New Testament manuscripts four ancient systems of division have been preserved. The oldest system which is known to us is that contained in codex Vati-

[99] For the Greek text of these subscriptions, with identification of manuscript variations, see B. M. Metzger, *A Textual Commentary on the Greek New Testament* (London, 1971), at the close of each Epistle.

[100] For a discussion, see chap. 15 of William Paley's *Horae Paulinae* (London, 1790).

[101] H. B. Swete, op. cit. (footnote 90 above), p. 354.

canus.[102] Of unknown origin, the division into sections was made with reference to breaks in the sense. There are 170 in Matthew, 62 in Mark, 152 in Luke, 80 in John. The chapters in the several Pauline Epistles are numbered continuously as though the Epistles were regarded as comprising one book. This circumstance enables us to say something about the order of the Epistles in a manuscript, now lost, from which the capitulation was copied, for the present arrangement in codex Vaticanus has suffered some dislocation. Sections 1 to 58 cover regularly Romans, 1 and 2 Corinthians, and Galatians; but Ephesians, instead of beginning with 59, begins with 70, and then there is no further break in sequence until 93, which stands near the end of 2 Thessalonians, after which follows the Epistle to the Hebrews, beginning with 59 and going on to 64 in 9:11, after which the manuscript is defective (from 9:14 onward). Obviously an ancestor of B contained the Epistle to the Hebrews between Galatians and Ephesians.

Next in antiquity to the sections in Vaticanus, if, indeed, not equally ancient, are the *κεφάλαια majora* and the *τίτλοι*. The former are chapter divisions, and the latter are summary headings briefly describing the contents (see Plates 23, 29, 31, 35). These divisions, of which there are 68 in Matthew, 48 in Mark, 83 in Luke, and 18 in John, are not found in Vaticanus and Sinaiticus, but are present in Alexandrinus (see Plate 18), so that their use in the fifth century is quite certain. For the New Testament a standardized list of *τίτλοι* occurs in many manuscripts;[103] for the Old Testament, besides the previously mentioned diversity of systems of chapter divisions, there is a great diversity of titles which await further investigation.[104]

The division of the Bible into chapters, which, with small modification, are still in use today, was introduced into the Latin Bible by Stephen Langton at the beginning of the thirteenth century while a lecturer at the University of Paris (Langton, who died Archbishop of Canterbury in 1228, is famous in history for wresting the Magna Carta from King John). Verse division in the Hebrew Bible by פסוקים is witnessed to as early as the Mishnah (Megillah iv.4). Numbered verses (for a Hebrew concordance to the Masoretic text) were first worked out by Rabbi Isaac Nathan in about 1440.[105] The current verse division in the New Testament is due to Robert Stephanus (Estienne),[106] who in 1551 published at Geneva a Greek and

[102] See H. K. McArthur, 'The Earliest Divisions of the Gospels,' *Studia Evangelica*, iii, Part 2, ed. by F. L. Cross (*Texte und Untersuchungen*, lxxxviii; Berlin, 1964), pp. 266–72.

[103] See Hermann von Soden, *Die Schriften des Neuen Testaments in ihrer ältesten erreichbaren Textgestalt*, I, i (Berlin, 1902), pp. 405–11 (the Gospels), 449–57 (Acts), 457–60 (Catholic Epistles), and 462–69 (Pauline Epistles). Cf. also Paul Gächter, 'Zur Textabteilung von Evangelienhandschriften,' *Biblica*, xv (1934), pp. 301–20.

[104] See, besides Swete, op. cit. (footnote 90 above), pp. 351–56, Robert Devreesse, *Introduction à l'étude des manuscrits grecs* (Paris, 1954), pp. 139–41.

[105] See G. F. Moore, 'The Vulgate Chapters and Numbered Verses in the Hebrew Bible,' *Journal of Biblical Literature*, xii (1893), pp. 73–8. In early printed Hebrew Bibles every fifth verse (1, 5, 10, etc.) is marked by its Hebrew numeral.

[106] According to Stephanus's son, his father made the divisions into verse *inter equitandum* on a journey from Paris to Lyons. Although some have understood this to mean 'on horseback' (and have explained inappropriate verse-divisions as originating when the horse bumped his pen into the wrong place!), the inference most natural and best supported by the evidence is that the task was accomplished while resting at inns along the road.

Latin edition of the New Testament with the text of the chapters divided into separate verses.[107] The first Bible in English to contain verse numbers was the Geneva Version, translated by William Whittingham and others in 1560.

(For the other two ancient systems of divisions in New Testament manuscripts, see §26 and §27.)

§26. THE EUSEBIAN CANON TABLES

It is to Eusebius of Caesarea that we owe an important innovation introduced into manuscripts of the Gospels. This was a device for showing which passages in each Gospel are similar to passages in other Gospels.[108] Taking over the system (usually attributed to Ammonius of Alexandria) of dividing the text of the Gospels into numbered sections[109] (355 in Matthew, 233 in Mark, 342 in Luke, and 232 in John), Eusebius drew up ten tables of canons (*κανόνες*), presenting in Canon I the references by numerals to more or less parallel passages found in all four Gospels; in Canon II, passages common to Matthew, Mark, and Luke; in Canon III, passages common to Matthew, Luke, and John; and so on for almost all possible combinations of Gospels (not, however, Mark, Luke, and John; or Mark and John). The final table gives references to matter peculiar to each Gospel alone.

Many manuscripts of the Gospels, not only in Greek, but also in Latin, Syriac, Coptic, Gothic, Armenian, and Georgian, include at the beginning the ten Canon Tables (often artistically ornamented with vines, leaves, flowers, birds, etc.[110]) along with Eusebius's Epistle to Carpianus, in which the system is explained to the user.[111]

In later centuries a simplification was introduced into some manuscripts. Using information from the Canon Tables, scribes copied at the bottom of each page the references to the appropriate parallels in other Gospels (see Plate 36).

§27. THE EUTHALIAN APPARATUS

Greek manuscripts of the Book of Acts and of the Epistles sometimes contain a collection of editorial materials that circulated under the name of Euthalius (or Evagrius), now generally dated to the middle of the fourth century. These con-

[107] For a list of differences in verse-division among about fifty editions of the Greek New Testament, see Ezra Abbot's Latin excursus in Caspar René Gregory's *Prolegomena* volume (Leipzig, 1894) to C. von Tischendorf's *Novum Testamentum Graece*, 8th ed. maior, pp. 167–82, translated into English in Abbot's posthumously published volume entitled, *The Authorship of the Fourth Gospel and Other Critical Essays* (Boston, 1888), pp. 464–77. For information about verse-division in versions of the Bible, see W. Wright in John Kitto, *A Cyclopædia of Biblical Literature*, 3rd ed., iii (Philadelphia, 1866), pp. 1066–70; reprinted with minor changes in John McClintock and James Strong, *Cyclopædia of Biblical, Theological and Ecclesiastical Literature*, x (New York, 1881), pp. 756–62.

[108] Eusebius's intention went beyond that of providing a harmony of the Gospels, for he sometimes linked passages which could not conceivably be identical but which express some common concept or activity (that is, his system represented a primitive form of marginal references); for the distinction, see H. K. McArthur, 'The Eusebian Sections and Canons,' *Catholic Biblical Quarterly*, xxvii (1965), pp. 250–56.

[109] These sections are very much shorter than the chapter divisions described above in section §25.

[110] See Carl Nordenfalk, *Die spätantiken Kanontafeln; Kuntsgeschichtliche Studien über die Eusebianische Evangelien-Konkordanz in die vier ersten Jahrhunderten ihrer Geschichte*, 2 vols. (Göteborg, 1938).

[111] For an English translation of the Epistle, see H. H. Oliver in *Novum Testamentum*, iii (1959), pp. 138–45.

sist of prologues, lists of quotations from other parts of the Bible, tables of lections, and lists of chapters, with summary headings of their contents.[112] Attached to the Euthalian prologue to the Pauline Epistles is a 'Martyrium Pauli,' which has been thought to date from 396 (F. C. Conybeare) or from 458 (L. A. Zacagni) or 670 (H. von Soden); but the reasons for identifying the author of this text with that of the rest of the Euthalian material now seem insufficient.[113] Several manuscripts contain a variety of other miscellaneous 'Helps for the Reader.'[114]

§28. HYPOTHESES

THE hypothesis (ὑπόθεσις) is a prologue or brief introduction to a book, supplying the reader with certain information concerning the author, the contents, and the character of the work. In some manuscripts the hypotheses for the Gospels are ascribed to Eusebius, but more often they are anonymous.

For the Acts and the Epistles a variety of prologues and prefatory materials occur in minuscule manuscripts (see Plate 44). Some are anonymous; others are attributed to Chrysostom, to Theodoret, and to Euthalius.[115]

§29. LECTIONARY EQUIPMENT

A lectionary is a book, or a list, of Scripture lessons to be read in divine services. The practice of assigning particular portions of the Bible to particular days began, it seems, as early as the fourth century.[116]

Originally the beginning (ἀρχή) and ending (τέλος) of each pericope were noted in the margin of the manuscript (see Plates 32 and 43), or even within the text itself (see Plates 23, 24, and 29). Later the Scripture passages were collected into service books, known as the Prophetologion (see Plate 34), the Evangelarium or Gospel Lectionary (see Plates 33 and 38), and the Apostolos (see Plate 39), depending on the nature of the Biblical passages.[117]

[112] The Euthalian materials were edited by L. A. Zacagni, *Collectanea Monumentorum Veteris Ecclesiae Graecae et Latinae*, i (Rome, 1698), pp. 401–708, most of which were reprinted in Migne, *Patrologia Graeca*, lxxxv, cols. 619–790. Among the considerable amount of secondary literature on Euthalius may be mentioned J. Armitage Robinson, *Euthaliana* (Cambridge, 1895); E. von Dobschütz, 'Euthaliusstudien,' *Zeitschrift für Kirchengeschichte*, xxix (1899), pp. 107–54; H. von Soden, op. cit. (footnote 103 above), I. i (1902), pp. 637–82; C. H. Turner in Hastings's *Dictionary of the Bible*, extra vol. (1904), pp. 524–9; G. Bardy in *Dictionnaire de la Bible, Supplément*, ii (1934), cols. 1215–18; and the dissertation mentioned in the following footnote.

[113] Cf. Louis Charles Willard, 'A Critical Study of the Euthalian Apparatus,' Ph.D. diss., Yale University, 1970.

[114] For these, see Willard's dissertation, pp. 98–126.

[115] For further information concerning hypotheses, see H. von Soden, op. cit. (footnote 103 above), I.i, pp. 314 ff.

[116] For a brief discussion of the development of the Greek lectionary system, see B. M. Metzger, *The Saturday and Sunday Lessons from Luke in the Greek Gospel Lectionary* (Chicago, 1944), pp. 11 ff.

[117] On the structure of each of three kinds of service books, see, respectively, Carsten Höeg and Günther Zuntz, 'Remarks on the Prophetologion,' *Quantulacumque; Studies Presented to Kirsopp Lake . . .*, ed. by Robert P. Casey, et al. (London, 1937), pp. 189–226; B. M. Metzger, 'Greek Lectionaries and a Critical Edition of the Greek New Testament,' *Die alten Übersetzungen des Neuen Testaments, die Kirchenväterzitate und Lektionare*, ed. by Kurt Aland (Berlin and New York, 1972), pp. 479–97; and Klaus Junack, 'Zu den griechischen Lektionaren und ihrer Überlieferung der katholischen Briefe,' ibid., pp. 497–591. For a convenient guide to the passages assigned to be read throughout the ecclesiastical year, see Irmgard M. de Vries, 'The Epistles, Gospels and Tones of the Liturgical Year,' *Eastern Churches Quarterly*, x (1953–54), pp. 41–9; 85–95; 137–49; 192–5; also published separately as Reprint No. 3 'Eastern Churches Quarterly' (Antwerp, n.d.).

Greek Gospel lectionaries have two main parts, the synaxarion and the menologion. Each supplies appointed lessons for a year, but the two are organized on different calendars. The synaxarion follows the movable, ecclesiastical calendar, beginning and ending with the variable date for Easter. About two out of five synaxaria present lessons for every day of the year; the rest present lessons for Saturdays and Sundays, except for the period between Easter and Pentecost, when daily lessons are provided by almost all Greek lectionaries (for information concerning the menologion, see Plate 38).

In lectionary manuscripts the wording of the Scripture text at the beginning and, more rarely, at the end of the lection very frequently has been slightly altered in order to provide a more intelligible commencement or conclusion. For example, αὐτός of the Scripture text might be replaced with the name of the person to whom it referred. Likewise, the reading was usually prefaced with a brief phrase, called an incipit; in the Gospels this was commonly τῷ καιρῷ ἐκείνῳ[118] (see Plates 33 and 38), in the Epistles, ἀδελφοί (see Plate 39).

§30. NEUMES

NEUMES are Byzantine musical notes which assisted the ἀναγνώστης (reader) in chanting or cantillating the Scripture lesson. Their form is that of hooks, dots, and oblique strokes (see Plates 24, 31, 34, 39), and they are usually written with red (or green) ink above the words to be sung. The most ancient system of neumes—that contained in older lectionaries of the ninth to twelfth centuries—is thought by Devreesse to go back to the first centuries of Christianity.[119] Three other systems of *notation ekphonétique*, as it is called,[120] were developed during the Byzantine period, and were applied to the text in various ecclesiastical books.[121] One such liturgical book in the Eastern Church is the Oktoëchos (ὀκτώηχος [βίβλος], 'book of eight tones'; also called Paraklētikē), which contains the variable parts of the service from the first Sunday after Pentecost till the tenth Sunday before Easter. Since these variables recur every eight weeks in the same order, only eight sets of tones (ὀκτὼ ἦχοι), one for each week, are provided (see the upper writing in Plate 30).

§31. MINIATURES

IN antiquity deluxe editions of the Greek and Latin classics were sometimes adorned with pictures (called miniatures because they often were colored with

[118] For five other, less frequently used incipits in Greek Gospel lectionaries, see footnote 153.

[119] Robert Devreesse, *Introduction à l'étude des manuscrits grecs* (Paris, 1954), pp. 197 f.

[120] Cf. J.-B. Thibaut, *Monuments de la Notation Ekphonétique et Hagiopolite de l'Eglise Grecque: Exposé documentaire des manuscrits de Jérusalem, du Mt. Sinai et de l'Athos conservés à la Bibliothèque Imperiale de Saint-Pétersbourg* (St. Petersburg, 1913); Carsten Höeg, *La notation ekphonétique* (Copenhagen, 1935); H. J. W. Tillyard, *Handbook of the Middle Byzantine Musical Notation* (Copenhagen, 1935); Oliver Strunk, *Specimina notationum antiquiorum, folia selecta ex variis codicibus saec. X, XI et XII phototypice depicta*, 2 vols. (Copenhagen, 1966); and I. D. Petresco, *Études de paléographie musicale byzantine* (Bucharest, 1967). On tones see also de Vries, op. cit. (footnote 117 above).

[121] For further information concerning this highly

minium, or red lead). In the course of time these were developed into rather elaborate cycles of illustrations following the narrative in the text.[122] It is not strange that eventually Christian scribes began to illustrate copies of books of the Bible, making use of patterns, scenes, and figures current among Hellenistic and Roman artists. In other words, early Christian book illumination was not a totally new branch of art, but from the start rested upon classical traditions. Christian artists adopted and adapted not only the prevailing iconographic style, but also, when this was possible, compositional schemes as well.[123]

Among noteworthy illuminated manuscripts of the Septuagint is the ill-fated Cotton Genesis dating from the fifth or sixth century.[124] Although only charred fragments of this manuscript survived the disastrous fire in the Cotton Library in 1751, these are sufficient to indicate the superior abilities of the artist who painted the 330 or so miniatures originally contained in the manuscript. Slightly later in date than the Cotton Genesis, the miniatures in the Vienna Genesis preserve that mode of the classical style which relates to impressionism. The illustrator also enriched the extensive Joseph cycle of miniatures with extraneous elements drawn from Jewish legends (see Plate 20).[125] In the case of the Psalms,[126] instead of cycles illustrating continuous narrative, the imagination of the artist moved from one kind of scene to another (see Plate 27).

The earliest New Testament codices that contain miniatures are two uncial manuscripts of the sixth century, codex Rossanensis (Σ)[127] and codex Sinopensis

specialized field, see Devreesse, op. cit.; E. Wellesz, *A History of Byzantine Music and Hymnography*, 2nd ed. (Oxford, 1961); Constantine Floros, *Universale Neumenkunde*, 3 vols. (Kassel-Wilhelmshöhe, 1970); and Oliver Strunk, *Essays on Music in the Byzantine World* (New York, 1977).

[122] For general discussions of manuscript illumination, see David Diringer, *The Illuminated Book, its History and Production* (New York, 1958), and P. D'Ancona and E. Aeschlimann, *The Art of Illumination; an Anthology of Manuscripts from the Sixth to the Sixteenth Century* (New York, 1969). For more technical discussions, see Kurt Weitzmann, *Ancient Book Illumination* (Cambridge, Massachusetts, 1959); idem, *Illustrations in Roll and Codex; a Study of the Origin and Method of Text Illustration* (Princeton, 1947; 2nd ed., 1970); and idem, 'The Study of Byzantine Book Illumination, Past, Present, and Future," in *The Place of Book Illumination in Byzantine Art*, by K. Weitzmann, W. C. Loerke, and H. Buchthal (Princeton, 1975), pp. 1–60.

[123] See the several studies by K. Weitzmann in *Studies in Classical and Byzantine Manuscript Illumination*, ed. by H. L. Kessler (Chicago, 1971), esp. (for the Septuagint), pp. 45–75.

[124] J. J. Tikkanen, 'Die Genesismosaiken von S. Marco in Venedig und ihr Verhaltnis zu den Miniaturen der Cottonbibel,' *Acta Societatis Scientiarum Fennicae*, xvii (Helsinki, 1889), pp. 99 ff., and K. Weitzmann, 'Observations on the Cotton Genesis Fragments,' *Late Classical and Mediaeval Studies in Honor of A. M. Friend, Jr.* (Princeton, 1955), pp. 112 ff.

[125] With reference to these two illustrated copies of Genesis, Gervase Mathew makes the point that, though they are 'essentially religious art, there is nothing to suggest that the artists were primarily religious. It is clear that they worked in groups; it has been calculated by stylistic analysis that either six, seven or eight painters collaborated on the Vienna Genesis. But it is only fantasy that they may have been monks. It is far more likely that they were the staff of a large workshop that produced paintings on secular or religious subjects to order' (*Byzantine Aesthetics* [London, 1963], p. 84). For a discussion of Palaeologan art in fifteen Greek manuscripts, see Hugo Buchthal and Hans Belting, *Patronage in Thirteen-Century Constantinople; an Atelier of Early Byzantine Book Illumination and Calligraphy* (Dumbarton Oaks Studies, xvi; Washington, 1978).

[126] Cf. Ernest T. DeWald, *The Illustrations in the Manuscripts of the Septuagint*; vol. iii, *Psalms and Odes*, Part 1 (Princeton, 1941); Part 2 (1942).

[127] See A. Haseloff, *Codex Purpureus Rossanensis* (Berlin, 1898), and A. Muñoz, *Il codice purpureo di Rossano* (Rome, 1907). According to Wm. C. Loerke, the miniatures of the trial of Christ are copies of monumental composition in Jerusalem of about the mid-fifth century, perhaps from the Domus Pilati, a *locum sanctum* which recreated for the Christian pilgrim the actual courtroom in which the trial was believed to have taken place ('The Miniatures of the Trial in the Rossano Gospels,' *Art Bulletin*, xliii [1961], pp. 171–95). For a representation of the scene of Christ before Pilate, see Plate VII in Metzger's *The Text of the New Testament*.

(O).[128] The former, which contains Matthew and Mark (up to 14:14) and is written on purple parchment with silver lettering (the first three lines of each Gospel are in gold), is noteworthy for a collection of seventeen pictures at the beginning of the volume. These represent scenes from the close of the earthly ministry of Christ, beginning with the raising of Lazarus and ending with the scene of Christ and his accusers before Pilate. Codex Sinopensis comprises forty-three leaves of Matthew, written in letters of gold on purple parchment, with five pictures illustrating the Gospel text. Each of the New Testament scenes is flanked by two Old Testament personages and texts. For example, the picture of Herodias and the decapitation of John the Baptist (Matt. 14:6–12) has on its left the bust of Moses with the text of Gen. 9:6 ('Whoever sheds the blood of man, by man shall his blood be shed'), and on its right the bust of David with the text of Psalm 116:15 [115:6 LXX] ('Precious in the sight of the Lord is the death of his saints').

Portraits of the Evangelists are of two varieties: (*a*) those in which the figures are standing, and (*b*) those in which they are seated, while writing or meditating or teaching and making gestures. According to A. M. Friend, Jr.,[129] because the architectural backgrounds that often appear behind the seated Evangelists embody details of the classical theater's *scenae frons*, it is probable that the antecedents of the seated Evangelist portraits were famous statues of poets and philosophers that often formed part of the decoration of the Roman theater.

§32. GLOSSES, LEXICA, ONOMASTICA, AND COMMENTARIES

A gloss, in the technical sense used here, is a marginal note employed for explanation or illustration. The use of marginal notes can be traced to classical times when they were employed to explain for Greek students the meaning of obsolete, dialectal, or foreign words, especially such as occurred in the Homeric poems. Subsequently these notes were collected and issued in the form of a kind of lexicon for a given author. It was Aristophanes of Byzantium who, in his important work entitled Λέξεις, raised glossography to the level of lexicography.[130] Thereafter significant advances in Greek lexicography were made by Hesychius of Alexandria (v century) in his Συναγωγὴ πασῶν λέξεων κατὰ στοιχεῖον, by Photius (ix century) in his Λεξικόν, and in the anonymous encyclopedia called the Suda (ἡ Σοῦδα, x century).

[128] See H. Omont, 'Notice sur un très ancien manuscrit grec de l'Évangile de S. Matthieu en onciales d'or sur parchemin pourpé et orné de miniatures, conservé à la Bibliothèque Nationale,' *Notices et Extracts des manuscrits de la Bibliothèque Nationale*, xxxvi (1900), pp. 599–675; idem, *Fac-similés des miniatures des plus anciens manuscrits grecs de la Bibliothèque Nationale du VIe au XIe siècle* (Paris, 1902), pp. 1 ff. For reproductions of the miniatures in color, see Omont in *Monuments et Mémoires* (Fondation Eugène Piot), vii (1901), pp. 175–185, and Plates XVI–XIX.

[129] 'The Portraits of the Evangelists in Greek and Latin Manuscripts,' *Art Studies*, v (1927), pp. 115–47, and vii (1929), pp. 3–29. See also U. Nilgen, 'Evangelisten,' in E. Kirschbaum's *Lexikon der christlichen Ikonographie*, i (Rome, Freiburg, Basel, Vienna, 1968), cols. 696–713, and R. P. Bergman, 'Portraits of the Evangelists in Greek Manuscripts,' *Illuminated Greek Manuscripts from American Collections*, ed. by Gary Vikan (Princeton, 1973), pp. 44–49.

A large number of representations of the Evangelists may now be conveniently found in the monumental Οἱ Θησαυροὶ τοῦ Ἁγίου Ὄρους. Εἰκονογραφημένα Χειρόγραφα, vols. i and ii (Athens 1973, 1975).

[130] See J. E. Sandys, *A History of Classical Scholarship: from the Sixth Century B. C. to the End of the Middle Ages*,

In the case of the transmission of the text of the Greek Bible there was a similar development from random glosses standing in the margins of manuscripts (see Plate 32) to the collection of such notes in alphabetic sequence. Fruits of such labors were subsequently added to Hesychius's Συναγωγή as a Biblical supplement to his classical Greek lexicon. In early Byzantine times Bible lexica, resting in part on the work of Hesychius and others, were drawn up and adapted for use in connection with specific parts of the Scriptures. There were, for example, a *Λέξεις τῆς Ὀκτατεύχου*,[131] a *Λέξεις* for each of the Gospels, for Acts (see below), and for other Biblical books.[132]

Onomastica are special collections of glosses explaining the meaning of the names of persons and places. The preponderance of Semitic names in the Old and New Testaments presented to Greek readers abundant subject matter for such inquiry. In common with all discussions in antiquity concerning the etymology of words—discussions which in the light of modern comparative linguistics are frequently naïve and/or absurd[133]—Biblical onomastica contain a high percentage of doubtful and/or erroneous information.

Onomastic traditions concerning names in the Septuagint were developed by Philo, carried forward by Origen and Eusebius, and translated into Latin by Jerome. Eventually such materials were classified, drawn up in tabular form, and included in manuscripts of the Bible. In minuscule manuscripts one now and then finds prefixed to each of the Gospels, or to the Book of Revelation, a list of the proper names contained in that book, each name being supplied with its supposed significance. As a sample, in addition to the lists included by Wutz in his magisterial monograph,[134] the following transcription of the first part of the onomasticon prefixed to the Gospel of Matthew in the twelfth-century codex 1315 will give some indication of this kind of 'Helps for Readers.'

Λεξικὸν τοῦ κατὰ Ματθαῖον ἁγίου Εὐαγγελίου

Βαρθολομαῖος, *υἱὸς κρεμάσας ὕδατα·* Βηθσαϊδᾶ, *οἶκος ἐπισιτισμοῦ·* Βαριωνᾶ, *υἱὸς περιστερᾶς·* Βηθσφαγή, *οἶκος στόματος ἢ φάραγγος·* Βηθανία, *οἶκος ὑπακοῆς·* Βαραχία, *εὐλόγησε κύριος·* Βαραββάν, *υἱὸν διδασκάλου ἢ υἱὸν πατρός·* Γενησαρέτ, *κῆποι ἀρχόντων·* Γεέννης, *φάραγχος·* Γεργεσίων, *προαστείων ἢ προσηλύτου·* Γαδαρηνῶν, *γενεὰς οἴκων αὔτη·* Γολγοθᾶ, *κρανίου . . . .*

In other lists, instead of an alphabetic order[135] the sequence is in accord with the order in which the words appear in the Scripture text. The following is the

2nd ed., i (Cambridge, 1908), p. 129, and Goetz, 'Glossographie,' Pauly-Wissowa-Kroll, *Real-Encyclopädie der classischen Altertumswissenschaft*, vii, 1 (1910), cols. 1433–66.

[131] Edited by Jacob Benediktsson in *Classica et Mediaevalia*, i (1938), pp. 243–80.

[132] For what appears to be an early Greek-Latin lexicon on the Apostle Paul, see Alfons Wouters, 'A Greek Grammar and a Graeco-Latin Lexicon on St. Paul (Rom., 2 Cor., Gal., Eph.): A Note on E. A. Lowe C.L.A. Supplement No. 1683,' *Scriptorium*, xxxi (1977), pp. 240–2.

[133] For examples, see William Dudley Woodhead, *Etymologizing in Greek Literature from Homer to Philo Judaeus*, Ph.D. diss., University of Toronto, 1928.

[134] Franz Wutz, *Onomastica sacra; Untersuchungen zum Liber interpretationis nominum Hebraicorum des hl. Hieronymus* (Texte und Untersuchungen, xli; Leipzig, 1914, 1915).

[135] It will be observed from the list given above that the alphabetizing has been imperfectly done; for the history of the development of the custom of alphabetizing, see Daly's monograph mentioned above in footnote 16.

opening section of the glossary prefixed to the Acts of the Apostles in codex 1315, in which words and expressions are defined briefly (chapter and verse numbers have been supplied):

Λέξεις τῶν Πράξεων τῶν Ἀποστόλων

[1:3] ὀπτανόμενος, ὁρώμενος ἤ φαινόμενος. [1:4] συναλιζόμενος, συναθροιζόμενος καὶ σὺν αὐτοῖς. [1:9] ὑπέλαβεν, ὑπεδέξατο. [1:10] ἀτενίζοντες, βλέποντες. [1:12] σαββάτου ἔχον ὁδόν, τοσοῦτον διάστημα εἰς ὃν δύνατον τὸν Ἰουδαῖον περιπατεῖν ἐν σαββάτῳ. [2:19] ἀτμίδα, τὴν αἴθμην . . . .

The following are the first six or seven items in the glossary prefixed to the Epistles in the same manuscript:

Λέξεις τῶν ἐπιστολῶν

[Rom. 1:1] ἀφορισμένος, ἐκλελεγμένος, διακριμένος. [Rom. 1:9] λατρεύω, δουλεύω. [Rom. 1:9] ἀδιαλείπτως, διηνεκῆς πάντων. [Rom. 1:11] στηριχθῆναι, βεβαιωθῆναι. [Rom. 1:20] ἀΐδιος, αἰώνια. [Rom. 1:30] θεοστυγεῖς, παρὰ θεοῦ μεμισημένοις. [Rom. 1:31] ἀστόργους, μὴ ἀγαπῶντας . . . .

In addition to such lexicographic glosses there also developed in ever fuller detail hermeneutic traditions presented in the form of scholia (σχόλια). A scholion is a marginal note, usually on a difficult passage, explaining its meaning.[136] The earliest patristic collection of such scholia appears to be the *Hypotyposes* of Clement of Alexandria, of which unfortunately only fragments are extant today (for one such fragment see Plate 31). Origen's scholia, to judge from those that have been preserved, were characterized by brevity and cogency. They contain notes on the text (see Plate 32), pertinent interpretations, and information on the subject matter, with relatively little allegorizing.

From such random notes accompanying the text of a Biblical book there developed ever more elaborate commentaries. Sometimes the comments were written in the margins around the Scripture text (see Plate 41); at other times the scribe alternated a section of the text with a section of comment (see Plate 42). In either case the scribe would often provide the name (or the abbreviation of the name) of the Church Father from whom the comment was borrowed. A compilation of such comments, extracted from a variety of exegetical commentaries, is called a catena ('a chain').[137] A total of twelve uncial manuscripts and 542 minuscule manuscripts of the New Testament are provided with commentary.[138]

[136] See G. Heinrici, 'Scholia,' *The New Schaff-Herzog Encyclopedia of Religious Knowledge*, x (1911), pp. 269–71, and A. Gudeman, 'Scholien,' Pauly-Wissowa-Kroll, *Real-Encyclopädie der klassischen Altertumswissenschaft*, 2te Reihe, iii (1921), cols. 625–705.

[137] Cf. Robert Devreesse, 'Chaînes, exégétiques grecques,' *Dictionnaire de la Bible, Supplément* i (Paris, 1928), cols. 1084–1233; Karl Staab, *Pauluskommentare aus der griechischen Kirche, aus Katenenhandschriften gesammelt und herausgegeben* (Münster, 1933); and R. Devreesse, 'Catenae,' *Twentieth Century Encyclopedia of Religious Knowledge*, i (Grand Rapids, 1955), pp. 217 f.

[138] For a classified list of commentary-codices of the New Testament, see H. von Soden, op. cit. (footnote 103 above), i, pp. 249–89; 525–637; 682–704; see especially the statistical summary, pp. 289–92.

APPENDIX I

How to Estimate the Date of a Greek Manuscript

In some manuscripts we find at the close a colophon (see §13) in which the scribe mentions the date when the work of copying was completed. The year is usually given according to the Mundane or Adamic era.[139] This was reckoned from September 1, 5509 B.C., which was believed to be the date of the creation of the world. In many cases the day of the month and sometimes the day of the week and even the hour of the day are also noted, and often the year of the current indiction is included (see Plates 31 and 35).[140]

Since most manuscripts, however, lack such chronological information, their approximate age must be determined on the basis of considerations of the style of the script. Now, the evolution of handwriting is a gradual process, and one form gives way to another almost imperceptibly. A considerable lapse of time is generally required to produce significant changes in the shapes of the letters and the general appearance of the script.[141]

It is understandable that one finds quite marked differences between the average hand of, say, A.D. 900 and that of 1300. For one thing, as time went on there was a very great increase in the number and kinds of ligatures (see Figs. 5 and 7). For another, what can be described only as a general decline in the minuscule hand occurred as scribes apparently devoted less care to their handiwork and preferred rapid to careful copying. Considerable diversity developed in handwriting, and in some cases the writing is irregular with letters that vary considerably in size.

At the same time, the beginning of certain features or practices can be identified. For example, infralinear writing appeared as early as A.D. 917, and it became common about the middle of the tenth century; however, the letters were sometimes still written on the line as late as 975.[142]

Taking account of the shape of breathing marks provides broad parameters in dating minuscule Greek manuscripts. According to a rule formulated by Gardthausen,[143] square breathing marks occur in codices written before the year 1000, whereas only round breathings are found after 1300. During the period between these two dates both kinds of breathings were used.

[139] The custom of dating events from the year in which Jesus Christ was supposed to have been born was introduced by Hippolytus of Rome, who flourished in the third century. This system, however, was not used by Byzantine scribes for the dating of manuscripts until the fourteenth century, and even then it was generally accompanied by the Anno Mundi reckoning.

[140] An indiction is a cycle or period of fifteen years. The Constantinian system of indictions was inaugurated by Constantine, the series of indictions beginning on September 1, 312. For tables of the indictions, see V. Gardthausen, op. cit. (footnote 2 above), ii, pp. 487–97.

[141] An exception to this statement is the appearance of the minuscule hand adopted for the writing of books at the beginning of the ninth century (see §16).

[142] So W. H. P. Hatch, *Facsimiles and Descriptions of Minuscule Manuscripts of the New Testament* (Cambridge, Massachusetts, 1951), p. 20, n. 16.

[143] Op. cit. (footnote 2), ii, pp. 386–8.

Another feature in the evolution of minuscule script is the intrusion, in ever greater numbers, of uncial forms of certain letters (notably Γ, Δ, Є, Η, Θ, Ν, and C), replacing the corresponding minuscule forms. By collecting statistics on the proportion of minuscule to uncial forms of ϵ, η, λ, and π in 111 dated New Testament manuscripts, Colwell and others[144] have been able to formulate certain generalizations of usage that are helpful in attempting to ascertain the approximate date of undated manuscripts.

The upshot of the preceding discussion of the development of the minuscule hand is that, though certain landmarks can be discerned, many scholars confess that it remains extremely difficult, if not impossible, to be confident in determining within narrow limits the date of a minuscule manuscript between 1050 and 1350.[145] Furthermore, whether the manuscript be uncial or minuscule two considerations must be kept in mind. (*a*) Sometimes a scribe took an earlier hand as his model, and consequently his work presents an archaic appearance that is not characteristic of his time.[146] (*b*) Since the style of a person's handwriting may remain more or less constant throughout life, it is unrealistic to seek to fix upon a date narrower than a fifty-year spread.[147]

In spite of the preceding caveats it still remains useful to attempt to date the handwriting of an undated manuscript by comparing it with dated manuscripts. Happily a considerable number of the latter have been identified and facsimile specimens of many have been made available. For a chronological list of several hundred dated Greek manuscripts, extending from about A.D. 512 to 1593, see Devreesse's *Introduction*,[148] and for reproductions of selected folios of dated manuscripts, see the collections published by the Lakes, by Turyn, and by others mentioned in the Bibliography (pp. 141 ff. below).

144 E. C. Colwell, 'Some Criteria for Dating Byzantine New Testament Manuscripts,' an Appendix in *The Four Gospels of Karahissar*, i, *History and Text* (Chicago, 1936), pp. 225–41; reprinted in Colwell, *Studies in Methodology in Textual Criticism of the New Testament* (Leiden and Grand Rapids, 1969), pp. 125–41. See also E. Folieri, 'La reintroduzione di lettere semionciali nei più antichi manoscritti greci in minuscola,' *Bollettino dell'Archivio Paleografico Italiano*, III, 1 (1962), pp. 15–36, who examines specimen folios of 56 manuscripts dated between 835 and 975, and R. Valentini, 'La reintroduzione dell'onciale e la datazione dei manoscritti greci in minuscola,' *Scritti in onore di †Carlo Diano* (Bologna, 1975), pp. 455–70, who presents statistics concerning the use of various forms of Β, Δ, Η, Κ, and Λ, as well as several sigla and compendia, in 123 specimens of manuscripts included in the Lakes' album of dated minuscule manuscripts.

145 Paul Maas observes that in calligraphic books the 'mixed minuscule' remains without noticeable variation from the eleventh to the fifteenth century (*Griechische Palaeographie*, 3te Aufl., in Alfred Gercke and Eduard Norden, *Einleitung in der Altertumswissenschaft* [Leipzig, 1927], pp. 28 and 80 f.).

146 On scribes who deliberately archaize the style of their handwriting, see Hunger's article cited above in footnote 50.

147 On the need to allow at least half a century leeway in dating manuscripts, see B. A. van Groningen's strongly worded comment: 'There is just one thing that I would like to mention because I think it is rather too often forgotten. Now my age is 70, and I write practically in the same way as when I was 20. If after 2,000 years there is a scrap of manuscript which was written by me, it could not possibly be said whether it was written in 1964 or in 1914, and I say that we must always be careful and not be too precise in our datings because you always have the difference of half a century in one man's life' (*Bulletin of the American Society of Papyrologists*, ii [1964–65], p. 16).

148 Robert Devreesse, *Introduction à l'étude des manuscrits grecs* (Paris, 1954), pp. 286–320; it should be observed that Turyn's collections of dated Greek manuscripts were published subsequently. For an examination of 213 dated Greek manuscripts (only seven of which, strangely enough, were written between 1200 and 1250), see Howard C. Kee, 'Palaeography of Dated New Testament Manuscripts before 1300,' unpublished Ph.D. dissertation, Yale University, 1951. Kee, who in general confirms Colwell's investigations (see footnote 144 above), finds slightly more conservatism in resisting the introduction of uncial letters in straight Gospel manuscripts than in lectionary manuscripts (p. 181). See also Kurt Treu, 'Die Schreiber der datierten byzantinischen Handschriften des 9. und 10. Jahrhunderts,' *Beiträge zur byzantinischen Ge-*

In conclusion, whether one is estimating the age of an undated manuscript or attempting to determine if two manuscripts were written by the same scribe,[149] the counsel of two eminent palaeographers, Kirsopp and Silva Lake, is appropriate:

> Palaeographers are divided into two schools. One dates manuscripts by the shape of individual letters, the other by the general impression of the script. In our opinion both are correct in part. The general impression is the starting-point, but this must be checked by a study of the individual letters. A combination of the two methods is perhaps the only way of deciding whether the same scribe did or did not write any two manuscripts.[150]

schichte im 9.–11. Jahrhundert, ed. by Vladimír Vavřínek (Prague, 1978), pp. 235–51.

[149] For a list of the names of scribes, see Marie Vogel and Viktor Gardthausen, *Die griechischen Schreiber des Mittelalters und der Renaissance* (Leipzig, 1909; reprinted, Hildesheim, 1966), pp. 124 f. Supplements to the list have been published by Ch. G. Patrinélis in 'Επετηρὶς τοῦ Μεσαιωνικοῦ 'Αρχείου, viii–ix (1958–59), pp. 63–124; P. Canart in *Scriptorium*, xvii (1963), pp. 56–82; K. A. de Meyier, ibid., xviii (1964), pp. 258–66; and B. L. Fonkitch in *Vizantijskij Vremennik*, xxvi (1965), pp. 266–71.

[150] 'The Scribe Ephraim,' *Journal of Biblical Literature*, lxii (1943), p. 264.

APPENDIX II

How to Collate a Greek Manuscript

An editor can report the text of a manuscript in two ways: either the text can be reproduced in its entirety (by photography or by transcription) or it can be collated. To collate means to compare the text of the manuscript with another text, chosen as a standard,[151] and to report each and every difference from the basic text.

The advantages of the collation process include (*a*) the ease with which one can then determine the distinctive elements of the new manuscript, (*b*) the relatively compact form of the report of those distinctive elements, and (*c*) the utility of such evidence in preparing a critical apparatus of variant readings.

In recording a collation one should, of course, mention the name and edition of the text chosen as the collating base. Chapter and verse numbers ought to be given with each separate item in the collation (see example on p. 116 below).

The first element in each entry is the reading of the collating base, followed by a square bracket (]); the second element is the reading of the manuscript being collated. No unnecessary words should be included in the collation. For example, if the printed text reads εν ουρανῳ and the manuscript reads εν τῳ ουρανῳ, the collation should read simply εν] + τῳ. If the manuscript lacks a word that is present in the printed text, that word is entered in the collation preceded by a minus sign. In case the word or phrase occurs more than once in the same verse, a small superscript numeral following the word or phrase will indicate which occurrence is intended; for example, − και^2. If the variation involves the sequence of two or more words, the collation should read, for example, ειπε ο Ιησους] ο Ιησους ειπε.

When two or more successive words differ from the collating base, they should be recorded together as one variant reading if they are grammatically or logically associated (for example, εν αυτῳ] εις αυτον), but should be recorded separately if they could occur independently of one another.

Abbreviations, symbols, and the like in the manuscript should be read as though the scribe had spelled them fully, and they therefore need not be mentioned in the collation if this spelling agrees with that of the collating base. An exception is the *nomen sacrum* $\overline{\delta\alpha\delta}$, which can represent any of the several spellings of the Greek word for David. This contraction therefore must be recorded as a contraction, to show that it cannot be assumed to support a particular spelling. Sometimes it is

[151] It has been customary to collate New Testament manuscripts against the so-called Textus Receptus (for example, against the Oxford edition of the Greek New Testament prepared by Charles Lloyd in 1825 and reprinted many times thereafter). Inasmuch as the Textus Receptus represents the later Byzantine type of text, a collation made against such a base will disclose the non-Byzantine elements of the manuscript.

also useful to indicate whether numerals are expressed by words or by letters of the alphabet.

For some purposes in collating, differences involving *nu*-moveable need not be recorded. If, however, there is any doubt about the wisdom of omitting information concerning such differences, they should be cited throughout the collation.

If any words or letters in the manuscript being collated are uncertain or illegible, the following procedures should be observed:

A letter partially legible but still somewhat doubtful should be written with a dot under it; for example, *επιου̣σ̣ιον*.[152]

A letter that is totally illegible should be represented by a dot; for example, *επιο*[· ·]*ιον*.

When the state of preservation of a manuscript makes complete verification of a reading impossible (for example, *τιη* in Plate 5), it should be marked *vid* (standing for the Latin *videtur*, 'it seems') to indicate apparent support.

When a reading in a manuscript has been corrected, both readings should be recorded; for example,

> *κυριος*] omitted by first hand and added in margin
> *ειπον*] *ειπα*, corrected to *ειπαν*

In collating Greek lectionary manuscripts one should indicate the day for which the lection is appointed to be read. Furthermore, the conventional introductory phrase (incipit) is ordinarily represented in a collation by a roman numeral,[153] followed by whatever modification in the Scriptural wording has taken place. For example, the Textus Receptus of Matt. 11:2 reads *ὁ δὲ 'Ιωάννης ἀκούσας ἐν τῷ δεσμωτηρίῳ τὰ ἔργα τοῦ Χριστοῦ*, whereas certain lectionaries begin the lection for the second day of the fourth week after Easter as follows: *τῷ καιρῷ ἐκείνῳ ἀκούσας ὁ 'Ιωάννης ἐν τῷ δεσμωτηρίῳ τὰ ἔργα τοῦ Χριστοῦ*. The collation of the beginning of this lection, therefore, should be represented as follows: *β̄ τῆς δ̄ ἑβδ* Matt. 11:2 Inc I *ακουσας ο Ιωαννης εν* (followed by the siglum of the lectionary that is being collated).

[152] On the difficulty of deciding when it is appropriate to use a dot under a letter, and what the user of the collation may be expected to understand concerning the degree of (un)certainty of the reading, see the discussion by Herbert C. Youtie, 'Text and Context in Transcribing Papyri,' *Greek, Roman, and Byzantine Studies*, vii (1966), pp. 251–8, reprinted in his *Scriptiunculae*, i (Amsterdam, 1973), pp. 25–32.

[153] The six incipits customarily found in Greek Gospel lections are as follows:

Inc I = *τῷ καιρῷ ἐκείνῳ*
Inc II = *εἶπεν ὁ κύριος τοῖς ἑαυτοῦ μαθηταῖς*
Inc III = *εἶπεν ὁ κύριος πρὸς ἐληλυθότας πρὸς αὐτὸν 'Ιουδαίους*
Inc IV = *εἶπεν ὁ κύριος πρὸς τοὺς πεπιστευκότας αὐτῷ 'Ιουδαίους*
Inc V = *εἶπεν ὁ κύριος*
Inc VI = *εἶπεν ὁ κύριος τὴν παραβολὴν ταύτην*

APPENDIX III

Statistics Relating to the Manuscripts of the Greek New Testament

In addition to the brief comment in the text concerning the relative numbers of uncial and minuscule manuscripts of the Greek New Testament (§16), the following statistics provide more precise details. As generally reckoned today,[154] there are four categories of New Testament manuscripts: papyri, uncial manuscripts, minuscule manuscripts, and lectionaries. Statistics concerning each of these categories (as of 1976) are as follows:[155]

Manuscripts Catalogued		*Uncial Script*	*Minuscule Script*
Papyri $\mathfrak{p}^{1}$–$\mathfrak{p}^{88}$		88	
Uncial MSS 01–0274		274	
Minuscule MSS 1–2795			2795
Lectionaries *l*1–*l*2209		245	1964
	totals	607	4759

Total number of N.T. lectionaries: 2209

Total number of N.T. manuscripts: 5366

A manuscript that contains the entire Bible was sometimes called a *pandect* (πανδέκτης). None have survived intact in Greek, though at one time the uncial manuscripts ℵ A B C were complete in both Testaments. Today the only uncial manuscript that contains all the books of the New Testament is codex Sinaiticus (Plate 14). Of the total number of minuscule manuscripts only 34 are complete and without lacunae for the entire New Testament; a list of these by century indicates that 14 belong to the fourteenth century. (In the following list the designation 'abs' attached to MS. 205 signifies that the manuscript is known to be a copy, or *Abschrift*, of MS. 205. Instances of a known copy of another manuscript are exceedingly rare, which suggests that only a very small percentage of manuscripts have survived).

154 Earlier this century two additional categories of New Testament witnesses, namely talismans and ostraca, were listed by Ernst von Dobschütz in *Eberhard Nestle's Einführung in das Griechische Neue Testament*, 4te Aufl. (Göttingen, 1923), pp. 80 and 85 f. Today these categories are no longer utilized; $\mathfrak{T}^{1}$ is now identified as 0152, and $\mathfrak{O}^{1-20}$ as 0153 (see Kurt Aland, *Kurzgefasste Liste der griechischen Handschriften des Neuen Testaments*, i [Berlin, 1963]). Ostraca are fragments of unglazed pottery vessels (which could be picked up from any rubbish heap) and were used in antiquity as we use scrap paper today. A series of twenty ostraca, written in three different hands probably in the seventh century, preserve portions of the Greek text of the four Gospels, the longest continuous text of which is Luke 22:40–71. See G. Lefebvre, *Fragments grecs des Évangiles sur Ostraka* (Bulletin de l'Institut français d'archéologie orientale, iv [Cairo, 1904]), and A. Deissmann, *Light from the Ancient East*, new ed. (New York, 1927), pp. 57–60.

155 The official list of New Testament Greek manuscripts is Kurt Aland's *Kurzgefasste Liste*, supplemented by continuations in his *Materialien zur neutestamentlichen Handschriften* (Berlin, 1969), pp. 1–37, and in *Bericht der Stiftung zur Förderung der neutestamentlichen Textforschung für die Jahre 1972 bis 1974* (Munster/Westfalen, 1974), pp. 9–16, and *Bericht . . . 1975 und 1976* (1977), pp. 10–12.

century	*manuscripts*
xi	35, 241, 1384
xii	242, 922
xii/xiii	180
xiii	339, 1597
xiii/xiv	1785
xiv	18, 201, 367, 386, 582, 680, 824, 925, 1075, 1503, 1637, 1678, 2200, 2494
xiv/xv	209
xv	149, 205, 205[abs], 644, 886, 1617, 2554
xvi	61, 296, 1704

Whether manuscripts contain the whole or only part of the New Testament, the order of books in most copies is Gospels, Acts, Catholic Epistles, Pauline Epistles (with Hebrews between 2 Thessalonians and 1 Timothy), Revelation.[156] The sequence of Pauline Epistles preceding Catholic Epistles occurs in a few Greek minuscule manuscripts as well as in a good many Latin manuscripts, from which it was adopted in editions of the Latin Vulgate (according to the decree of the Council of Trent in 1546) and in versions in modern languages. In half a dozen manuscripts, including codex Sinaiticus (Plate 14) and MS. 69 (Plate 45), the Pauline Epistles precede Acts. In 𝔓[46] (Plate 6) Hebrews follows Romans, and in an ancestor from which codex Vaticanus was copied (see p. 41 above) Hebrews followed Galatians. The four Gospels usually stand in their familiar order, but in codex Bezae (Plate 19), as well as in several Old Latin manuscripts and in the Gothic version, they are in the sequence Matthew, John, Luke, Mark.[157]

A considerable number of New Testament Greek manuscripts present the text in more than one language.[158] In a few cases the second language is interlinear (see Plate 28); in the great majority, however, the two texts stand in adjoining columns (see Plates 22 and 40) or on facing pages (see Plate 19). When Greek is one of the two languages, it customarily stands in the left-hand column or on the left-hand page, and the other language on the right (for an exception, see Plate 22). The following lists identify ninety-seven New Testament Greek manuscripts that present the text in two or more languages:

[156] This sequence was adopted in the editions published by Lachmann (1842–50), Tischendorf (1869–72), Tregelles (1857–79), Westcott-Hort (1881), Baljon (1898), von Gebhardt (1901), and von Soden (1913).

[157] For information about still other sequences in Greek and versional manuscripts, see Caspar René Gregory, *Textkritik des Neuen Testamentes*, ii (Leipzig, 1902; reprinted 1976), pp. 848–58.

[158] For information concerning these manuscripts, as well as lists of other bilingual and polylingual New Testament manuscripts that have no Greek text, see the present writer's contribution to the forthcoming Festschrift in honor of Prof. Bo Reicke.

BILINGUAL NEW TESTAMENT GREEK MSS.

Languages	*Gregory–Aland numbers*
Greek and Arabic	0136, 0137, 211, 609, *l*6, *l*225, *l*311, *l*762, *l*804, *l*937, *l*1023, *l*1343, *l*1344, *l*1746, *l*1733, *l*1774
Greek and Armenian	256
Greek and Coptic	$\mathfrak{p}^{6}$, $\mathfrak{p}^{41}$, $\mathfrak{p}^{42}$, $\mathfrak{p}^{62}$, T, 070, 086, 0100, 0110, 0113, 0124, 0125, 0129, 0139, 0164, 0177, 0178, 0179, 0180, 0184, 0190, 0191, 0193, 0200, 0202, 0203, 0204, 0205, 0236, 0237, 0238, 0239, 0260, *l*143, *l*961, *l*962, *l*963, *l*964a, *l*964b, *l*965, *l*1353, *l*1355, *l*1575, *l*1602, *l*1603, *l*1604, *l*1606, *l*1607, *l*1614, *l*1678, *l*1739, *l*1994
Greek and Latin	D (Bezae), D (Claromontanus), E (Laudianus), F, G (Boernerianus), Δ, 0130, 0230, 9^{abs}, 16, 17, 74, 130, 165, 620, 628, 629, 694, 866b, *l*925
Greek and Slavonic	525, 2136, 2137
Greek and Turkish	1325

TRILINGUAL NEW TESTAMENT GREEK MSS.

Coptic, Greek, and Arabic	*l*1993
Greek, Coptic, and Arabic	*l*1605
Greek, Latin, and Arabic	460

According to statistics published in 1967, of a total of 5236 manuscripts of the Greek New Testament, 80 percent are in eight countries. In first place, as would be expected, is Greece, with 1458 manuscripts; then follow Italy with 729; Great Britain, 474; France, 390; Soviet Union, 299; USA, 295; Egypt, 254; and Germany, 128. Listed according to location, more than 500 manuscripts are on Mount Athos; between 200 and 500 are at London, Paris, Rome, Athens, and Mount Sinai; between 100 and 200, at Oxford, Leningrad, and Jerusalem; between 50 and 100, at Cambridge, Berlin, Venice, Florence, Grottaferrata, Patmos, Moscow, Ann Arbor, and Chicago.[159]

In all of Central and South America there is, so far as is reported in Aland's official listing, only one manuscript of the Greek New Testament.[160]

[159] For these statistics, see K. Aland, *Studien zur Überlieferung des Neuen Testamentes und seines Textes* (Berlin, 1967), pp. 208 and 227.

[160] In 1952 the present writer made inquiry of twelve large libraries and museums in South America concerning their holdings of New Testament manuscripts. Of the four replies received, only one (from the National Library at Rio de Janeiro) stated that the library had one Greek manuscript, the content of which was unknown. Later that year a visit to the library disclosed that the manuscript is a twelfth-century parchment codex of the four Gospels, lacking the early chapters of Matthew. A brief description of the manuscript was sent to Professor Kurt Aland (who assigned the number 2437 to the manuscript) and a more lengthy description was published in an article (tranlated into Portuguese by Philip S. Landes), 'Un manuscrito grego dos quatro evangelhos na Biblioteca Nacional do Río de Janeiro,' *Revista teológica do Seminario Presbiteriano do Sul* (Campinas), N.F. ii (1952–53), pp. 5–10. A microfilm of the manuscript is in Speer Library, Princeton Theological Seminary.

PART TWO

Plates and Descriptions

Plates and Descriptions

THE following plates depict specimen pages from a variety of manuscripts of the Greek Bible, chosen because of some special feature, whether palaeographic, historical, or textual. Cross-references to and from the first section of the volume will assist the reader to correlate the systematic discussion there with specific points illustrated in the several plates.

The description of each manuscript follows a certain pattern. The heading supplies information as to the passage of Scripture reproduced in the plate and the name and/or number of the manuscript, with its date. In the case of Old Testament manuscripts, the identification is in accord with the system developed by Alfred Rahlfs in his *Verzeichnis der griechischen Handschriften des Alten Testaments* (Göttingen, 1914), and continued by Robert Hanhart of the University of Göttingen. In the case of New Testament manuscripts the identification is in accord with the system devised by Caspar René Gregory and continued by Kurt Aland in his *Kurzgefasste Liste der griechischen Handschriften des Neuen Testaments*, i. *Gesamtübersicht* (Berlin, 1963).

The line following the heading presents information concerning the place, the collection, the number within that collection, and the folio of the manuscript shown in the plate. The opening paragraph ordinarily provides a summary of palaeographic and codicological features of the manuscript as a whole. The dates assigned to undated manuscripts are generally in accord with those suggested by Rahlfs or Aland, or, in the case of recently discovered items, by the editor of the document. All dates are to be understood as belonging to the Christian era except those that are expressly designated as B.C. In giving the measurements of a manuscript, the height is followed by the width.

In the discussion that follows the opening paragraph of each description, attention is drawn to features that make the manuscript important palaeographically, historically, or textually. In most cases the description closes with a brief bibliography bearing on one or another aspect of the given manuscript.

The script of each of the several manuscripts shown in the plates is reproduced in its actual size unless the area of writing on a folio exceeds the height and width of a page in the present book (11 × 8½ inches; 28 × 21.6 cm.). In a few cases the empty margins of a folio have been cropped by the photographer so that the script could be shown more nearly in its actual size.

In the transcription of texts shown in the plates, instances of itacism as well as erroneous accent and breathing marks have been corrected; likewise, capitalization and punctuation (when introduced) follow modern editorial conventions. A dot under a Greek letter signifies that there is some amount of doubt as to the reading. A letter that is totally illegible is represented by a centered dot.

1. Deuteronomy 25:1–3. Rahlfs 957. ii cent. B.C.

MANCHESTER, JOHN RYLANDS LIBRARY, P. RYL. 458, FRAG. B.

In 1917 the John Rylands Library of Manchester acquired two pieces of cartonnage (wrapping used for encasing mummies), made of an amalgam of small papyrus scraps that included fragments of four separate columns of a roll containing the Greek text of Deuteronomy. The verso of the roll was used for taking an account before it went to the scrap-merchant to be made into cartonnage. Fragment *b*, shown in the Plate, measures 3⅛ × 3¼ in. (8 × 8.4 cm.).

The writing, dated by the editor to the ii century B.C., is carefully executed and heavily ornamented; cf. *kappa* (line 5), *mu* (line 4), *nu* (line 5), and *tau* (line 1). The scribe left a small space at the end of a group of words and a slightly larger one at the end of a clause or end of a sentence (as in fragment *a*, not shown in the Plate). In line 4 a dot is visible between the *α* and *σ* of *μαστιγωσιν*; the editor thinks that 'apparently the scribe wrote *ματ*, then corrected the *τ* to a *σ*, erasing the left horizontal stroke of the *τ*, and the apparent dot is the remnant of the hook of the original *τ*.'

καιον   και καταγνωσι̣[ν του ασεβους]
[κ]α̣ι εσται εαν αξι̣[ος η πληγων ο ασε]
[βη]ς   και καθιει αυτον ε̣ν̣[αντιον]
[αυτ]ο̣υ   και μαστιγωσιν [αυτον εναντι]
[ον αυ]τ̣ων   κατα την ασεβ̣[ειαν αυτου]
[αριθμω]ι τεσσαρακο̣ντα [μαστιγωσου]
[σιν αυτο]ν   ου προσθησου[σιν εαν δε]
[προσθω]σιν   μαστιγω[σαι αυτον κτλ.]

BIBLIOGRAPHY: C. H. Roberts, *Two Biblical Papyri in the John Rylands Library* (Manchester, 1936), pp. 9–46; idem, *Catalogue of the Greek and Latin Papyri in the John Rylands Library*, iii (Manchester, 1938), pp. 3–8; H. G. Opitz and H. H. Schaeder, 'Zum Septuaginta-Papyrus Rylands Greek 458,' *Zeitschrift für die neutestamentliche Wissenschaft*, xxxv (1936), pp. 115–17; A. Vaccari, S.J., 'Fragmentum Biblicum saeculi II ante Christum,' *Biblica*, xvii (1936), pp. 501–4. Cf. Paul E. Kahle, *The Cairo Geniza*, 2nd ed. (Oxford, 1959), pp. 220–2.

2. Exodus 28:4–6. Rahlfs 803. About 100 B.C.

JERUSALEM, PALESTINE ARCHAEOLOGICAL MUSEUM, 7Q1 LXX EX.

Cave VII at Qumran is unique in that it contained only Greek documents, with no Hebrew or Aramaic texts (except רומא written twice on a large jar). Among the Greek documents, the text of which can be identified with certainty, are two papyrus fragments which, after an examination of the fibres, appear to belong near to each other; they measure (together), about 2 × ⅞ inches (5 × 2.3 cm.) and contain Exodus 28:4–6. Since only one side has writing, it is probable that the scraps are from a roll.

The uncial script is ornamented with small hooks or serifs at the extremities of certain letters (similar to Schubart's 'Zierstil'; see §15), and can be dated to about 100 B.C. (so C. H. Roberts). *Alpha*, *kappa*, and *omega* are each made with two strokes of the pen.

(Frag. 1)
[ρῶν τῷ ἀ]δ̣[ελ]φ[ῷ σου καὶ τοῖς]
[υἱοῖς α]ὐ̣τοῦ ἱερα[τεύειν αὐ-]
[τὸν ἐμ]οί. [5]Καὶ αὐ[τοὶ λήμψον-]
[ται] τ̣ὸ χρυσίο̣ν̣ [καὶ τὸν ὑά-]
[κιν]θον καὶ τ̣ὴ̣[ν πορφύραν]
[καὶ] τ̣ὸ κόκκι[νον καὶ τὴν]
[βύσσο]ν̣. [6]Κα̣[ὶ ποιήσου-]
[σιν τὴν ἐ]π̣ω[μίδα ἐκ χρυ-]
[σίου καὶ ὑα]κ̣ί̣ν̣[θου καὶ πορ-]
[φύρας καὶ κοκκίνου νενη-]
[σμένου καὶ βύσσου κεκλω-]
[σμένης, ἔργον ὑφάντου ποι-]
[κιλτοῦ· [7]δύο ἐπωμίδες συν-]
(Frag. 2) [έχουσαι ἔ]σ̣ο̣ν̣[ται αὐτῷ ἑ-]
[τέρα τὴν ἑ]τέ̣ρ̣α̣[ν, ἐπὶ τοῖς]

BIBLIOGRAPHY: M. Baillet, J. T. Milik, and R. de Vaux, O.P., *Les 'Petits Grottes' de Qumrân* (Discoveries in the Judaean Desert of Jordan, iii; Oxford, 1962), Textes, pp. 142 f.; Planches, xxx.

3. Deuteronomy 31:28–30; 32:1–7. Rahlfs 848. i cent. B.C.

CAIRO, UNIVERSITY LIBRARY, P. FOUAD INV. 266, FRAG. 104–106.

In 1943 the Société Égyptienne de Papyrologie obtained 113 fragments of a papyrus roll (or rolls) estimated to have been originally about 47 feet (15 meters) long, with 88 columns of writing. Fragments 104–106, shown in the Plate, have a top margin of 1 inch (2.5 cm.) and intercolumniation of 9/16 inch (1.5 cm.). It has been computed (by Turner) that to complete chap. 31 an additional 12 lines are needed in col. *a*, making a total of 33 lines to the column, with a writing height of 9 to 9½ inches (23 to 24 cm.). The ends of the lines are not even. The letters, which seem to have been written with care, are upright, rounded uncials with ornamental serifs. *Iota* adscript, which occurs throughout the fragments (e.g. col. *a*, line 4), seems to be required by the space in lines 8 and 13 of col. *b*.

Wherever the name of God appears in the text, the original scribe carefully reserved sufficient space for the addition of the Hebrew Tetragrammaton (see §20).

The bibliography is on p. 140.

Column *a*

λογου τουτου και δια]μαρτυρ[ομαι
αυτοις το]ν [τε ουρανον] και την γη[ν
οι]δα [οτι] εσχατον τ[ης τελ]ευτης μου
ε]ν ανομιαι ονομησ[ετε κ]αι εκκλινειτε
εκ] της οδου ης εντελλ[ομ]αι υμιν και
συ]ναντησετα υμιν τα [κ]ακα εσχατον
τ]ων ημερων οτι ποιησ[ετ]ε το πονηρον
εν]αντι יהוה παροργισα[ι α]υτον εν τοι
ερ]γοις των χει[ρων υμων και ελ]αλησεν
Μω]σης ε[ις τα ωτα πασης εκκλησιας

Column *b*

προσεχε ουρα[νε και λαλησω
και ακουετω η [γη ρηματα εκ στοματος μου
προσδοκεισθω ω[ς υετος το αποφθεγμα μου
και καταβητω ω[ς δροσος τα ρηματα μου
ωσει δροσος επ [αγρωστιν
κ]αι ωσει νιφε[τος επι χορτον
ο]τι ονομα יהוה [εκαλεσα
δ]οτε μεγαλωσσ[υνην τωι θε]ω[ι ημων
θε]ος αληθινα τα [εργα αυ]του
κ]αι πασαι αι οδοι [αυτου κ]ρισις

Column *b* (continued)

θε]ος πιστος κα[ι ουκ εστι]ν αδικια
δι]καιος και οσι[ος יהוה
η[μ]αρτοσαν ο[υκ αυτωι τεκνα μωμητα
γ[εν]εα σκολια κ[αι διεστραμμενη
τ[αυ]τα יהוה απ[οδιδοτε
ουτως λαος μωρο[ς και ουχι σοφος
ουκ αυτος ουτο[ς σου πατηρ
εκτησατο [σε και εποιησεν σε
μν[ησθητε ημερας αιωνος
συ[νετε ετη γενεων γενεαι

1

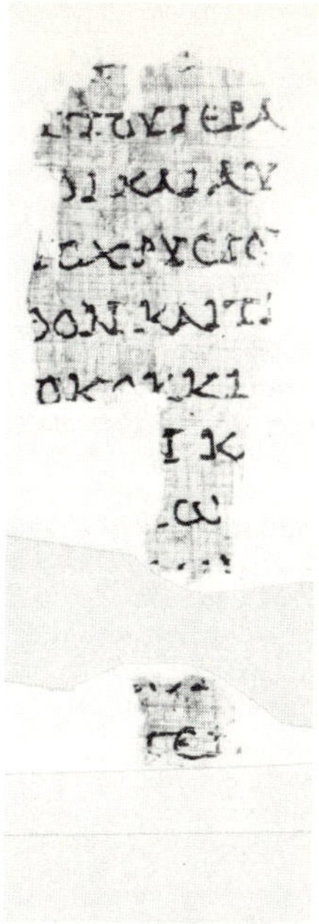

2

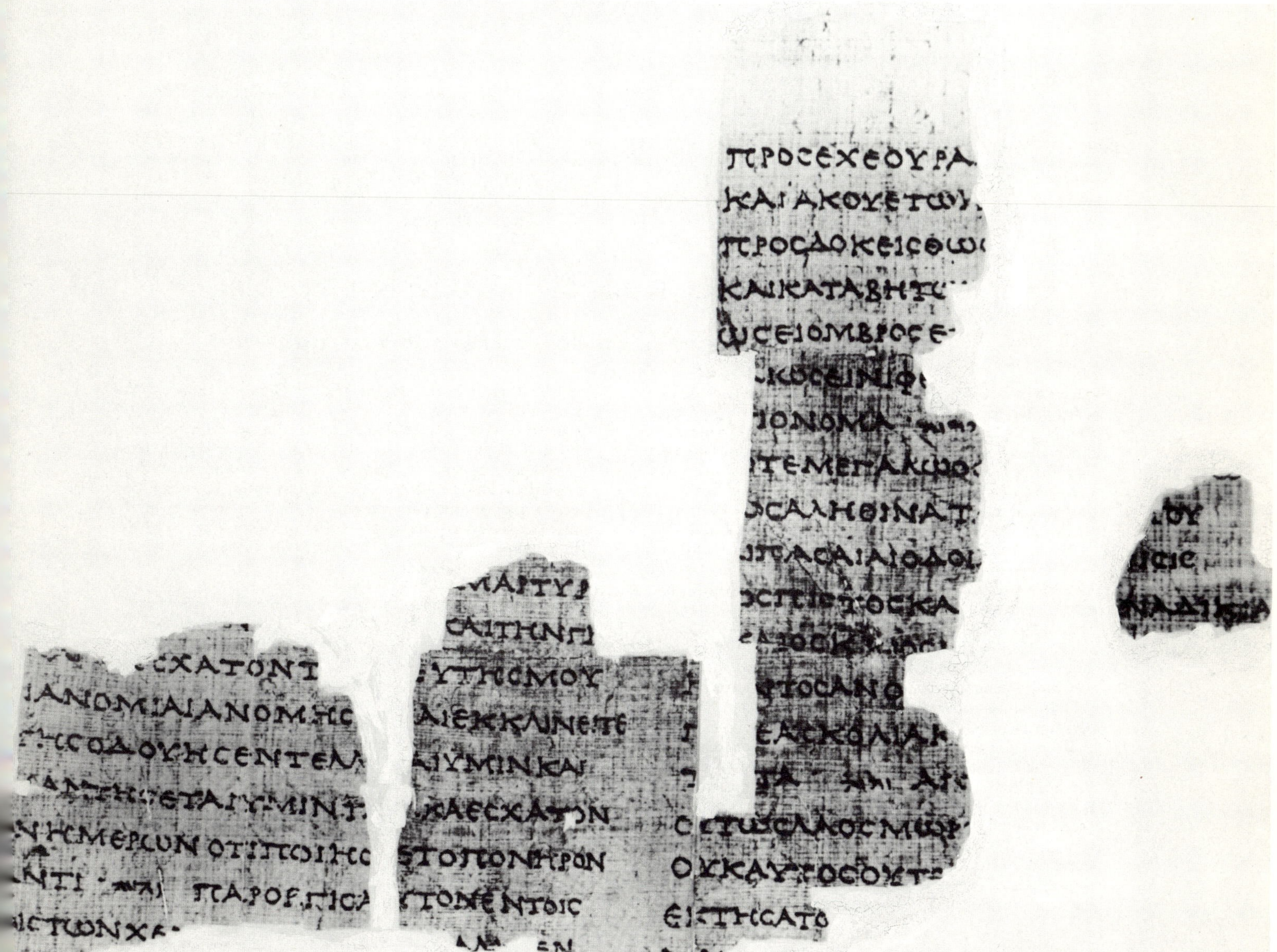

3

4. John 18:31–34; 37–38. Gregory–Aland $\mathfrak{p}^{52}$. First half ii cent.

MANCHESTER, JOHN RYLANDS LIBRARY, P. RYL. 457.

Acquired in Egypt in 1920, this papyrus fragment, measuring 3½ × 2¼ inches (8.9 × 6 cm.), is generally assigned to about A.D. 100–150.[1] Since the upper margin and part of the inner margin are preserved, it can be estimated that eleven lines of text would be required to fill the gap between recto and verso, giving a page of eighteen lines, and that the entire Gospel would have required a codex of 130 pages, each measuring about 8½ × 8 inches (21.5 × 20 cm.).

Apart from a few itacisms, the scribe's orthography is good and his hand, if not that of a practised scribe, is painstaking and regular. In the employment of the diaeresis both properly (as in line 2 recto *ουδεναϊνα*) and improperly (as in line 2 verso *ϊνα* following a consonant), and in the omission of the *iota* adscript (line 4 verso *αυτω*), the papyrus is in accord with other early examples of Greek texts.

The only textual variation of significance is the probable omission of the second instance of *εἰς τοῦτο* in verse 37. If the full text of that verse is supplied, line 3 verso has 38 letters rather than the average 29/30. Consequently it is fairly certain that $\mathfrak{p}^{52}$ represents a shorter version, perhaps the result of the scribe's having accidentally omitted the second instance of the phrase. In reading *πάλιν* before *εἰς τὸ πραιτώριον* (ver. 33) $\mathfrak{p}^{52}$ agrees with $\mathfrak{p}^{66}$ B C* D^{suppl} L W Δ 054 0109 fam^{13} *al.*; the reverse order is read by א A C^{2} Γ Θ 087 fam^{1}, the Byzantine text, and the Textus Receptus.

The bibliography is on p. 140.

Recto (John 18:31–34)

οι ϊουδαι[οι] ημε[ιν ουκ εξεστιν αποκτειναι]
ουδενα ϊνα ο λο̣[γος του ιησου πληρωθη ον ει]
πεν σημαινω[ν ποιω θανατω ημελλεν απο]
θνησκειν ισ[ηλθεν ουκ παλιν εις το πραιτω]
ριον ο Π[ιλατος και εφωνησεν τον Ιησουν]
και ειπ[εν αυτω συ ει ο βασιλευς των ιου]
[δ]αιω[ν απεκριθη Ιησους . . .

Verso (John 18:37–38)

[λευς ειμι εγω εις το]υτο γ[ε]γεννη̣μαι
[και <εις τουτο> εληλυθα εις τον κο]σμον ϊνα μαρτυ
[ρησω τη αληθεια πας ο ων] εκ της αληθε̣[ι]
[ας ακουει μου της φωνης] λεγει αυτω
[ο Πιλατος τι εστιν αληθεια κ]α̣ι τουτο
[ειπων παλιν εξηλθεν προς] τους ιο̣[υ]
[δαιους και λεγει αυτοις εγω ουδ]εμι[αν]

[1] It is thus the earliest known manuscript of any identifiable portion of the New Testament. José O'Callaghan's attempt (see footnote 41) to identify several tiny scraps of Greek papyri, found in Cave VII at Qumran, as portions of Mark, Acts, Romans, 1 Timothy, James, and 2 Peter, and to date them earlier than the date of $\mathfrak{p}^{52}$, is widely regarded as unsuccessful; cf. discussions by C. H. Roberts, *Journal of Theological Studies*, n.s. xxiii (1972), pp. 446–7; P. Benoit, *Revue Biblique*, lxxix (1972), pp. 321–4; lxxx (1973), pp. 5–12; Gordon D. Fee, *Journal of Biblical Literature*, xcii (1973), pp. 109–12; and Kurt Aland in *Studies in New Testament Language and Text*, ed. by J. K. Elliott (Leiden, 1976), pp. 14–38.

5. Genesis 14:12–15. Rahlfs 814. Second half ii cent.

NEW HAVEN, YALE UNIVERSITY, BEINECKE LIBRARY, P. YALE 1, VERSO.

In 1931 Yale University acquired from a dealer in Egypt a fragmentary papyrus leaf, measuring 3⅝ × 5¾ inches (9.3 × 14.5 cm.) and containing Genesis 14:5–8 and 12–15. Since the fragment preserves the lower margin, the editor was able to estimate from the amount of text lost between ver. 8 and ver. 12 that the codex had 30 lines to the page and would have been complete in about 188 pages. This leaf would have been the 21st, that is, pages 41 and 42.

The hand of P. Yale 1 is clear, unpretentious, and easily read except where the papyrus is frayed or eaten away. Letters are all of about the same height and width, and it is rare that the pen runs on from one letter to another. Occasionally the scribe indulges in decorative finials, some strokes beginning or ending with slight curves or hooks. The central stroke of *epsilon* is often extended to the right, touching the next letter. The non-Greek name ⲖⲰⲦ (line 8) is followed by a mark resembling a grave accent, indicating division of words (see §18).

Except for several orthographic and other minor variants, the fragment contains the generally accepted text of the Septuagint. At Gen. 14:14 in most Greek manuscripts the number of Abraham's servants (318) is spelled out (*τριακοσίους δέκα καὶ ὀκτώ*, but in six or seven others it is represented by Greek letters used as numerals, *τιη*. Although the script of the Yale fragment is illegible at this point, considerations of space make it altogether probable that it too had *τιη*. Because of the Christological interpretation given in the early Church to the text of Gen. 14:14 when the numeral was written with Greek letters (see §5), Welles regarded P. Yale 1 as the oldest Christian document and a portion of the oldest papyrus codex known, dating from 'perhaps between A.D. 80 and 100.' This opinion, unsupported by any detailed study of the writing, has not found acceptance among papyrologists. E. G. Turner, for example, ascribes the fragment to the end of the second or the beginning of the third century,[1] and C. H. Roberts to the second half of the second century.[2]

[γ]ὰ̣[ρ] κ̣α̣τ̣ο̣ι̣κ̣ῶ̣ν̣ ἐ̣ν̣ Σ̣ο̣δ̣ό̣μ̣ο̣ι̣ς̣ π̣α̣ρ̣[α]γ̣ε̣ν̣ό̣-
[μ]ε̣ν̣ο̣ς̣ δὲ τ̣ῶ̣ν̣ ἀνασωθέ̣ν̣τ̣ω̣ν̣ [τι]ς ἀ̣π̣ή̣[γ-]
[γει]λεν Ἀβ̣ρ̣ὰ̣μ τ̣ῷ̣ π̣ε̣ρ̣ά̣τ̣η̣· α̣ὐ̣τ̣ὸ̣ς̣ δ̣ὲ̣
[κατῴ]κει πρ[ὸ]ς τῇ̣ δ̣ρ̣υ̣ὶ τῇ Μαμβρῇ[ὁ Ἀ-]
μορὶς τοῦ ἀ̣δ̣ε̣λ̣φοῦ Ἐσχὼλ [καὶ τοῦ ἀδελφοῦ]
Α̣ὐ̣ν̣ά̣ν̣, οἳ ἦσαν συνωμόται το̣ῦ̣ [Ἀβράμ,]
ἀ̣κ̣ο̣ύσας δὲ Ἀβρὰ[μ] ὅτι ἠχμαλ[ωτεύ-]
θη Λὼτ ὁ ἀδελφὸς αὐτο̣ῦ̣, ἠρείθ̣[μησεν]
τ̣ο̣ὺ̣ς̣ ἰδίους ο[ἰ]κογενεῖς̣ αὐ̣τ̣ο̣ῦ̣, [τιη,]
[κ[αὶ κατεδίωξεν ὀπίσω αὐ[τ]ῶν ἕ̣ω̣ς̣ Δάν.
[κ]α̣[ὶ] ἐπέπεσεν ἐπ' αὐτοὺς τὴν νύκτ[α αὐ-]
[τὸ]ς̣ κ̣αὶ οἱ παῖδες αὐτοῦ κ̣αὶ ἐπέ[τ]α[ξεν]

In line 12 the scribe erroneously writes *πεδες*, for *αι* and *ε* had come to be pronounced alike (see §8).

The bibliography is on p. 140.

[1] *The Typology of the Early Codex* (Philadelphia, 1977), p. 19.
[2] *Manuscript, Society and Beliefs in Early Christian Egypt* (London, 1979), p. 13.

4

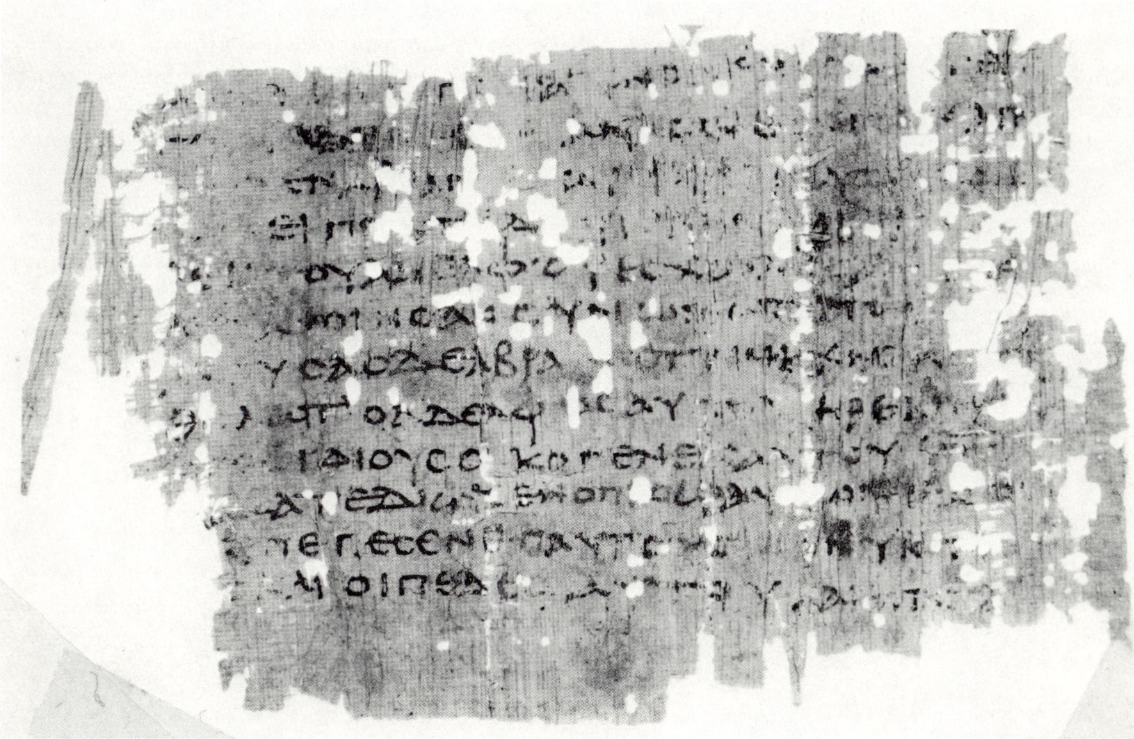

5

6. Romans 16:23; Hebrews 1:1–7. Gregory–Aland 𝔭46. About A.D. 200.

ANN ARBOR, UNIVERSITY OF MICHIGAN, INV. 6238, FOL. 21 RECTO.

Single-quire papyrus codex, originally with 104 leaves of which 86 survive today (56 at Dublin in the Chester Beatty Library and 30 at Ann Arbor), containing the Pauline Epistles (but not the Pastorals), about A.D. 200, original size of page about 11 × 6⅜ inches (28 × 16.2 cm.), one column, 25 to 32 lines to a page, tending to increase as the manuscript progresses.

The order of the Epistles in this, the earliest known copy of the Pauline correspondence, is remarkable: Romans (beginning at 5:17), Hebrews, 1 and 2 Corinthians, Ephesians, Galatians, Philippians, Colossians, and 1 Thessalonians. Seven leaves are lost from the beginning and seven from the ending of the codex. The seven leaves lost from the end probably contained 2 Thessalonians, but would have been insufficient for the Pastoral Epistles. The inclusion of Hebrews among the Pauline Epistles reflects the high regard accorded this Epistle in the Eastern Church, where its Pauline authorship was generally accepted. The sequence of the Epistles, with Hebrews immediately after Romans, seems to have been dictated in accord with the decreasing lengths of the Epistles.

The script is large, free, and flowing, with some pretensions to style and elegance. The upper termination of several letters (*α*, *δ*, *ι*, *κ*, *υ*) frequently is made with a slight curve or hook; the shaft of *epsilon* often extends to the right. Diaeresis generally stands over initial *ι* and *υ* (not shown in the Plate) and occasionally over medial *ι* (*υϊω* line 7). A square breathing mark occurs occasionally. Pauses in sense are sometimes indicated by slight space-intervals between words.

A cursive hand (apparently of the early third century) has added at the end of each book a statement concerning the number of *στίχοι* (see §23); for the Epistle to the Romans the number given is 1000 (standing between lines 1 and 2, *στι*ˣ *ᾱ*). The page number MA (=41) is placed centrally in the upper margin. Above line 4 a second hand has inserted *ημων* following *πατρασιν* (Heb. 1:1).

Textually 𝔭46 is frequently in agreement with the Alexandrian group of witnesses (B ℵ A C), less often with the Western (D F G), and occasionally with the later Byzantine witnesses. The doxology in Romans, which in the great uncials stands at the end of the Epistle, and at the end of chap. 14 in the vast number of the minuscules, is here placed at the end of chap. 15.

As regards Western readings in 𝔭46, according to A. W. Adams the codex 'offers no support for those attested by D alone, and thus raises the question whether the "Western" readings it supports are properly so called, and are not rather very early elements common to both East and West which have disappeared from the Alexandrian and Eastern traditions. In relation to the Byzantine text 𝔭46 shows that some readings (faulty as well as genuine) go back to a very early period.'[1]

BIBLIOGRAPHY: Frederic C. Kenyon, *The Chester Beatty Biblical Papyri . . .* Fasciculus III Supplement, *Pauline Epistles*, Text (London, 1936); Plates (1937); W. H. P. Hatch, 'The Position of Hebrews in the Canon of the New Testament,' *Harvard Theological Review*, xxix (1936), pp. 133–51; G. Zuntz, *The Text of the Epistles, a Disquisition on the Corpus Paulinum* (London, 1953); Harry Gamble, Jr., *The Textual History of the Letter to the Romans* (Grand Rapids, 1977); and S. Giversen, 'The Pauline Epistles on Papyrus,' *Die Paulinische Literatur und Theologie*, ed. by Sigfred Pedersen (Göttingen, 1980), pp. 201–12.

[1] F. G. Kenyon, *The Text of the Greek Bible*, 3rd ed., revised and augmented by A. W. Adams (London, 1975), p. 71.

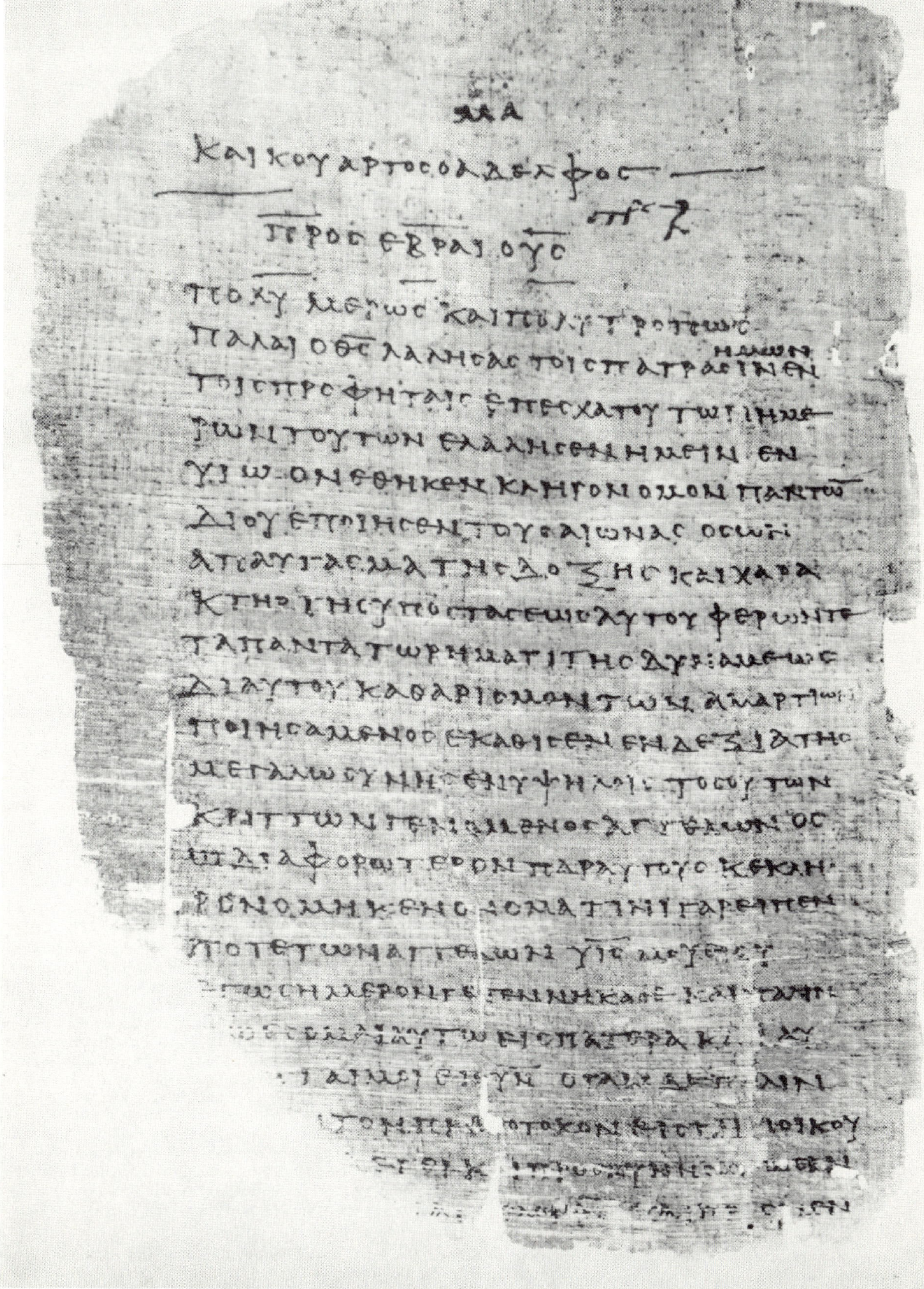

7. John 11:31–37. Gregory–Aland 𝔭[66]. About A.D. 200.

Cologny-Geneva, Bibliotheca Bodmeriana, Pap. 2, page 79.

Papyrus codex, containing the Gospel according to John (with lacunae), *c.* A.D. 200,[1] 6⅜ × 5⅝ inches (16.2 × 14.2 cm.), one column, 17 lines to a page.

Page format is nearly square; written in a medium-sized, rounded uncial, some letters having serifs. Page number οθ (=79) stands in upper right-hand corner. *Nomina sacra* shown in the Plate are Ἰ[ησοῦ]ς lines 3, 6, and 13; κ(ύρι)ε line 5, and πν(εύματ)ι line 10. A line-filler at the end of line 4 resembles an apostrophe. Final *nu* is indicated by a horizontal line (end of lines 5 and 6); *καί*-compendium occurs at the close of lines 7 and 17 and between lines 11 and 12. Two prickings near the top margin and two near the bottom served to guide the scribe in placing his writing area.

One of the special features of 𝔭[66] is the large number of corrections made to its text—about 450 in all. Plate 7 shows corrections made (*a*) by insertions above the line (lines 2 and 12) or within the line (*ο* inserted before ιϲ, line 13); (*b*) by deletion with a sponge and then re-writing (line 9 *εταραχθη* replaces *εβρ(ε)ιμη | σατο*, the last four letters of which are still visible at the beginning of line 10); (*c*) by using expunging dots and curved brackets to mark a relic of an earlier reading (line 11 [*εαυ*]*τον*).

Like codex W (see discussion of Plate 16) 𝔭[66] varies in textual type from one part of the manuscript to another. In chapters 1–5 it shows close relationship to the three major Alexandrian witnesses, 𝔭[75] B C, while in the rest of the book it exhibits a mixture of Western readings—abundant in chapters 6–7 and again in 11–12. It also possesses a certain number of readings that agree with the Byzantine type of text; most of such readings appear to be secondary, creating an easier text or a more common Greek style.

Bibliography: Victor Martin, *Papyrus Bodmer II, Évangile de Jean*, chap. 1–14 (grec) (Cologny-Geneva, 1956); idem, *Supplément*, chap. 14–21 (grec) (1958); (enlarged ed., with facsimile of entire MS., 1962); J. N. Birdsall, *The Bodmer Papyrus of the Gospel of John* (London, 1960); G. D. Fee, 'The Corrections of Papyrus Bodmer II,' *Novum Testamentum*, vii (1965), pp. 247–57; E. F. Rhodes, 'The Corrections of P. Bodmer II,' *New Testament Studies*, xiv (1968), pp. 271–81; G. D. Fee, *Papyrus Bodmer II* (P[66]): *its Textual Relationships and Scribal Characteristics* (Studies and Documents, xxxiv, Salt Lake City, 1968).

[1] Herbert Hunger dates 𝔭[66] to a time not later than the middle of the second century (*Anzeiger des phil.-hist. Klasse der Österreichischen Akademie der Wissenschaften*, 1960, Nr. 4, pp. 12–23), whereas E. G. Turner prefers a date *c.* A.D. 200–250 (*Greek Manuscripts of the Ancient World*, p. 108).

8. Tatian's Diatessaron. Gregory–Aland 0212. First half iii cent.

New Haven, Yale University, Beinecke Library, Dura Parch. 24 (D pg. 24).

In 1933 a fragment of fairly heavy parchment, measuring 4⅛ × 3¾ inches (10.5 × 9.5 cm.), was found at Dura Europos, a Roman border-town destroyed A.D. 256 by the Persian troops of King Shapur I. Written on only one side, the fragment may have once been part of a roll. It is the only surviving Greek witness of Tatian's Diatessaron, an edition of the four Gospels in a continuous narrative.

The text is written in a good book-hand, the words frequently set off from each other by blank spaces. An extra wide space in line 3 may be intended to mark a paragraph. The tips of the letters are frequently decorated with a small hook or apex turning to the left. There are three kinds of *alpha*: the older capital, the uncial, and the third-century cursive-type. *Mu* is characterized by a deep saddle. The *tau* and *eta* of τῆς in line 2 are written in ligature, apparently to save space. *Nomina sacra* are indicated by a line above them, and by a medial dot following them (lines 3, 10, 13).

A singular reading of Luke 23:49 seems to be preserved in lines 1 and 2 (partly reconstructed: *αἱ γυναῖκες τῶν συνακολουθησάντων αὐτῷ* ('the wives of those who had been his disciples').

The text, restored by the editor, is as follows (*v* indicates an empty space one letter in width).

[Ζεβεδ]αι̣ο̣υ και Σαλωμη κ[α]ι̣ α̣ι γ̣υ̣ν̣αικες
[των συ]ν̣ακολουθησαντων α̣[υτ]ω *v* απο της
[Γαλιλαι]α̣ς ορωσαι τον στ(αυρωθεντ)α. *vvvv* ην δε
[η ημερ]α Παρασκευη. *v* Σαββατον επεφω̣-
[σκεν. ο]ψ̣ιας δε γενομενης επι τ̣[η Π]α̣ρ̣[α]σ-
[κευη], *v* ο εστιν Προσαββατον, π̣ρ̣ο̣σ-
[ηλθεν] ανθρωπος βουλευτη̣[ς *v*]π̣α̣ρ-
[χων α]π̣ο Ερινμαθαια[ς] π̣[ο]λ̣ε̣ω̣ς της
[Ιουδαι]ας, ονcμα Ιω̣[σηφ], α̣[γ]αθος̣ δι-
[καιος], ων μαθητης τ[ο]υ̣ Ιη(σου), κ̣ε- *vvvv*
[κρυμ]μενος δε δια τ̣ο̣ν φ̣ο̣βον των
[Ιουδαιω]ν, και αυτος προσεδεχτο
[την] *v* β̣[ασιλειαν] του̣ Θ(εο)υ ο̣υτος ουκ
[ην συνκατατ] ιθεμ̣εν̣[ο]ς̣ τη β̣[ουλη̣]

TRANSLATION

[. . . the mother of the sons of Zebed]ee (Matt. xxvii. 56) and Salome (Mark xv. 40) and the wives [of those who] had followed him from [Galile]e to see the crucified (Luke xxiii. 49b–c). And [the da]y was Preparation: the Sabbath was daw[ning] (Luke xxiii. 54). And when it was evening (Matt. xxvii. 57), on the Prep[aration], that is, the day before the Sabbath (Mark xv. 42), [there came] up a man (Matt. xxvii. 57), be[ing] a member of the council (Luke xxiii. 50), from Arimathea (Matt. xxvii. 57), a c[i]ty of [Jude]a (Luke xxiii. 51b), by name Jo[seph] (Matt. xxvii. 57), g[o]od and ri[ghteous] (Luke xxiii. 50), being a disciple of Jesus, but se[cret]ly, for fear of the [Jew]s (John xix. 38). And he (Matt. xxvii. 57) was looking for [the] k[ingdom] of God (Luke xxiii. 51c). This man [had] not [con]sented to [their] p[urpose] (Luke xxiii. 51a) . . .

Bibliography: Carl H. Kraeling, *A Greek Fragment of Tatian's Diatessaron from Dura* (Studies and Documents, iii; London, 1935); C. Bradford Welles, R. O. Fink, and J. Frank Gilliam, *The Parchments and Papyri* (The Excavations at Dura-Europos . . , Final Report V, Part i (New Haven, 1959), pp. 23–4; B. M. Metzger, *The Early Versions of the New Testament* (Oxford, 1977), pp. 10–36.

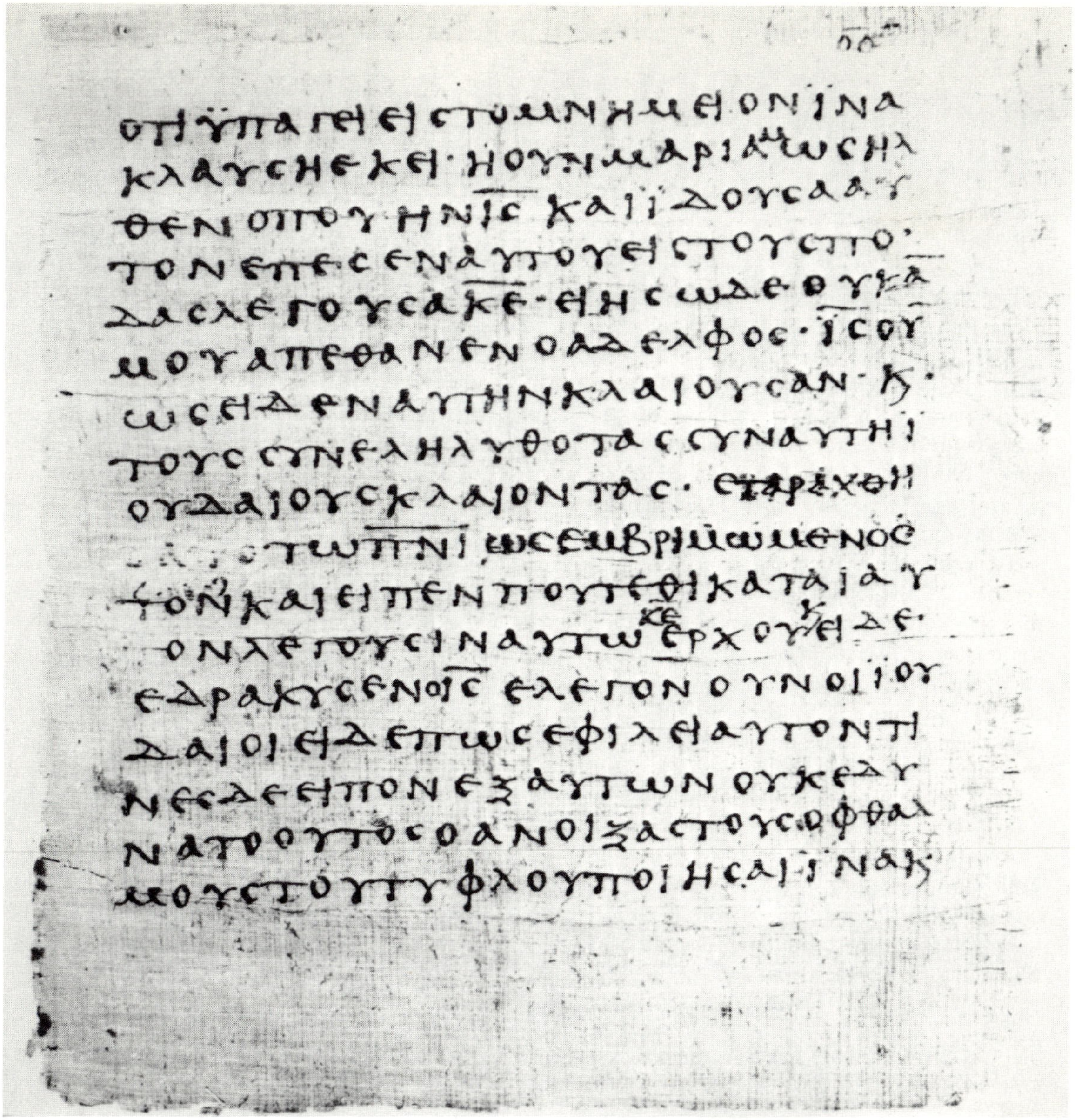

7

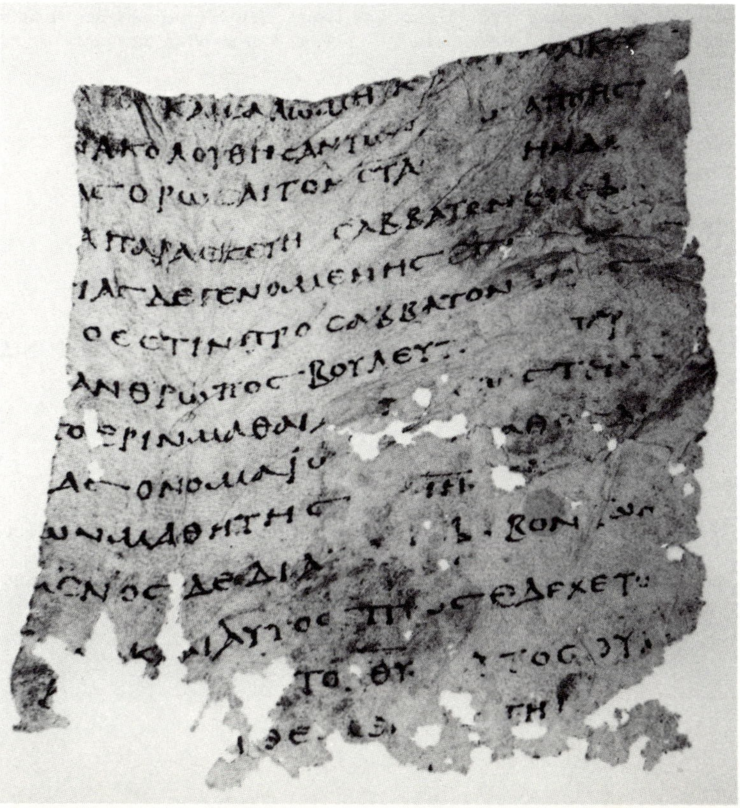

8

9. Luke 16:9–21. Gregory–Aland $\mathfrak{p}^{75}$. Early iii cent.

Cologny-Geneva, Bibliotheca Bodmeriana, Pap. XIV, page 45.

Papyrus codex, containing most of the Gospel according to Luke, early iii century, 10¼ × 5⅛ inches (26 × 13 cm.), one column, averaging 42 lines to the page.

This, the earliest known copy of Luke, is written in a medium-sized, rounded uncial, though some letters (particularly *omicron* and *sigma*) are much smaller than the average size. The scribe marks paragraphs by leaving blank a space of one or two letters, and extends into the left-hand margin the first letter of the following line (see lines 17–18 and 34–35). Final *nu* is indicated by horizontal line over the last letter (lines 10, 28, 29). Apostrophe is used after *ουκ* (line 8) and as a separator (*ευαγ'γελιζεται*, line 27). Diaeresis occasionally occurs over *ι* and *υ* (lines 2 and 3). What appears to be intended as a rough breathing mark stands over *η* in line 26.

Textually the manuscript is of importance in showing that the Alexandrian type of text characteristic of the fourth-century codices Vaticanus (B) and Sinaiticus (א) was current at the beginning of the third century (see studies mentioned in the bibliography). Furthermore, not only is the text of $\mathfrak{p}^{75}$ Alexandrian, but it is closer to B than that of any other manuscript, while the influence of readings of the Western type is almost non-existant. This goes a long way, as A. W. Adams remarks, 'to showing that the B-type of text was already in existence in Egypt, and in a relatively pure form, before the end of the second century. If so, the view, much canvassed in recent years, that the Alexandrian text-type was a third or fourth century recension—i.e. a deliberately revised or "made" text formed out of the "popular" texts of the second century—will need considerable revision.'[1]

A noteworthy variant reading is the name given to the Rich Man mentioned in Luke 16:19. Following the words *Ανθρωπος δε τις ην πλουσιος*, $\mathfrak{p}^{75}$ is the only known Greek manuscript that adds *ονοματι Νευης* (Plate 9, line 8 from bottom). Inasmuch as the Sahidic version of this verse gives the name Nineveh to the anonymous Rich Man,[2] it is probable that ONOMATINEYHC is a scribal blunder for ONOMATININEYHC.

Bibliography: Victor Martin and Rodolphe Kasser, *Papyrus Bodmer XIV, Evangile de Luc chap. 3–24* (Cologny-Geneva, 1961); C. L. Porter, 'Papyrus Bodmer XV (P75) and the Text of Codex Vaticanus,' *Journal of Biblical Literature*, lxxxi (1962), pp. 363–76; Kurt Aland, *Studien zur Überlieferung des Neuen Testaments und seines Textes* (Berlin, 1967), pp. 155–72; and especially Carlo M. Martini, *Il problema della recensionalità del codice B alla luce del papiro Bodmer XIV* (Rome, 1966). For a collation of $\mathfrak{p}^{75}$ against the United Bible Societies' Greek New Testament, see [Raymond Lejoly], *Annotations pour une étude du Papyrus 75 . . .* (Dison, 1976).

[1] F. G. Kenyon, *The Text of the Greek Bible*, 3rd ed., revised and augmented by A. W. Adams (London, 1975), p. 77.

[2] For other examples in early Christian tradition of names being given to those who are nameless in the New Testament, see chap. 2 in the present writer's volume *New Testament Studies, Philological, Versional, and Patristic* (Leiden, 1980).

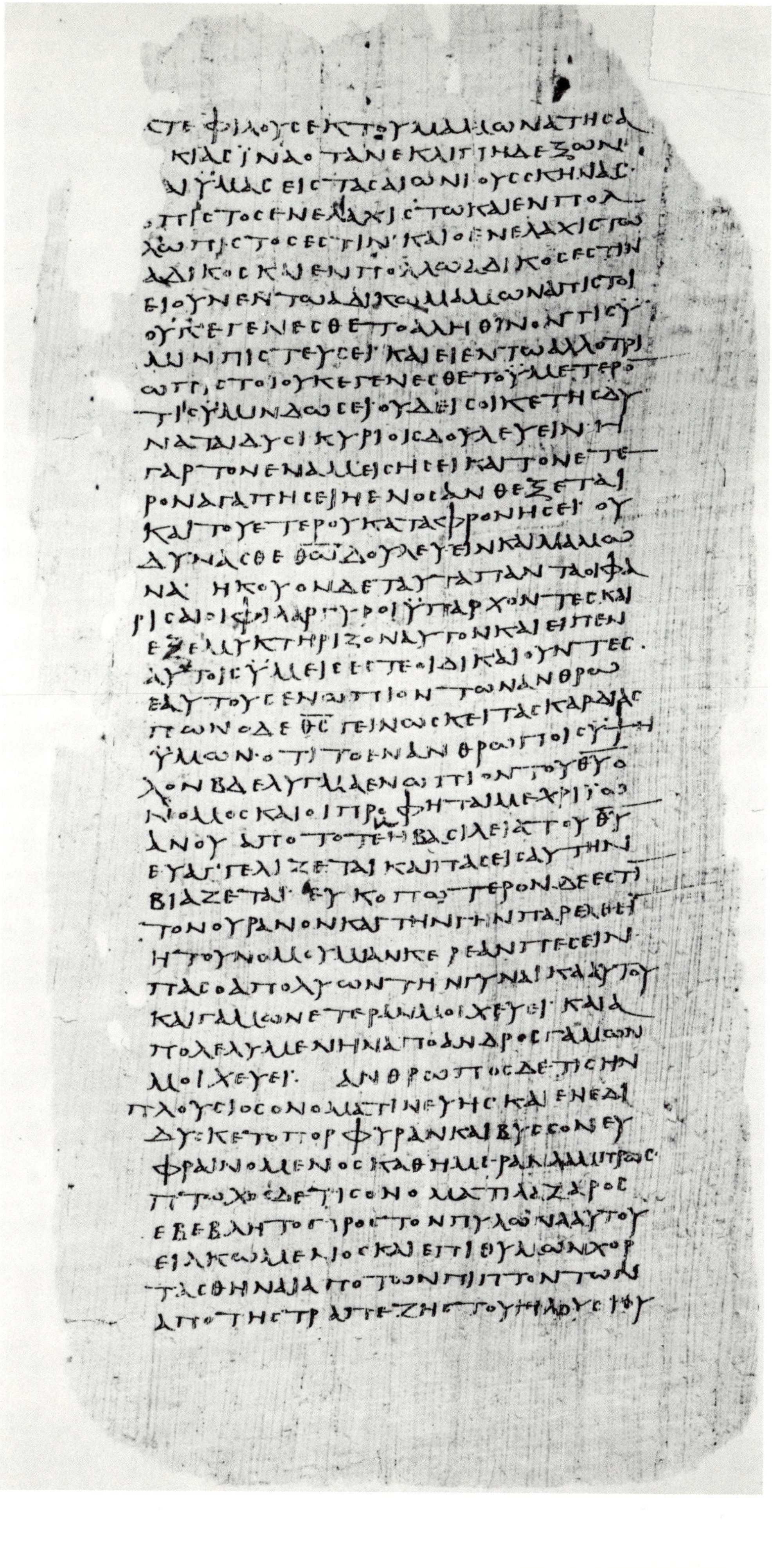

ΣΤΕ ΦΙΛΟΥΣ ΕΚ ΤΟΥ ΜΑΜΜΩΝΑ ΤΗΣ Α
ΚΙΑΣ ΙΝΑ ΟΤΑΝ ΕΚΛΙΠΗ ΔΕΞΩΝ
ΥΜΑΣ ΕΙΣ ΤΑΣ ΑΙΩΝΙΟΥΣ ΣΚΗΝΑΣ·
ΠΙΣΤΟΣ ΕΝ ΕΛΑΧΙΣΤΩ ΚΑΙ ΕΝ ΠΟΛ
ΛΩ ΠΙΣΤΟΣ ΕΣΤΙΝ ΚΑΙ Ο ΕΝ ΕΛΑΧΙΣΤΩ
ΑΔΙΚΟΣ ΚΑΙ ΕΝ ΠΟΛΛΩ ΑΔΙΚΟΣ ΕΣΤΙΝ
ΕΙ ΟΥΝ ΕΝ ΤΩ ΑΔΙΚΩ ΜΑΜΜΩΝΑ ΠΙΣΤΟΙ
ΟΥΚ ΕΓΕΝΕΣΘΕ ΤΟ ΑΛΗΘΙΝΟΝ ΤΙΣ Υ
ΜΙΝ ΠΙΣΤΕΥΣΕΙ ΚΑΙ ΕΙ ΕΝ ΤΩ ΑΛΛΟΤΡΙ
Ω ΠΙΣΤΟΙ ΟΥΚ ΕΓΕΝΕΣΘΕ ΤΟ ΥΜΕΤΕΡΟ
ΤΙΣ ΥΜΙΝ ΔΩΣΕΙ ΟΥΔΕΙΣ ΟΙΚΕΤΗΣ ΔΥ
ΝΑΤΑΙ ΔΥΣΙ ΚΥΡΙΟΙΣ ΔΟΥΛΕΥΕΙΝ Η
ΓΑΡ ΤΟΝ ΕΝΑ ΜΕΙΣΗΣΕΙ ΚΑΙ ΤΟΝ ΕΤΕ
ΡΟΝ ΑΓΑΠΗΣΕΙ Η ΕΝΟΣ ΑΝΘΕΞΕΤΑΙ
ΚΑΙ ΤΟΥ ΕΤΕΡΟΥ ΚΑΤΑΦΡΟΝΗΣΕΙ ΟΥ
ΔΥΝΑΣΘΕ ΘΩ ΔΟΥΛΕΥΕΙΝ ΚΑΙ ΜΑΜΜΩ
ΝΑ ΗΚΟΥΟΝ ΔΕ ΤΑΥΤΑ ΠΑΝΤΑ ΟΙ ΦΑ
ΡΙΣΑΙΟΙ ΦΙΛΑΡΓΥΡΟΙ ΥΠΑΡΧΟΝΤΕΣ ΚΑΙ
ΕΞΕΜΥΚΤΗΡΙΖΟΝ ΑΥΤΟΝ ΚΑΙ ΕΙΠΕΝ
ΑΥΤΟΙΣ ΥΜΕΙΣ ΕΣΤΕ ΟΙ ΔΙΚΑΙΟΥΝΤΕΣ·
ΕΑΥΤΟΥΣ ΕΝΩΠΙΟΝ ΤΩΝ ΑΝΘΡΩ
ΠΩΝ Ο ΔΕ ΘΣ ΓΕΙΝΩΣΚΕΙ ΤΑΣ ΚΑΡΔΙΑΣ
ΥΜΩΝ· ΟΤΙ ΤΟ ΕΝ ΑΝΘΡΩΠΟΙΣ ΥΨΗ
ΛΟΝ ΒΔΕΛΥΓΜΑ ΕΝΩΠΙΟΝ ΤΟΥ ΘΥ Ο
ΝΟΜΟΣ ΚΑΙ ΟΙ ΠΡΟΦΗΤΑΙ ΜΕΧΡΙ ΙΩ
ΑΝΟΥ ΑΠΟ ΤΟΤΕ Η ΒΑΣΙΛΕΙΑ ΤΟΥ ΘΥ
ΕΥΑΓΓΕΛΙΖΕΤΑΙ ΚΑΙ ΠΑΣ ΕΙΣ ΑΥΤΗΝ
ΒΙΑΖΕΤΑΙ· ΕΥΚΟΠΩΤΕΡΟΝ ΔΕ ΕΣΤΙ
ΤΟΝ ΟΥΡΑΝΟΝ ΚΑΙ ΤΗΝ ΓΗΝ ΠΑΡΕΛΘΕΙ
Η ΤΟΥ ΝΟΜΟΥ ΜΙΑΝ ΚΕΡΕΑΝ ΠΕΣΕΙΝ·
ΠΑΣ Ο ΑΠΟΛΥΩΝ ΤΗΝ ΓΥΝΑΙΚΑ ΑΥΤΟΥ
ΚΑΙ ΓΑΜΩΝ ΕΤΕΡΑΝ ΜΟΙΧΕΥΕΙ ΚΑΙ Ο
ΑΠΟΛΕΛΥΜΕΝΗΝ ΑΠΟ ΑΝΔΡΟΣ ΓΑΜΩΝ
ΜΟΙΧΕΥΕΙ· ΑΝΘΡΩΠΟΣ ΔΕ ΤΙΣ ΗΝ
ΠΛΟΥΣΙΟΣ ΟΝΟΜΑΤΙ ΝΕΥΗΣ ΚΑΙ ΕΝΕΔΙ
ΔΥΣΚΕΤΟ ΠΟΡΦΥΡΑΝ ΚΑΙ ΒΥΣΣΟΝ ΕΥ
ΦΡΑΙΝΟΜΕΝΟΣ ΚΑΘΗΜΕΡΑΝ ΛΑΜΠΡΩΣ·
ΠΤΩΧΟΣ ΔΕ ΤΙΣ ΟΝΟΜΑΤΙ ΛΑΖΑΡΟΣ
ΕΒΕΒΛΗΤΟ ΠΡΟΣ ΤΟΝ ΠΥΛΩΝΑ ΑΥΤΟΥ
ΕΙΛΚΩΜΕΝΟΣ ΚΑΙ ΕΠΙΘΥΜΩΝ ΧΟΡ
ΤΑΣΘΗΝΑΙ ΑΠΟ ΤΩΝ ΠΙΠΤΟΝΤΩΝ
ΑΠΟ ΤΗΣ ΤΡΑΠΕΖΗΣ ΤΟΥ ΠΛΟΥΣΙΟΥ

9

10. Ezekiel 31:8–15. Rahlfs 967. Early iii cent.

Princeton, University Library, Scheide Pap. 1, page 71.

Early third-century papyrus codex, 13½ × 5 inches (34.4 × 12.8 cm.), containing Ezekiel, Daniel, and Esther, originally embracing 118 leaves, of which 109 are known today: 21 in the Scheide collection, the others in Barcelona, Cologne, Dublin, and Madrid. Daniel and Esther are in a hand different from Ezekiel, and the sequence of the books agrees with that of codex Alexandrinus. Page **οα** (=71) is shown in the Plate.

Verso pages average 51.1 lines, recto pages average 53.8 lines. Lines vary from 16 to 27 letters, but rarely exceed 22 letters in length. When a long line would have ended in the letter *nu*, the scribe saved space by indicating this letter with a horizontal line over the preceding vowel (lines 7, 38, 40). In the case of short lines, sometimes a space-filler in the form of an angular bracket is inserted; more often the scribe widened letters, particularly a final *nu* (line 15).

Here and there are marks of punctuation (the high point sometimes resembles an acute accent), but there seems to be no consistent plan of their use. The ending of a paragraph is usually indicated by two short sloping parallel lines (lines 10 and 46), with the initial letter of the following line extending slightly into the left-hand margin. According to Revell (see Bibliography below), the paragraphing of the Greek text is related somehow to the *petuḥot* and *setumot* ('open' and 'closed' divisions) of the Hebrew Bible; the two-stroke sign occurs in 24 of the 31 cases where the Masoretic text has *petuḥa* (77%), and in 38 of the 62 cases where *setuma* occurs (66%).

Among the special features of the Scheide text is the use of the single κ̅ς̅ in designating the *nomen sacrum* when the other uncial manuscripts more closely represent the present Masoretic text by a doublet of some form or other. Of other singular readings one of the more interesting is εγγιζουσι for ελπιζουσι (Ezek. 36:8); this is the reading of the Hebrew text, but curiously enough it occurs (according to Ziegler's *apparatus criticus*) in no other Greek manuscript, and seems to have been unknown to Origen.

According to Johnson, Gehman, and Kase (see Bibliography), 'the use of οτι and διοτι in the Scheide text calls for special comment since Herrmann and Baumgärtel sought to support their theory of different translators for Ezekiel by the variations in the use of these conjunctions which are to be found in Vaticanus. In B certain sections usually show διοτι in the oracular phrase επιγνωσεσθε διοτι εγω κ̅ς̅ while others are consistent in using οτι. In this phrase or its variants the new text uses οτι throughout with but one exception (xxii. 22). Elsewhere οτι and διοτι are used indifferently without regard to the avoidance of hiatus' (pp. 14 f.).

The Plate shows the page slightly reduced in size.

Bibliography: *The John H. Scheide Biblical Papyri: Ezekiel*, ed. by Allan C. Johnson, Henry S. Gehman, Edmund H. Kase, Jr. (Princeton, 1938); Sir F. G. Kenyon, *The Chester Beatty Biblical Papyri*, fasc. vii (London, 1937), Part 2, *Plates* (1938); Manuél Fernández-Galiano, 'Nuevas páginas del códice 967 del A. T. griego (Ez 28,19–43,9) (P. Matr. bibl. 1),' *Studia Papyrologica*, x (1971), pp. 7–77; E. J. Revell, 'A Note on Papyrus 967,' ibid., xv (1976), pp. 131–6.

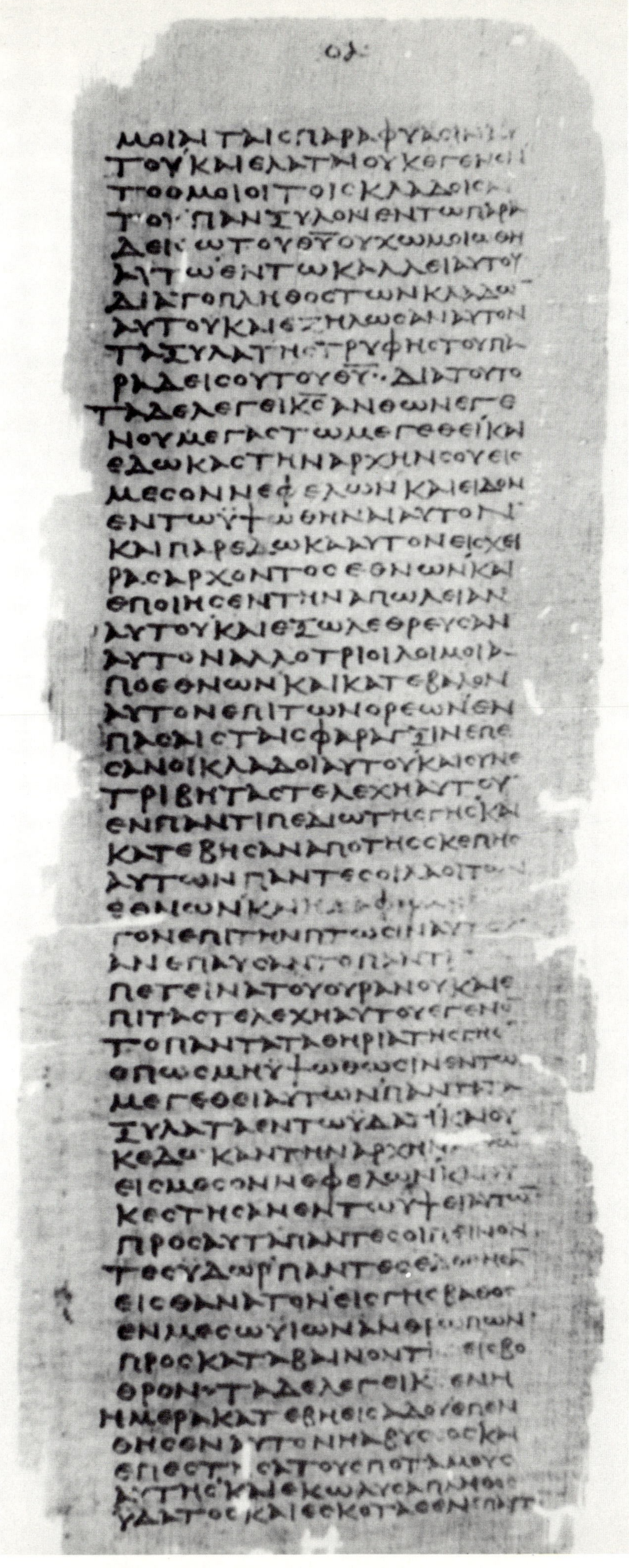

11. Genesis 42:7–19. Rahlfs 962. Second half of iii cent.

Dublin, Chester Beatty Library, Pap. V, fol. 19 recto.

Papyrus codex of 27 fragmentary leaves (of an original 84), containing part of the Book of Genesis, second half of iii century A.D., having an estimated original measurement of 8¼ × 6 inches (about 21 × 15.2 cm.), one column, average of 18 or 19 lines to the page.

The writing of codex 962 is markedly different from the hands of all the other manuscripts in the Beatty collection, in being of a definitely non-literary type. It is a good documentary hand, upright and somewhat compressed laterally. Several of the letters are exaggerated in size, notably β, ξ, ρ, φ, and ψ. The letter ϵ is made in two distinct halves, the upper portion (which includes the cross-bar) being often noticeably large. The scribe concludes some letters (e.g. β and ξ) with a flourish; he also extends the horizontal line over *nomina sacra* far to the right, beyond the *nomen sacrum* (lines 6 and 18).

The word κύριος is contracted when used in the secular sense of 'master' (line 6) as well as when referring to the Deity. The rough breathing occurs occasionally (line 13 ὧδε, line 15 ἡ [for ἦ]). Initial ι and υ often have the diaeresis. There is no punctuation.

A very few corrections have been entered between the lines; e.g., the addition of δε after ειπαν (line 8).

Page-enumeration has been added in the middle of the upper margin in a large cursive hand other than that of the original scribe.

Bibliography: Frederic G. Kenyon, *The Chester Beatty Biblical Papyri; Descriptions and Texts of Twelve Manuscripts on Papyrus of the Greek Bible*, Fasciculus iv, *Genesis*, Text (London, 1934); Fasciculus iv, *Genesis* (*Pap. V*), Plates (London, 1936); Albert Pietersma, *Chester Beatty Biblical Papryi IV and V; a New Edition, with Text-Critical Analysis* (American Studies in Papyrology, 16; Toronto and Sarasota, 1977).

12. Revelation 3:19–4:1. Gregory–Aland 0169. iv cent.

Princeton, Theological Seminary Library, Pap. 5, recto.

A parchment leaf (=P.Oxy. 1080) from a small, pocket-sized codex of the Book of Revelation, iv century, 3¾ × 2⅞ inches (9.5 × 7.8 cm.), one column, 14 lines to the page. Since this is page 33 (ΛΓ stands in the upper right-hand corner), the complete text of Revelation would have made a pudgy, pocket-sized volume.[1]

The hand of 0169 is a fair-sized upright uncial, fairly regular, and having a certain amount of ornamental finish. The scribe forms *sigma* with two strokes of the pen, and *epsilon* with three strokes; *kappa* and *upsilon* have serifs.

A corrector has altered ζηλευε (line 1) to ζηλευσον, in agreement with ℵ P 1 and the Byzantine text. By oversight the eye of the scribe passed from the first to the second instance of την θυραν και in 4:20, omitting the intervening words. Later, having noticed the omission, the scribe or someone else placed a conventional mark (indicating insertion) in line 3 between και and εισελευσομαι and wrote the missing words in the lower margin—of which only traces remain today: κρ̣ουω ε[α]ν̣ τ[ις] α̣κου[ση της φων]ης μ[ου και ανοιξη την θυραν και].

Of the approximately 250 manuscript witnesses to the Book of Revelation, ten are uncials; only three of these are complete (ℵ, A, and 046), and three others comprise but a single leaf each (0163, 0169, and 0207). According to R. H. Charles, the text of the Princeton fragment agrees 'much more closely with ℵ than with any other uncial.'[2]

Bibliography: *The Oxyrhynchus Papyri*, ed. by A. S. Hunt, viii (London, 1911), pp. 14 f.

[1] On pocket-sized codices, see W. H. Worrell, *The Coptic Manuscripts in the Freer Collection* (New York, 1923), pp. xi–xiii; A. Henrichs and L. Koenen, 'Ein griechischer Mani-Codex,' *Zeitschrift für Papyrologie und Epigraphik*, v (1970), pp. 100–3; and Eric G. Turner, *The Typology of the Early Codex* (Philadelphia, 1977), pp. 30 ff. Since all but one of the forty-five pocket-sized codices dating from the third and fourth centuries contain works of Christian literature, Roberts is certainly justified in concluding that 'the miniature codex would seem to be a Christian invention' (*Manuscript, Society and Belief in Early Christian Egypt* [London, 1979], p. 12).

[2] *The Revelation of St. John* (International Critical Commentary), ii (New York, 1920), p. 450.

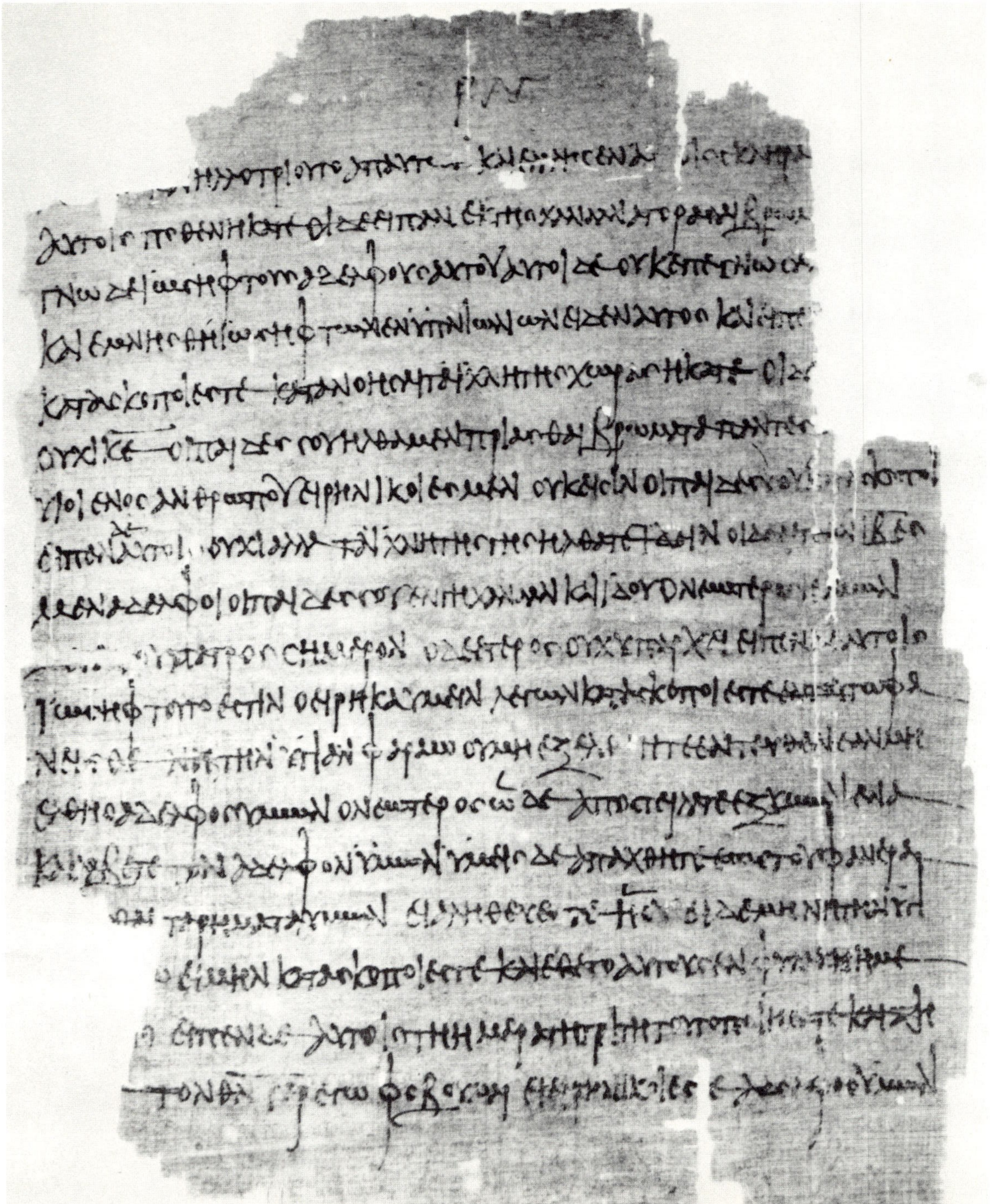

11

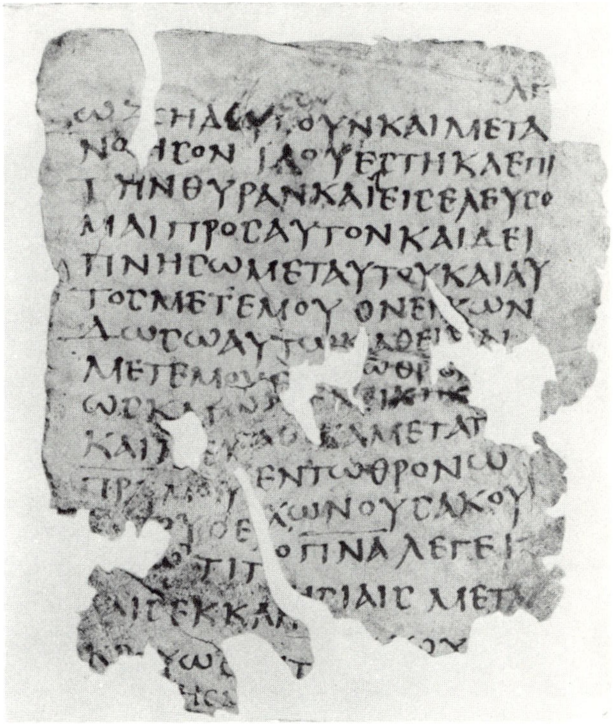

12

13. 2 Thess. 3:11–18; Heb. 1:1–2:2. Gregory–Aland B (Codex Vaticanus). iv cent.

ROME, BIBLIOTECA VATICANA, GR. 1209, PAGE 1512.

Fourth-century vellum codex of the Bible, 759 leaves (617 of Old Testament, 142 of New Testament), averaging 10⅞ × 10⅞ inches (27.5 × 27.5 cm.), three columns, 42 lines to a column. New Testament defective after Heb. 9:14 (lacks 1 and 2 Tim., Titus, Philem., Rev.). Every book of the Greek Old Testament is included, except 1–4 Maccabees and the Prayer of Manasseh, which never found a place in the manuscript.

The writing is small and neat, without ornamentation or capitals. Unfortunately the beauty of the original has been spoiled by a later scribe who found the ink faded and traced over every letter afresh, omitting only those letters and words that he believed to be incorrect. A few passages therefore remain to show the original appearance of the first hand.

There appear to have been two scribes of the Old Testament and one of the New Testament, and two correctors, one (B^2) about contemporary with the scribes, the other (B^3) of about the tenth or eleventh century.

In the Old Testament the type of text varies, with a good text in Ezekiel, and a bad one in Isaiah. In Judges the text differs substantially from that of the majority of manuscripts, but agrees with the Old Latin and Sahidic versions and Cyril of Alexandria. In Job it has the additional 400 half-verses from Theodotion, which are not in the Old Latin and Sahidic versions.

In the New Testament the text of the Gospels and Acts is the purest known example of the Alexandrian type of text, preserved also in $\mathfrak{p}^{75}$, which dates from about A.D. 200 (see Plate 9). In the Pauline Epistles there is a distinctly Western element.

Accent and breathing marks, as well as punctuation, have been added by a later hand. In the New Testament, quotations from the Old Testament are indicated by marks in the left-hand margin of the column (see the lower part of col. *b*).

The Ammonian section and Eusebian canon numbers do not appear, which points to a date before they were generally known. The chapter divisions in the Gospels (a system found in only one other manuscript, the sixth-century MS. Ξ) are topical; the Acts and the Epistles have two independent numerations (for one of them see §25). Because no numeration is applied to 2 Peter, it has been concluded that the system of divisions dates from a time before this Epistle came to be commonly regarded as canonical.

As to the place of origin of codex Vaticanus, Hort was inclined to assign it to Rome; others to southern Italy or to Caesarea. But the similarity of its text in significant portions of both Testaments with the Coptic versions and with Greek papyri, and the style of writing (notably the Coptic forms used in some of the titles) point rather to Egypt and Alexandria.

In the Plate the first column concludes with the subscription and a note *ἐγράφη ἀπὸ Ἀθηνῶν* (see §24 end). The scribe began the text of the second column with a small initial *π* for the first word *πολυμερως*, but a later scribe inserted a large initial Π, which he decorated with blue ink; this ink is used as well for the horizontal bar over the column. Above the bar stand three crosses made with red ink, which was used also to decorate the top of the large Π.

The left-hand margin opposite Heb. 1:3 preserves a curiously indignant note by a rather recent scribe who restored the original (but erroneous) reading of the manuscript *φανερων*, for which a corrector had substituted the usual reading, *φερων*. The note reads *ἀμαθέστατε καὶ κακέ, ἄφες τὸν παλαιόν, μὴ μεταποίει* ('Fool and knave, can't you leave the old reading alone, and not alter it!')

The Plate shows the page slightly reduced in size.

BIBLIOGRAPHY: Photographic facsimile, *Bibliorum ss. Graecorum Codex Vaticanus* 1209 . . . (Milan, 1904; 1907); in 1968 the New Testament portion was issued by the Vatican in photographic facsimile in color (with an introduction by Carlo M. Martini, S.J.) and a copy given to each bishop attending Vatican Council II; E. Tisserant, 'Notes sur la preparation de l'édition en fac-simile typographique du Codex Vaticanus (B),' *Angelicum*, xx (1943), pp. 237–48; Sakae Kubo, *P*[72] *and the Codex Vaticanus* (Studies and Documents, 27; Salt Lake City, 1965); Janco Šagi, S.J., 'Problema historiae codicis B,' *Divus Thomas; commentarium de philosophia et theologica*, lxxv (1972), pp. 3–29; and Jean Duplacy, 'Les divisions du texte de l'Épitre de Jacques dans B (03) du Nouveau Testament (Vatic. Gr. 1209),' *Studies in New Testament Language and Text*, ed. by J. K. Elliott (Leiden, 1976), pp. 122–36. Cf. also bibliography cited for Plate 9.

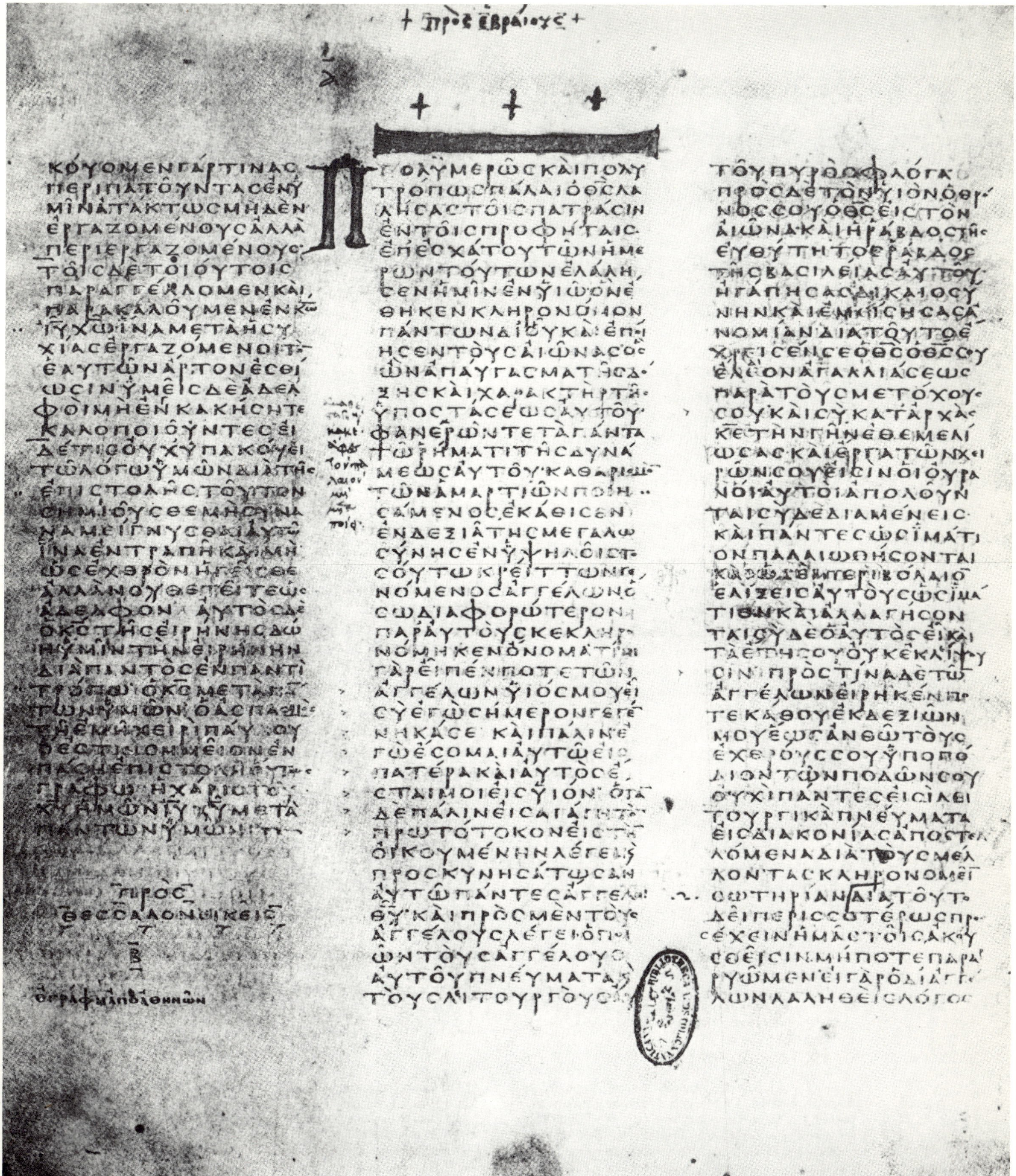

13

14. Luke 24:23–53. Gregory–Aland א (Codex Sinaiticus). iv cent.

LONDON, BRITISH LIBRARY, ADD. 43725, FOL. 246 VERSO.

Fourth-century vellum codex of the Bible, preserving part of the O.T. and all of the N.T.,[1] with the Epistle of Barnabas and part of the Shepherd of Hermas (as far as Mandate iv.3.6), 43 leaves at Leipzig, fragments of three others at Leningrad, and 347 at the British Library (199 of the Old Testament, 148 of the New Testament), measuring when found, according to Gregory, 16⅞ × 14⅞ inches (43 × 37.8 cm.), but now, according to Milne and Skeat, 15 × 13½ inches (38.1 × 34.5 cm.), four columns (two in Psalms, Proverbs, Ecclesiastes, Song of Songs, Wisdom of Solomon, Ecclesiasticus, and Job), 48 lines to a column.

The codex Sinaiticus gets its name from the place of its discovery, the famous monastery of St. Catherine on Mount Sinai, built in the middle of the sixth century A.D. by the Emperor Justinian. The romantic story of how in the mid-nineteenth century Constantine von Tischendorf found the manuscript, some leaves of which were in a waste-basket waiting to be burnt, has often been told and need not be repeated here.[2] Taken in 1859 to St. Petersburg and presented to Alexander II, the Czar of Russia, in 1933 the codex was purchased by the British Museum for the sum of £100,000, raised largely by public appeal in Britain and America, supplemented by a grant from the British government.

In its original state the manuscript probably comprised at least 730 leaves (1460 pages) of fine vellum, made from both sheepskin and goatskin. Since the size of the double sheets of vellum, each making two leaves (four pages), must originally have measured about 17 × 30 inches (43 × 76 cm.), and since each no doubt represents the skin of a single animal, the expense of providing the necessary animals (about 360) must have come to a considerable sum.[3]

Sinaiticus is written in a simple and dignified 'Biblical uncial' hand, the letters being free from ornamental serifs. There are no accents and breathing marks. A new paragraph is indicated by extending the initial letter (which is not enlarged) slightly into the left-hand margin; the preceding line is often not filled out to the right-hand margin. Before the manuscript left the scriptorium[4] the Eusebian apparatus (see §26) was entered with red ink in the margins of the Gospels, except in Luke, where the numerals terminate at 9:61 with section number 106 (fol. 37r).

Tischendorf, followed by Lake, identified four different scribes in the production of the codex, whom he named A, B, C, and D. On the basis, however, of more recent detailed scrutiny of the manuscript by Milne and Skeat it has become clear that there were only three. These three hands are extraordinarily alike, suggesting that the scribes must have received their training in some large writing school with a definite tradition of its own. At the same time, however, they disclose individual peculiarities, apart from the formation of letters, which make it possible to distinguish them. One of these is the difference in the correctness of the spelling of each scribe. In Greek, as in English, pronunciation continued to develop (see §8) after the spelling of words had become fixed, with the result that correct spelling had to be learned in the main by sheer force of memory.

[1] Of the 274 uncial manuscripts of the New Testament, Sinaiticus is the only one that contains the entire twenty-seven books of the New Testament. They stand in the order of Gospels, Pauline Epistles (including Hebrews following 2 Thessalonians), Acts, Catholic Epistles, Revelation.

[2] See, e.g., B. M. Metzger, *The Text of the New Testament*, pp. 42 ff. The news that 'at least 8—perhaps even 14—folios from Codex Sinaiticus' have recently turned up at St. Catherine's Monastery has been reported by James H. Charlesworth; see 'The Manuscripts of St. Catherine's Monastery,' *Biblical Archaeologist*, xliii (1980), p. 27; see also 'Die neuen Sinai-Funde,' *Bericht der Hermann Kunst-Stiftung zur Forderung der neutestamentlichen Textforschung für die Jahre 1977 bis 1979* (Münster/Westf., 1979), pp. 46–58, esp. 49, and Linos Politis, 'Nouveaux manuscrits grecs découverts au Mont Sinaï. Rapport preliminaire,' *Scriptorium*, xxxiv (1980), pp. 5–17.

[3] The further cost of transcribing the manuscript is estimated by J. Rendel Harris to have come to 28,960 denarii (*New Testament Autographs*, supplement to the American Journal of Philology, no. 12; [Baltimore, n.d.], p. 23).

[4] The Eusebian apparatus must have been added before the cancel-leaves in Matthew (folios 10 and 15) were prepared by Scribe D, for these, and only these in Matthew, lack the section and canon numbers.

The spelling of scribe D of Sinaiticus is well-nigh faultless; scribe B, by contrast, is an exceedingly poor speller, while scribe A is not very much better.

These and other points make it possible to show that scribe A wrote most of the historical and poetical books of the Old Testament, almost the whole of the New Testament, and the Epistle of Barnabas, while scribe B was responsible for the Prophets and the Shepherd of Hermas. The work of scribe D was curiously spasmodic: in the Old Testament he wrote the whole of Tobit and Judith, the first half of 4 Maccabees, and the first two-thirds of the Psalms. In the New Testament, besides writing the first five verses of Revelation, he rewrote six pages where, apparently, scribe A had made some unusually serious mistake.

Besides errors in spelling, here and there in the work of all three scribes one finds other faults, particularly accidental omissions. In the light of such carelessness in transcription, it is not surprising that a good many correctors (apparently as many as nine) have been at work on the manuscript, some contemporary (or identical) with the original scribes (א^{a}), and others as late as the twelfth century. Tischendorf's edition of the manuscript enumerates some 14,800 places where some alteration has been made to the text. By far the most extensive of the corrections are those made by a group of scholars in the seventh century (denoted by the sigla א$^{c.a}$ or א$^{c.b}$ —the latter representing at least three scribes). The most important of these is א$^{c.a}$, who carefully revised the entire manuscript (except the Epistle of Barnabas), bringing it into general conformity with the Byzantine texts familiar to him. Another corrector, called א$^{c. Pamph}$ by Kirsopp Lake, added two extremely imtant notes at the end of 2 Esdras (=Nehemiah) and Esther. These state that the manuscript was collated with a very early copy bearing an autograph note by Pamphilus the martyr to the effect that he himself had corrected this manuscript in prison from Origen's own copy of the Hexapla. If this is so, the corrections of this hand (which begin with 1 Samuel and end with Esther) are based on a manuscript only one step removed from Origen himself.

By the use of the ultra-violet lamp, Milne and Skeat discovered that the original reading in the manuscript was erased at a few places and another written in its place by the same scribe. In Matt. 6:28, for example, instead of 'Consider the lilies of the field how they grow; they neither toil nor spin,' the first hand of א seems to have read '. . . how they neither card nor spin nor toil' (*πως ου ξενουσιν* [itacism for *ξαιν-*] *ουδε νηθουσιν ουδε κοπιωσιν*, instead of the usual text, *πως αυξανουσιν· ου κοπιωσιν ουδε νηθουσιν*). This reading of א*, not otherwise attested in New Testament manuscripts, is included in the New English Bible as a marginal reading. R.V.G. Tasker explains the reasoning of the NEB committee in his textual notes to the edition of the Greek New Testament which inferentially lies behind the English rendering: 'As ΟΥΞΕΝΟΥΣΙΝ, wrongly read as ΑΥΞΑΝΟΥΣΙΝ, could have given rise to the other variants, and as *αὐξάνουσιν* seemed unnatural in the present context, the translators thought that the posssibility that the reading of א* is original should be left open, but *αὐξάνουσιν* was retained in the text.'

The last verse of the Gospel according to John (21:25) is another passage where the use of ultraviolet light has confirmed Tischendorf's surmise as to the original reading. It is now known that the scribe for some reason finished the Gospel with ver. 24, adding the subscription *Εὐαγγέλιον κατὰ Ἰωάννην* and drawing, as usual, a coronis (tail-piece) in the left-hand margin between the text and the subscription. Later, however, the same scribe washed the vellum clean of the coronis and subscription and added the concluding verse, repeating the coronis and subscription in a correspondingly lower position.

The place of the writing of codex Sinaiticus has been greatly debated. Hort thought that it was produced in the West, probably Rome; Milne and Skeat, following J. Rendel Harris, preferred Caesarea; other scholars, including Kenyon, Gardthausen, Ropes, and Jellicoe, found reasons to connect it with Alexandria.

The date of Sinaiticus is ordinarily given as the fourth century, though Gardthausen, on the basis of epigraphical evidence, argued vigorously for the first half of the fifth century. On the other hand, as Milne and Skeat point out, palaeographically the hand resembles papyrus documents that have been dated between about A.D. 200 and the second half of the fourth century. The one objective criterion of the *terminus post quem* is the presence of the Eusebian apparatus which was inserted, as it seems, by two of the scribes of the manuscript itself. The *terminus ante quem* is less certain, but, according to Milne and Skeat, is not likely to be much later than about 360.

The character of the text of Sinaiticus varies from book to book in accord with the varying characters of the separate rolls or codices from which its text was ultimately derived. In the Old Testament it agrees, on the whole, with codex Vaticanus (B), which is usually regarded as the best all-round manuscript of the Greek Old Testament. As compared with B it contains additionally 1 and 4 Maccabees. In certain books, notably 1 Chronicles, 2 Esdras, and the Prophets, Sinaiticus has the better text, its superiority being especially marked in Isaiah. In Tobit, Sinaiticus has a considerably longer recension than that of Vaticanus and Alexandrinus, but there is no general agreement as to which is superior.

In the New Testament, particularly in the Gospels and Acts, Sinaiticus and Vaticanus very frequently agree against the overwhelming majority of later manuscripts. In the Book of Revelation, on the other hand, the character of the text of Sinaiticus is distinctly inferior to that of codex Alexandrinus of the following century.

In Plate 14, col. *a*, lines 24 f., the original reading και διερμηνευειν has been corrected to διερμηνευσεν (Luke 24:27); line 32, πορρωτερωτερω, corrected to πορρωτερω (24:28); col. *b*, line 1, διηνοιγησαν, to διηνοιχθησαν (24:31); line 2, after οφθαλμοι, the words και επεγνωσαν (omitted by the original scribe) have been added in the margin by a later corrector; col. *c*, line 14, ωδε is corrected to ενθαδε (24:41); line 1 from bottom, αποστελλω, corrected to εξαποστελλω (24:49); col. *d*, line 16, after αυτων, the corrector has inserted an arrow, which is repeated in the upper margin followed by the words και ανεφερετο εις τον ουρανον (24:51).

The Plate shows the page slightly reduced in size.

BIBLIOGRAPHY: Photographic facsimile of the New and Old Testaments, by Helen and Kirsopp Lake, *Codex Sinaiticus Petropolitanus* . . . 2 vols., N.T. 1911, O.T. 1922 (Oxford), with Introduction by K. Lake; H. J. M. Milne and T. C. Skeat, *Scribes and Correctors of the Codex Sinaiticus* (British Museum, 1938); T. C. Skeat, 'The Lilies of the Field,' *Zeitschrift für die neutestamentliche Wissenschaft*, xxxvii (1938), pp. 211–4; Christian Tindall, ed. by T. B. Smith, *Contributions to the Statistical Study of the Codex Sinaiticus* (Edinburgh and London, 1961) [statistics based on the number of letters in the 552 columns of N.T. text; author's conclusions to be used with caution; cf. J. Duplacy in *Recherches de science religieuse*, l (1962), pp. 260 ff.]; Gordon P. Fee, 'Codex Sinaiticus in the Gospel of John: a Contribution to Methodology in Establishing Textual Relationships,' *New Testament Studies*, xv (1968–69), pp. 22–44 [in John, up to 8:38, ℵ is Western, not Alexandrian].

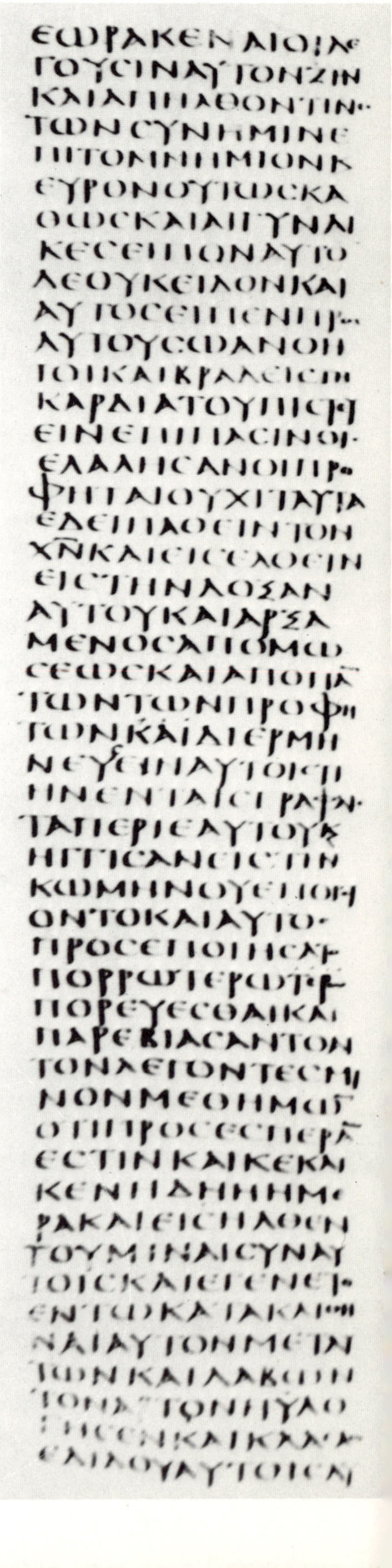

14

ΚΑΙΑΝΕΦΕΡΕΤΟΕΙΣΤΟΝΟΥΝΟΝ

ΤΩΝΔΕΔΙΗΝΥΓΗ
ΣΑΝΟΙΟΦΘΑΛΜΟΙ
ΚΑΙΑΥΤΟΣΑΦΑΝ
ΤΟΣΕΓΕΝΕΤΟΑΠΑΥ
ΤΩΝ
ΚΑΙΕΙΠΑΝΠΡΟΣΑΛ
ΛΗΛΟΥΣΟΥΧΙΗΚΑΡ
ΔΙΑΗΜΩΝΚΕΟΜΕ
ΝΗΗΝΕΝΗΜΙΝ
ΩΣΕΛΑΛΕΙΗΜΙΝ
ΕΝΤΗΟΔΩΩΣΔΙ
ΗΝΥΓΕΝΗΜΙΝ
ΤΑΣΓΡΑΦΑΣΚΑΙΑ
ΝΑΣΤΑΝΤΕΣΑΥΤΗ
ΤΗΩΡΑΥΠΕΣΤΡΕ
ΨΑΝΕΙΣΙΕΡΟΥΣΑ
ΛΗΜΚΑΙΕΥΡΟΝΗ
ΘΡΟΙΣΜΕΝΟΥΣΤΟΥΣ
ΕΝΔΕΚΑΚΑΙΤΟΥΣ
ΣΥΝΑΥΤΟΙΣΛΕΓΟΝ
ΤΑΣΟΤΙΟΝΤΩΣΗ
ΓΕΡΘΗΟΚΣΚΑΙΩ
ΦΘΗΤΩΣΙΜΩΝΙ
ΚΑΙΑΥΤΟΙΕΞΗΓΟΥ
ΤΟΤΑΕΝΤΗΟΔΩ
ΚΑΙΩΣΕΓΝΩΣΘΗ
ΑΥΤΟΙΣΕΝΤΗΚΛΑ
ΣΕΙΤΟΥΑΡΤΟΥ
ΤΑΥΤΑΔΕΑΥΤΩΝ
ΛΑΛΟΥΝΤΩΝΑΥ
ΤΟΣΕΣΤΗΕΝΜΕΣΩ
ΑΥΤΩΝΚΑΙΛΕΓΕΙ
ΑΥΤΟΙΣΕΙΡΗΝΗ
ΥΜΙΝΦΟΒΗΘΕΝ
ΤΕΣΔΕΚΑΙΕΜΦΟ
ΒΟΙΓΕΝΟΜΕΝΟΙ
ΕΔΟΚΟΥΝΠΝΑΘΕ
ΩΡΕΙΝΚΑΙΕΙΠΕ
ΑΥΤΟΙΣΤΙΤΕΤΑΡΑΓ
ΜΕΝΟΙΕΣΤΕΚΑΙ
ΔΙΑΤΙΔΙΑΛΟΓΙΣΜΟΙ
ΑΝΑΒΑΙΝΟΥΣΙΝ
ΕΝΤΑΙΣΚΑΡΔΙΑΙΣ
ΥΜΩΝΕΙΔΕΤΕΤΑΣ
ΠΟΔΑΣΜΟΥΚΑΙ
ΤΑΣΧΙΡΑΣΜΟΥΟΤΙ
ΕΓΩΕΙΜΙΑΥΤΟΣ
ΨΗΛΑΦΗΣΑΤΕΜΕ

ΚΑΙΙΔΕΤΕΟΤΙΠΝΑ
ΣΑΡΚΑΚΑΙΟΣΤΕΑ
ΟΥΚΕΧΕΙΚΑΘΩΣ
ΕΜΕΘΕΩΡΕΙΤΑΙΕ
ΧΟΝΤΑΚΑΙΤΟΥΤΟΕΙ
ΠΩΝΕΔΙΞΕΝΑΥΤΟΙΣ
ΤΑΣΧΙΡΑΣΚΑΙΤΟΥΣ
ΠΟΔΑΣ
ΕΤΙΔΕΑΠΙΣΤΟΥΝΤΩΝ
ΑΥΤΩΝΑΠΟΤΗΣΧΑ
ΡΑΣΚΑΙΘΑΥΜΑΖΟΝ
ΤΩΝΕΙΠΕΝΑΥΤΟΙΣ
ΕΧΕΤΕΤΙΒΡΩΣΙΜΟΝ
ΩΔΕΟΙΔΕΕΠΕΔΩ
ΚΑΝΑΥΤΩΙΧΘΥΟΣ
ΟΠΤΟΥΜΕΡΟΣΚΑΙ
ΛΑΒΩΝΕΝΩΠΙΟΝ
ΑΥΤΩΝΕΦΑΓΕΝ
ΕΙΠΕΝΔΕΠΡΟΣΑΥ
ΤΟΥΣ
ΟΥΤΟΙΟΙΛΟΓΟΙΜΟΥ
ΟΥΣΕΛΑΛΗΣΑΠΡΟΣΥ
ΜΑΣΕΤΙΩΝΣΥΝΥ
ΜΙΝΟΤΙΔΕΙΠΛΗ
ΡΩΘΗΝΑΙΠΑΝΤΑ
ΤΑΓΕΓΡΑΜΜΕΝΑΕΝ
ΤΩΝΟΜΩΜΩΣΕ
ΩΣΕΝΤΟΙΣΠΡΟΦΗ
ΤΑΙΣΚΑΙΨΑΛΜΟΙΣΠΕ
ΡΙΕΜΟΥ
ΤΟΤΕΔΙΗΝΥΞΕΝΑΥ
ΤΩΝΤΟΝΝΟΥΝΤΟΥ
ΣΥΝΙΕΝΑΙΤΑΣΓΡΑ
ΦΑΣΚΑΙΕΙΠΕΝΑΥ
ΤΟΙΣΟΤΙΟΥΤΩΣΓΕ
ΓΡΑΠΤΑΙΠΑΘΕΙΝ
ΤΟΝΧΝΚΑΙΑΝΑΣΤΗ
ΝΑΙΕΚΝΕΚΡΩΝ
ΤΗΤΡΙΤΗΗΜΕΡΑΚΑΙ
ΚΗΡΥΧΘΗΝΑΙΕΠΙ
ΤΩΟΝΟΜΑΤΙΑΥΤΟΥ
ΜΕΤΑΝΟΙΑΝΕΙΣΑ
ΦΕΣΙΝΑΜΑΡΤΙΩΝ
ΕΙΣΠΑΝΤΑΤΑΕΘΝΗ
ΑΡΞΑΜΕΝΟΙΑΠΟΙ
ΕΡΟΥΣΑΛΗΜΥΜΕΙΣ
ΕΣΤΕΜΑΡΤΥΡΕΣΤΟΥ
ΤΩΝΚΑΙΕΓΩΑΠΟΣΤΕ

ΛΩΤΗΝΕΠΑΓΓΕΛΙ
ΑΝΤΟΥΠΡΣΜΟΥ
ΕΦΥΜΑΣΥΜΕΙΣ
ΔΕΚΑΘΙΣΑΤΕΕΝΤΗ
ΠΟΛΕΙΕΩΣΟΥΕΝ
ΔΥΣΗΣΘΕΕΞΥΨΟΥΣ
ΔΥΝΑΜΙΝ
ΕΞΗΓΑΓΕΝΔΕΑΥΤΟΥΣ
ΕΩΣΠΡΟΣΒΗΘΑ
ΝΙΑΝΚΑΙΕΠΑΡΑΣ
ΤΑΣΧΙΡΑΣΑΥΤΟΥΕΥ
ΛΟΓΗΣΕΝΑΥΤΟΥΣ
ΚΑΙΕΓΕΝΕΤΟΕΝ
ΤΩΕΥΛΟΓΙΝΑΥΤΟΝ
ΑΥΤΟΥΣΔΙΕΣΤΗ
ΑΠΑΥΤΩΝΚΑΙΑΥ
ΤΟΙΠΡΟΣΚΥΝΗΣΑΝ
ΤΕΣΑΥΤΟΝΥΠΕΣ
ΤΡΕΨΑΝΕΙΣΙΕΡΟΥ
ΣΑΛΗΜΜΕΤΑΧΑ
ΡΑΣΜΕΓΑΛΗΣΚΑΙ
ΗΣΑΝΔΙΑΠΑΝΤΟΣ
ΕΝΤΩΙΕΡΩΕΥΛΟ
ΓΟΥΝΤΕΣΤΟΝΘΝ

ΕΥΑΓΓΕΛΙΟΝ

ΚΑΤΑΛΟΥΚΑΝ

15. Joshua 11:9–16. Rahlfs G (Codex Colberto-Sarravianus). iv/v cent.

LEIDEN, UNIVERSITY LIBRARY, VOSS. GR. Q8, FOL. 109 RECTO.

Parchment codex, containing the Octateuch (with lacunae), iv/v century, 9⅞ × 9$\frac{1}{16}$ inches (25 × 23 cm.), comprising 153 leaves, 130 at Leiden, 22 at Paris (Bibliothèque Nationale, Gr. 17), and one at Leningrad (Public Library, Gr. 3), two columns, 27 lines to a column.

The title of the codex perpetuates the names of earlier owners of the Paris and Leiden portions; the former belonged to Jean Baptiste Colbert, finance minister and chief adviser of Louis XIV, and the latter to Claude Sarràve of Paris, from whose hands the folios passed eventually into the possession of the University of Leiden.

A new paragraph is indicated by extending the initial letter (which is not enlarged) into the left-hand margin. In order to make the right-hand margin as even as possible, the scribe (*a*) uses a horizontal line to indicate final *nu*, (*b*) writes one or more letters very small, (*c*) combines *eta* with the preceding or following letter (see Fig. 6), and/or (*d*) frequently uses *καί*-compendium.

Occasionally a rough breathing mark is added by one or another corrector (of whom Tischendorf identified seven). The three most important are (A) a contemporary hand, (B) another fifth-century hand that revised Deuteronomy and Judges, and (C) a hand of the sixth century which has been busy in the text of Numbers.

Codex G is noteworthy as being the oldest and best witness to an Origenic text that retains many of the Hexaplaric signs (see §22).

TRANSCRIPTION OF PLATE 15

αρ]ματα αυτων ενεπρη|σεν πυρι (erasure) | *και επεστρεψεν ι̅ς̅ εν* | *τω καιρω εκεινω* ϗ | *κατελαβετο * την:* *ασωρ* | *και τον βασιλεα αυτης* | * *απεκτεινεν εν ρομ*| * *φαια: ην δε ασωρ το προ|τερον αρχουσα πασω̄* | *των βασιλειων του|των και απεκτειναᾱ* | *παν ενπνεον * ο: εν* | *αυτη εν στοματι ξιφους* | *και εξωλεθρευσαν:* | —*παντας: και ου κατελι|φθη εν αυτη ενπνε|ον και την ασωρ ενε|πρησεν εν πυρι και πα|σας τας πολεις των* | *βασιλειων * τουτω̄:* | *και * παντας: τους βασι|λεις αυτων ελαβεν ι̅ς̅* | *και ανειλεν αυτους* | *εν στοματι ξιφους* ϗ | *εξωλεθρευσεν αυτους* | *ον τροπον συνεταξε̄* | Μωσης *ο παις κ̅υ̅· αλλα* | *πασας τας πολεις τας* ‖ *κεχωματισμενας* | * *αυτων: ουκ ενεπρη|σεν ι̅η̅λ̅ πλην * την: α|σωρ μονην :̄ αυτην: ενεπρησεν ι̅ς̅ και πᾱ|τα τα σκυλα αυτης ** ϗ | * *τα κτηνη: επρονομευ|σαν εαυτοις οι ϋϊοι ι̅η̅λ̅* | * *κατα το ρημα κ̅υ̅ ο ενε*| * *τειλατο τω ι̅υ̅: αυτους* | *δε παντας εξωλεθρευ|σεν εν στοματι ξιφους* | *εως απωλεσεν αυτους* | *ου κατιλιπον :̄ αυτω̄: ουδε εν ενπνεον ο̄* | *τροπον συνεταξεν* | *κ̅ς̅ τω* Μωση *τω παι|δι αυτου ωσαυτως* | *ενετειλατο* Μωσης | *τω ι̅υ̅ και ουτως εποι|ησεν|ις| ου παρεβη ου|δεν απο παντωνω̄* | *συνεταξεν κ̅ς̅ τω* Μωση | *και ελαβεν ι̅ς̅ * την: πα|σαν την γην * ταυτη:̄* | *την ορεινην και * τη:̄* | *πασαν την γην νε|γεβ και πασαν την γη̄*

BIBLIOGRAPHY: *Vetus Testamentum Graece. Codicis Sarraviani-Colberti quae supersunt in Bibliothecis Leidensi Parisensi Petropolitana phototypice edita.* Praefatus est Henricus Omont (Leiden, 1897).

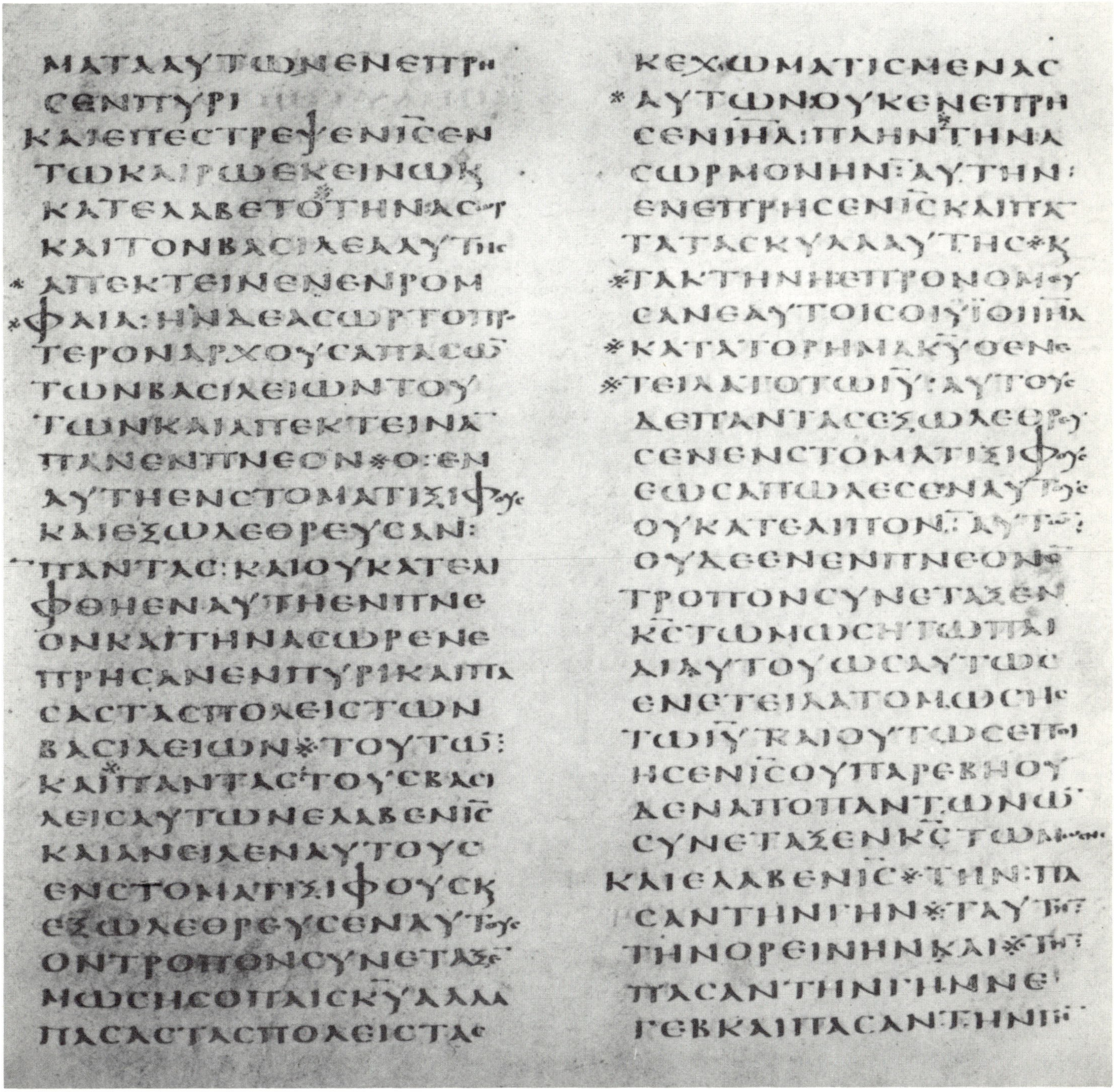
ΜΑΤΑΑΥΤΩΝΕΝΕΠΡΗ
ΣΕΝΠΥΡΙ
ΚΑΙΕΠΕΣΤΡΕΨΕΝΙΣΕΝ
ΤΩΚΑΙΡΩΕΚΕΙΝΩΚ
ΚΑΤΕΛΑΒΕΤΟΤΗΝΑΣΩΡ
ΚΑΙΤΟΝΒΑΣΙΛΕΑΑΥΤΗΣ
* ΑΠΕΚΤΕΙΝΕΝΕΝΡΟΜ
*ΦΑΙΑ:ΗΝΔΕΑΣΩΡΤΟΠΡΟ
ΤΕΡΟΝΑΡΧΟΥΣΑΠΑΣΩΝ
ΤΩΝΒΑΣΙΛΕΙΩΝΤΟΥ
ΤΩΝΚΑΙΑΠΕΚΤΕΙΝΑΝ
ΠΑΝΕΝΠΝΕΟΝ*Ο:ΕΝ
ΑΥΤΗΕΝΣΤΟΜΑΤΙΞΙΦΟΥΣ
ΚΑΙΕΞΩΛΕΘΡΕΥΣΑΝ:
ΠΑΝΤΑΣ:ΚΑΙΟΥΚΑΤΕΛΙ
ΦΘΗΕΝΑΥΤΗΕΝΠΝΕ
ΟΝΚΑΙΤΗΝΑΣΩΡΕΝΕ
ΠΡΗΣΑΝΕΝΠΥΡΙΚΑΙΠΑ
ΣΑΣΤΑΣΠΟΛΕΙΣΤΩΝ
ΒΑΣΙΛΕΙΩΝ*ΤΟΥΤΩΝ:
ΚΑΙΠΑΝΤΑΣΤΟΥΣΒΑΣΙ
ΛΕΙΣΑΥΤΩΝΕΛΑΒΕΝΙΣ
ΚΑΙΑΝΕΙΛΕΝΑΥΤΟΥΣ
ΕΝΣΤΟΜΑΤΙΞΙΦΟΥΣΚ
ΕΞΩΛΕΘΡΕΥΣΕΝΑΥΤΟΥΣ
ΟΝΤΡΟΠΟΝΣΥΝΕΤΑΞΕ
ΜΩΣΗΣΟΠΑΙΣΚΥΑΛΛΑ
ΠΑΣΑΣΤΑΣΠΟΛΕΙΣΤΑΣ

ΚΕΧΩΜΑΤΙΣΜΕΝΑΣ
*ΑΥΤΩΝΟΥΚΕΝΕΠΡΗ
ΣΕΝΙΗΛ:ΠΛΗΝΤΗΝΑ
ΣΩΡΜΟΝΗΝ:ΑΥΤΗΝ:
ΕΝΕΠΡΗΣΕΝΙΣΚΑΙΠΑ
ΤΑΤΑΣΚΥΛΑΑΥΤΗΣ*Κ
*ΤΑΚΤΗΝΗΕΠΡΟΝΟΜΕΥ
ΣΑΝΕΑΥΤΟΙΣΟΙΥΙΟΙΙΗΛ
*ΚΑΤΑΤΟΡΗΜΑΚΥΟΕΝ
*ΤΕΙΛΑΤΟΤΩΙΥ:ΑΥΤΟΥΣ
ΔΕΠΑΝΤΑΣΕΞΩΛΕΘΡΕΥ
ΣΕΝΕΝΣΤΟΜΑΤΙΞΙΦΟΥΣ
ΕΩΣΑΠΩΛΕΣΕΝΑΥΤΟΥΣ
ΟΥΚΑΤΕΛΙΠΟΝ:ΑΥΤΩΝ:
ΟΥΔΕΕΝΕΝΠΝΕΟΝ*
ΤΡΟΠΟΝΣΥΝΕΤΑΞΕΝ
ΚΣΤΩΜΩΣΗΤΩΠΑΙ
ΔΙΑΥΤΟΥΩΣΑΥΤΩΣ
ΕΝΕΤΕΙΛΑΤΟΜΩΣΗΣ
ΤΩΙΥΚΑΙΟΥΤΩΣΕΠΟΙ
ΗΣΕΝΙΣΟΥΠΑΡΕΒΗΟΥ
ΔΕΝΑΠΟΠΑΝΤΩΝΩΝ
ΣΥΝΕΤΑΞΕΝΚΣΤΩΜΩΣΗ
ΚΑΙΕΛΑΒΕΝΙΣ*ΤΗΝ:ΠΑ
ΣΑΝΤΗΝΓΗΝ*ΤΑΥΤΗΝ
ΤΗΝΟΡΕΙΝΗΝΚΑΙ*ΤΗΝ
ΠΑΣΑΝΤΗΝΓΗΝΝΕ
ΓΕΒΚΑΙΠΑΣΑΝΤΗΝΓΗ

15

16. Mark 16:12–17. Gregory–Aland W (Codex Washingtonianus). iv/v cent.

WASHINGTON, FREER GALLERY OF ART, COD. 06.274, PAGE 371.

Parchment codex, containing the four Gospels (except Mark 15:13–38, John 14:25–16:7) in the so-called Western order (Matthew, John, Luke, Mark), late iv or (more probably) early v century, average size of leaves 8⅛ × 5⅝ inches (20.8 × 14.3 cm.), 187 leaves, one column, 30 lines to the page.

Codex W is the work of two scribes; the first quire of John (1:1–5:11) is in a different hand, with a different system of punctuation and on a different kind of parchment, from that of the rest of the manuscript. The writing of the major portion of the manuscript is a graceful, sloping uncial of small size. It was evidently written with ease and rapidity. The letters ρ and υ are usually about twice the height, and φ and ψ nearly three times the height of the other letters. The other scribe was a less-practised penman, whose letters vary a little more in size and shape, and the line is followed less carefully.

A remarkable feature of codex W is the lack of homogeneity in its text. In Matthew and part of Luke (8:13–24:53) the text is of the common Byzantine variety; in Mark 1:1–5:30 it is Western, resembling the Old Latin; Mark 5:31–16:20 is Caesarean, akin to 𝔭[45]; and Luke 1:1–8:12 and John 5:12–21:25 are Alexandrian. The text of John 1:1–5:11, which fills a quire that was added about the seventh century, presumably to replace one which was damaged, is a mixed text with some Alexandrian and a few Western readings. The stratification of text is matched by similar variations in paragraphing. According to Sanders, this variegation is to be explained by the theory that the codex is derived from a patchwork ancestor made up of fragments from different manuscripts pieced together after the attempt made by the Emperor Diocletian in 303 to crush Christianity by destroying its sacred books.

One of the most noteworthy of the variant readings in codex W is a remarkable addition near the close of the Gospel according to Mark (following 16:14), part of which was known to Jerome, who declares that it was present 'in certain copies and especially in Greek codices.'[1] The logion, which is doubtless of apocryphal origin, comprises lines 9–24 of the Plate.

Transcription

κακεινοι απελογουντο [MS. *-τε*] *λεγοντες οτι ο* | *αιων ουτος της ανομιας και της απιστιας* | *υπο τον σαταναν εστιν ο μη εων τα υπο* | *των πν*[*ευμ*]*ατων ακαθαρτα την αληθειαν* | *του θ*[*εο*]*υ καταλαβεσθαι δυναμιν δια* | *τουτο αποκαλυψιν σου την δικαιοσυ*|*νην ηδη εκεινοι ελεγον τω Χ*[*ριστ*]*ω και ο* | *Χ*[*ριστο*]*ς εκεινοις προσελεγεν οτι πεπληρω*|*ται ο ορος των ετων της εξουσιας του* | *σατανα αλλα εγγιζει αλλα δεινα* (MS. *δινα*) *και υ*|*περ ων εγω αμαρτησαντων παρεδοθην εις θανατον ϊνα υποστρεψωσιν εις την* | *αληθειαν και μηκετι αμαρτησωσιν* | *ϊνα την εν τω ουρανω πν*[*ευματ*]*ικεν και α*|*ψθαρτον της δικαιοσυνης δοξαν* | *κληρονομησωσιν.*

Translation

And they excused themselves, saying, 'This age of lawlessness and unbelief is under Satan, who does not allow the truth and power of God to prevail over the unclean things of the spirits.[2] Therefore reveal thy righteousness now'—thus they spoke to Christ. And Christ replied to them, 'The term of years for Satan's power has been fulfilled, but other terrible things draw near. And for those who have sinned I was delivered over to death, that they may return to the truth and sin no more; that they may inherit the spiritual and incorruptible glory of righteousness which is in heaven.'

BIBLIOGRAPHY: Caspar René Gregory, *Das Freer-Logion* (Leipzig, 1908); Henry A. Sanders, *Facsimile of the Washington Manuscript of the Four Gospels in the Freer Collection* (Ann Arbor, 1912); idem, *The New Testament Manuscripts in the Freer Collection*; Part I, *The Washington Manuscript of the Four Gospels* (New York, 1912); B. H. Streeter, 'W and the Caesarean Text,' *The Four Gospels*, 2nd impression (London, 1926), pp. 598–600; Eugen Helzle, 'Der Schluss der Markusevangeliums und das Freer-Logion (Mk. 16, 14 W),' Dissertation, Tübingen, 1959 [cf. *Theologische Literaturzeitung*, 1960, cols. 470 f.]; and Larry Weir Hurtado, 'Codex Washingtonianus in the Gospel of Mark; its Textual Relationships and Scribal Characteristics,' Ph.D. diss., Case Western Reserve Univ., 1973.

[1] Cf. B. M. Metzger, 'St. Jerome's Explicit References to Variant Readings in Manuscripts of the New Testament,' *Text and Interpretation; Studies in the New Testament Presented to Matthew Black*, ed. by Ernest Best and R. McL. Wilson (Cambridge, 1979), pp. 179–90.

[2] Or, who does not allow what lies under the unclean spirits to understand the truth and power of God.

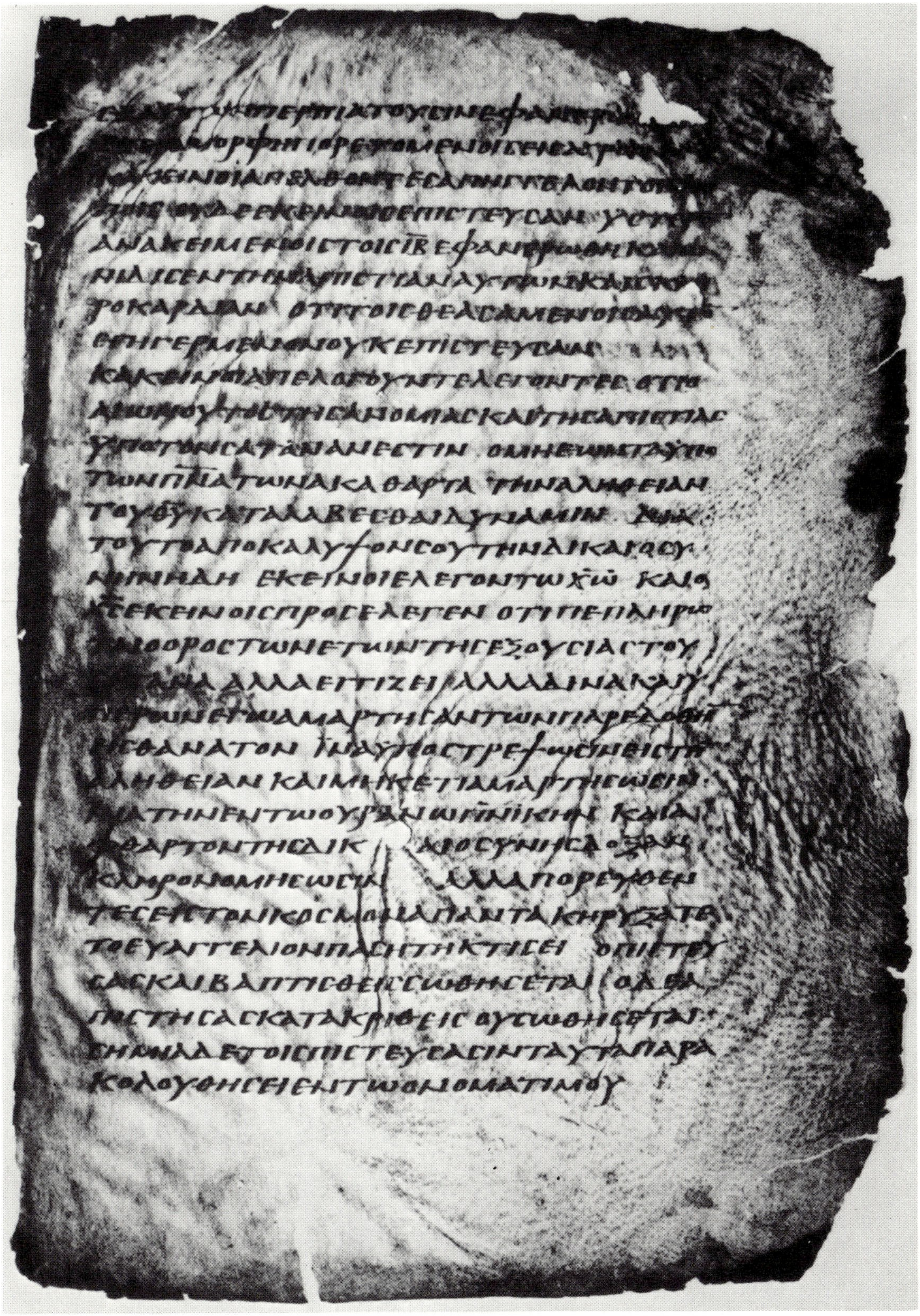

16

17. Deuteronomy 10:6–15. Rahlfs W (Sanders Θ). v cent.

Washington, Freer Gallery of Art, cod. Wash. i, page 35.

Parchment codex, containing Deuteronomy and Joshua, v century, 12 × 10⅛ inches (30.6 × 25.8 cm.), 102 leaves, two columns, 31 lines to a column (the first three lines of Deuteronomy and the first two and the title of Joshua are in red ink).

This is one of four manuscripts bought in 1906 by Mr. Charles L. Freer, an industrialist of Detroit, from a dealer in Gizah, near Cairo. It was subsequently given to the Smithsonian Institution in Washington. The codex is written on fairly thick parchment, which has wrinkled and hardened with age and exposure. At the bottom the leaves are somewhat decayed, but only in the case of three leaves has this decay extended to the text.

The codex consists of fourteen quires numbered in the upper right-hand corner of the first page of each with the numbers ΛZ to N (37 to 60). The preceding portion presumably contained Genesis through Numbers.

The writing is an upright square uncial of good size. Occasionally the letter *tau* is taller than other letters (e.g. col. *a*, line 1, and col. *b*, line 2). As is the case with other examples of 'Biblical uncial,' the scribe's pen makes relatively thick lines vertically but relatively slender lines horizontally. The central stroke of *epsilon* terminates in a thickening.

Paragraph or chapter divisions are indicated by an enlarged letter set out in the left-hand margin. Punctuation by the first hand is a single dot in the middle (or slightly above middle) position. The scribe is quite haphazard in employing punctuation, and it is often omitted if a vacant space occurs at the end of a line.

There are no accent marks, though an apostrophe sometimes occurs after words ending in any consonant except ν and ς. It is used most frequently after proper names (e.g. col. *a*, lines 2 and 3 after Γαλγαλ· [twice]; col. *b*, line 9 after the contraction for Ἰσραήλ), as well as to indicate elision (col. *b*, line 11 αλλ').

A somewhat later hand (the editor attributes it to the end of the sixth or the beginning of the seventh century) added in cursive script the directives for ecclesiastical lections. On the page shown in the Plate, opposite line 7 from the bottom of col. *b* stands the abbreviation for ἀρχή, indicating that the Scripture lesson begins with ἰδού in the line to the right (Deut. 10:14 ff.). In the upper margin stands the staurogram,[1] followed by the directive *εις την μνημην των αγιων π(α)τρων εις το λυχνηκον* (for λυχνικον), 'to the memory of the holy fathers, for the evening reading.'

The Plate shows the page slightly reduced in size.

Bibliography: Henry A. Sanders, *A Facsimile Edition of the Washington Manuscript of Deuteronomy and Joshua* (Ann Arbor, 1910); idem, *The Old Testament Manuscripts in the Freer Collection* (New York, 1917).

[1] The staurogram, which is a contraction of the Greek word *σταυρός*, occurs as early as A.D. 200 (in 𝔓[66] and 𝔓[75]). Along with the Christogram (*chi-rho* monogram; see description of Plate 35), the staurogram came into widespread usage in Greek, Latin, and Coptic; cf. Erich Dinkler, *Signum Crucis* (Tübingen, 1967), pp. 177 f.; Kurt Aland, 'Bemerkungen zum Alter und zur Entstehung des Christogrammes,' *Studien zur Überlieferung des Neuen Testamentes und seines Textes* (Berlin, 1967), pp. 173–9; and Wolfgang Wischmeyer, 'Christogramm und Staurogramm in den lateinischen Inschriften altkirchlicher Zeit,' *Theologia Crucis—Signum Crucis; Festschrift für Erich Dinkler*, ed. by Carl Andresen and Günter Klein (Tübingen, 1979), pp. 539–50.

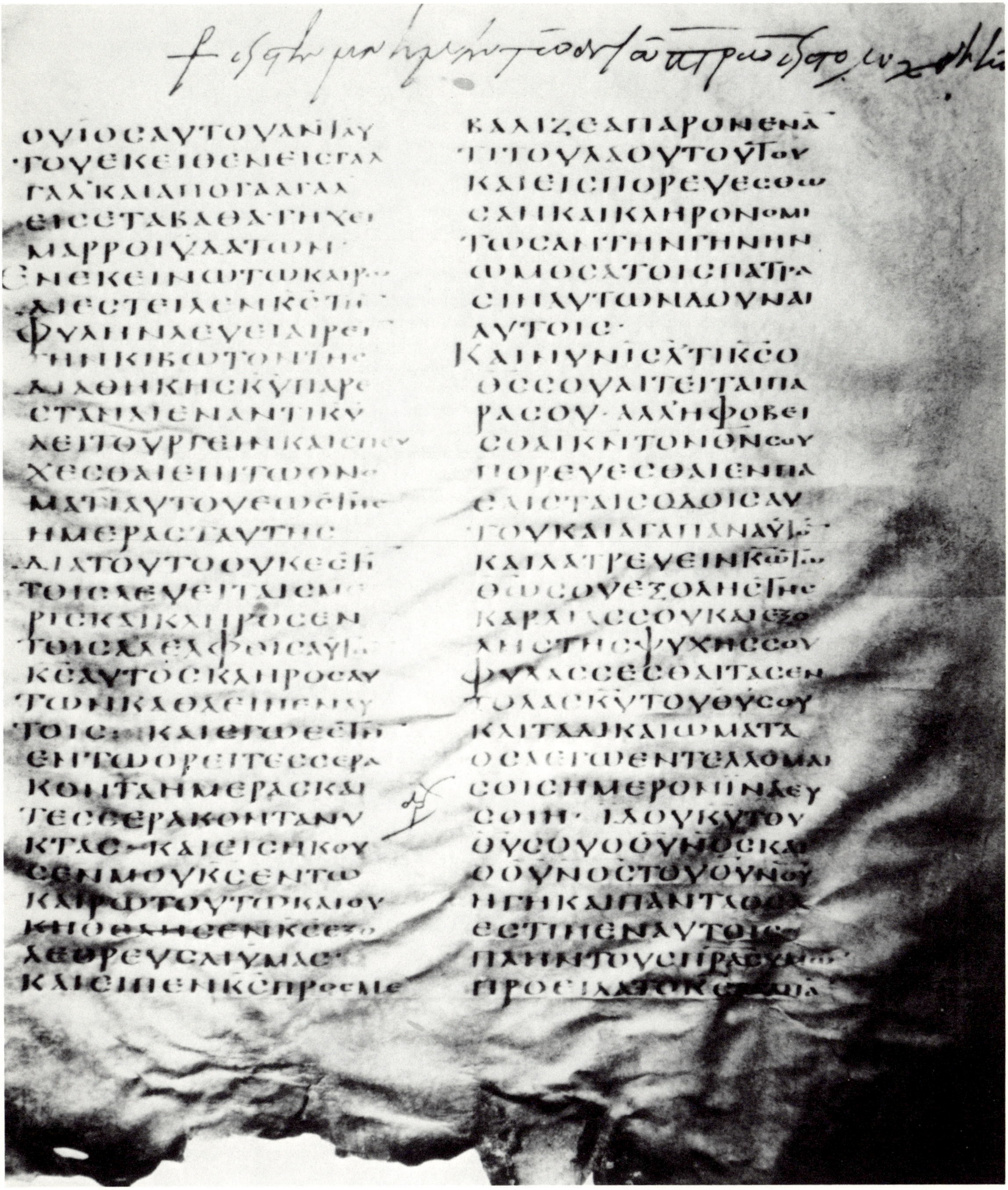
ΟΥΙΟΣ ΑΥΤΟΥ ΑΝΤ' ΑΥ
ΤΟΥ ΕΚΕΙΘΕΝ ΕΙΣ ΓΑΔ
ΓΑΔ ΚΑΙ ΑΠΟ ΓΑΔΓΑΔ
ΕΙΣ ΕΤΑΒΑΘΑ ΓΗ ΧΕΙ
ΜΑΡΡΟΙ ΥΔΑΤΩΝ
ΕΝ ΕΚΕΙΝΩ ΤΩ ΚΑΙΡΩ
ΔΙΕΣΤΕΙΛΕΝ ΚΣ ΤΗΝ
ΦΥΛΗΝ ΛΕΥΕΙ ΑΙΡΕΙΝ
ΤΗΝ ΚΙΒΩΤΟΝ ΤΗΣ
ΔΙΑΘΗΚΗΣ ΚΥ ΠΑΡΕ
ΣΤΑΝΑΙ ΕΝΑΝΤΙ ΚΥ
ΛΕΙΤΟΥΡΓΕΙΝ ΚΑΙ ΕΠΕΥ
ΧΕΣΘΑΙ ΕΠΙ ΤΩ ΟΝΟ
ΜΑΤΙ ΑΥΤΟΥ ΕΩΣ ΤΗΣ
ΗΜΕΡΑΣ ΤΑΥΤΗΣ
ΔΙΑ ΤΟΥΤΟ ΟΥΚ ΕΣΤΙ
ΤΟΙΣ ΛΕΥΕΙΤΑΙΣ ΜΕ
ΡΙΣ ΚΑΙ ΚΛΗΡΟΣ ΕΝ
ΤΟΙΣ ΑΔΕΛΦΟΙΣ ΑΥΤΩ
ΚΣ ΑΥΤΟΣ ΚΛΗΡΟΣ ΑΥ
ΤΩΝ ΚΑΘΑ ΕΙΠΕΝ ΑΥ
ΤΟΙΣ· ΚΑΙ ΕΓΩ ΕΣΤΗΝ
ΕΝ ΤΩ ΟΡΕΙ ΤΕΣΣΕΡΑ
ΚΟΝΤΑ ΗΜΕΡΑΣ ΚΑΙ
ΤΕΣΣΕΡΑΚΟΝΤΑ ΝΥ
ΚΤΑΣ· ΚΑΙ ΕΙΣΗΚΟΥ
ΣΕΝ ΜΟΥ ΚΣ ΕΝ ΤΩ
ΚΑΙΡΩ ΤΟΥΤΩ ΚΑΙ ΟΥ
ΚΗΘΕΛΗΣΕΝ ΚΣ ΕΞΟ
ΛΕΘΡΕΥΣΑΙ ΥΜΑΣ·
ΚΑΙ ΕΙΠΕΝ ΚΣ ΠΡΟΣ ΜΕ
ΒΑΔΙΖΕ ΑΠΑΡΟΝ ΕΝΑ
ΝΤΙ ΤΟΥ ΛΑΟΥ ΤΟΥΤΟΥ
ΚΑΙ ΕΙΣΠΟΡΕΥΕΣΘΩ
ΣΑΝ ΚΑΙ ΚΛΗΡΟΝΟΜΙ
ΤΩΣΑΝ ΤΗΝ ΓΗΝ ΗΝ
ΩΜΟΣΑ ΤΟΙΣ ΠΑΤΡΑ
ΣΙΝ ΑΥΤΩΝ ΔΟΥΝΑΙ
ΑΥΤΟΙΣ·
ΚΑΙ ΝΥΝ ΙΣΛ ΤΙ ΚΣ Ο
ΘΣ ΣΟΥ ΑΙΤΕΙΤΑΙ ΠΑ
ΡΑ ΣΟΥ· ΑΛΛ' Η ΦΟΒΕΙ
ΣΘΑΙ ΚΝ ΤΟΝ ΘΝ ΣΟΥ
ΠΟΡΕΥΕΣΘΑΙ ΕΝ ΠΑ
ΣΑΙΣ ΤΑΙΣ ΟΔΟΙΣ ΑΥ
ΤΟΥ ΚΑΙ ΑΓΑΠΑΝ ΑΥΤΟΝ
ΚΑΙ ΛΑΤΡΕΥΕΙΝ ΚΩ ΤΩ
ΘΩ ΣΟΥ ΕΞ ΟΛΗΣ ΤΗΣ
ΚΑΡΔΙΑΣ ΣΟΥ ΚΑΙ ΕΞ Ο
ΛΗΣ ΤΗΣ ΨΥΧΗΣ ΣΟΥ
ΦΥΛΑΣΣΕΣΘΑΙ ΤΑΣ ΕΝ
ΤΟΛΑΣ ΚΥ ΤΟΥ ΘΥ ΣΟΥ
ΚΑΙ ΤΑ ΔΙΚΑΙΩΜΑΤΑ
Ο ΕΓΩ ΕΝΤΕΛΛΟΜΑΙ
ΣΟΙ ΣΗΜΕΡΟΝ ΙΝΑ ΕΥ
ΣΟΙ Η· ΙΔΟΥ ΚΥ ΤΟΥ
ΘΥ ΣΟΥ Ο ΟΥΝΟΣ ΚΑΙ
Ο ΟΥΝΟΣ ΤΟΥ ΟΥΝΟΥ
Η ΓΗ ΚΑΙ ΠΑΝΤΑ ΟΣΑ
ΕΣΤΙΝ ΕΝ ΑΥΤΟΙΣ·
ΠΛΗΝ ΤΟΥΣ ΠΑΤΕΡΑΣ ΥΜΩΝ
ΠΡΟΕΙΛΑΤΟ ΚΣ ΑΓΑΠΑΝ

18. Mark 9:2–29. Gregory–Aland A (Codex Alexandrinus). v cent.

LONDON, BRITISH LIBRARY, ROYAL I.D.V-VIII, VOL. IV, FOL. 36 VERSO.

Vellum codex of the Bible (now bound in four volumes), with lacunae, v century, 12⅝ × 10⅜ inches (32 × 26.3 cm.), 773 leaves (279+238+118 in O.T. vols.; 144 in N.T. vol.), two columns, generally 49–51 lines to a column.

This codex was sent as a gift to James I of England by Cyril Lucar, Patriarch successively of Alexandria (1602–1621) and Constantinople (1621–1638).[1] It did not, however, reach Britain till 1627, after the succession of Charles I. A collation of the New Testament was made for the London Polyglot Bible (1657) by Alexander Huish, Prebendary of Wells.

The Old Testament includes (in addition to the usual books of Greek Bibles) 3 and 4 Maccabees, Psalm 151, and (after the Psalter) the fourteen liturgical canticles, or Odes. The twelve Minor Prophets precede the Book of Isaiah. In the New Testament the Catholic Epistles precede the Pauline Epistles. At the close of the New Testament are appended the two Epistles of Clement. According to the table of contents, the Psalms of Solomon were originally included at the end of the manuscript, but these have been lost with the end of 2 Clement (after 12:4).

The codex is written in a large, square uncial hand by two scribes (so Milne and Skeat, who dispute Kenyon's opinion that there were five scribes). There are no accent and breathing marks, except a few added by a later hand; but the punctuation (limited to a single point, usually high) is by the first hand. Except in the poetical books, which are written *στιχηρῶς*, new sections are indicated by the use of enlarged ('capital') letters. The first letter of each paragraph, or, if the paragraph begins in the middle of a line, the first letter of the first complete line in it (e.g., col. *a*, lines 33, 45), is enlarged and projects into the left-hand margin. The Ammonian section and Eusebian canon numbers stand in the margins of the Gospels.

Many corrections have been made in the manuscript, some of them by the original scribe and others by more recent hands. In line 30 of col. *b* of the page reproduced, the original reading was simply *ο πατηρ του παιδιου ελεγεν* (9:24, as in 𝔭⁴⁵ ℵ B C* L W Δ Ψ 28 700), but the corrector has inserted the phrase *μετα δακρυων* by writing *παιδιου μετα* in the margin, and in the next line by erasing *παιδιου* and substituting *δακρυων*. The corrected form of text agrees with D N X Y Γ Θ Π Σ Φ and the great majority of the minuscule manuscripts, on which the Textus Receptus depends. The type of text of Alexandrinus varies as to section in both Testaments: in the Gospels it is Byzantine; in the Acts and Epistles, Alexandrian, though with some Western readings; in the Apocalypse, and in several Old Testament books (so Jellicoe), it has the best text of all manuscripts.

The Plate shows the page slightly reduced in size.

BIBLIOGRAPHY: For a full description of the manuscript, see E. Maunde Thompson's introduction to his photographic facsimile edition (London, 1879–1883); a reduced photographic facsimile of the New Testament (and Epistles of Clement), with introduction by Frederic G. Kenyon, was published by the British Museum in 1909; the Old Testament followed, in four parts, Octateuch, 1915; 1 Sam.-2 Chron., 1930; Hosea-Judith, 1936; 1 Esdras-Ecclus., 1957. For palaeographical details of codex Alexandrinus, see H. J. M. Milne and T. C. Skeat, *Scribes and Correctors of the Codex Sinaiticus* (London, 1938), Appendix ii.

[1] See Matthew Spinka, 'Acquisition of the Codex Alexandrinus by England,' *Review of Religion*, xvi (1936), pp. 10–29.

ΚΑΙ ΙΩΑΝΝΗΝ ΚΑΙ ΑΝΑΦΕΡΕΙ ΑΥ
ΤΟΥΣ ΕΙΣ ΟΡΟΣ ΥΨΗΛΟΝ ΚΑΤ ΙΔΙΑΝ
ΜΟΝΟΥΣ ΚΑΙ ΜΕΤΕΜΟΡΦΩΘΗ
ΕΜΠΡΟΣΘΕΝ ΑΥΤΩΝ ΚΑΙ ΤΑ ΙΜΑ
ΤΙΑ ΑΥΤΟΥ ΕΓΕΝΟΝΤΟ ΣΤΙΛΒΟΝ
ΤΑ ΛΕΥΚΑ ΛΙΑΝ ΩΣ ΧΙΩΝ ΟΙΑ ΓΝΑ
ΦΕΥΣ ΕΠΙ ΤΗΣ ΓΗΣ ΟΥ ΔΥΝΑΤΑΙ ΛΕΥ
ΚΑΝΑΙ ΚΑΙ ΩΦΘΗ ΑΥΤΟΙΣ ΗΛΙΑΣ
ΣΥΝ ΜΩΣΕΙ ΚΑΙ ΗΣΑΝ ΣΥΛΛΑΛΟΥΝ
ΤΕΣ ΤΩ ΙΥ· ΚΑΙ ΑΠΟΚΡΙΘΕΙΣ Ο ΠΕ
ΤΡΟΣ ΛΕΓΕΙ ΤΩ ΙΥ ΡΑΒΒΕΙ ΚΑΛΟΝ
ΕΣΤΙΝ ΗΜΑΣ ΩΔΕ ΕΙΝΑΙ ΚΑΙ ΠΟΙ
ΗΣΩΜΕΝ ΣΚΗΝΑΣ ΤΡΕΙΣ ΣΟΙ ΜΙΑ
ΚΑΙ ΜΩΣΕΙ ΜΙΑΝ ΚΑΙ ΗΛΙΑ ΜΙΑΝ
ΟΥ ΓΑΡ ΗΔΕΙ ΤΙ ΛΑΛΗΣΕΙ ΗΣΑΝ ΓΑΡ
ΕΚΦΟΒΟΙ ΚΑΙ ΕΓΕΝΕΤΟ ΝΕΦΕ
ΛΗ ΕΠΙΣΚΙΑΖΟΥΣΑ ΑΥΤΟΙΣ ΚΑΙ ΗΛ
ΘΕΝ ΦΩΝΗ ΕΚ ΤΗΣ ΝΕΦΕΛΗΣ ΛΕ
ΓΟΥΣΑ ΟΥΤΟΣ ΕΣΤΙΝ Ο ΥΣ ΜΟΥ Ο ΑΓ
ΑΠΗΤΟΣ ΑΥΤΟΥ ΑΚΟΥΕΤΕ ΚΑΙ ΕΞΑ
ΠΙΝΑ ΠΕΡΙΒΛΕΨΑΜΕΝΟΙ ΟΥΚΕΤΙ
ΟΥΔΕΝΑ ΕΙΔΟΝ ΑΛΛΑ ΤΟΝ ΙΝ ΜΟ
ΝΟΝ ΜΕΘ ΕΑΥΤΩΝ
ΚΑΤΑΒΑΙΝΟΝΤΩΝ ΔΕ ΑΥΤΩΝ ΑΠΟ
ΤΟΥ ΟΡΟΥΣ ΔΙΕΣΤΕΙΛΑΤΟ ΑΥΤΟΙΣ
ΙΝΑ ΜΗΔΕΝΙ ΔΙΗΓΗΣΩΝΤΑΙ Α ΕΙ
ΔΟΝ ΕΙ ΜΗ ΟΤΑΝ Ο ΥΙΟΣ ΤΟΥ ΑΝΟΥ
ΕΚ ΝΕΚΡΩΝ ΑΝΑΣΤΗ
ΚΑΙ ΤΟΝ ΛΟΓΟΝ ΕΚΡΑΤΗΣΑΝ ΠΡΟΣ
ΕΑΥΤΟΥΣ ΣΥΝΖΗΤΟΥΝΤΕΣ ΤΙ
ΕΣΤΙΝ ΤΟ ΕΚ ΝΕΚΡΩΝ ΑΝΑΣΤΗ
ΝΑΙ · ΚΑΙ ΕΠΗΡΩΤΗΣΑΝ ΑΥ
ΤΟΝ ΛΕΓΟΝΤΕΣ ΟΤΙ ΛΕΓΟΥΣΙΝ
ΟΙ ΓΡΑΜΜΑΤΕΙΣ ΟΤΙ ΗΛΙΑΝ ΔΕΙ
ΕΛΘΕΙΝ ΠΡΩΤΟΝ · Ο ΔΕ ΑΠΟΚΡΙ
ΘΕΙΣ ΕΙΠΕΝ ΑΥΤΟΙΣ ΗΛΕΙΑΣ ΜΕΝ
ΕΛΘΩΝ ΠΡΩΤΟΝ ΑΠΟΚΑΘΙΣΤΑ
ΝΕΙ ΠΑΝΤΑ ΚΑΘΩΣ ΓΕΓΡΑΠΤΑΙ
ΕΠΙ ΤΟΝ ΥΝ ΤΟΥ ΑΝΟΥ ΙΝΑ ΠΟΛΛΑ
ΠΑΘΗ ΚΑΙ ΕΞΟΥΔΕΝΩΘΗ · ΑΛΛΑ
ΛΕΓΩ ΥΜΙΝ ΟΤΙ ΚΑΙ ΗΛΕΙΑΣ ΕΛΗ
ΛΥΘΕΝ ΚΑΙ ΕΠΟΙΗΣΑΝ ΑΥΤΩ ΟΣΑ
ΗΘΕΛΗΣΑΝ ΚΑΘΩΣ ΓΕΓΡΑΠΤΑΙ
ΕΠ ΑΥΤΟΝ · ΚΑΙ ΕΛΘΩΝ ΠΡΟΣ
ΤΟΥΣ ΜΑΘΗΤΑΣ ΕΙΔΕΝ ΟΧΛΟΝ ΠΟ
ΛΥΝ ΠΕΡΙ ΑΥΤΟΥΣ ΚΑΙ ΓΡΑΜΜΑ
ΤΕΙΣ ΣΥΝΖΗΤΟΥΝΤΑΣ ΑΥΤΟΙΣ
ΚΑΙ ΕΥΘΕΩΣ ΠΑΣ Ο ΟΧΛΟΣ ΙΔΟΝΤΕΣ
ΑΥΤΟΝ ΕΞΕΘΑΜΒΗΘΗ · ΚΑΙ ΠΡΟ
ΤΡΕΧΟΝΤΕΣ ΗΣΠΑΖΟΝΤΟ ΑΥΤΟΝ

ΚΑΙ ΕΠΗΡΩΤΗΣΕΝ ΤΟΥΣ ΓΡΑΜΜΑ
ΤΕΙΣ ΤΙ ΣΥΝΖΗΤΕΙΤΕ ΠΡΟΣ ΑΥΤΟΥΣ
ΚΑΙ ΑΠΟΚΡΙΘΕΙΣ ΕΙΣ ΕΚ ΤΟΥ ΟΧΛΟΥ
ΕΙΠΕΝ ΔΙΔΑΣΚΑΛΕ ΗΝΕΓΚΑ ΤΟΝ ΥΝ
ΜΟΥ ΠΡΟΣ ΣΕ ΕΧΟΝΤΑ ΠΝΕΥΜΑ ΑΛΑ
ΛΟΝ · ΚΑΙ ΟΠΟΥ ΕΑΝ ΑΥΤΟΝ ΚΑΤΑΛΑ
ΒΗ ΡΗΣΣΕΙ ΑΥΤΟΝ ΚΑΙ ΑΦΡΙΖΕΙ ΚΑΙ
ΤΡΙΖΕΙ ΤΟΥΣ ΟΔΟΝΤΑΣ ΑΥΤΟΥ ΚΑΙ ΞΗ
ΡΑΙΝΕΤΑΙ · ΚΑΙ ΕΙΠΟΝ ΤΟΙΣ ΜΑΘΗ
ΤΑΙΣ ΣΟΥ ΙΝΑ ΑΥΤΟ ΕΚΒΑΛΩΣΙΝ ΚΑΙ
ΟΥΚ ΙΣΧΥΣΑΝ · Ο ΔΕ ΑΠΟΚΡΙΘΕΙΣ
ΑΥΤΟΙΣ ΛΕΓΕΙ Ω ΓΕΝΕΑ ΑΠΙΣΤΟΣ
ΕΩΣ ΠΟΤΕ ΠΡΟΣ ΥΜΑΣ ΕΣΟΜΑΙ
ΕΩΣ ΠΟΤΕ ΑΝΕΞΟΜΑΙ ΥΜΩΝ ΦΕ
ΡΕΤΕ ΑΥΤΟΝ ΠΡΟΣ ΜΕ · ΚΑΙ ΗΝΕΓΚΑ
ΑΥΤΟΝ ΠΡΟΣ ΑΥΤΟΝ · ΚΑΙ ΙΔΩΝ ΑΥ
ΤΟΝ ΕΥΘΕΩΣ ΤΟ ΠΝΕΥΜΑ ΕΣΠΑ
ΡΑΞΕΝ ΑΥΤΟΝ · ΚΑΙ ΠΕΣΩΝ ΕΠΙ ΤΗΣ
ΓΗΣ ΕΚΥΛΙΕΤΟ ΑΦΡΙΖΩΝ
ΚΑΙ ΕΠΗΡΩΤΗΣΕΝ ΤΟΝ ΠΡΑ ΑΥΤΟΥ
ΠΟΣΟΣ ΧΡΟΝΟΣ ΕΣΤΙΝ ΩΣ ΤΟΥΤΟ
ΓΕΓΟΝΕΝ ΑΥΤΩ · Ο ΔΕ ΕΙΠΕΝ ΠΑΙ
ΔΙΟΘΕΝ · ΚΑΙ ΠΟΛΛΑΚΕΙΣ ΑΥΤΟΝ
ΚΑΙ ΕΙΣ ΤΟ ΠΥΡ ΕΒΑΛΕΝ · ΚΑΙ ΕΙΣ
ΥΔΑΤΑ ΙΝΑ ΑΠΟΛΕΣΗ ΑΥΤΟΝ · ΑΛΛ ΕΙ ΤΙ
ΔΥΝΑΣΑΙ ΒΟΗΘΗΣΟΝ ΗΜΙΝ ΣΠΛΑ
ΓΧΝΙΣΘΕΙΣ ΕΦ ΗΜΑΣ · Ο ΔΕ ΙΣ ΕΙΠΕ
ΑΥΤΩ ΤΟ ΕΙ ΔΥΝΑΣΑΙ ΠΙΣΤΕΥΣΑΙ
ΠΑΝΤΑ ΔΥΝΑΤΑ ΤΩ ΠΙΣΤΕΥΟΝΤΙ
ΚΑΙ ΕΥΘΕΩΣ ΚΡΑΞΑΣ Ο ΠΗΡ ΤΟΥ ΠΑΙΔΙΟΥ ΜΕΤΑ
ΔΑΚΡΥΩΝ ΕΛΕΓΕΝ ΠΙΣΤΕΥΩ ΒΟ
ΗΘΕΙ ΜΟΥ ΤΗ ΑΠΙΣΤΕΙΑ
ΙΔΩΝ ΔΕ Ο ΙΣ ΟΤΙ ΕΠΙΣΥΝΤΡΕΧΕΙ
Ο ΟΧΛΟΣ ΕΠΕΤΙΜΗΣΕΝ ΤΩ ΠΝΕΥ
ΜΑΤΙ ΤΩ ΑΚΑΘΑΡΤΩ ΛΕΓΩΝ ΑΥ
ΤΩ ΤΟ ΠΝΕΥΜΑ ΤΟ ΑΛΑΛΟΝ ΚΑΙ ΚΩΦΟΝ
ΕΓΩ ΣΟΙ ΕΠΙΤΑΣΣΩ ΕΞΕΛΘΕ ΕΞ ΑΥ
ΤΟΥ ΚΑΙ ΜΗΚΕΤΙ ΕΙΣΕΛΘΗΣ ΕΙΣ
ΑΥΤΟΝ · ΚΑΙ ΚΡΑΞΑΝ ΚΑΙ ΠΟΛΛΑ ΣΠΑ
ΡΑΞΑΝ ΑΥΤΟΝ ΕΞΗΛΘΕΝ ΚΑΙ ΕΓΕ
ΝΕΤΟ ΩΣΕΙ ΝΕΚΡΟΣ ΩΣΤΕ ΤΟΥΣ
ΠΟΛΛΟΥΣ ΛΕΓΕΙΝ ΟΤΙ ΑΠΕΘΑΝΕΝ
Ο ΔΕ ΙΣ ΚΡΑΤΗΣΑΣ ΑΥΤΟΝ ΤΗΣ ΧΕΙΡΟΣ
ΗΓΕΙΡΕΝ ΑΥΤΟΝ ΚΑΙ ΑΝΕΣΤΗ
ΚΑΙ ΕΙΣΕΛΘΟΝΤΑ ΑΥΤΟΝ ΕΙΣ ΤΟΝ
ΟΙΚΟΝ ΟΙ ΜΑΘΗΤΑΙ ΑΥΤΟΥ ΕΠΗΡΩ
ΤΩΝ ΑΥΤΟΝ ΚΑΤ ΙΔΙΑΝ ΟΤΙ
ΗΜΕΙΣ ΟΥΚ ΗΔΥΝΗΘΗΜΕΝ ΕΚ
ΒΑΛΕΙΝ ΑΥΤΟ · ΚΑΙ ΕΙΠΕΝ ΑΥΤΟΙΣ
ΤΟΥΤΟ ΤΟ ΓΕΝΟΣ ΕΝ ΟΥΔΕΝΙ ΔΥΝΑ

19. Luke 5:38–6:9. Gregory–Aland D (Codex Bezae). v cent.

Cambridge, University Library, Nn.2.41, fols. 205 verso and 206 recto.

Bilingual parchment codex, containing the Gospels in the so-called Western order (Matthew, John, Luke, Mark),[1] a small portion of 3 John (in Latin),[2] and Acts, the Greek text standing on the left-hand page, the Latin on the right-hand page, v century,[3] 10¼ × 8⅜ inches (26 × 21 cm.), 510 leaves, one column with text written in cola, 33 lines to a page, the first three lines of each book in red ink.

In 1562 Théodore de Bèze, the French reformer of Geneva, acquired from the loot of the monastery of St. Irenaeus at Lyon the famous codex which now bears his name. A few years earlier it had been taken to the Council of Trent by William à Prato (Guillaume du Prat), Bishop of Clermont in Auvergne, and used there in 1546 as evidence for several unique or unusual Greek readings relating to matters under debate by members of the council. While the manuscript was in Italy a friend made a list of more than 350 noteworthy variant readings, which were communicated to Robert Estienne (Stephanus), the famous Parisian printer and editor, who incorporated them with variant readings of other manuscripts in his 1550 Greek New Testament, the first printed edition to have a critical apparatus. From here several were represented in the margin of the Geneva Bible of 1560.[4] In 1581 the manuscript was presented to the Library of Cambridge University.

J. R. Harris and J. H. Ropes, following J. J. Wettstein, have called attention to latinizing corruptions in the Greek text due to influence from the adjoining Latin. There is, however, no generally accepted view of the nature of the relation of the two texts, for, though they present many features of similarity, they are by no means identical (Scrivener found 2000 divergencies between the Greek and the Latin). The result is that D can neither be rejected as secondary, contaminated with corruptions from the Latin, nor yet used as in every respect a trustworthy witness, as it stands, to the Western text. A striking characteristic of D is the frequent harmonization of parallel passages, which often do not agree with similar harmonizations of the Byzantine text.

The place of origin of the codex has long been debated. The south of France, where it was found; southern Italy, where both Greek and Latin were current; and Sicily, where Latin was the official language, but the mass of people continued to speak Greek—each of these places has been urged with more or less persuasive arguments.

The codex, which is badly written, seems to be the work of one scribe. On the Greek side he is guilty of many obvious blunders and misspellings on nearly every page; at the same time, his ignorance of Latin is also extraordinary. Scrivener detected the work of nine correctors, ranging from the sixth to the eleventh or twelfth century. A variety of comments and glosses, often written in a scrawl, stand in the margins of many pages; they include not only section numbers and *τίτλοι*, but also, written by a later hand in the lower margins of the Gospel of Mark, a series of sixty-nine brief sentences or comments, used, it appears, for divination or telling fortunes (*sortes sanctorum*).[5]

1 On the basis of palaeographic and other considerations, Chapman thought it probable that an ancestor of codex Bezae had the Gospels in the order Matthew, Mark, John, and Luke, the same sequence as in the Curetonian Syriac manuscript and in Mommsen's Cheltenham list of canonical books (see John Chapman, 'The Order of the Gospels in the Parent of Codex Bezae,' *Zeitschrift für die neutestamentlichen Wissenschaft*, vi [1905], pp. 339–46).

2 According to Chapman the text of the Book of Revelation and of 1, 2, and 3 John would just fill the space (66 leaves) between the end of Mark and the last verses (still extant) of 3 John (see John Chapman, 'The Original Contents of Codex Bezae,' *The Expositor*, Sixth series, xii [1905], pp. 46–53).

3 Codex Bezae has been variously dated: to the vi century (Tischendorf, Gregory, von Soden, Nestle, Bover, Merk, Aland in *Kurzgefasste Liste*, 1963); to the v century (Burkitt, Souter, Ropes, Lake, Kenyon, Hatch, Aland in Nestle–Aland *NT*²⁶, 1979); to the early v century (E. A. Lowe, *Codices Latini Antiquiores*, ii, 2nd ed.); to the iv century (P. Mallon, H. J. Frede).

4 Cf. B. M. Metzger, 'Codex Bezae and the Genevan Version of the English Bible,' *Historical and Literary Studies* (Leiden and Grand Rapids, 1968), pp. 138–44.

5 Cf. J. Rendel Harris, *Codex Bezae* (Cambridge, 1891), pp. 9–11, and Otto Stegmüller, 'Zu den Bibelorakeln im Codex Bezae,' *Biblica*, xxxiv (1953), pp. 13–22. See also Harris, 'The "Sortes Sanctorum" in the St. Germain Codex,' *American Journal of Philology*, ix (1888), pp. 58–63.

Textually, no known New Testament manuscript contains so many distinctive readings, chiefly the free addition (and occasional omission) of words, sentences, and even incidents. Thus, in Luke chap. 6 this manuscript has ver. 5 after ver. 10, and between verses 4 and 6 it puts into the mouth of Jesus a warning against thoughtless transgression of the Sabbath commandment. The agraphon, not otherwise transmitted, reads, 'When on the same day he [Jesus] saw a man doing work on the Sabbath, he said to him, "Man, if you know what you are doing, you are blessed; but if you do not know, you are accursed and a transgressor of the law" ' (the Greek text is shown in lines 16–20: *τῇ αὐτῇ ἡμέρᾳ θεασάμενός τινα ἐργαζόμενον τῷ σαββάτῳ εἶπεν αὐτῷ· ἄνθρωπε, εἰ μὲν οἶδάς τι ποιεῖς, μακάριος εἶ· εἰ δὲ μὴ οἶδας, ἐπικατάρατος καὶ παραβάτης εἶ τοῦ νόμου*).

At the top of the page shown in the Greek Plate stands the *τίτλος* belonging to the section of text marked M̅Λ̅ (=41), namely (retaining the scribe's orthography), *περι Δαυγι ωτε ισηλθεν εν το θυσιαστιρηον και φαγεν τōς αρτōς τις προθεσεος* ('Concerning David when he went into the sanctuary and ate the bread of the Presence').

In both Plates are traces of writing showing through the parchment from the opposite side of the leaf. The hole in the left-hand leaf was present prior to receiving writing, which is carefully adjusted around it.

Bibliography: Transcription, F. H. [A.] Scrivener, *Bezae Codex Cantabrigiensis* (Cambridge, 1864; reprinted by the Pickwick Press, Pittsburgh, 1978); J. Rendel Harris, *Codex Bezae* (Cambridge, 1891); photographic reproduction, *Codex Bezae Cantabrigiensis . . . phototypice repraesentatus* (Cambridge, 1899); J. R. Harris, *The Annotations of Codex Bezae (with some Notes on Sortes Sanctorum)* (London, 1901); James H. Ropes, *The Text of Acts* (London, 1926), pp. lvi–lxxxiv; Albert C. Clark, *The Acts of the Apostles* (Oxford, 1933), pp. 173–220; and James D. Yoder, *Concordance to the Distinctive Greek Text of Codex Bezae* (Leiden, 1961).

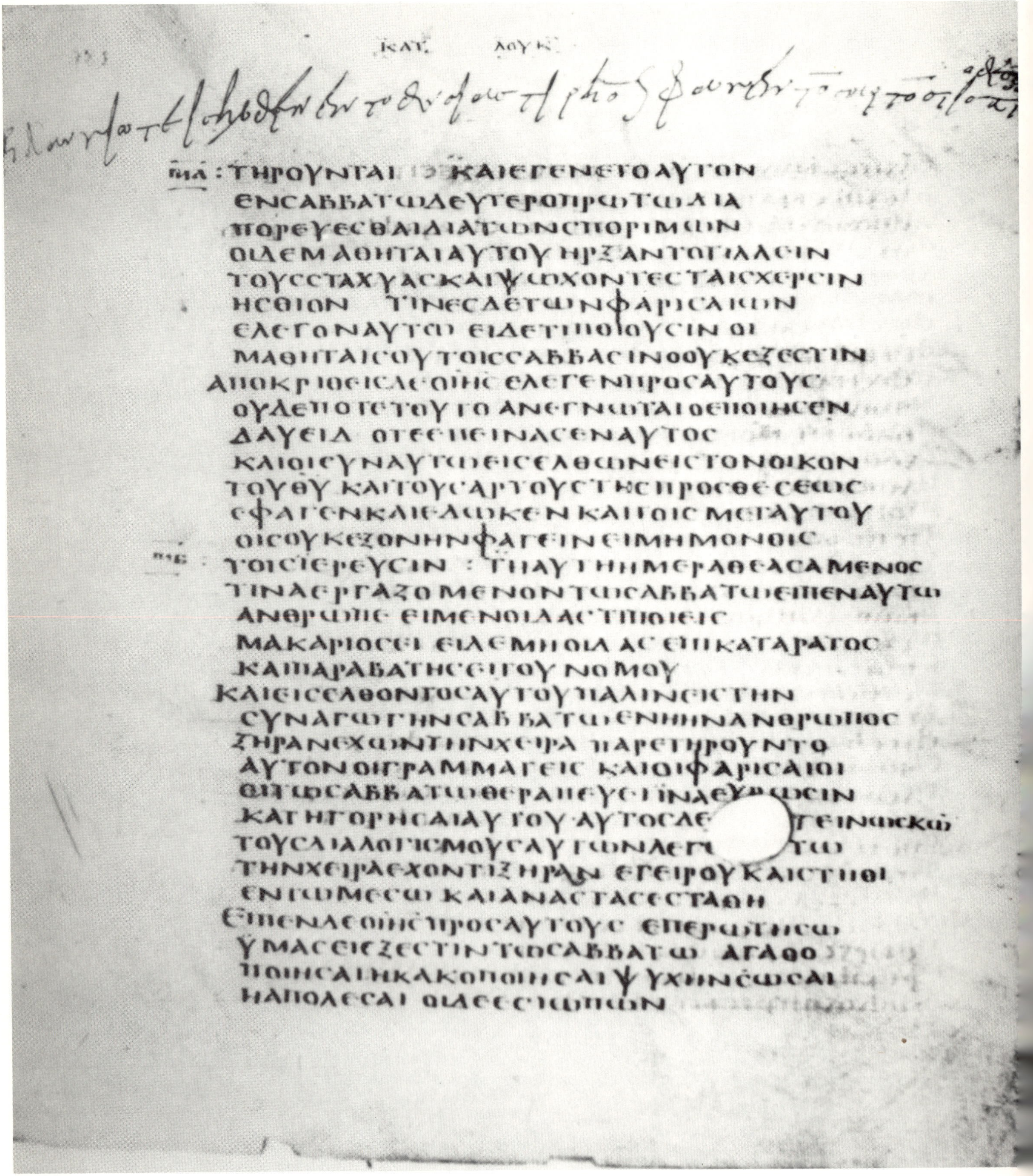

μα: ΤΗΡΟΥΝΤΑΙ : ΚΑΙΕΓΕΝΕΤΟΑΥΤΟΝ
ΕΝϹΑΒΒΑΤѠΔΕΥΤΕΡΟΠΡѠΤѠΔΙΑ
ΠΟΡΕΥΕϹΘΑΙΔΙΑΤѠΝϹΠΟΡΙΜѠΝ
ΟΙΔΕΜΑΘΗΤΑΙΑΥΤΟΥΗΡΞΑΝΤΟΤΙΛΛΕΙΝ
ΤΟΥϹϹΤΑΧΥΑϹΚΑΙΨѠΧΟΝΤΕϹΤΑΙϹΧΕΡϹΙΝ
ΗϹΘΙΟΝ ΤΙΝΕϹΔΕΤѠΝΦΑΡΙϹΑΙѠΝ
ΕΛΕΓΟΝΑΥΤѠ ΕΙΔΕΤΙΠΟΙΟΥϹΙΝ ΟΙ
ΜΑΘΗΤΑΙϹΟΥΤΟΙϹϹΑΒΒΑϹΙΝΟΟΥΚΕΞΕϹΤΙΝ
ΑΠΟΚΡΙΘΕΙϹΔΕΟΙΗϹ ΕΛΕΓΕΝΠΡΟϹΑΥΤΟΥϹ
ΟΥΔΕΠΟΤΕΤΟΥΤΟ ΑΝΕΓΝѠΤΑΙΟΕΠΟΙΗϹΕΝ
ΔΑΥΕΙΔ ΟΤΕΕΠΕΙΝΑϹΕΝΑΥΤΟϹ
ΚΑΙΟΙϹΥΝΑΥΤѠΕΙϹΕΛΘѠΝΕΙϹΤΟΝΟΙΚΟΝ
ΤΟΥΘΥ ΚΑΙΤΟΥϹΑΡΤΟΥϹΤΗϹΠΡΟϹΘΕϹΕѠϹ
ΕΦΑΓΕΝΚΑΙΕΔѠΚΕΝ ΚΑΙΤΟΙϹ ΜΕΤΑΥΤΟΥ
ΟΙϹΟΥΚΕΞΟΝΗΝΦΑΓΕΙΝΕΙΜΗΜΟΝΟΙϹ
μβ: ΤΟΙϹΙΕΡΕΥϹΙΝ : ΤΗΑΥΤΗΗΜΕΡΑΘΕΑϹΑΜΕΝΟϹ
ΤΙΝΑΕΡΓΑΖΟΜΕΝΟΝΤѠϹΑΒΒΑΤѠΕΙΠΕΝΑΥΤѠ
ΑΝΘΡѠΠΕ ΕΙΜΕΝΟΙΔΑϹΤΙΠΟΙΕΙϹ
ΜΑΚΑΡΙΟϹΕΙ ΕΙΔΕΜΗΟΙΔΑϹ ΕΠΙΚΑΤΑΡΑΤΟϹ
ΚΑΙΠΑΡΑΒΑΤΗϹΕΙΤΟΥ ΝΟΜΟΥ
ΚΑΙΕΙϹΕΛΘΟΝΤΟϹΑΥΤΟΥΠΑΛΙΝΕΙϹΤΗΝ
ϹΥΝΑΓѠΓΗΝϹΑΒΒΑΤѠΕΝΗΝΑΝΘΡѠΠΟϹ
ΞΗΡΑΝΕΧѠΝΤΗΝΧΕΙΡΑ ΠΑΡΕΤΗΡΟΥΝΤΟ
ΑΥΤΟΝΟΙΓΡΑΜΜΑΤΕΙϹ ΚΑΙΟΙΦΑΡΙϹΑΙΟΙ
ΕΙΤѠϹΑΒΒΑΤѠΘΕΡΑΠΕΥϹΙ ΙΝΑΕΥΡѠϹΙΝ
ΚΑΤΗΓΟΡΗϹΑΙΑΥΤΟΥ ΑΥΤΟϹΔΕ [illegible] ΓΕΙΝѠϹΚѠ
ΤΟΥϹΔΙΑΛΟΓΙϹΜΟΥϹΑΥΤѠΝΛΕΓΕΙ [illegible] ΤѠ
ΤΗΝΧΕΙΡΑΕΧΟΝΤΙΞΗΡΑΝ ΕΓΕΙΡΟΥΚΑΙϹΤΗΘΙ
ΕΝΤѠΜΕϹѠ ΚΑΙΑΝΑϹΤΑϹΕϹΤΑΘΗ
ΕΙΠΕΝΔΕΟΙΗϹΠΡΟϹΑΥΤΟΥϹ ΕΠΕΡѠΤΗϹѠ
ΥΜΑϹΕΙΕΞΕϹΤΙΝΤѠϹΑΒΒΑΤѠ ΑΓΑΘΟ
ΠΟΙΗϹΑΙΗΚΑΚΟΠΟΙΗϹΑΙΨΥΧΗΝϹѠϹΑΙ
ΗΑΠΟΛΕϹΑΙ ΟΙΔΕΕϹΙѠΠѠΝ

19A

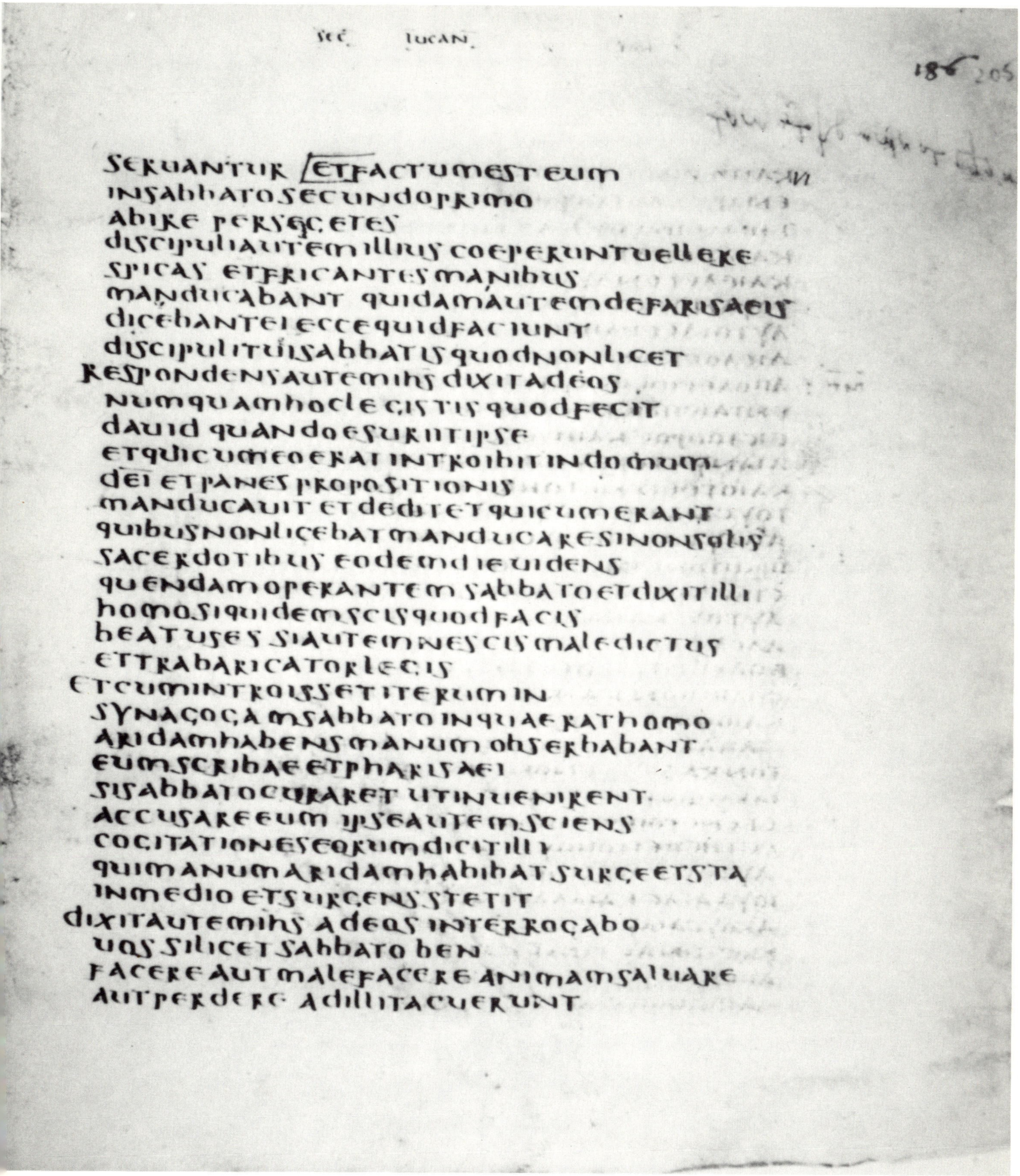
SEC LUCAN

186 205

SERUANTUR ET FACTUM EST EUM
IN SABBATO SECUNDO PRIMO
ABIRE PER SEGETES
DISCIPULI AUTEM ILLIUS COEPERUNT UELLERE
SPICAS ET FRICANTES MANIBUS
MANDUCABANT QUIDAM AUTEM DE FARISAEIS
DICEBANT EI ECCE QUID FACIUNT
DISCIPULI TUI SABBATIS QUOD NON LICET
RESPONDENS AUTEM IHS DIXIT AD EOS
NUMQUAM HOC LEGISTIS QUOD FECIT
DAUID QUANDO ESURIIT IPSE
ET QUI CUM EO ERAT INTROIBIT IN DOMUM
DEI ET PANES PROPOSITIONIS
MANDUCAUIT ET DEDIT ET QUI CUM ERANT
QUIBUS NON LICEBAT MANDUCARE SI NON SOLIS
SACERDOTIBUS EODEM DIE UIDENS
QUENDAM OPERANTEM SABBATO ET DIXIT ILLI
HOMO SI QUIDEM SCIS QUOD FACIS
BEATUS ES SI AUTEM NESCIS MALEDICTUS
ET TRABARICATOR LEGIS
ET CUM INTROISSET ITERUM IN
SYNAGOGAM SABBATO IN QUA ERAT HOMO
ARIDAM HABENS MANUM OBSERBABANT
EUM SCRIBAE ET PHARISAEI
SI SABBATO CURARET UT INUENIRENT
ACCUSARE EUM IPSE AUTEM SCIENS
COGITATIONES EORUM DICIT ILLI
QUI MANUM ARIDAM HABIBAT SURGE ET STA
IN MEDIO ET SURGENS STETIT
DIXIT AUTEM IHS AD EOS INTERROGABO
UOS SI LICET SABBATO BEN
FACERE AUT MALE FACERE ANIMAM SALUARE
AUT PERDERE AD ILLI TACUERUNT

19B

20. Genesis 39:9–18. Rahlfs L (Vienna Genesis). v/vi cent.

VIENNA, NATIONALBIBLIOTHEK, THEOL. GR. 31, FOL. 31.

The Vienna Genesis is a handsome illuminated purple parchment manuscript of the v/vi century, consisting today of 24 leaves, 13¾ × 10¼ inches (35 × 26 cm.), with 48 water-color miniatures in the classical style. Each page contains one or more pictures and the Greek text of Genesis (sometimes abbreviated to provide more space for the picture), written in well-formed uncials with silver ink, which here and there has eaten through the parchment.

Initial ι and υ have the diaeresis. *Nomina sacra* occur (e.g. end of line 3). To save space at the end of a line the scribe uses ligatures, e.g. writing *αὐτῆς* with the first three letters in ligature (line 5) and the last two letters of *τοιαύτη* in ligature (line 6). The *καί*-compendium occurs at the end of line 11.

This fragmentary manuscript, one of the chief specimens of early Christian book illumination, was probably designed to contain two hundred illustrations, though only forty-eight survive today. It is the work of several master-craftsmen, two of whom had apprentices working under them. The provenance of the artists is uncertain, but there are notes in the manuscript which show that in the fourteenth century it was at Venice. In 1664 it was acquired by the Imperial Library in Vienna.

The Plate depicts the episode of the temptation of Joseph by Potiphar's wife. Dressed in a diaphanous garment, the temptress sits on the edge of a gilded bed before a double-rowed collonade, suggesting a stately palace chamber. She is grasping the edge of Joseph's mantle, while he is attempting to leave. In the next scene Joseph, without the mantle, is looking back at the open door through which he has just escaped.

The other scenes portray extra-Biblical, legendary accretions to the Joseph-cycle. The figure at the top right in a star-studded mantle and holding a spindle has been explained as an astrologer. The woman bending over the cradle and holding a rattle may be once more Potiphar's wife; the baby has been thought, on the basis of Jewish traditions, to be Osnath (Asenath in Greek), an adopted daughter whom Joseph will later marry. Less surely identified are the figures in the lower register: a woman holding a naked baby and two seated women spinning, the one on the right clad like Potiphar's wife in the first scene. The two trees can be dismissed as 'space fillers.'

The Plate shows the page slightly reduced in size.

BIBLIOGRAPHY: Facsimile editions by Wilhelm Ritter von Hartel and Franz Wickhoff, *Die Wiener Genesis* (Vienna/Prague/Leipzig, 1895), and by Hans Gerstinger, *Die Wiener Genesis* (Vienna, 1931); Kurt Weitzmann, 'Zur Frage des Einflusses jüdischer Bilderquellen auf die Illustration des Alten Testamentes,' *Mullus; Festschrift Theodor Klauser* (Münster/W., 1964), pp. 401–15, trans. into English, 'The Question of the Influence of Jewish Pictorial Sources in Old Testament Illustrations,' *Studies in Classical and Byzantine Manuscript Illumination*, ed. by Herbert L. Kessler (Chicago, 1971), pp. 75–95; and Michael D. Levin, 'Some Jewish Sources for the Vienna Genesis,' *The Art Bulletin*, liv (1972), pp. 241–4.

21. Isaiah 13:3–10. Rahlfs Q (Codex Marchalianus). vi cent.

ROME, BIBLIOTECA VATICANA, GR. 2125, PAGE 205.

Parchment codex of the Old Testament prophets (the minor prophets precede the others), vi cent., 11⅜ × 7⅛ inches (29.5 × 17.9 cm.), 416 leaves, one column, 29 lines to the page.

One of the most important manuscripts for Septuagint studies, codex Marchalianus (its name is derived from a former owner, René Marchal)[1] is written in a bold uncial of the so-called Coptic style (see §15). The letters *τ* and *υ* have serifs; *φ* and *ω* are dilated. The circumflex accent is often placed medially over diphthongs (e.g. lines 11 and 14 [twice], but not line 21).

The margins contain a variety of 'helps for the reader' derived from the researches of Origen. About seventy items of an onomasticum (lexicon of proper names; see §32) stand in the margins of Ezekiel and Lamentations.[2] Of greater importance are the Hexaplaric readings (see §22) found on most pages; these are written in tiny uncials by a hand not much later than the original scribe, and are keyed by a short wavy line standing over the designated word in the text. Prefixed to these readings are *α'*, *σ'*, *θ'*, signifying Aquila, Symmachus, and Theodotion respectively. Collectively the three versions are identified as *οἱ γ* (or sometimes simply *γ*). Of the Hexaplaric sigla, only the asterisk occurs on the page reproduced (line 3 from bottom).

A noteworthy feature in some of the books is the representation of the Tetragrammaton written in the inner margin in Greek letters (*πιπι*, see §20). This symbol is keyed by a short wavy line that is repeated in the text near the contraction of *κύριος* (lines 8, 11, 13, and 22).

The following is a transcription of the Hexaplaric readings that stand in the inner and outer margins of page 205, linked in each case by a conventional mark to words within the line:

line 4	*σ'*	*χαιροντας τη υβρει μου*
line 7	*οἱ γ'*	*βασιλειων*
line 11	*σ'*	*κ(υριο)ς κ(υριο)ς σκευη οργης αυτου*
line 18	*οἱ γ'*	*ωδινησουσιν*
line 22	*θ'*	*μηνιδος κ(αι) οργης κ(αι) θυμου*
line 27	*	*αυτῶ*
line 28	*σ' θ'*	*ο ηλιος εν τη εξοδω αυτου*

Above *ἄγω* in line 1 a subsequent scribe added from the Latin Vulgate the word *mandavi* ('I have commanded').

BIBLIOGRAPHY: Facsimile edition, *Prophetarum codex Graecus Vaticanus 2125* . . . heliotypice editus curante Iosepho Cozza-Luzi (Rome, 1890); a companion volume with commentary by Antonio Ceriani was published the same year with the title *De codice Marchaliano seu Vaticano Graeco 2125* . . . The full title of each volume is given in H. B. Swete's edition of the Septuagint, iii, p. viii n. 3.

[1] Marchal obtained the manuscript from the Abbey of St. Denis near Paris. From the library of Marchal it passed into the hands of Cardinal Rochefoucauld, who in turn presented it to the Collège de Clermont, the celebrated Jesuit house at Paris. Finally, in 1785 it was purchased for the Vatican Library, where it now reposes.

[2] Cf. Erich Klostermann, 'Onomasticum Marchalianum,' *Zeitschrift für die alttestamentliche Wissenschaft*, xxiii (1903), pp. 135–40.

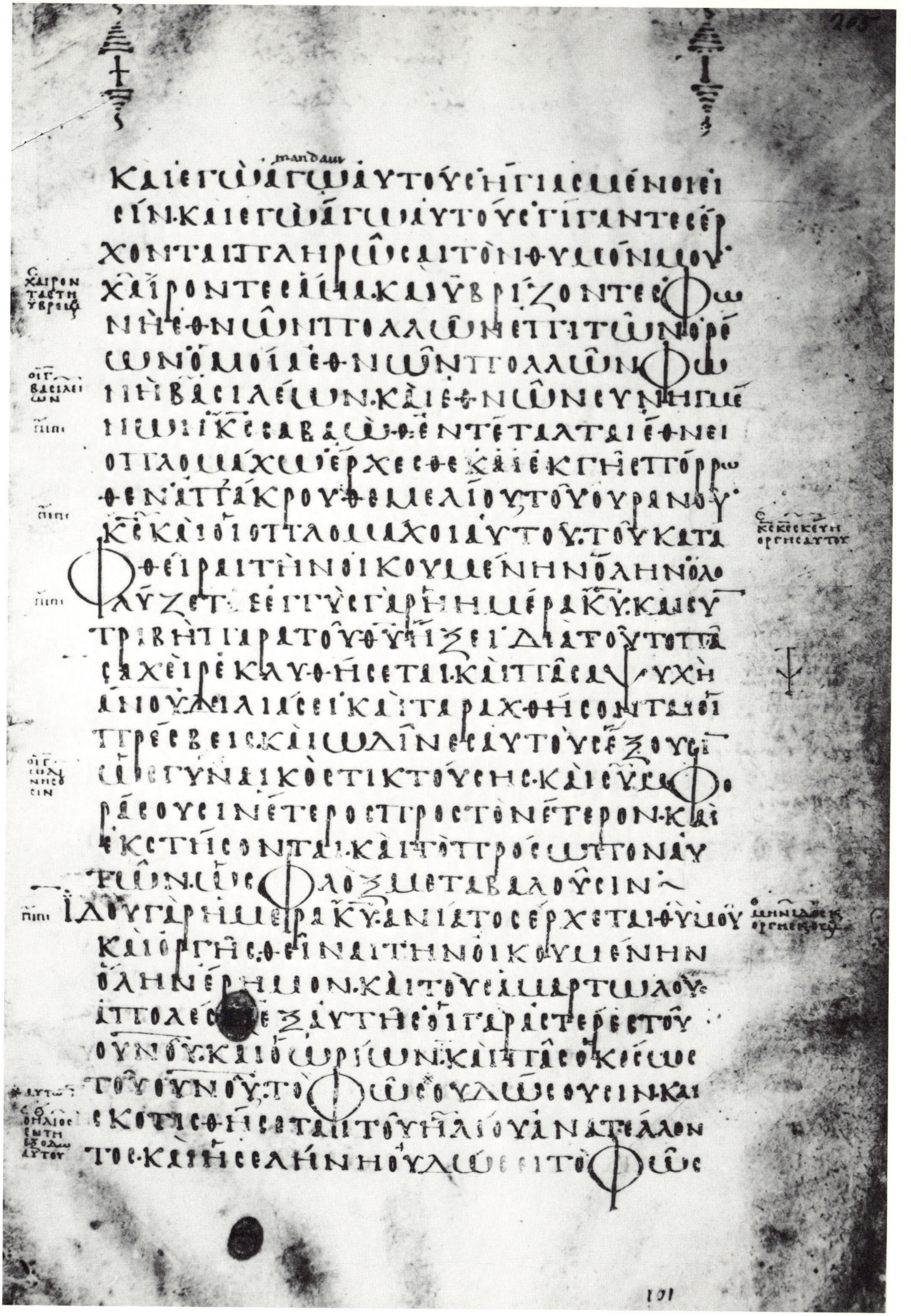
ΚΑΙ ΕΓΩ ΑΓΩ ΑΥΤΟΥΣ ΗΓΙΑΣΜΕΝΟΙ ΕΙ
ΣΙΝ· ΚΑΙ ΕΓΩ ΑΓΩ ΑΥΤΟΥΣ ΓΙΓΑΝΤΕΣ ΕΡ
ΧΟΝΤΑΙ ΠΛΗΡΩΣΑΙ ΤΟΝ ΘΥΜΟΝ ΜΟΥ
ΧΑΙΡΟΝΤΕΣ ΑΜΑ ΚΑΙ ΥΒΡΙΖΟΝΤΕΣ ΦΩ
ΝΗ ΕΘΝΩΝ ΠΟΛΛΩΝ ΕΠΙ ΤΩΝ ΟΡΕ
ΩΝ ΟΜΟΙΑ ΕΘΝΩΝ ΠΟΛΛΩΝ ΦΩ
ΝΗ ΒΑΣΙΛΕΩΝ ΚΑΙ ΕΘΝΩΝ ΣΥΝΗΓΜΕ
ΝΩΝ ΚΣ ΣΑΒΑΩΘ ΕΝΤΕΤΑΛΤΑΙ ΕΘΝΕΙ
ΟΠΛΟΜΑΧΩ ΕΡΧΕΣΘΑΙ ΕΚ ΓΗΣ ΠΟΡΡΩ
ΘΕΝ ΑΠ ΑΚΡΟΥ ΘΕΜΕΛΙΟΥ ΤΟΥ ΟΥΡΑΝΟΥ
ΚΣ ΚΑΙ ΟΙ ΟΠΛΟΜΑΧΟΙ ΑΥΤΟΥ ΤΟΥ ΚΑΤΑ
ΦΘΕΙΡΑΙ ΤΗΝ ΟΙΚΟΥΜΕΝΗΝ ΟΛΗΝ ΟΛΟ
ΛΥΖΕΤΕ ΕΓΓΥΣ ΓΑΡ Η ΗΜΕΡΑ ΚΥ ΚΑΙ ΣΥΝ
ΤΡΙΒΗ ΠΑΡΑ ΤΟΥ ΘΥ ΗΞΕΙ ΔΙΑ ΤΟΥΤΟ ΠΑ
ΣΑ ΧΕΙΡ ΕΚΛΥΘΗΣΕΤΑΙ ΚΑΙ ΠΑΣΑ ΨΥΧΗ
ΑΝΟΥ ΔΕΙΛΙΑΣΕΙ ΚΑΙ ΤΑΡΑΧΘΗΣΟΝΤΑΙ ΟΙ
ΠΡΕΣΒΕΙΣ ΚΑΙ ΩΔΙΝΕΣ ΑΥΤΟΥΣ ΕΞΟΥΣΙ
ΩΣ ΓΥΝΑΙΚΟΣ ΤΙΚΤΟΥΣΗΣ ΚΑΙ ΣΥΜΦΟ
ΡΑΣΟΥΣΙΝ ΕΤΕΡΟΣ ΠΡΟΣ ΤΟΝ ΕΤΕΡΟΝ ΚΑΙ
ΕΚΣΤΗΣΟΝΤΑΙ ΚΑΙ ΤΟ ΠΡΟΣΩΠΟΝ ΑΥ
ΤΩΝ ΩΣ ΦΛΟΞ ΜΕΤΑΒΑΛΟΥΣΙΝ
ΙΔΟΥ ΓΑΡ ΗΜΕΡΑ ΚΥ ΑΝΙΑΤΟΣ ΕΡΧΕΤΑΙ ΘΥΜΟΥ
ΚΑΙ ΟΡΓΗΣ ΘΕΙΝΑΙ ΤΗΝ ΟΙΚΟΥΜΕΝΗΝ
ΟΛΗΝ ΕΡΗΜΟΝ ΚΑΙ ΤΟΥΣ ΑΜΑΡΤΩΛΟΥΣ
ΑΠΟΛΕΣΑΙ ΕΞ ΑΥΤΗΣ ΟΙ ΓΑΡ ΑΣΤΕΡΕΣ ΤΟΥ
ΟΥΝΟΥ ΚΑΙ Ο ΩΡΙΩΝ ΚΑΙ ΠΑΣ Ο ΚΟΣΜΟΣ
ΤΟΥ ΟΥΝΟΥ ΤΟ ΦΩΣ ΟΥ ΔΩΣΟΥΣΙΝ ΚΑΙ
ΣΚΟΤΙΣΘΗΣΕΤΑΙ ΤΟΥ ΗΛΙΟΥ ΑΝΑΤΕΛΛΟΝ
ΤΟΣ ΚΑΙ Η ΣΕΛΗΝΗ ΟΥ ΔΩΣΕΙ ΤΟ ΦΩΣ

21

22. Acts 8:36–38. Gregory–Aland E (Codex Laudianus). vi/vii cent.

Oxford, Bodleian Library, Laud. 35, fol. 70 verso.

Parchment codex, containing the Book of Acts[1] in Latin and Greek, vi/vii century, 10⅜ × 8⅝ inches (27 × 22 cm.), 227 leaves, two columns, 23–26 lines to a column.

An inscription on a fly-leaf at the end indicates that at some time after A.D. 534 the codex was in Sardinia, an island on which Greek and Latin elements met. It next turns up in the north of England, where the Venerable Bede[2] used it in the compilation of his commentary on Acts (between 709 and 716). Given soon after among other precious books to Boniface, when he started on his mission to the Continent, it was probably later transferred by him to Burchard, when Boniface consecrated him Bishop of Würzburg (Bavaria). In 1631 during the Thirty Years' War, Würzburg was captured by the Swedes, and subsequently this manuscript among others was acquired from the Swedish army by agents of Archbishop Laud, who in due course, as Chancellor of Oxford University, presented it to the Bodleian Library (1636).

The manuscript is written in very large, thick, and clumsy-looking uncials, without punctuation, accents, or breathings, except that *iota* and *upsilon* are often written with diaeresis (lines 2, 3, 18). The shape of *xi* (e.g. line 11) is more complicated than usual. The alteration of light and dark letters suggests that the scribe frequently needed to dip his pen into the ink.

The parchment is of fair quality and often very thin, so that often the writing on the opposite side shows through the sheet. The Latin version occupies the place of honor in the left-hand column on each page. The text of both columns is arranged colometrically with very short κῶλα, which often contain but a single word, and rarely as many as three or four.[3] A peculiar chapter-division, containing fifty-eight chapters up to 26:24, has been added by a corrector of the seventh century.

Textually E has basically an Antiochian, or Byzantine, type of text with a sizeable number of Western readings. It was formerly held that the Latin text had been accommodated to the Greek, but Ropes and Clark maintain that the more striking Greek Western readings are due to retranslation from the Old Latin.

Codex Laudianus is the earliest known copy of Acts that contains 8:37, the Ethiopian eunuch's confession of faith: ειπεν δε | αυτω | ο φιλιππος, | Εαν πιστευεις | εξ ολης | της καρδιας σου | σωθησει.[4] | αποκριθεις δε | ειπεν, | Πιστευω | εις τον Χ(ριστο)ν | τον υιον | του Θ(εο)υ (lines 7–19). This passage is absent from $\mathfrak{p}^{45}$ $\mathfrak{p}^{74}$ ℵ A B C 33 81 614 vg $syr^{p,h}$ $cop^{sa,bo}$ eth, but present, with many minor variations, in many minuscules, $it^{gig,h}$ vg^{mss} $syr^{h\ with\ *}$ cop^{G67} arm. There is no reason why scribes should have omitted the confession if it had originally stood in the text. On the other hand, its insertion into the text seems to have been due to the feeling that Philip could not have baptized the Ethiopian without securing a confession of faith, which needed to be expressed in the narrative.

Bibliography: Edited by C. Tischendorf, *Codex Laudianus* (Monumenta sacra inedita, novæ collectionis appendix, ix; Leipzig, 1870); James H. Ropes, 'The Greek Text of Codex Laudianus,' *Harvard Theological Review*, xvi (1923), pp. 175–86; idem, *The Text of Acts* (London, 1926), pp. lxxxiv–lxxxviii; Albert C. Clark, *The Acts of the Apostles* (Oxford, 1933), pp. 234–46; and O. Kenneth Walther, 'Codex Laudianus G 35: A Re-Examination of the Manuscript, Including a Reproduction of the Text and an Accompanying Commentary,' unpublished Ph.D. diss., University of St. Andrews, 1979.

[1] The manuscript lacks the last seven or eight leaves, which contained Acts 26:29–28:26.

[2] In his essay *Expositio Retracta* Bede gives seventy and more readings, all of which are in this manuscript, and often only in this. The manuscript must have been complete when Bede used it, for he cites the Latin of 27:5 and 28:2. See M. L. W. Laistner, 'The Latin Versions of Acts Known to the Venerable Bede,' *Harvard Theological Review*, xxx (1937), pp. 37–50, esp. 43–9.

[3] It is probable that the manuscript was copied from a bilingual predecessor constructed in the same manner, for on several occasions a line or lines at the foot of a page are repeated at the beginning of the next page in the same formation.

[4] In the Latin column (line 13) a corrector expunged the first four letters of *suscepis* (which represented εξεστιν, found in other Greek witnesses), and wrote in the left margin *salvus* (the remaining letters of *suscepis* were understood as *eris* (Latin *p* taken as Greek ρ).

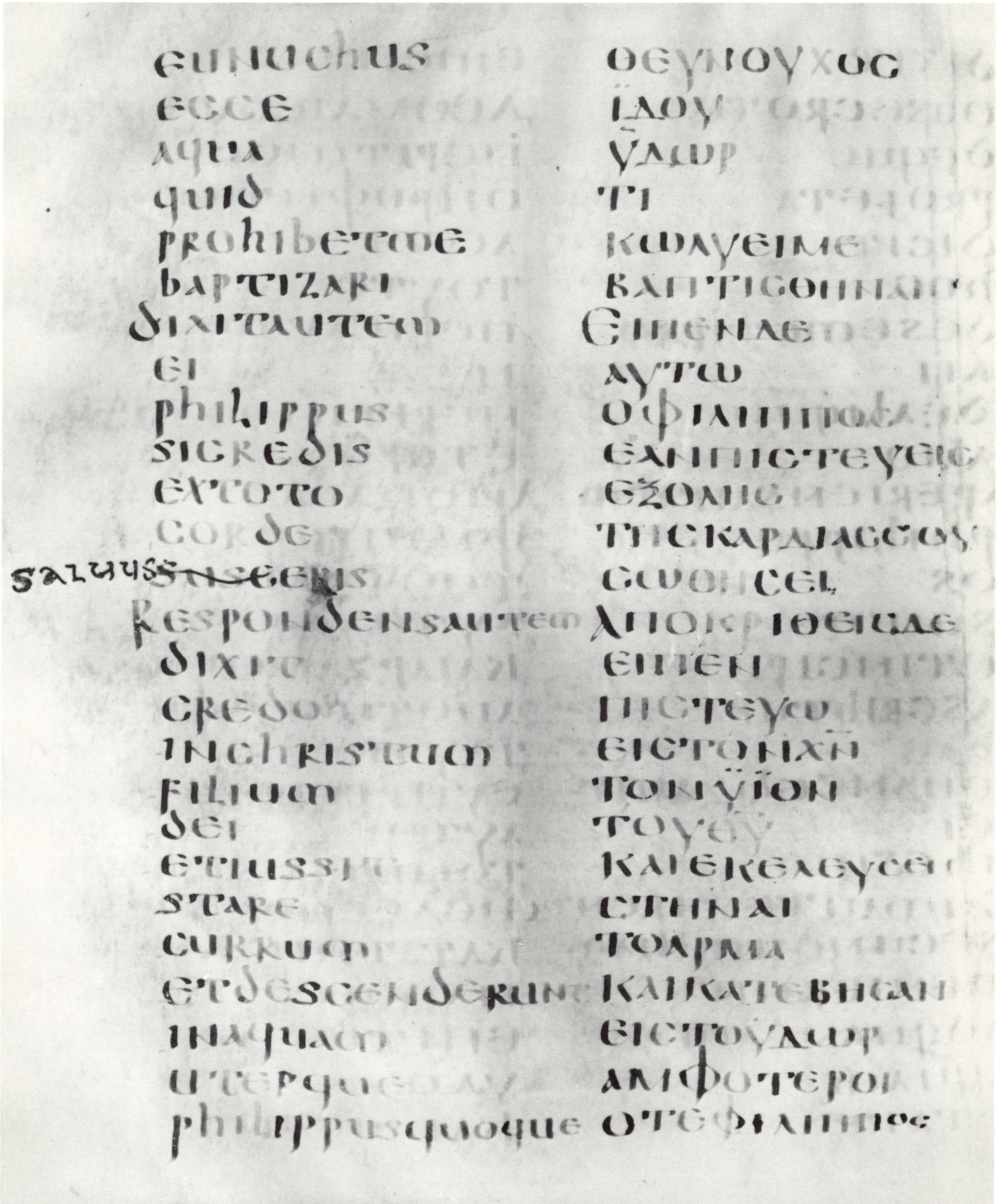

eunuchus	ο ευνουχος
ecce	ιδου
aqua	υδωρ
quid	τι
prohibet me	κωλυει με
baptizari	βαπτισθηναι
dixit autem	ειπεν δε
ei	αυτω
philippus	ο φιλιππος
si credis	εαν πιστευεις
ex toto	εξ ολης
corde	της καρδιας σου
salvus ~~sus~~ eris	σωθησει
respondens autem	αποκριθεις δε
dixit	ειπεν
credo	πιστευω
in christum	εις τον χν
filium	τον υιον
dei	του θυ
et iussit	και εκελευσεν
stare	στηναι
currum	το αρμα
et descenderunt	και κατεβησαν
in aquam	εις το υδωρ
uterque	αμφοτεροι
philippus quoque	ο τε φιλιππος

23. John 4:47–5:6. Gregory–Aland 047. viii cent.

PRINCETON, UNIVERSITY LIBRARY, GARRETT MS. 1, FOL. 131 RECTO.

Parchment codex, containing the four Gospels, viii century, 8 × 6⅛ inches (20.3 × 15.4 cm.), 152 leaves, one column, 37 or 38 lines written in the form of a cross.

The manuscript was formerly in the monastery (Skete) of St. Andrew on Mount Athos. It was brought to the United States by T. Whittemore, purchased in 1924 by Robert Garrett of Baltimore, and given by him to Princeton University Library in 1942.

Manuscripts with cruciform text throughout are uncommon; two others are Greek lectionaries, one of the eleventh century in the British Library (cod. add. 39603; Gregory–Aland *l*233), and the other of the thirteenth century in the Pierpont Morgan Library in New York (cod. M692; Gregory–Aland *l*1635). A little-known Gospel lectionary of the twelfth century in the Dumbarton Oaks Collection (cod. 1; Gregory–Aland *l*2139) is written partly in double-columns and partly in cruciform format.

The upper margin contains the τίτλος (in red ink) for the seventh κεφάλαιον, namely περὶ τοῦ τριάκοντα καὶ ὀκτὼ ἔτη ἔχοντος ἐν τῇ ἀσθενείᾳ. Near the close of line 19 of the text stands the abbreviation of τέλος (in red ink), signifying the close of the sixth κεφάλαιον. In the left-hand margin ἀρ Ζ̄ (in red ink) signifies the beginning of the seventh κεφάλαιον (John 5:1–15), to which the τίτλος at the top of the page applies. In the Greek lectionary system this passage is appointed to be read on the third Sunday after Easter, which is identified as either κυριακῇ γ̄ or κυριακῇ τῆς γ̄ ἑβδομάδος. In the line following the τίτλος the scribe combines both to produce the curious directive 'for the third Sunday of the third week' (also spelling the abbreviation for week with ἑνδ, which in some dialects was pronounced like ἑβδ).

A subsequent scribe marked the text of lines 27–33 (John 5:4) with asterisks in the left-hand margin, indicating that the passage is doubtful or spurious. A number of early and good witnesses omit the passage, including $\mathfrak{p}^{66}$ $\mathfrak{p}^{75}$ ℵ B C* D W^{supp} 33, as well as several early versions; more than twenty other Greek manuscripts mark the passage with asterisks or obeli (including S Λ Π 1079 2174).

BIBLIOGRAPHY: Artistic features of the manuscript are discussed in *Illuminated Greek Manuscripts from American Collections*, ed. Gary Vikan (Princeton, 1973), p. 57.

24. Mark 16:2–11. Gregory–Aland Ψ. viii/ix cent.

MOUNT ATHOS, LAURA 172 (Β′ 52), FOL. 14 VERSO.

Parchment codex, containing part of Mark (9:5–16:20), Luke, John, Acts, Catholic Epistles,[1] and Pauline Epistles (including Hebrews, though lacking one leaf), viii/ix century, 8¼ × 6 inches (21 × 15.3 cm.), 261 leaves, one column, 30 and 31 lines to a page.

Written in a typical hand of the eighth and ninth centuries, the scribe enlarges letters that begin a new section, and extends them, when possible, into the left-hand margin. Accents and square breathing marks are used throughout. The Ammonian section and Eusebian canon numbers stand in the margin, and the abbreviation of τέλος, marking the close of a liturgical lesson, appears within the text itself (e.g., end of line 17, after Mark 16:8). Besides punctuation involving high, middle, and low points, the text is also furnished with neumes.

After Mark 16:8 the manuscript agrees with several other Greek and versional witnesses (including L 099 0112 274^{mg} 579 *l*1602 $syr^{h\ (mg)}$ $cop^{sa\ (mss),\ bo\ (mss)}$ eth^{mss})[2] in providing the shorter ending of the Gospel before the longer ending (16:9–20). Following ἐφοβοῦντο γάρ (16:8) and the abbreviation of τέλος, the manuscript continues (line 18):

> Πάντα δὲ τὰ παρηγγελμένα τοῖς περὶ τὸν | Πέτρον συντόμως ἐξήγγειλαν : Μετὰ | Δὲ ταῦτα καὶ αὐτὸς Ἰ(ησοῦ)ς ἐφάνη ἀπὸ ἀνατολῆς | καὶ μέχρι δύσεως ἐξαπέστειλεν δι' αὐτῶν | τὸ ἱερὸν καὶ ἄφθαρτον κήρυγμα τῆς αἰω|νίου σωτηρίας ἀμήν.[3]

Following the shorter ending, a heading (lines 25–26) states that after the words ἐφοβοῦντο γάρ there is also current (φερόμενα) the ending beginning Ἀναστὰς δέ, which are the opening words of the longer ending of Mark (16:9–20). At the conclusion of the longer ending (on the next page) stands the subscription εὐαγγέλιον κατὰ Μᾶρκαν.

In the lower left-hand margin is a liturgical rubric stating that the reading is for Easter morning, ἀναστάσιμ[ον] ἑωθινόν. In the right-hand margin are smudges from the Ammonian section and Eusebian canon numbers that stand in the left-hand margin of the facing page.

BIBLIOGRAPHY: Kirsopp Lake, 'Texts from Mount Athos,' *Studia Biblica et Ecclesiastica*, v (Oxford, 1903), pp. 89–185, esp. 94–131; Hermann von Soden, *Die Schriften des Neuen Testaments in ihrer ältesten erreichbaren Textgestalt*, I, iii (Berlin, 1910), pp. 1664–6, 1841, 1921, and 1928; M.-J. Lagrange, *La critique rationnelle* (Paris, 1935), pp. 109 f.

[1] The Epistle of James comes next after 2 Peter.

[2] For the evidence of the Ethiopic version, see B. M. Metzger's *New Testament Studies, Philological, Versional, and Patristic* (Leiden, 1980), pp. 127–47.

[3] 'But they reported briefly to Peter and those with him all that they had been told. And after this Jesus himself also appeared; he sent out through them, from the east even to the west, the sacred and imperishable proclamation of eternal salvation. Amen.'

23

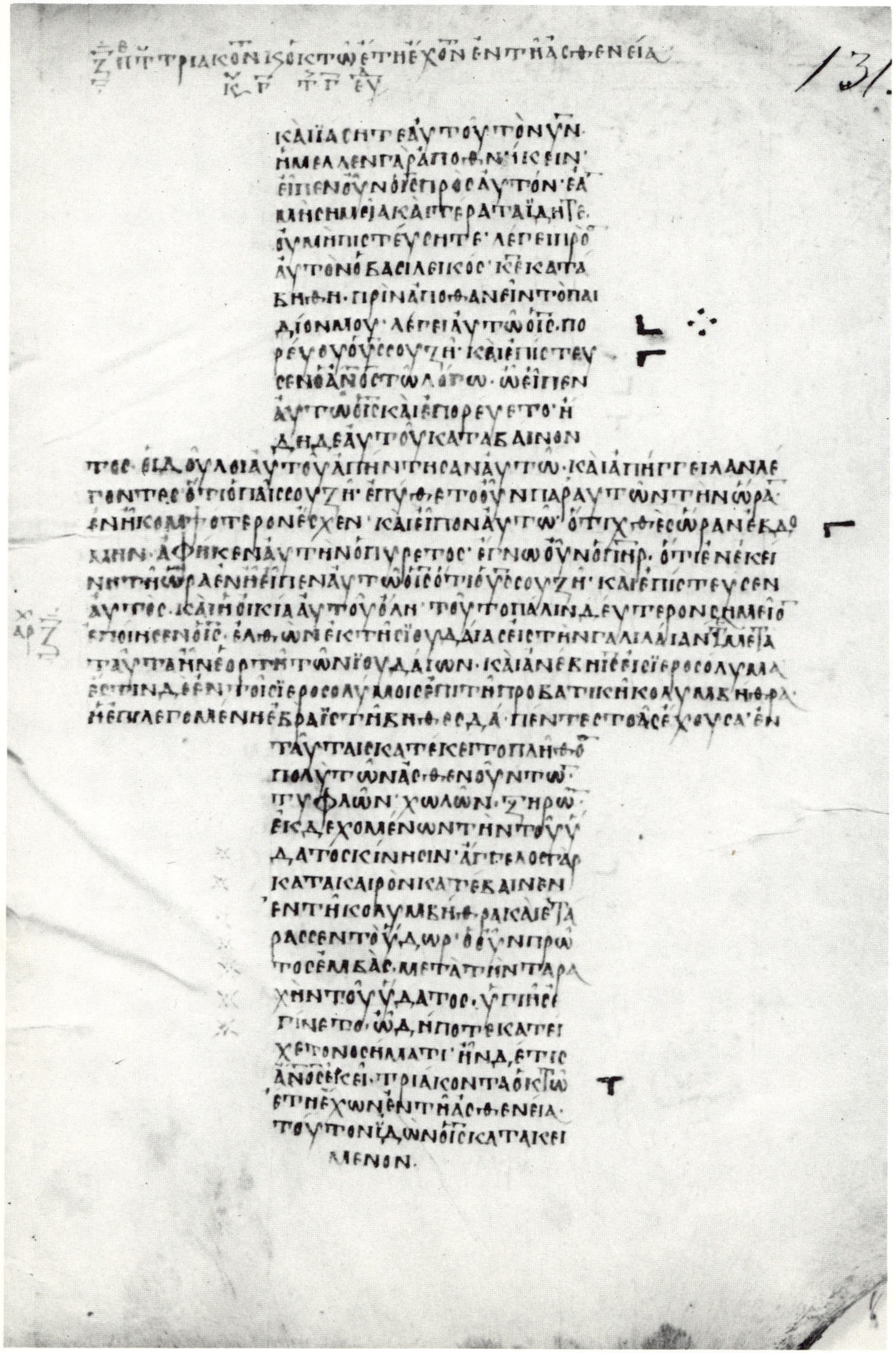

24

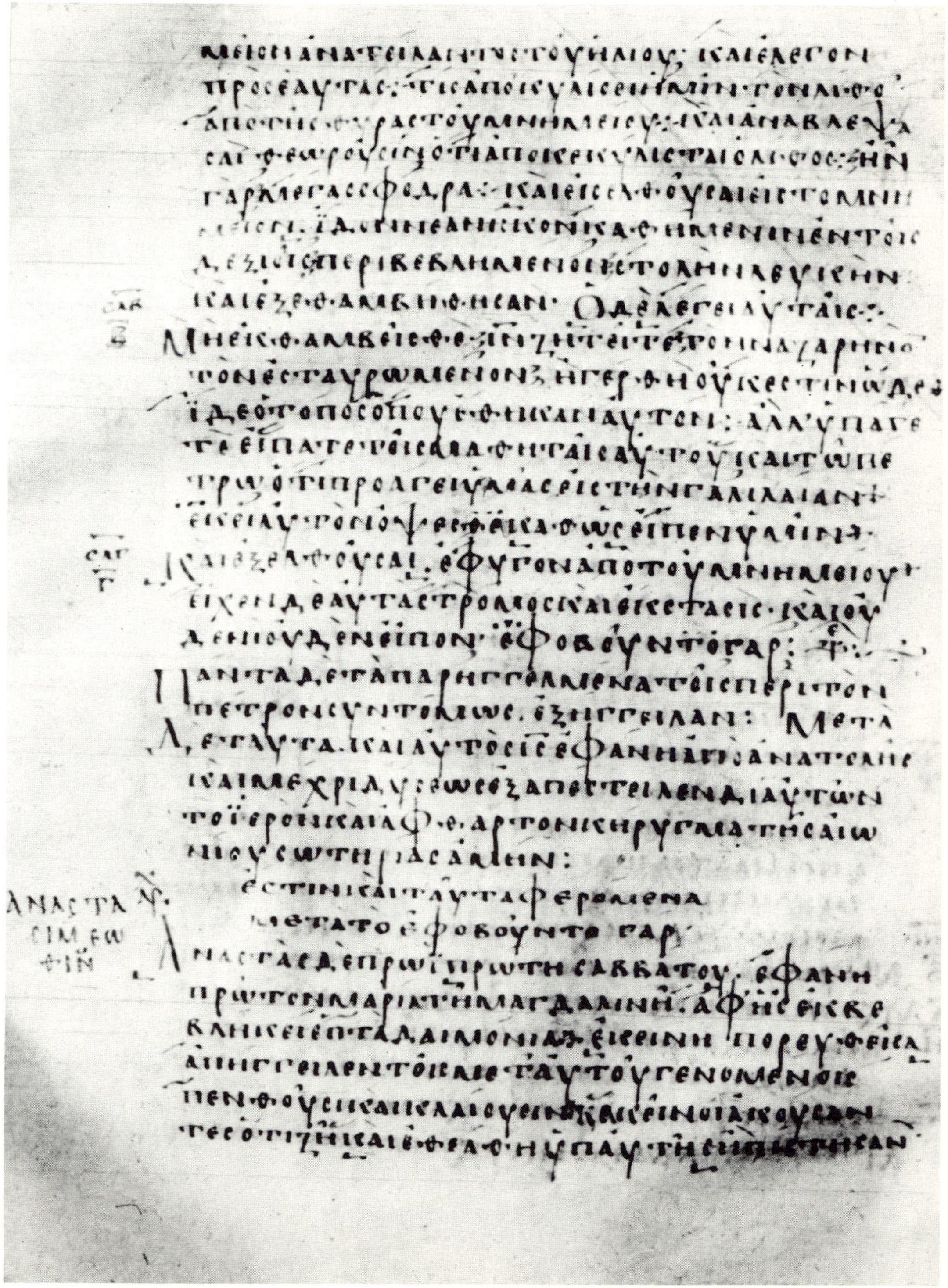

25. Matthew 27:16–23. Gregory–Aland Θ (Koridethi Codex). ix cent. ?

TIFLIS, INST. RUKOP., GR. 28, FOL. 67 VERSO.

Parchment codex, containing the four Gospels (with a few lacunae in Matthew), generally attributed to the ix century (though Lake declared, 'This MS. cannot be dated because no other specimen of the same kind of writing has ever been found'[1]), 11 × 9 inches (28 × 23 cm.), 249 leaves, two columns, 19–32 lines to a column.

The manuscript once belonged to a monastery in Koridethi in the ancient country of Lazoi, located at the eastern end of the Black Sea, not very far from Batum. It came to the attention of the scholarly world about the middle of the nineteenth century, but later that century it fell out of sight for about thirty years. In 1901 it was rediscovered by Bishop Kirion in the treasure-room of St. Andrew's Cathedral in Kutais. Bishop Kirion brought the manuscript to Tiflis.

The physiognomy of codex Koridethi is rustic. The script gives the impression that the scribe drew rather than wrote his letters, which vary considerably in size. Furthermore, the letters are sometimes on the line, sometimes pendant from the line, and sometimes the line runs through the letters. The scribe was probably a Georgian not very familiar with Greek. On the inner-side of the back cover is an inscription written with Greek and several Georgian and, as some have (erroneously) thought, Coptic letters; it is the text Heb. 10:7 (=Ps. 40:7), 'In the head of the book it is written about me to do thy will.'

What is the character of the text of this unusual manuscript? In Matthew, Luke, and John the text is frequently similar to the type of text in most Byzantine manuscripts (though occasionally it presents notable readings), but in Mark it is quite different. Here it is akin to the type of text that Origen and Eusebius used in the third and fourth centuries at Caesarea.

A remarkable reading occurs at Matt. 27:16, 17 (Plate 25, col. *a*, lines 4 and 11), where the Koridethi manuscript has Pilate ask the crowds whether he should release Jesus Bar Rabbas (ΙΝ̄ ΒΑΡ ΡΑΒΒΑΝ) or Jesus who is called the Christ. Several other witnesses (1*, 118, 209, 241*, 299**, 700*, 1582 syr[s, pal] arm geo[2]) also insert Ἰησοῦν before Βαραββᾶν. The tenth-century uncial manuscript S (Plate 31) and about twenty minuscule manuscripts contain a marginal note stating that in very ancient manuscripts Barabbas is called Jesus; in one of these the note is attributed to Origen. Since Origen himself calls attention to the variant reading in his Commentary on Matthew (*in loc.*),[2] the reading must be of great antiquity.

From the standpoint of transcriptional probability, in ver. 17 the word Ἰησοῦν could have been accidentally either added or deleted by scribes owing to the presence of υμιν before it (ΥΜΙΝΙΝ̄).

In support of the reading with Ἰησοῦν as original in both verses are the following considerations: (*a*) the double name adds point to the passage ('Whom shall I release to you? Jesus Barabbas or Jesus who is called the Christ?'); (*b*) Although scribes would have had no reason deliberately to add the name, it may well have been suppressed from reverential motives; (*c*) the reading τὸν before Βαραββᾶν in B and 1010 appears to presuppose the presence of Ἰησοῦν in an ancestor of these two manuscripts.

On the other hand, in support of the traditional reading are such considerations as (*a*) the evidence of nearly all Greek manuscripts, including the best, and of nearly all versions; (*b*) the fact that even the few witnesses that prefix 'Jesus' to Barabbas in verses 16 and 17 do not do so in verses 20, 21, and 26, where one might expect to find it repeated; (*c*) no trace of any such reading is found in any text of Mark, Luke, or John.

BIBLIOGRAPHY: Facsimile edition of the text of Mark, *Materialy po Arkheologii Kavkaza . . .*, xi (Moscow, 1907); transcription of the entire text in Gustav Beermann and Caspar René Gregory, *Die Koridethi Evangelien* Θ 038 (Leipzig, 1913); Kirsopp Lake and Robert P. Blake, 'The Text of the Gospels and the Koridethi Codex,' *Harvard Theological Review*, xvi (1923), pp. 267–86; J. de Zwaan, 'No Coptic in the Koridethi Codex', ibid., xviii (1925), pp. 112–4; cf. Blake's 'Rejoinder,' ibid., p. 114.

[1] K. Lake, *The Text of the New Testament*, 6th ed. (London, 1928), p. 19.

[2] Cf. B. M. Metzger, 'Explicit References in the Works of Origen to Variant Readings in New Testament Manuscripts,' *Historical and Literary Studies* (Leiden and Grand Rapids, 1968), pp. 88–103, esp. 94.

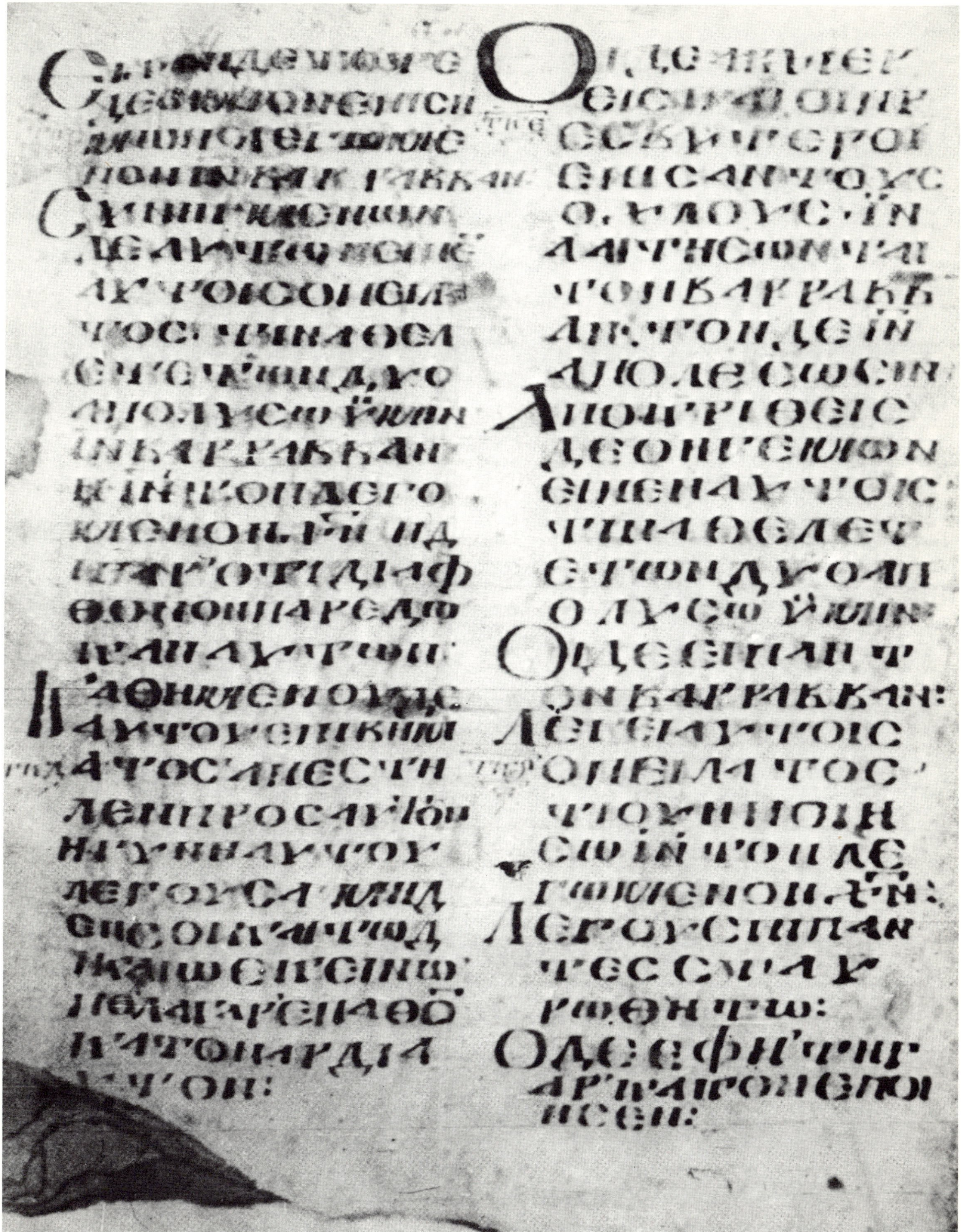

26. Mark 1:1–6. Gregory–Aland 461 (Uspenski Gospels). A.D. 835.

LENINGRAD, STATE PUBLIC LIBRARY, GR. 219, PAGE 100.

Parchment codex, containing the four Gospels, dated A.D. 835, 6½ × 4⅛ inches (16.7 × 10.7 cm.), 344 leaves, one column, 19 lines to a page.

This, the earliest dated minuscule Greek manuscript (see §16), was formerly in the Monastery of Mar Saba in Palestine; later it belonged to Bishop Porfiri Uspenski of Kiev. It is written in a small, upright hand. The writing is on the ruled lines at the top and middle of a column, and pendant from the bottom line. In order to indicate new sections the scribe brings the text of the first full line of the section into the left-hand margin. Ligatures combine consecutive letters as well as, occasionally, separate words. The heading of each Gospel and the lection notes are written in uncials.

The colophon at the end of the text (fol. 344 verso), written in the same hand and ink, provides the date of the manuscript and the name of the scribe: ἐτελειώθη θ(εο)ῦ χάριτι ἡ ἱερὰ αὐτὴ καὶ θεοχάρακτος βίβλος μηνὶ μαΐῳ ζ̄ ἰνδικτιῶνος ιγ̄ ἔτους κόσμου ϛτμγ̄. δυσωπῶ δὲ πάντας τοὺς ἐντυγχάνοντας μνίαν (*sic*) μου ποιεῖσθαι τοῦ γράψαντος Νικολάου ἁμαρτ(ωλοῦ) μοναχ(οῦ) ὅπως εὕροιμι ἔλεος ἐν ἡμέρᾳ κρίσεως, γένοιτο κ(ύρι)ε ἀμήν. This Nicolaus has been plausibly identified with the monk of that name who later became the second abbot of the Studion monastery at Constantinople, and who may have written (so Diller thinks) another New Testament manuscript extant today (Gregory–Aland MS. K).

The type of text is Byzantine (von Soden classifies it as K^1); the *pericope de adultera*, omitted by the original scribe, has been added in the margin by a much later hand.

The liturgical note in the upper right-hand margin specifies that the passage (Mark 1:1–8) is appointed to be read on the Sunday before the Feast of Lights (i.e. January 6): τῇ κυριακῇ πρὸ τῶν Φώτων ἐὰν φθάσουν δύο κυριακὰς μέσον λέγεται τοῦτο εἰς τὴν β̄ κυριακήν.

BIBLIOGRAPHY: G. Cereteli, 'Wo ist das Tetraevangelism von Porphyrius Uspenskij aus dem Jahr 835 erstanden?' *Byzantinische Zeitschrift*, ix (1900), pp. 649–53; T. W. Allen, 'The Origin ot the Greek Minuscule Hand,' *Journal of Hellenic Studies*, xl (1920), pp. 1–12; A. Diller, 'A Companion to the Uspenski Gospels' [Gregory–Aland MS. K], *Byzantinische Zeitschrift*, xlix (1956), pp. 332–5. Cf. also Bp. Mikhail, 'Četveroevangelie 891 goda,' *Zhurnal moskovskoj patriarkhii*, xiv, 4 (1956), pp. 43–9, esp. p. 46 and the two plates, and L. P. Žukovskaja, *Tekstologija i jazyk drevnejskich slavjanskich pamjatnikov* (Moscow, 1976), who discusses the oldest Greek Gospel manuscripts found in Russia (pp. 234–41).

27. Psalm 72 [73]:1–10*a*. Rahlfs 1101 (Khludov Psalter). ix cent.

MOSCOW, HISTORICAL MUSEUM, COD. 129, FOL. 70 VERSO.

Parchment codex, containing the Psalms, ix-century, 7⅝ × 5¾ inches (19.4 × 14.5 cm.), 169 leaves, one column, about 23 lines to the page.

In 1847 this richly illustrated Psalter, containing more than 200 miniatures, was brought by V. I. Grigorovič from Mount Athos to Moscow, where it eventually became the property of Alexei Ivanovič Khludov. Originally written during the ninth century in a beautiful uncial hand (see the caption in the left-hand margin of the Plate), in the twelfth century, the ink having became rather faint, the Scripture text was re-written with darker ink in contemporary minuscules. Here and there the under-writing is visible, detracting from the aesthetic qualities of the manuscript.

Accent and breathing marks are supplied throughout; occasionally diaeresis stands over iota (lines 9, 18, 19). Among *nomina sacra* θ[εό]ς and Ἰ[σρα]ήλ occur in line 1 and οὐ[ρα]νόν in line 20; there is an anomalous contraction of the plural of ἄνθρωπος in lines 10 and 11.

The initial letter of each Psalm is considerably enlarged, and the initial letter of each verse is somewhat enlarged; they are written with red ink, as is also the number of the Psalm (οβ̄ = 72 [Masoretic text 73]). A conventional sign (semi-circle and dot) above the upper picture, which shows two men falling headlong, is repeated at the beginning of line 8 over the last syllable of θανατω in the clause ὅτι οὐκ ἔστιν ἀνάνευσις τῷ θανάτῳ αὐτῶν ('For there is no movement upward at their death'). The lower picture illustrates the text of lines 20–22, Ἔθεντο εἰς οὐ(ρα)νὸν τὸ στόμα αὐτῶν καὶ ἡ γλῶσσα αὐτῶν διῆλθεν ἐπὶ τῆς γῆς ('They set their mouth against heaven, and their tongue has gone about upon the earth'), which is interpreted with grotesque literalism, showing the mouths of the wicked gaping toward heaven (which is surmounted by a cross) and their tongues reaching to the earth. The caption, written by the original scribe and not re-written by a later scribe, reads οι αιρε|τιζον|τες και| λαλουν|τες κα|τα του | θ(εο)υ. The wavy, colored line above the caption is repeated in the text above στόμα αὐτῶν, thus correlating picture with text.

The verses shown in the Plate agree with the printed text of Rahlfs except for ver. 1, where instead of τῷ Ἰσραὴλ ὁ θεός, MS. 1101 agrees with the reading of ℵ^c.a, ὁ θεὸς τῷ Ἰσραήλ.

BIBLIOGRAPHY: Facsimile edition (in full color), M. V. Schepkins, *Miniatiury Khludovskoĭ Psaltyri, grecheskiĭ illiustriovannyi kodeks ix veka* (Moscow, 1977); cf. J. J. Tikkanen, *Die Psalterillustration im Mittelalter* (Acta Societatis Fennicae, xxxi; Helsinki, 1895; reprinted, Soest, 1975), pp. 1 ff.

26

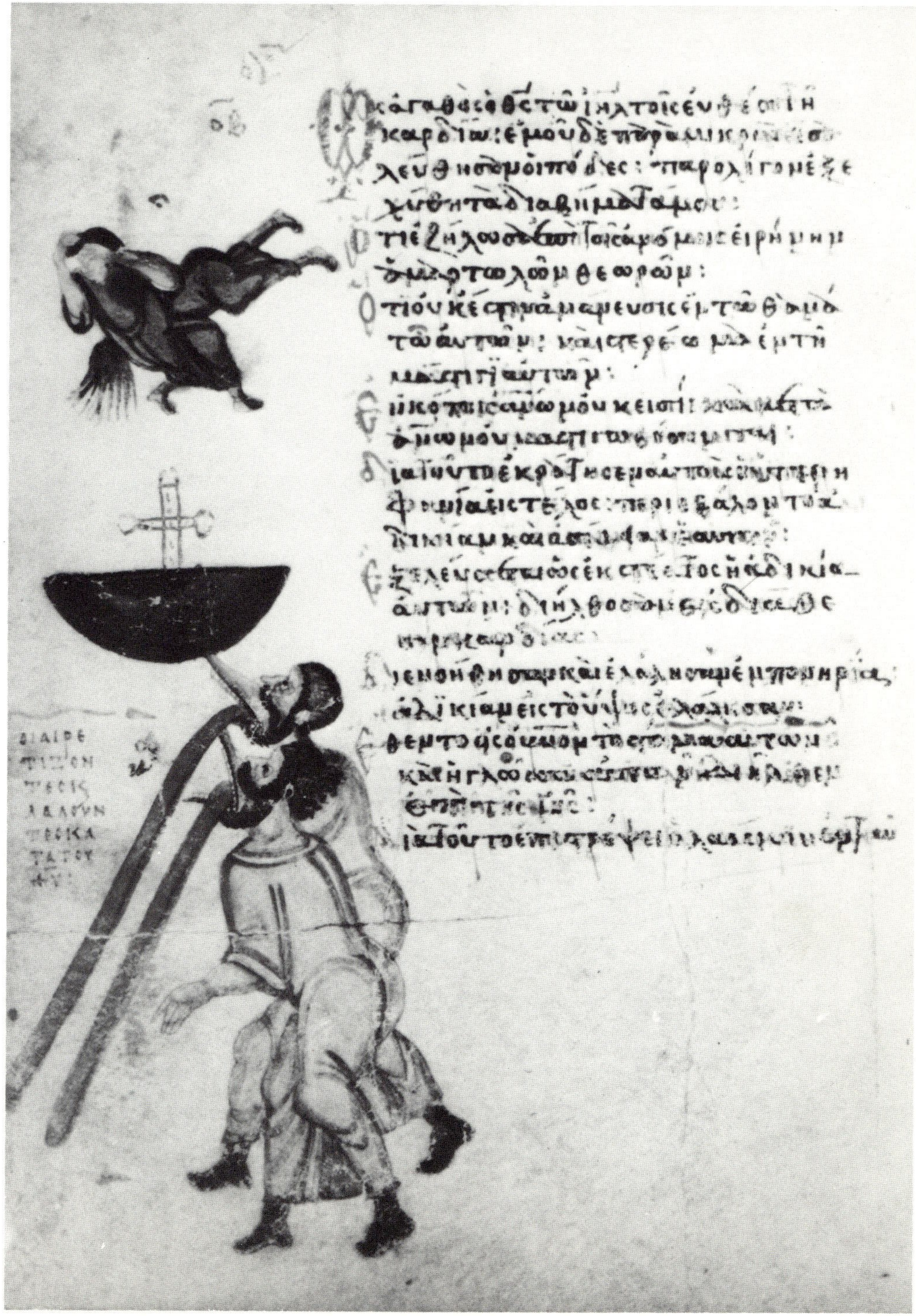

27

28. I Corinthians 2:9–3:3. Gregory–Aland G (Codex Boernerianus). ix cent.

DRESDEN, SÄCHISCHE LANDESBIBLIOTHEK, A 145B, FOL. 23 RECTO.

Bilingual parchment codex, containing the Greek and Latin texts of the Pauline Epistles (without Hebrews), ix century, 9⅞ × 7½ inches (25 × 19 cm.), 99 leaves, one column, 20 lines to the column.

The manuscript was formerly the property of Christian Friedrich Börner, professor of theology at Leipzig, who purchased it in 1705. After the end of Philemon, and lower on the page, there stands the title *προς Λαουδακησας*[1] *αρχεται επιστολη*, with the Latin words standing above the Greek, *ad Laudicenses incipit epistola*, but neither that apocryphal epistle nor the Epistle to the Hebrews follows.

The Greek uncials are coarse and peculiar. There are no breathing or accent marks. Capital letters are decorated with colored inks (yellow, red, pink). In these and in other respects codex Boernerianus resembles codex Sangallensis (Δ) of the Gospels,[2] at one time thought to be the first portion of G.

The text from which G was copied seems to have been arranged in *στίχοι*, for almost every line has at least one Greek capital letter. If the capital letters be assumed to commence the lines of the exemplar, the text divides itself into regular *στίχοι* (see §23). Quotations from the Old Testament are indicated by marks placed in the left-hand margin (lines 1 and 14–15), and a Latin notation identifies the origin of a quotation (*Iesaia*, opposite line 14).

The Latin translation, which follows the Greek word for word, is written above the latter. The Latin text is for the most part the Vulgate, but here and there it has been conformed to the Greek. Occasionally a Greek word is supplied with alternative Latin renderings, connected with the word meaning 'or'; sometimes the two renderings are synonymns, sometimes one is a literal rendering followed by one congruent with Latin syntax (for an example of the latter kind, see line 3 from the bottom of the Greek text shown in the Plate, where *ὑμας* is rendered *vos t* [=*vel*] *vobis*).

There is no question that this manuscript was written in the west of Europe (very possibly in the monastery of St. Gall in northeast Switzerland, where codex Δ still remains) by some of the Irish monks who emigrated to those parts. At the foot of the page reproduced in the Plate are several lines of Irish verse which refer to making a pilgrimage to Rome:[3]

Téicht do róim [téicht do róim] Mór saido becic torbai Inrí chondaigi hifoss Manimbera latt ni fog bai.	To come to Rome, to come to Rome, Much of trouble, little of profit, The thing thou seekest here, If thou bring not with thee, thou findest not.
Mór báis mór baile Mór coll ceille mór mise Olais aurchenn teicht dóecaib Beith fó étoil maic Maire.	Great folly, great madness, Great ruin of sense, great insanity, Since thou has set out for death, That thou shouldest be in disobedience to the Son of Mary.

BIBLIOGRAPHY: Facsimile edition, *Der Codex Boernerianus der Briefe des Apostels Paulus . . .*, mit einem Vorwort von Dr. Alexander Reichardt . . . (Leipzig, 1909); Wm. H. P. Hatch, 'On the Relationship of Codex Augiensis and Codex Boernerianus of the Pauline Epistles,' *Harvard Studies in Classical Philology*, lx (1951), pp. 187–99; Hermann J. Frede, *Altlateinische Paulus-Handschriften* (Freiburg, 1964), pp. 50–77.

[1] Here *αου* standing to represent *au* shows that the Greek is derived from the Latin, not vice versa.

[2] For a specimen of codex Sangallensis, see Plate XIII (*a*) in Metzger, *The Text of the New Testament*, 2nd ed. (Oxford, 1968).

[3] The transcription and translation are taken from F. H. A. Scrivener, *A Plain Introduction to the Criticism of the New Testament*, 4th ed., i (London, 1894), p. 180, n. 2.

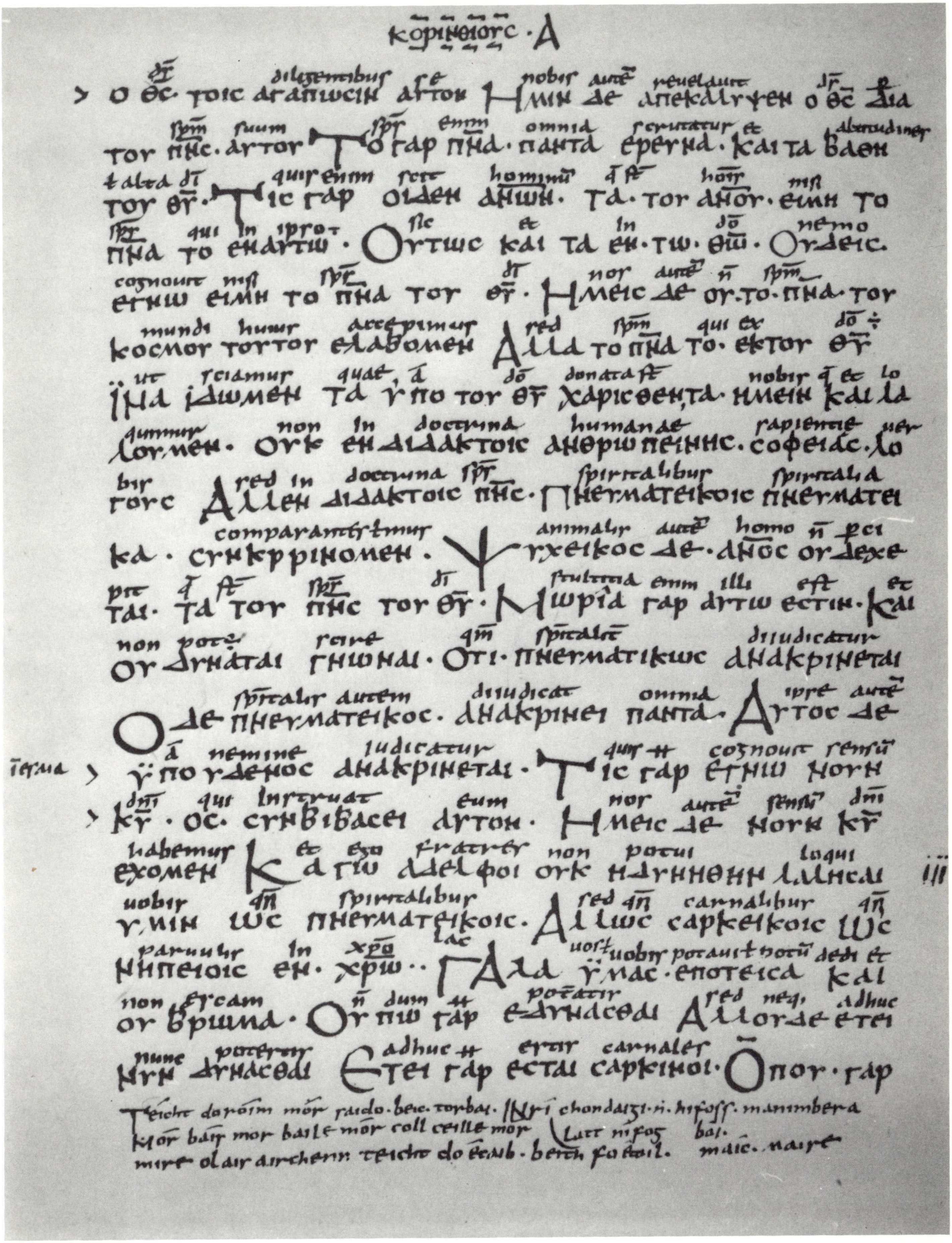

κοριnθιουc · Α

ο θc τοιc αγαπωcιν αυτον Ημιν δε απεκαλυψεν ο θc δια
του πνc αυτου Το γαρ πνα παντα ερευνα και τα βαθη
του θυ · Τιc γαρ οιδεν ανων τα του ανου ειμη το
πνα το εν αυτω · Ουτωc και τα εν τω θω · Ουδειc
εγνω ειμη το πνα του θυ · Ημειc δε ου το πνα του
κοcμου τουτου ελαβομεν Αλλα το πνα το εκ του θυ
ινα ιδωμεν τα υπο του θυ χαριcθεντα · ημειν και λα
λουμεν · ουκ εν διδακτοιc ανθρωπεινηc · cοφειαc · λο
γοιc Αλλ εν διδακτοιc πνc · πνευματεικοιc πνευματει
κα · cυνκρινομεν · Ψυχεικοc δε · ανοc ου δεχε
ται · τα του πνc του θυ · Μωρια γαρ αυτω εcτιν · και
ου δυναται γνωναι · οτι · πνευματικωc ανακρινεται
Ο δε πνευματεικοc · ανακρινει παντα · Αυτοc δε
υπο ουδενοc ανακρινεται · Τιc γαρ εγνω νουν
κυ · οc · cυνβιβαcει αυτον · Ημειc δε νουν κυ
εχομεν Καγω αδελφοι ουκ ηδυνηθην λαληcαι
υμιν ωc πνευματεικοιc · Αλλ ωc cαρκεικοιc ωc
νηπειοιc εν · χρω · · Γαλα υμαc · εποτειcα και
ου βρωμα · Ουπω γαρ εδυναcθαι Αλλ ουδε ετει
νυν δυναcθαι Ετει γαρ εcται cαρκινοι · Οπου · γαρ

Teicht doroim mor saido · becc · torbai · In ri chondaigi hi foss · manimbera
latt nifog bai ·
Mor baile mor coll ceille mor mire olair airchenn teicht do écaib · beith fo étoil · maic · Maire

29. Luke 22:38–45. Gregory–Aland 892. ix (or x) cent.

LONDON, BRITISH LIBRARY, ADD. 33277, FOL. 261 VERSO.

Parchment[1] codex, containing the four Gospels, ix (or x) century, 6 × 4⅛ inches (17.2 × 11.5 cm.), 353 leaves, one column, 20 lines to a page.

The scribe of this manuscript was careful to preserve the line and page dimensions of its uncial ancestor. The scribe sometimes leaves the lower part of a page blank so that he may begin the next page in harmony with his copy. Square breathing marks are used throughout the Scripture text. The manuscript is furnished with lectionary equipment for both synaxarion and menologion (see §29). In the upper margin of the page shown in the Plate stands the rubric stating that the lesson (Luke 22:39–23:1) is for the third day of Cheese-Week (the week immediately preceding Lent), *τῇ γ̄ τυροφάγου*, and that the incipit for the lesson is *τῷ καιρῷ ἐξελθὼν ὁ Ἰησοῦς*. The lesson begins in line 2 at the place marked with the abbreviation of *ἀρχή*. In line 5 the abbreviation of *τέλος* marks the close of the lesson for the preceding day (Luke 19:29–40; 22:7–39). The Ammonian section and Eusebian canon numbers stand in the left-hand margin.

Textually, the manuscript contains many remarkable readings of an early type. In chap. 5 of Mark, for example, Harris found 35 readings in which 892 agrees with ℵ 30 times, with B 29 times, with C 28 times, with Δ 27 times, and with D 12 times. Von Soden, on the basis of a more representative analysis of the manuscript, classified its text as Hesychian with a certain amount of influence from the Koine and Jerusalem types of text.

On the page shown in the Plate the passage concerning the Bloody Sweat (Luke 22:43–44) is marked in the left-hand margin (lines 13 to 19) to signify that it is regarded as doubtful or spurious. Some ancient witnesses omit the verses entirely ($\mathfrak{p}^{75}$ $\aleph^{a}$ B T W syr^{s} $cop^{sa,bo}$ arm^{mss} geo Marcion Clement Origen *al*); in other manuscripts (family 13) the passage is transferred to follow Matt. 26:39. On the other hand, its presence in many manuscripts (ℵ* D L X Δ* Θ Π* Ψ family 1 *al*), as well as its citation by Justin, Irenaeus, Hippolytus, Eusebius, and many other Fathers, is proof of the antiquity of the account. In the judgment of the editors of the United Bible Societies' *Greek New Testament*, 'On the grounds of transcriptional probability it is less likely that the verses were deleted in several different areas of the church by those who felt that the account of Jesus overwhelmed with human weakness was incompatible with his sharing the divine omnipotence of the Father, than that they were added from an early source, oral or written, of extra-canonical traditions concerning the life and passion of Jesus.'[2]

BIBLIOGRAPHY: Collation by J. Rendel Harris, 'An Important MS of the New Testament,' *Journal of Biblical Literature*, ix (1890), pp. 31–59; Hermann von Soden, *Die Schriften des Neuen Testaments in ihrer ältesten erreichbaren Textgestalt*, I, ii (Berlin, 1907), pp. 973–8.

[1] John 10:6–12:18 and 14:23–21:35 are written on paper by a sixteenth-century hand.
[2] B. M. Metzger, *A Textual Commentary on the Greek New Testament* (London, 1971), p. 177.

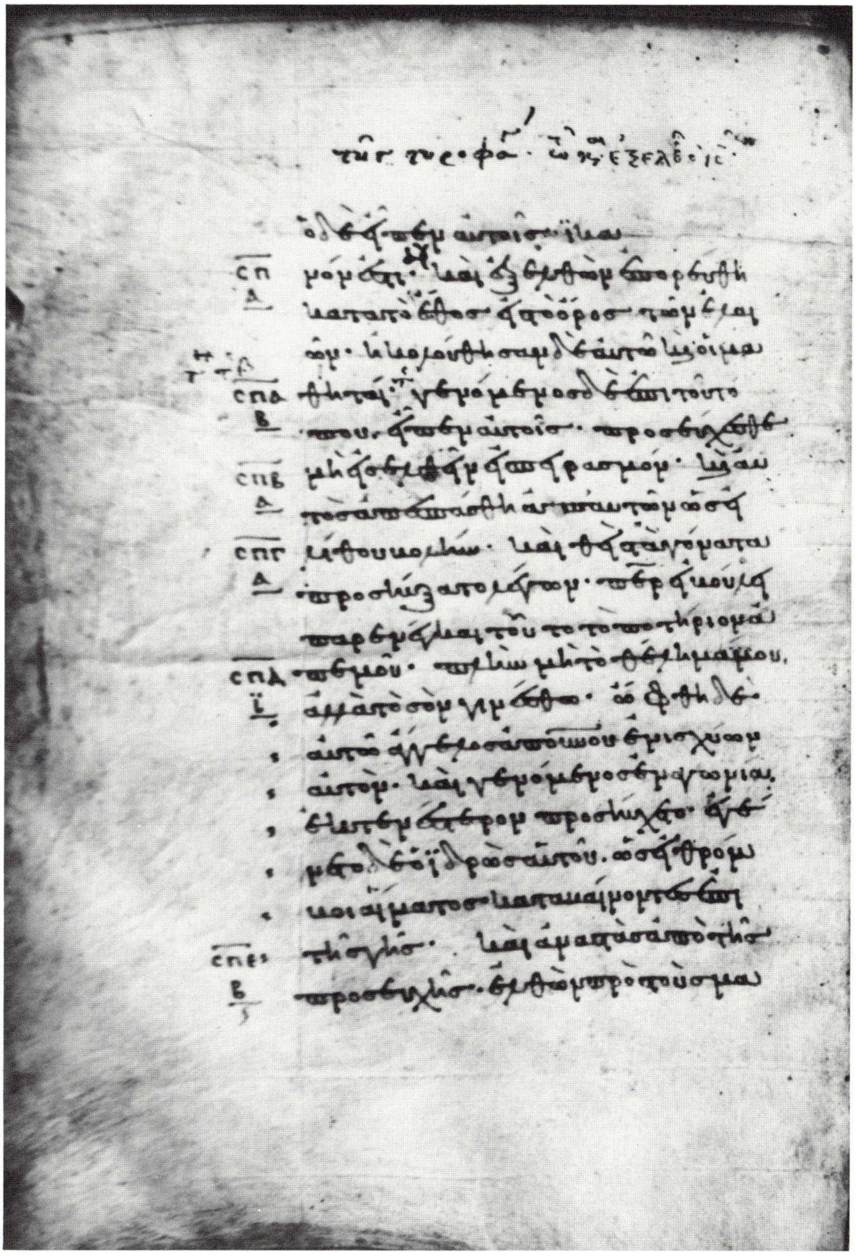

ὁ δὲ εἶπεν αὐτοῖς· ἱκα
νόν ἐστι. καὶ ἐξελθὼν ἐπορεύθη
κατὰ τὸ ἔθος εἰς τὸ ὄρος τῶν ἐλαι
ῶν· ἠκολούθησαν δὲ αὐτῷ καὶ οἱ μα
θηταί. γενόμενος δὲ ἐπὶ τοῦ τό
που, εἶπεν αὐτοῖς· προσεύχεσθε
μὴ εἰσελθεῖν εἰς πειρασμόν. καὶ αὐ
τὸς ἀπεσπάσθη ἀπ' αὐτῶν ὡσεὶ
λίθου βολήν· καὶ θεὶς τὰ γόνατα
προσηύχετο λέγων· πάτερ εἰ βούλει
παρενέγκαι τοῦτο τὸ ποτήριον ἀπ'
ἐμοῦ· πλὴν μὴ τὸ θέλημά μου,
ἀλλὰ τὸ σὸν γινέσθω. ὤφθη δὲ
αὐτῷ ἄγγελος ἀπ' οὐρανοῦ ἐνισχύων
αὐτόν. καὶ γενόμενος ἐν ἀγωνίᾳ,
ἐκτενέστερον προσηύχετο· ἐγέ
νετο δὲ ὁ ἱδρὼς αὐτοῦ ὡσεὶ θρόμ
βοι αἵματος καταβαίνοντες ἐπὶ
τὴν γῆν. καὶ ἀναστὰς ἀπὸ τῆς
προσευχῆς, ἐλθὼν πρὸς τοὺς μα

29

30. Psalm 27 [28]:6–7. Rahlfs 1098. ix or x cent.

Milan, Biblioteca Ambrosiana, O 39 Sup., fol. 105 recto and 100 verso.

Palimpsest parchment leaves, originally measuring about 15⅜ × 11 inches (39 × 28 cm.), containing in the under-writing about 150 verses of the Hexaplaric Psalter, written in a hand of the ninth or tenth century. In the thirteenth or fourteenth century the codex was dismantled and the parchment reused for another book. The leaves were (partially) erased and cut in half laterally, each half making two leaves and four pages of the new codex. The Plate shows one such leaf (formerly the upper half of a page of the original codex), the under-writing, in five columns, giving for Psalm 27 [28]:6–7 the transliteration of the Hebrew text and the translations made by Aquila, Symmachus, the Seventy, and, instead of Theodotion as might have been expected, the Quinta (see footnote 87 above). The first column of the Hexapla, giving the Hebrew text (see §22), is lacking.

By oversight ver. 7 is repeated. *Iota* adscript occurs (lines 9 and 20); accent and breathing marks are provided even for the transliteration of the Hebrew. The Tetragrammaton is written in square Hebrew letters, followed, in the Septuagint column, by the contraction for *κύριος* (in ver. 8 on the next page κ̅ς̅ is followed by *πιπι*; see §20 end).

יהוה	יהוה	יהוה	יהוה κ̅ς̅	יהוה
χι	ὅτι	ὁ	ὅτι	ὅτι
σμας	ἤκουσε	ἐπακούσας	εἰσήκουσε	εἰσήκουσε
κωλ	φωνῆς	τῆς φωνῆς	τῆς φωνῆς	τῆς φωνῆς
θανουναϊ	δεήσεώς μου.	τῆς ἱκεσίας μου.	τῆς δεήσεώς μου.	τῆς δεήσεώς μου.
יהוה	יהוה	יהוה	יהוה κ̅ς̅	יהוה
ὀζει	κράτος μου	ἰσχύς μου	βοηθός μου	βοηθός μου
οὐμαγεννη	(καὶ) θυρεός μου·	καὶ ὑπερα·σπιστής μου·	καὶ <ὑ>περασπιστής μου·	(καὶ) ὑπερασπιστής μου·
βω·	ἐν αὐτῶι	αὐτῶι	ἐν αὐτῶι	ἐν αὐτῶι
βατε	ἐπεποίθησεν	ἐπεποίθησεν	ἤλπισεν	ἤλπισεν
λεββὶ	καρδία μου,	ἡ καρδία μου,	ἡ καρδία μου,	καρδία μου,
ου·νάζερθι	(καὶ) ἐβοηθήθην,	καὶ ἐβοηθήθην,	καὶ ἐβοηθήθην,	(καὶ) ἐβοηθήθην,
ουαϊαλεζ	καὶ ἠγαυριάσατο	(καὶ) ἰλαρύνθ(η)	καὶ ἀνέθαλεν	καὶ ἐκραταιώθ(η)
λεββὶ	καρδία μου·	ἡ καρδία μου·	ἡ σάρξ μου·	ἡ καρδία μου·
οὐμεσσιρι	(και) ἀπὸ αἴσματό(s) μου	καὶ ἐν ὠιδαῖς μου	καὶ ἐκ θελήματό(s) μου	(καὶ) ἀπὸ τοῦ ἄσματό(s) μου
αωδεννου	ἐξομολογήσωμ(αι) αὐτ(ῷ.)	ὑμνήσω αὐτόν.	ἐξομολογήσομαι αὐτ(ῷ.)	ἐξομολογήσομ(αι) αὐτ(ῷ.)
יהוה	יהוה	יהוה	יהוה κ̅ς̅	יהוה
ὀζει	κράτος μου	ἰσχύς μου	βοηθός μου	βοηθός μου
οὐμαγεννι	καὶ θυρεός μου	καὶ ὑπερασπιστής μου·	καὶ ὑπερασπιστής μου·	καὶ ὑπερασπιστής μου·
βω	ἐν αὐτῶι	αὐτῶι	ἐν αὐτῶι	ἐν αὐτῶ

Bibliography for Hexaplaric text: Giovanni Mercati (ed.), *Psalterii Hexapli Reliquiae . . .*, Pars Prima: *Codex Rescriptus Bybliothecae Ambrosianae* O 39 *sup. phototypice expressus et transcriptus* (Vatican City, 1958); idem, Pars Prima: *'Osservazioni' Commento critico al testo dei frammenti esaplari* (Vatican City, 1965); P. E. Kahle, 'The Greek Bible Manuscripts used by Origen,' *Journal of Biblical Literature*, lxxiv (1960), pp. 111–18; J. A. Emerton, 'A Further Consideration of the Purpose of the Second Column of the Hexapla,' *Journal of Theological Studies*, n.s. xxii (1971), pp. 15–29.

Oktoëchos. Upper-writing, xiii/xiv cent.

In the thirteenth or fourteenth century the leaves of the codex were re-used for the text of the Oktoëchos (Ὀκτώηχος), a service-book of the Greek Orthodox Church (see §30). Each sheet of parchment made two leaves and four pages, a page measuring 7¼ × 5½ inches (18.5 × 14 cm.). The left-hand page of the Plate shows part of a Theotokos hymn; the first three 'stanzas' are transcribed as follows:

Παρθενικῆς ἐκ νηδύος, σαρκω|θεὶς ἐπεφάνης εἰς σ(ωτη)ρίαν ἡμῶν· | διό σου τὴν Μ(ητέ)ρα, εἰδότες Θ(εοτό)κον | εὐχαρίστως κραυγάζομεν· εὐ(λογητὸς εἶ).

Ῥάβδος ἔφυς παρθένε, Ἰεσσαὶ ἐκ | τῆς ῥίζης ἡ παμμακάριστος, καρ | πὸν ἀνθηφοροῦσα σ(ωτή)ριον τοῖς πί|στει, τῷ υἱῷ σου κραυγάζουσιν : ὁ τῶν (πατέρων ἡμῶν, θεὸς εὐλογητὸς εἶ).

Τῆς Ἰ(ησο)ῦ Θεότητος, ἡ ὑπέρθεος δύ|ναμις, ἐν τοῖς καθ' ἡμᾶς θεοπρε|πῶς ἐξέλαμψε· σαρκὶ γὰρ γευσά|μενος, ὑπὲρ παντὸς θανάτου στ(αυ)ροῦ, | ἔλυσε τοῦ ᾅδου τὴν ἰσχύν· ὃν ἀπαύ|στως, οἱ παῖδες εὐλογεῖτε.

On the right-hand page, line 3, stands the rubric *ἑωθινὸν β'* (i.e. the second troparion sung at the end of Lauds), and, line 3 from the bottom, *Ἐξαποστειλάριον γ'* (i.e. the third troparion sung immediately before Lauds). In the right-hand margin the abbreviation Ἠ β' signifies the second of the eight tones used in successive weeks (see §30).

Bibliography for Oktoëchos: *Ὀκτώηχος τοῦ ἐν ἁγίοις πατρὸς ἡμῶν Ἰωάννου τοῦ Δαμασκηνοῦ* (Athens, 1976, and other editions); H. J. W. Tillyard, *Hymns of the Octoëchos*, Parts I and II (Copenhagen, 1940, 1949); Oliver Strunk, 'Antiphons of the Oktoëchos,' *Journal of the American Musicological Society*, xiii (1960), pp. 50–67; reprinted in Strunk, *Essays on Music in the Byzantine World* (New York, 1977), pp. 165–90.

31. Matthew 8:1–10. Gregory–Aland S. A.D. 949. 948

Rome, Biblioteca Vaticana, Gr. 354, fol. 30 recto.

Parchment codex, containing the four Gospels, dated A.D. 949, 14⅛ × 8⅝ inches (36 × 22 cm.), 235 leaves, two columns, an average of 27 lines to a column.

Codex Vaticanus 354, the only extant uncial manuscript of the Greek New Testament which has a precise date, indicates in a colophon on fol. 234 verso that it was written by 'Michael, monk [and] sinner,' who finished his work 'in the month of March, the fifth day, the sixth hour, the year (of the world) 6457, the seventh indiction.'

The script, written in large oblong or compressed uncials, presents an extreme contrast of heavy and light strokes; the general aspect of the writing is one of excessive artificiality. (This type of Greek writing has received the name 'Slavic,' having been taken as a pattern for the alphabets of Eastern Europe.) The text is provided with accent and breathing marks as well as neumes (see §30). Chapter numbers with titles stand at the top of each column, ϛ̄ *πε(ρὶ) τοῦ λεπροῦ* and ζ̄ *πε(ρὶ) τοῦ ἑκατοντάρχ(ου)*; the same chapter numbers stand in the left-hand margin of col. *a* opposite 8:1 and 8:5, where also the Ammonian section and Eusebian canon numbers are given ($\frac{63}{2}$ and $\frac{64}{3}$). In the right-hand margin of col. *a*, opposite line 5 from the bottom, the abbreviation of *τέλος* marks the close of a lection, which is followed by the lection appointed to be read on the fourth Sunday after Pentecost, *κυ(ριακῇ)* δ̄.

In the right-hand margin, written in small uncials, stands a quotation (not otherwise preserved) from Clement of Alexandria's *Hypotyposes*, bk. vi, dealing with the passage concerning the leper (a conventional sign above *λεπρός*, col. *a*, line 5 of the Scripture text, is repeated above the quotation), the comment bearing particularly upon the meaning of the phrase *εἰς μαρτύριον* (lines 6 and 5 from the bottom of col. *a*), which is marked with several dots above the first and last letters of the phrase.

Κλ(ήμεντος) ἐκ τῆς ϛ̄ | *τῶν ὑποτυπώσεων* (MS. *-πόσεων*). |

Καὶ τὸν λεπρὸν | ἐθεράπευσεν καὶ | εἶπεν, "Δεῖξον σεαυ|τὸν τοῖς ἱερεῦσιν | εἰς μαρτύριον" διὰ | τοιαύτην παράδο|σιν. Ἔθος εἶχον οἱ | ἱερεῖς δυνάμει θ(εο)ῦ | λεπροὺς ἰᾶσθαι | ἡμέραις τακταῖς. | τοῦτον οὖν τὸν | λεπρὸν πολλῷ | χρόνῳ μὴ δυνη|θέντες ἰάσασθαι | ἔλεγον, Τοῦτον | οὐδεὶς ἰάσεται | ἢ μόνος ὁ Χ(ριστὸ)ς ἐὰν ἔλ|θῃ. Πολλὰ τοίνυν | δεηθέντος τοῦ | λεπροῦ ὁ σ(ωτ)ὴρ "ἐπι|σπλαγχισθείς," ἰα|σάμενος αὐτόν, | διὰ τοῦτο εἶπεν, | ""Απελθε καὶ δεῖξον | σεαυτὸν τοῖς ἱερεῦσιν | εἰς μαρτύριον" ὅτι, | εἰ τεθεράπευται οὗ|τος ἐφ' οὗ εἰρήκατε, | "Οὐδεὶς ἀλλ' ἢ ὁ Χ(ριστὸ)ς | μόνος αὐτὸν (MS. *αὐτὸς*) *ἰά|σεται, ἦλθεν | ὁ Χ(ριστό)ς, καὶ πιστεύσα|τε αὐτῷ."*

The Plate shows the page somewhat reduced in size.

Bibliography: G. Mercati, *Un frammento delle Ipotiposi di Clemente Alessandrino* (Studi e testi, 12; Rome, 1904).

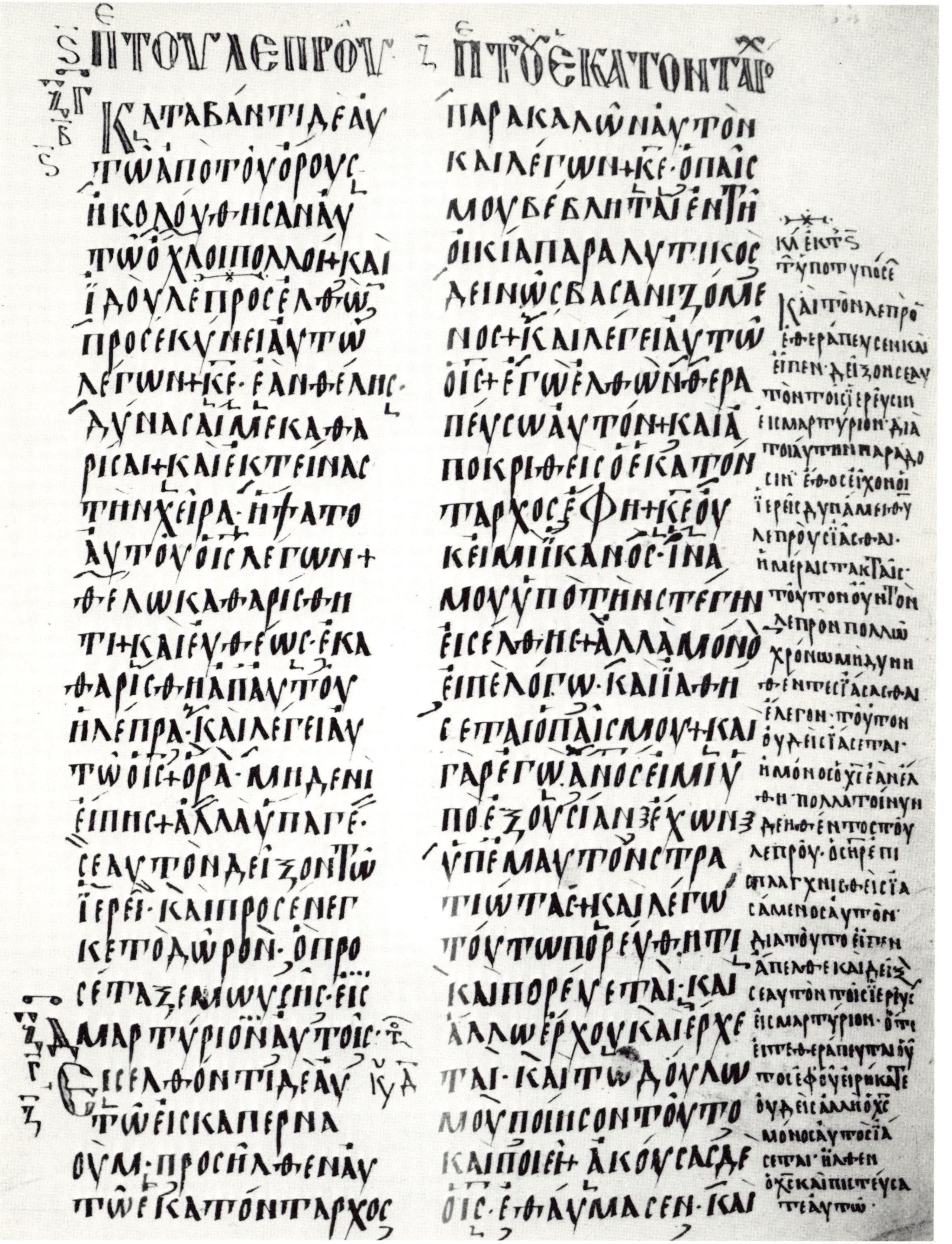
ΠΕΡΙ ΤΟΥ ΛΕΠΡΟΥ

ΚΑΤΑΒΑΝΤΙ ΔΕ ΑΥ
ΤΩ ΑΠΟ ΤΟΥ ΟΡΟΥΣ
ΗΚΟΛΟΥΘΗΣΑΝ ΑΥ
ΤΩ ΟΧΛΟΙ ΠΟΛΛΟΙ· ΚΑΙ
ΙΔΟΥ ΛΕΠΡΟΣ ΕΛΘΩΝ
ΠΡΟΣΕΚΥΝΕΙ ΑΥΤΩ
ΛΕΓΩΝ· ΚΕ· ΕΑΝ ΘΕΛΗΣ·
ΔΥΝΑΣΑΙ ΜΕ ΚΑΘΑ
ΡΙΣΑΙ· ΚΑΙ ΕΚΤΕΙΝΑΣ
ΤΗΝ ΧΕΙΡΑ· ΗΨΑΤΟ
ΑΥΤΟΥ Ο ΙΣ ΛΕΓΩΝ·
ΘΕΛΩ ΚΑΘΑΡΙΣΘΗ
ΤΙ· ΚΑΙ ΕΥΘΕΩΣ· ΕΚΑ
ΘΑΡΙΣΘΗ ΑΠ ΑΥΤΟΥ
Η ΛΕΠΡΑ· ΚΑΙ ΛΕΓΕΙ ΑΥ
ΤΩ Ο ΙΣ· ΟΡΑ· ΜΗΔΕΝΙ
ΕΙΠΗΣ· ΑΛΛ ΥΠΑΓΕ·
ΣΕΑΥΤΟΝ ΔΕΙΞΟΝ ΤΩ
ΙΕΡΕΙ· ΚΑΙ ΠΡΟΣΕΝΕΓ
ΚΕ ΤΟ ΔΩΡΟΝ· Ο ΠΡΟ
ΣΕΤΑΞΕ ΜΩΥΣΗΣ· ΕΙΣ
ΜΑΡΤΥΡΙΟΝ ΑΥΤΟΙΣ·
ΕΙΣΕΛΘΟΝΤΙ ΔΕ ΑΥ
ΤΩ ΕΙΣ ΚΑΠΕΡΝΑ
ΟΥΜ· ΠΡΟΣΗΛΘΕΝ ΑΥ
ΤΩ ΕΚΑΤΟΝΤΑΡΧΟΣ

ΠΕΡΙ ΤΟΥ ΕΚΑΤΟΝΤΑΡΧΟΥ

ΠΑΡΑΚΑΛΩΝ ΑΥΤΟΝ
ΚΑΙ ΛΕΓΩΝ· ΚΕ· Ο ΠΑΙΣ
ΜΟΥ ΒΕΒΛΗΤΑΙ ΕΝ ΤΗ
ΟΙΚΙΑ ΠΑΡΑΛΥΤΙΚΟΣ
ΔΕΙΝΩΣ ΒΑΣΑΝΙΖΟΜΕ
ΝΟΣ· ΚΑΙ ΛΕΓΕΙ ΑΥΤΩ
Ο ΙΣ· ΕΓΩ ΕΛΘΩΝ ΘΕΡΑ
ΠΕΥΣΩ ΑΥΤΟΝ· ΚΑΙ Α
ΠΟΚΡΙΘΕΙΣ Ο ΕΚΑΤΟΝ
ΤΑΡΧΟΣ ΕΦΗ· ΚΕ ΟΥΚ
ΕΙΜΙ ΙΚΑΝΟΣ· ΙΝΑ
ΜΟΥ ΥΠΟ ΤΗΝ ΣΤΕΓΗΝ
ΕΙΣΕΛΘΗΣ· ΑΛΛΑ ΜΟΝΟ(Ν)
ΕΙΠΕ ΛΟΓΩ· ΚΑΙ ΙΑΘΗ
ΣΕΤΑΙ Ο ΠΑΙΣ ΜΟΥ· ΚΑΙ
ΓΑΡ ΕΓΩ ΑΝΟΣ ΕΙΜΙ Υ
ΠΟ ΕΞΟΥΣΙΑΝ· ΕΧΩΝ
ΥΠ ΕΜΑΥΤΟΝ ΣΤΡΑ
ΤΙΩΤΑΣ· ΚΑΙ ΛΕΓΩ
ΤΟΥΤΩ ΠΟΡΕΥΘΗΤΙ
ΚΑΙ ΠΟΡΕΥΕΤΑΙ· ΚΑΙ
ΑΛΛΩ ΕΡΧΟΥ ΚΑΙ ΕΡΧΕ
ΤΑΙ· ΚΑΙ ΤΩ ΔΟΥΛΩ
ΜΟΥ ΠΟΙΗΣΟΝ ΤΟΥΤΟ
ΚΑΙ ΠΟΙΕΙ· ΑΚΟΥΣΑΣ ΔΕ
Ο ΙΣ· ΕΘΑΥΜΑΣΕΝ· ΚΑΙ

ΚΑ ΕΚ ΤΟΥ Ϛ
ΤΥΠΟΣ ΤΥΠΟΣ Ε
ΚΑΙ ΤΟΝ ΛΕΠΡΟ(Ν)
ΕΘΕΡΑΠΕΥΣΕΝ ΚΑΙ
ΕΙΠΕΝ· ΔΕΙΞΟΝ ΣΕΑΥ
ΤΟΝ ΤΟΙΣ ΙΕΡΕΥΣΙΝ
ΕΙΣ ΜΑΡΤΥΡΙΟΝ· ΔΙΑ
ΤΟ ΙΑΥΤΗΝ ΠΑΡΑΔΟ
ΣΙΝ ΕΘΟΣ ΕΙΧΟΝ ΟΙ
ΙΕΡΕΙΣ ΔΥΝΑΜΕΝΟΥ
ΛΕΠΡΟΥΣ ΙΑΣΘΑΙ·
ΗΜΕΡΑΙΣ ΤΑΚΤΑΙΣ·
ΤΟΥΤΟΝ ΟΥΝ ΤΟΝ
ΛΕΠΡΟΝ ΠΟΛΛΩ
ΧΡΟΝΩ ΜΗ ΔΥΝΗ
ΘΕΝΤΕΣ ΙΑΣΑΣΘΑΙ
ΕΛΕΓΟΝ· ΤΟΥΤΟΝ
ΟΥΔΕΙΣ ΙΑΣΕΤΑΙ·
Η ΜΟΝΟΣ Ο ΧΣ ΕΑΝ ΕΛ
ΘΗ· ΠΟΛΛΑ ΤΟΙΝΥΝ
ΔΕΗΘΕΝΤΟΣ ΤΟΥ
ΛΕΠΡΟΥ· Ο ΣΗΡ ΕΠΙ
ΣΠΛΑΓΧΝΙΣΘΕΙΣ ΙΑ
ΣΑΜΕΝΟΣ ΑΥΤΟΝ·
ΔΙΑ ΤΟΥΤΟ ΕΙΠΕΝ
ΑΠΕΛΘΕ ΚΑΙ ΔΕΙΞ(ΟΝ)
ΣΕΑΥΤΟΝ ΤΟΙΣ ΙΕΡΕΥΣ(Ι)
ΕΙΣ ΜΑΡΤΥΡΙΟΝ· ΟΤΙ
ΕΙ ΤΕΘΕΡΑΠΕΥΤΑΙ ΟΥ
ΤΟΣ ΕΦ ΟΥ ΕΙΡΗΚΑΤΕ
ΟΥΔΕΙΣ ΑΛΛ Η Ο ΧΣ
ΜΟΝΟΣ ΑΥΤΟΝ ΙΑ
ΣΕΤΑΙ· ΗΛΘΕΝ
Ο ΧΣ ΚΑΙ ΠΙΣΤΕΥΣΑ
ΤΕ ΑΥΤΩ·

32. Philemon 10–25. Gregory–Aland 1739. x cent.

MOUNT ATHOS, LAURA 184 (B'64), FOL. 102 RECTO.

Parchment codex, containing the Acts of the Apostles, the Catholic and Pauline Epistles, x century, 9⅟16 × 6⅞ inches (23 × 17.5 cm.), 102 leaves, one column, an average of 35 lines to the page.

This interesting and important manuscript was written by a monk named Ephraim, from whose pen at least three other manuscripts have survived. He copied MS. 1739 from an uncial exemplar that contained a large number of notes drawn from Irenaeus, Clement of Alexandria, Origen, Eusebius, and Basil. Since no comment is assigned to a writer more recent than Basil (A.D. 329–379), it appears that the ancestor of 1739 was written toward the close of the fourth century. A superscription to the Pauline Epistles (fol. 44 verso) indicates that the scribe of this fourth-century exemplar used a manuscript which contained an Origenian type of text. This, however, was not of the Caesarean type but of a relatively pure form of the Alexandrian type. For example, along with 𝔭[46] B* ℵ* in Eph. 1:1 MS. 1739 lacks ἐν Ἐφέσῳ. Zuntz finds close links between the archetype of 1739 and 𝔭[46] and B.

Above line 1 after ἐν τοῖς δεσμοῖς a corrector has added μου, thereby conforming the text to that of ℵ[c] C D[c] E K L P *al* and the Textus Receptus. Several notes stand in the right-hand margin: opposite line 1, ὁμ(οίως) Ὠρ(ι)γ(ένης); opposite line 3, καὶ αὐτό(ς) ὁμοίως τοῦ προσλαβοῦ οὐκ ἐμνημόνευσε, with a horizontal line (*obelos*) extending into the left-hand margin and a mark of reference in the text before προσλαβοῦ (ver. 12), a word which is lacking in ℵ* A F[gr] G[gr] *al*; opposite line 5, τ(έ)λ(ος) ⌈ with the abbreviation of τέλος in the text following τοῦ εὐαγγελίου (ver. 13); opposite line 12, ἑρμ(ενεία), and opposite lines 13 and 14, ⁒ ἐγώ σου ἀπολαύσω ἐν κ(υρί)ῳ [this is an interpretation of the second part of ver. 20, to which it is linked by ⁒ over ὀναίμην].

Following the text are several superscriptions: lines 21–22, πρὸς Φιλήμονα ἐγράφη ἀπὸ Ῥώμης διὰ Τυχικοῦ καὶ Ὀνησίμου. In smaller letters to the left of lines 21–22, and to the right of line 22, τέλος σὺν θ(ε)ῷ ἀγ (ἅγιον ?) τῶν καθολικῶν ἐπιστολῶν τῶν ἁγίων ἀποστόλων.

Lines 23–29, μετελήφθησαν καὶ αἱ ιδ̄ Παύλου ἐπιστολ(αί). ἐκ τοῦ αὐτοῦ ἀντιγρά|φου· πρὸς ὃ καὶ ἀντεξητάσθησαν ἐπιμελῶς ὡς ἐνεδέχετο· | ὅπερ ἀντίγραφον πρὸς τῶι τέλει τὴν ὑποσημείωσιν εἶχε ταύτη(ν): | δόξα τῶι ἐλεήμονι θεῶι. ἀμήν: | διὰ τὴν ἀγάπην τοῦ Χ(ριστο)ῦ ὁ ἀναγινώσκων. ὑπερευξάσθω τῆς | ἁμαρτωλῆς ψυχῆς τοῦ γράψαντος. Ἐφραὶμ μοναχοῦ:— | ὁ θ(εό)ς ἱλάσθητί μοι τῶι ἁμαρτωλῶι. ἀμήν.

The lower portion of this, the final leaf, has been cut off.

BIBLIOGRAPHY: E. von der Goltz, *Eine textkritische Arbeit des zehnten bezw. sechsten Jahrhunderts* (Texte und Untersuchungen, N.F. ii. 4; Berlin, 1899); Otto Bauernfeind, *Der Römerbrieftext des Origens* (Texte und Untersuchungen, 3te Reihe, xiv. 3; Berlin, 1923); *Six Collations of New Testament Manuscripts*, ed. by Kirsopp Lake and Silva New (Harvard Theological Studies, xvii; Cambridge, Massachusetts, 1932), pp. 141–219; Kirsopp and Silva Lake, 'The Scribe Ephraim,' *Journal of Biblical Literature*, lxii (1943), pp. 263–8; Aubrey Diller, 'Notes on Greek Codices of the Tenth Century,' *Transactions and Proceedings of the American Philological Association*, lxxvii (1947), pp. 184–8, esp. 186; K. W. Kim, 'Codices 1582, 1739, and Origen,' *Journal of Biblical Literature*, lxix (1950), pp. 167–75; G. Zuntz, *The Text of the Epistles; a Disquisition upon the* Corpus Paulinum (London, 1953), pp. 68–84; idem, 'A Piece of Early Christian Rhetoric in the New Testament Manuscript 1739,' *Opuscula Selecta . . .* (Manchester, 1972), pp. 284–90; and J. Neville Birdsall, 'A Study of MS. 1739 of the Pauline Epistles and its Relationship to MSS. 6, 424, 1908, and M,' unpublished Ph.D. dissertation, University of Nottingham, 1959; and idem, 'The Text and Scholia of the Codex von der Goltz and its Allies, and their Bearing upon the Texts of the Works of Origen, especially the Commentary on Romans,' *Origeniana, premier colloque international des études origéniennes*, Monserrat 1973 (Quaderni di 'Vetera christianorum,' 12; Bari, 1975), pp. 215–21.

For the work and influence of the scribe Ephraem, see J. Irigoin, 'Le scriptorium d'Ephrem,' *Scriptorium*, xiii (1959), pp. 181–95, and A. Diller, 'The Age of Some Early Greek Classical Manuscripts,' *Serta Turyniana*, ed. by John L. Heller (Urbana, 1974), pp. 514–24.

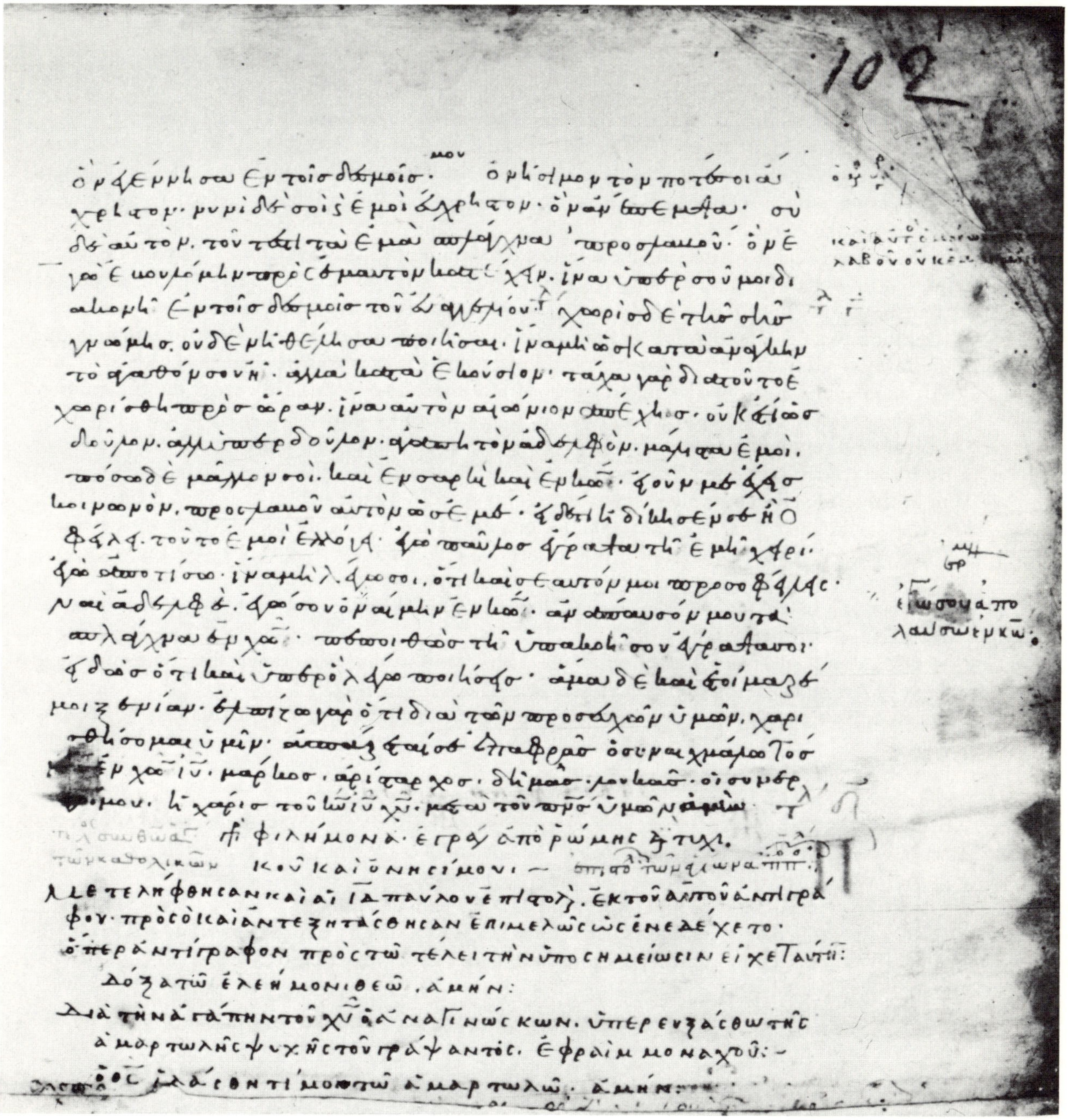

ὃν ἐγέννησα ἐν τοῖς δεσμοῖς μου Ὀνήσιμον τὸν ποτέ σοι ἄ-
χρηστον· νυνὶ δὲ σοὶ καὶ ἐμοὶ εὔχρηστον· ὃν ἀνέπεμψα· σὺ
δὲ αὐτόν, τοῦτ᾽ ἔστι τὰ ἐμὰ σπλάγχνα προσλαβοῦ· ὃν ἐ-
γὼ ἐβουλόμην πρὸς ἐμαυτὸν κατέχειν· ἵνα ὑπὲρ σοῦ μοι δι-
ακονῇ ἐν τοῖς δεσμοῖς τοῦ εὐαγγελίου· χωρὶς δὲ τῆς σῆς
γνώμης οὐδὲν ἠθέλησα ποιῆσαι· ἵνα μὴ ὡς κατὰ ἀνάγκην
τὸ ἀγαθόν σου ᾖ· ἀλλὰ κατὰ ἑκούσιον· τάχα γὰρ διὰ τοῦτο ἐ-
χωρίσθη πρὸς ὥραν· ἵνα αἰώνιον αὐτὸν ἀπέχῃς· οὐκ ἔτι ὡς
δοῦλον· ἀλλ᾽ ὑπὲρ δοῦλον· ἀδελφὸν ἀγαπητόν· μάλιστα ἐμοί·
πόσῳ δὲ μᾶλλον σοὶ καὶ ἐν σαρκὶ καὶ ἐν κυρίῳ· εἰ οὖν με ἔχεις
κοινωνόν, προσλαβοῦ αὐτὸν ὡς ἐμέ· εἰ δέ τι ἠδίκησέ σε ἢ ὀ-
φείλει, τοῦτο ἐμοὶ ἐλλόγα· ἐγὼ Παῦλος ἔγραψα τῇ ἐμῇ χειρί·
ἐγὼ ἀποτίσω· ἵνα μὴ λέγω σοι, ὅτι καὶ σεαυτόν μοι προσοφείλεις·
ναὶ ἀδελφέ· ἐγώ σου ὀναίμην ἐν κυρίῳ· ἀνάπαυσόν μου τὰ
σπλάγχνα ἐν χῷ· πεποιθὼς τῇ ὑπακοῇ σου ἔγραψά σοι·
εἰδὼς ὅτι καὶ ὑπὲρ ὃ λέγω ποιήσεις· ἅμα δὲ καὶ ἑτοίμαζέ
μοι ξενίαν· ἐλπίζω γὰρ ὅτι διὰ τῶν προσευχῶν ὑμῶν χαρι-
σθήσομαι ὑμῖν· ἀσπάζεταί σε Ἐπαφρᾶς ὁ συναιχμάλωτός
μου ἐν χῷ ἰῦ· Μάρκος· Ἀρίσταρχος· Δημᾶς· Λουκᾶς· οἱ συνερ-
γοί μου. ἡ χάρις τοῦ κῦ ἰῦ χῦ μετὰ τοῦ πνεύματος ὑμῶν· ἀμήν

πρὸς Φιλήμονα ἐγράφη ἀπὸ Ῥώμης διὰ Τυχικοῦ καὶ Ὀνησίμου —

ἐτελειώθησαν καὶ αἱ ιδ΄ Παύλου ἐπιστολ(αί). ἐκ τοῦ αὐτοῦ ἀντιγρά-
φου· πρὸς ὃ καὶ ἀντεξητάσθησαν ἐπιμελῶς ὡς ἐνεδέχετο.
ὅπερ ἀντίγραφον πρὸς τῷ τέλει τὴν ὑποσημείωσιν εἶχε ταύτην:
δόξα τῷ ἐλεήμονι θεῷ. ἀμήν:
διὰ τὴν ἀγάπην τοῦ χῦ οἱ ἀναγινώσκοντες, ὑπερεύξασθε τῆς
ἁμαρτωλῆς ψυχῆς τοῦ γράψαντος. Ἐφραὶμ μοναχοῦ:-
[illegible] ἁμαρτωλῷ. ἀμήν:

33. John 19:10–16; Matthew 27:3–5. Gregory–Aland *l*562. A.D. 991.

ROME, BIBLIOTECA VATICANA, GR. 2138, FOL. 29 VERSO.

Parchment codex, containing a Gospel lectionary (with lacunae), dated A.D. 991, 10⅛ × 7½ inches (25.9 × 18.5 cm.), 91 leaves, two columns, 29 lines to a column.

This carefully written Gospel lectionary has elaborate initials in yellow, blue, green, and carmine; some of them are zoomorphic. The scribe has also occasionally colored the interior of letters in the text, e.g. *omicron* (col. *a*, lines 12 and 19; col. *b*, line 2) and *pi* (col. *a*, line 4). The writing is pendent from the ruled lines.

The title ευαγγελιον ε̄, written in uncial letters (col. *b*, lines 13–14), refers to the fifth of the twelve lections of the Passion of Jesus Christ, read on Holy Thursday (Matt. 27:3–32). The latter part of the fourth lection (John 18:28–19:16) stands in col. *a* and the first part of col. *b*.

According to a colophon on fol. 52 recto, Kyriakos, monk and presbyter, wrote the manuscript in the town of Capua, and another on fol. 91 recto states that it was finished in the year (of the world) 6499, in the fourth indiction, on the twelfth of June. The equivalent year of the Incarnation is also given: ἀπὸ δὲ τῆς ἐνανθρωπήσεως τοῦ κυρίου Ἰησοῦ Χριστοῦ ἔτη ἐννακόσια ἐνενήκοντα ἕν : ϡϟα.

Several kinds of modifications have been made in the text. Wishing to give emphasis to οὐδεμίαν in John 19:11, someone erased the words κα|τ' ἐμοῦ at the end of the clause (col. *a*, lines 5–6), wrote them in the left-hand margin, and keyed the marginal note by the siglum ·|· (which is also placed after ἐξουσίαν in line 5), thus directing the lector to read the text in the sequence οὐκ εἶχες ἐξουσίαν κατ' ἐμοῦ οὐδεμίαν. This order of words is also read by 𝔭[66 vid] ℵ B D[supp] K L X 1, 33, 124, 157 *et al.*

In line 12, in order to make doubly certain that no one will misunderstand to whom the pronoun αὐτόν refers, it is deleted by a stroke and the lector is advised by a note in the margin to replace it with τὸν Ἰ(ησοῦ)ν.

At the end of line 2 from the bottom of col. *a* the word δέ has been erased, thereby conforming the text (John 19:14) to that of MS. 157 and several other witnesses.

In col. *b*, lines 15–16, a new lection opens with the conventional incipit τῷ καιρῷ ἐκείνῳ (see §29 end), followed by a lozenge. At the opening of the new lection (Ἰδὼν Ἰούδας ὅτι κατεκρίθη, Matt. 27:3) the text is expanded by an addition, written in small letters, so as to read Ἰδὼν ὁ Ἰούδας ὁ παραδιδοὺς αὐτὸν ὅτι κατεκρίθη.

In the lower margin stands τριάκοντα which, by a conventional siglum, the lector is advised to insert between τὰ and ἀργύρια in line 3 from the bottom of col. *b*, thus conforming the text of Matt. 27:5 to that of ℵ 047, 122.

The scribe uses καί-compendium (col. *a*, lines 22 and 29; col. *b*, line 21). The question mark after σε (col. *a*, line 3) is partly combined with the *epsilon.* Occasionally double accent marks (see footnote 20 above) stand on δέ̋ (col. *b*, line 3 from top and line 5 from bottom).

BIBLIOGRAPHY: See the literature mentioned in §29.

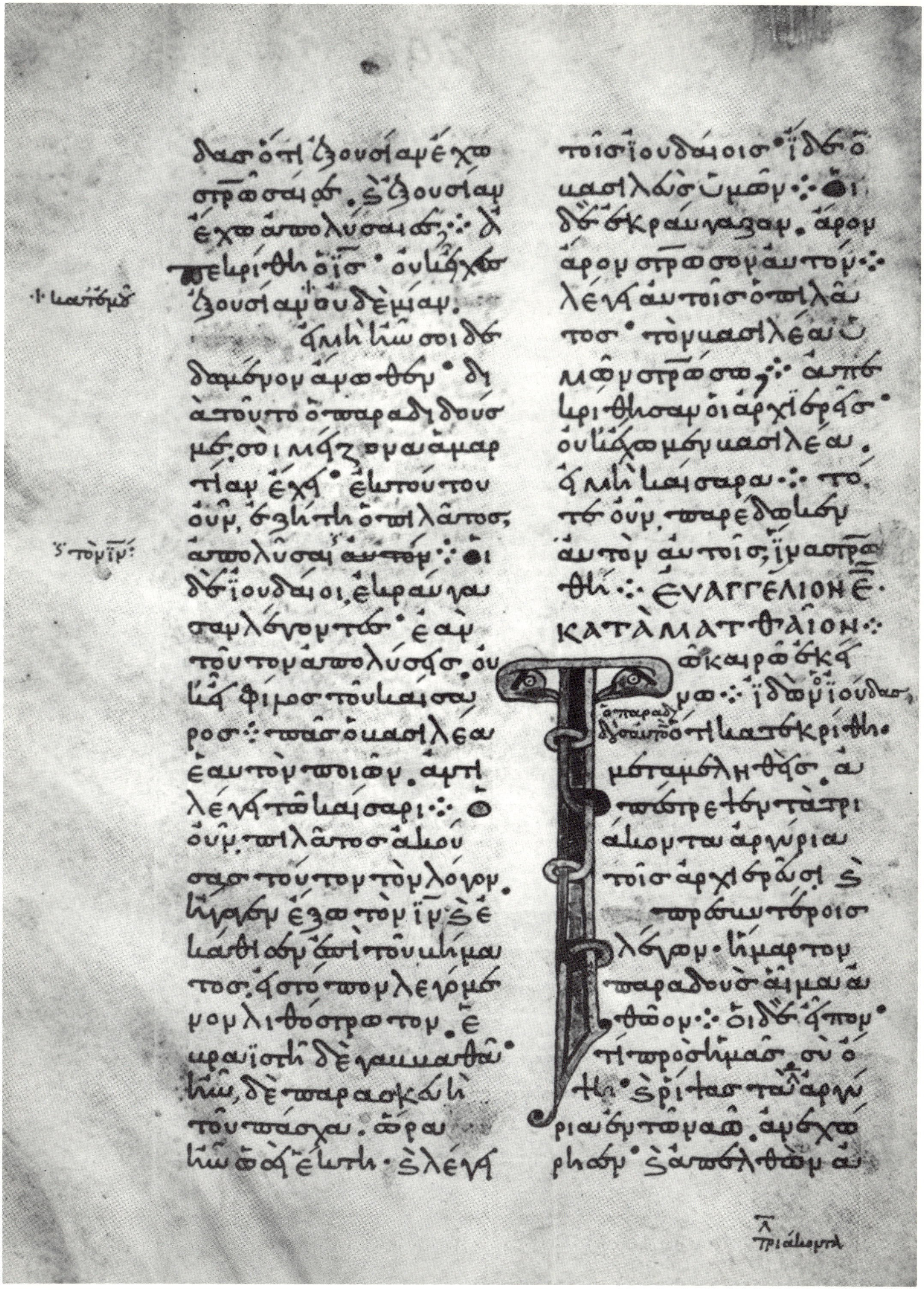

κατ᾿ ἐμοῦ

δας ὅτι ἐξουσίαν ἔχω
σταυρῶσαί σε, καὶ ἐξουσίαν
ἔχω ἀπολῦσαί σε; ὁ δὲ
ἀπεκρίθη ὁ ἰς· οὐκ εἶχες
ἐξουσίαν οὐδεμίαν·
εἰ μὴ ἦν σοι δε-
δομένον ἄνωθεν· διὰ
τοῦτο ὁ παραδιδούς
με σοι μείζονα ἁμαρ-
τίαν ἔχει· ἐκ τούτου
οὖν ἐζήτει ὁ Πιλᾶτος,
καὶ τὸν ἰν
ἀπολῦσαι αὐτόν· οἱ
δὲ ἰουδαῖοι ἐκραύγα-
ζον λέγοντες· ἐὰν
τοῦτον ἀπολύσῃς, οὐκ
εἶ φίλος τοῦ καίσα-
ρος· πᾶς ὁ βασιλέα
ἑαυτὸν ποιῶν, ἀντι-
λέγει τῷ καίσαρι· ὁ
οὖν Πιλᾶτος ἀκού-
σας τοῦτον τὸν λόγον,
ἤγαγεν ἔξω τὸν ἰν καὶ ἐ-
κάθισεν ἐπὶ τοῦ βήμα-
τος εἰς τόπον λεγόμε-
νον λιθόστρωτον· ἑ-
βραϊστὶ δὲ γαββαθᾶ·
ἦν δὲ παρασκευὴ
τοῦ πάσχα· ὥρα
ἦν ὡσεὶ ἕκτη· καὶ λέγει

τοῖς ἰουδαίοις· ἴδε ὁ
βασιλεὺς ὑμῶν· οἱ
δὲ ἐκραύγασαν· ἆρον
ἆρον σταύρωσον αὐτόν·
λέγει αὐτοῖς ὁ Πιλᾶ-
τος· τὸν βασιλέα ὑ-
μῶν σταυρώσω; ἀπε-
κρίθησαν οἱ ἀρχιερεῖς·
οὐκ ἔχομεν βασιλέα,
εἰ μὴ καίσαρα· τό-
τε οὖν παρέδωκεν
αὐτὸν αὐτοῖς, ἵνα σταυ-
ρωθῇ· ΕΥΑΓΓΕΛΙΟΝ Ε
ΚΑΤΑ ΜΑΤΘΑΙΟΝ·
Τῷ καιρῷ ἐκεί-
νῳ· ἰδὼν ἰούδας,
ὁ παραδι-
δοὺς αὐτὸν ὅτι κατεκρίθη·
μεταμεληθεὶς ἀ-
πέστρεψε τὰ τρι-
άκοντα ἀργύρια
τοῖς ἀρχιερεῦσι καὶ
πρεσβυτέροις
λέγων· ἥμαρτον
παραδοὺς αἷμα ἀ-
θῷον· οἱ δὲ εἶπον·
τί πρὸς ἡμᾶς; σὺ ὄ-
ψει· καὶ ῥίψας τὰ ἀργύ-
ρια ἐν τῷ ναῷ· ἀνεχώ-
ρησεν· καὶ ἀπελθὼν ἀ-

λ
τριάκοντα

33

34. Isaiah 61:1–5. Prophetologion. xi cent.

JERUSALEM, GREEK PATRIARCHAL LIBRARY, SABA 247, FOL. 124 RECTO.

Parchment codex, containing a Prophetologion (with lacunae), xi century, 11 × 8⅝ inches (28 × 22 cm.), 188 leaves, two columns, 23 lines to a column.

Prophetologion is the term used to designate a collection of Scripture lessons drawn from the Greek Old Testament. The name indicates the great part played by the lessons taken from the prophets, among whom Isaiah is prominent, but there are also many lessons from the Octateuch and Proverbs and a few from other books of the Old Testament. In comparison with the number of Greek lectionaries of the New Testament (namely 2209; see Appendix III), the number of copies of the Prophetologion known to scholars is relatively few—only about 160 manuscripts, dating from the ninth to the sixteenth century. According to Höeg and Zuntz, a very marked uniformity characterizes the manuscripts of the Prophetologion. This uniformity is all the more striking when one considers that a lesson is a veritable cento made up of verses separated in the original text. No less obvious is the uniformity of the liturgical instructions, which are much fuller here than in the Gospel lectionaries.

Written in a typical minuscule hand of the eleventh century, Saba MS. 247 is equipped with neumes for the cantillation of the Scripture text. The Plate shows the decorative headpiece at the beginning of the reading for September 1st (*μηνὶ*[1] *Σεπτεμβρίῳ α̅*). Within the headpiece it is indicated that at the 'beginning of the Indiction,' *ἀρχ(ὴ) τῆς ἰνδ(ικτιῶνος)* the passage from Isaiah[2] is to be used in memory of 'St. Simeon the Stylite,' *εἰς ὅσ(ιον) Συμε(ῶνα) τὸν στυλί(την)*.

A collation of the Scripture text shown on the Plate against the text of the edition of the Prophetologion prepared by Höeg and Zuntz (pp. 469 f.) discloses the following variant readings:

	column *a*		column *b*
line 10	*αναβλεψιν*] + *αποστειλαι τεθραυσμενους εν αφεσει*	line 17	*πολεις*] *πολης ερημους*
		line 19	*και*] *εις*

A collation against the text of Isaiah in the Göttingen Septuagint edited by Joseph Ziegler (*Isaias*, 1935) discloses the following variant readings:

Isaiah 61:1	*τη καρδια*] *την καρδιαν*
	αναβλεψιν] *αποστειλαι τεθραυσμενους εν αφεσει*
61:2	*ανταποδοσεως*] + *τῳ θ(ε)ῳ ημων*
61:3	*σποδου*] *σπονδου*
	αντι πενθους] *τοις πενθουσι*
	γεναι] *γενεα*
61:4	*προτερας*] *το προτερον*
	καινιουσι] *ανακαινιουσιν*
	πολεις] *πολη*
	εις γενεας] *απο γενεας εις γενεας*

BIBLIOGRAPHY: Alfred Rahlfs, *Die alttestamentlichen Lektionen der griechischen Kirche* (Göttingen, 1915); Carsten Höeg and Günther Zuntz, 'Remarks on the Prophetologion,' *Quantulacumque; Studies Presented to Kirsopp Lake by Pupils, Colleagues and Friends*, ed. by Robert P. Casey et al. (London, 1937), pp. 189–226; G. Zuntz, 'Das byzantinische Septuagint-Lektionar ("Prophetologion"),' *Classica et Mediaevalia*, xvii (1956), pp. 183–98; *Prophetologium*, ed. by Carsten Höeg and Günther Zuntz (Monumenta musicae byzantinae, Lectionaria, vol. 1, fasc. 1–6; Copenhagen, 1939–70).

[1] The first three letters of *μηνι* are written as a ligature.

[2] The passage begins with Is. 61:1–10; according to Rahlfs (*Die alttestamentlichen Lektionen der griechischen Kirche*, 1915, pp. 139 f.) it continues with Lev. 26 (abbreviated) and Wis. 4:7–15.

+ ΜΗΝΙ ΣΕΠΤΕΜΒΡΙΩ Α +

προφητείας ἡσαΐου.
Πνεῦμα κυρίου ἐπ' ἐμέ· οὗ
εἵνεκεν ἔχρισέν με·
εὐαγγελίσασθαι πτωχοῖς
ἀπέσταλκέν με· ἰάσα-
σθαι τοὺς συντετριμ-
μένους τὴν καρδίαν·
κηρύξαι αἰχμαλώ-
τοις ἄφεσιν· καὶ τυ-
φλοῖς ἀνάβλεψιν·
ἀποστεῖλαι τεθραυ-
σμένους ἐν ἀφέσει·
καλέσαι ἐνιαυτὸν
κυρίου δεκτόν· καὶ ἡμέ-
ραν ἀνταποδόσε-
ως· τῷ θεῷ ἡμῶν· πα-
ρακαλέσαι πάντας τοὺς πεν-
θοῦντας· τοῦ δοθῆναι
τοῖς πενθοῦσι σιὼν·
δόξαν ἀντὶ σποδοῦ·
ἄλειμμα εὐφροσύνης
τοῖς πενθοῦσι· κατα-
στολὴν δόξης ἀντὶ πνεύματος
ἀκηδίας· καὶ κληθή-
σονται γενεαὶ δικαι-
οσύνης· φύτευμα κυρίου
εἰς δόξαν· καὶ οἰκοδο-
μήσουσιν ἐρήμους αἰ-
ωνίας· ἐξηρημωμέν-
ας τὸ πρότερον· ἐ-
ξαναστήσουσι· καὶ ἀνα-
καινιοῦσιν· πόλεις
ἐρήμους ἐξηρημωμέ-
νας· ἀπὸ γενεῶν εἰς γε-
νεάς· καὶ ἥξουσιν ἀλ-
λογενεῖς· ποιμαίνοντες
τὰ πρόβατά σου·
καὶ ἀλλόφυλοι ἀροτῆρ-

35. Jude 3–25. Gregory–Aland 623. A.D. 1037.

ROME, BIBLIOTECA VATICANA, GR. 1650, FOL. 31 RECTO.

Parchment codex, containing the Acts of the Apostles, the Catholic and Pauline Epistles (followed by the homilies of St. John Chrysostom on the Acts of the Apostles), dated A.D. 1037, 13⅝ × 10⅝ inches (34.6 × 27 cm.), 187 leaves, two columns, average of 43 lines to a column.

A colophon on fol. 186 recto gives the name of the scribe, the place, the name of the bishop, and the date when he finished writing the manuscript: *ἐγράφη αὕτη ἡ | δέλτος διὰ χειρὸς Θεοδώρου | κληρικοῦ Σικελιώτου κατ' ἐ|πιτροπὴν Νικολάου ἐπισκόπου | κτήτορος ταύτης. ἐν ἔτει ἀπὸ | κτίσεως κόσμου ἔτ. ,ςφμε ἰνδ. ε̄ | κύκλῳ (σελήνης) θ̄ κύ(κλῳ) (ἡλίου) κα̅ κ(αὶ) ἐπληρώθ(η) μη(νὶ) | ἰαννουαρίῳ εἰς τὸν αὐτὸν ☧* [1] | *ἡμέ(ρᾳ) (πρώτῃ) ὥρᾳ γ̄.*

The numbers Β Γ Δ in the left-hand margin of the columns signify the beginning of the chapters, the titles of which stand in the upper and lower margins. The title at the top of col. *a* is the second part of the first title, continued from the preceding page; the second part refers to verses 5–10: *ἐν ᾧ πε(ρὶ) μελλούσης αὐτῶν κολάσεως καθ' ὁμοίωσιν τῶν πάλαι ἁμαρτημάτων τε καὶ πονηρῶν*. The title at the foot of col. *a* refers to verses 11–16: *Β̄ ταλανισμὸς αὐτῶν ἐπὶ τῇ πλάνῃ καὶ δυσεβείᾳ* (*sic*) *καὶ ἀσελγίᾳ καὶ βλασφημίᾳ καὶ ἐπιπλάστου ὑποκρίσεως τῇ εἰς ἀπάτην δοροδοκίᾳ*. The title at the foot of col. *b* refers to verses 17–23: *Γ̄ πε(ρὶ) ἀσφαλείας αὐτῶν ἐπὶ τῇ πίστει συμπαθείας τε καὶ φειδοῦς εἰς τὸν πλησίον ἐπὶ σωτηρίᾳ ἐν ἁγιασμῷ*. The title for Δ̄, verses 24–25, is lacking.

The notes that stand in the left-hand margin of each column are part of the Euthalian apparatus (see §27). In col. *a*, lines 27 f., the statement about Michael the archangel contending with the devil (ver. 9) is identified in the margin as from the apocryphal book known as the Assumption of Moses, and in col. *b*, lines 7 f., the quotation (verses 14–15) is identified as from the apocryphal book of Enoch.

At the conclusion of col. *b* is the subscription *Ἰούδα ἐπιστολὴ καθολική*. Between lines 10 and 11 of col. *a* a corrector has added the word *τοῦτο*, which is intended to replace *πάντα* in line 11 (ver. 5). Among other witnesses *πάντα* is read by ℵ A B *al*; *τοῦτο* is read by K L and the great mass of minuscule manuscripts.

The Plate shows the page reduced in size.

BIBLIOGRAPHY: For an encyclopedic survey of all known textual evidence for the Epistle of Jude, see C. A. Albin, *Judasbrevet, traditionen, texten, tolkningen* (Stockholm, 1962), pp. 143–590 (for a collation of MS. 623, see p. 389).

[1] For the Christogram (*chi-rho* monogram), see the literature cited in the footnote attached to the description of Plate 17.

ἐν ᾧ περὶ μελλούσης αὐτῶν κολάσεως καθομοιοῖ σιν τῶν πάλαι ἁμαρτημάτων τε καὶ πονηριῶν·

φ(ησὶ) μὲν ... περὶ τῆς κοινῆς ἡμῶν σωτηρί
ας ἀνάγκην ἔσχον γράψαι ὑμῖν παρα
καλῶν ἐπαγωνίζεσθαι τῇ ἅπαξ πα
ραδοθείσῃ τοῖς ἁγίοις πίστει· παρεισέ
δυσαν γάρ τινες ἄνθρωποι οἱ πάλαι προγε
γραμμένοι εἰς τοῦτο τὸ κρίμα ἀσε
βεῖς τὴν τοῦ θεοῦ ἡμῶν χάριν μετατι
θέντες εἰς ἀσέλγειαν· καὶ τὸν μόνον
δεσπότην θεὸν καὶ κύριον ἡμῶν Ἰησοῦν Χριστὸν ἀρνού
μενοι· ὑπομνῆσαι δὲ ὑμᾶς βούλομαι
εἰδότας ὑμᾶς ἅπαξ τοῦτο ὅτι ὁ θεὸς
λαὸν ἐκ γῆς Αἰγύπτου σώσας· τὸ δεύ
τερον τοὺς μὴ πιστεύσαντας ἀπώ
λεσεν· ἀγγέλους τε τοὺς μὴ τηρήσαν
τας τὴν ἑαυτῶν ἀρχὴν ἀλλὰ ἀπο
λείποντας τὸ ἴδιον οἰκητήριον· εἰς
κρίσιν μεγάλης ἡμέρας δεσμοῖς ἀϊδί
οις ὑπὸ ζόφον τετήρηκεν· ὡς Σό
δομα καὶ Γόμορρα καὶ αἱ περὶ αὐτὰς
πόλεις τὸν ὅμοιον τρόπον τούτοις ἐκ
πορνεύσασαι· καὶ ἀπελθοῦσαι
ὀπίσω σαρκὸς ἑτέρας· πρόκεινται
δεῖγμα πυρὸς αἰωνίου δίκην ὑπέ
χουσαι· ὁμοίως μέντοι καὶ οὗτοι ἐνυ
πνιαζόμενοι σάρκα μὲν μιαίνουσιν
κυριότητα δὲ ἀθετοῦσιν δόξας δὲ
βλασφημοῦσιν· ὁ δὲ Μιχαὴλ ὁ (Μωϋσέως ἀπόκρυφον)
ἀρχάγγελος ὅτε τῷ διαβόλῳ διακρι
νόμενος διελέγετο περὶ τοῦ Μωϋσέως
σώματος· οὐκ ἐτόλμησεν κρίσιν
ἐπενεγκεῖν βλασφημίας ἀλλ' εἶπεν
ἐπιτιμήσαι σοι κύριος· οὗτοι δὲ ὅσα
μὲν οὐκ οἴδασιν βλασφημοῦσιν· ὅσα
δὲ φυσικῶς ὡς τὰ ἄλογα ζῷα ἐπί
στανται ἐν τούτοις φθείρονται·

β̅ Οὐαὶ αὐτοῖς ὅτι τῇ ὁδῷ τοῦ Κάϊν ἐ
πορεύθησαν καὶ τῇ πλάνῃ τοῦ
Βαλαὰμ μισθοῦ ἐξεχύθησαν καὶ τῇ
ἀντιλογίᾳ τοῦ Κορὲ ἀπώλοντο·
οὗτοί εἰσιν οἱ ἐν ταῖς ἀγάπαις ὑμῶν
σπιλάδες συνευωχούμενοι ἀφόβως
ἑαυτοὺς ποιμαίνοντες· νεφέλαι
ἄνυδροι ὑπὸ ἀνέμων παραφερόμε
ναι·

δένδρα φθινοπωρινὰ ἄκαρπα δὶς
ἀποθανόντα ἐκριζωθέντα· κύματα
ἄγρια θαλάσσης ἐπαφρίζοντα τὰς ἑαυ
τῶν αἰσχύνας· ἀστέρες πλανῆται οἷς ὁ
ζόφος τοῦ σκότους εἰς αἰῶνα τετήρηται·
προεφήτευσεν δὲ καὶ τούτοις ἕβδομος (Ἐνὼχ ἀπόκρυφον)
ἀπὸ Ἀδὰμ Ἐνὼχ λέγων· ἰδοὺ ἦλθεν
κύριος ἐν ἁγίαις μυριάσιν αὐτοῦ ποιῆσαι
κρίσιν κατὰ πάντων καὶ ἐλέγξαι πάν
τας τοὺς ἀσεβεῖς περὶ πάντων τῶν
ἔργων ἀσεβείας αὐτῶν ὧν ἠσέβησαν
καὶ περὶ πάντων τῶν σκληρῶν ὧν ἐ
λάλησαν κατ' αὐτοῦ ἁμαρτωλοὶ ἀσεβεῖς·
οὗτοί εἰσιν γογγυσταί· μεμψίμοιροι·
κατὰ τὰς ἐπιθυμίας αὐτῶν πορευό
μενοι· καὶ τὸ στόμα αὐτῶν λαλεῖ ὑπέ
ρογκα· θαυμάζοντες πρόσωπα ὠ
γ̅ φελείας χάριν· ὑμεῖς δὲ ἀγαπη
τοὶ μνήσθητε τῶν ῥημάτων τῶν προει
ρημένων ὑπὸ τῶν ἀποστόλων τοῦ
κυρίου ἡμῶν Ἰησοῦ Χριστοῦ ὅτι ἔλεγον ὑμῖν ὅτι ἐπ' ἐσ
χάτου χρόνου ἔσονται ἐμπαῖκται
κατὰ τὰς ἑαυτῶν ἐπιθυμίας πορευ
όμενοι τῶν ἀσεβειῶν· οὗτοί εἰσιν
οἱ ἀποδιορίζοντες ἑαυτοὺς ψυχικοί
πνεῦμα μὴ ἔχοντες· ὑμεῖς δὲ ἀγαπη
τοὶ ἐποικοδομοῦντες ἑαυτοὺς τῇ
ἁγιωτάτῃ ὑμῶν πίστει ἐν πνεύματι ἁγίῳ
προσευχόμενοι· ἑαυτοὺς ἐν ἀγάπῃ
θεοῦ τηρήσατε· προσδεχόμενοι τὸ
ἔλεος τοῦ κυρίου ἡμῶν Ἰησοῦ Χριστοῦ εἰς ζωὴν αἰώ
νιον· καὶ οὓς μὲν ἐλεεῖτε διακρι
νομένους· οὓς δὲ σώζετε ἐκ πυρὸς
ἁρπάζοντες· οὓς δὲ ἐλεᾶτε ἐν φόβῳ·
μισοῦντες καὶ τὸν ἀπὸ τῆς σαρκὸς
δ̅ ἐσπιλωμένον χιτῶνα· τῷ δὲ δυ
ναμένῳ φυλάξαι ὑμᾶς ἀπταίστους
καὶ στηρίξαι κατενώπιον τῆς δόξης
αὐτοῦ ἀμώμους ἐν ἀγαλλιάσει μόνῳ σοφῷ
θεῷ σωτῆρι ἡμῶν διὰ Ἰησοῦ Χριστοῦ τοῦ κυρίου ἡμῶν·
δόξα· μεγαλωσύνη· κράτος καὶ ἐξου
σία πρὸ παντὸς τοῦ αἰῶνος· καὶ νῦν
καὶ εἰς πάντας τοὺς αἰῶνας· ἀμήν·

ἸΟΥΔΑ ἘΠΙΣΤΟΛΗ ΚΑΘΟΛΙΚΗ:

β̅ [illegible] αὐτῶν ἐπὶ τῇ πλάνῃ καὶ ἀσε
βείᾳ καὶ ἀσελγείαις βλασφημίᾳ κ(αὶ) ἐπιπλά
στῳ ὑποκρίσει τῇ εἰς ἀπάτην [illegible]

γ̅ Περὶ ἀσφαλείας αὐτῶν ἐπὶ τῇ πίστει σὺν ἀπαθεί
ᾳ τε καὶ ἀφειδοῦς εἰς τὸν πλησίον ἐπὶ σωτηρίᾳ ἐν
ἁγιασμῷ·

36. Luke 21:37–38; John 7:53–8:11; Luke 22:1–3. Gregory–Aland 124. xi cent.

VIENNA, NATIONALBIBLIOTHEK, THEOL. GR. 188, FOL. 122 RECTO.

Parchment codex, containing the four Gospels (with lacunae), xi century, 8½ × 7⅜ inches (21.5 × 18.8 cm.), 188 leaves, two columns, 25 to 28 lines to a column.

Initials at the beginning of books in codex 124 are ornamented with red, blue, green, brown, and black; initials elsewhere (at the beginning of sections) are ornamented with red and blue. The Ammonian section and Eusebian canon numbers stand in the left-hand margins of the columns. The lower margin contains information regarding parallel passages in Luke, John, Mark, and Matthew. At the top of the page shown in Plate 36 stand the chapter number $\overline{o\varsigma}$ (=76) and the title πε(ρὶ) τοῦ πάσχ(α).

Written in Calabria, southern Italy, MS. 124 was formerly the property of a certain Leo John Sambuky, 'Pannonii Caesaris consul et historicus,' who brought it from Naples to Vienna in the latter half of the sixteenth century. In the nineteenth century William Hugh Ferrar, professor of Latin in the University of Dublin, made the discovery that this manuscript and three others (13, 69, and 346) are related; his collations of the four were published posthumously by T. K. Abbott. Today it is known that this group, called the Ferrar group, comprises about a dozen members, more or less closely related. They were copied between the eleventh and fifteenth centuries, and are descendants of an archetype that came either from Calabria or from Sicily. Rendel Harris, on the ground of certain affinities with the Old Syriac version, attempted to establish a Syriac origin for the most characteristic readings of the group, while in a subsequent study he argued for an Arabic medium of transmission for this Syriac influence. During the twentieth century several scholars identified the group as a constituent part of the Caesarean type of text. (See also Plate 45.)

One of the noteworthy features of the Ferrar group of manuscripts is the presence of the *pericope de adultera* (John 7:53–8:11), not in the Fourth Gospel,[1] but after Luke 21:38 (see Plate 36, col. *a*, line 5, to line 16 of col. *b*), where the reference to Mount Olivet in Luke 21:37 makes a not inappropriate context for John 8:1.

Other features that members of the Ferrar group have in common include the transfer of Luke 22:43, 44 to follow after Matt. 26:39, as well as a set of four subscriptions attached to the Gospels. These state that Matthew was written in Hebrew eight years after the Lord's Ascension, and contains 2522 ῥήματα and 2560 στίχοι (see §23); that Mark was written in Latin (ῥωμαϊστί) ten years after the Ascension with 1675 ῥήματα and 1604 στίχοι; Luke, in Greek fifteen years after, with 3803 (should be 3083) ῥήματα and 2750 στίχοι; and John, thirty-two years after with 1938 ῥήματα.

BIBLIOGRAPHY: William Hugh Ferrar, *A Collation of Four Important Manuscripts of the Gospels . . .*, ed. by T. K. Abbott (Dublin, 1877); J. Rendel Harris, *On the Origin of the Ferrar-Group* (Cambridge, 1893); idem, *Further Researches into the History of the Ferrar-Group* (London, 1900), E. A. Hutton, 'Excursus on the Ferrar Group,' *An Atlas of Textual Criticism* (Cambridge, 1911), pp. 49–53; K. and S. Lake, *Family 13 . . .* (London, 1941); Jacob Geerlings, *The Lectionary Text of Family 13 . . .* (Salt Lake City, 1959); idem, *Family 13. The Ferrar Group* (1961–64).

[1] In some manuscripts the *pericope de adultera* stands after John 7:36 (MS. 225) or after John 7:44 (several Georgian MSS.) or after 21:25 (MSS. 1 565 1076 1570 1582). It is lacking altogether in the oldest witnesses ($\mathfrak{p}^{66, 75}$ ℵ B). For a discussion of the textual evidence, including that of the versions and the Fathers, see Metzger's *A Textual Commentary on the Greek New Testament* (London, 1971), pp. 219–22.

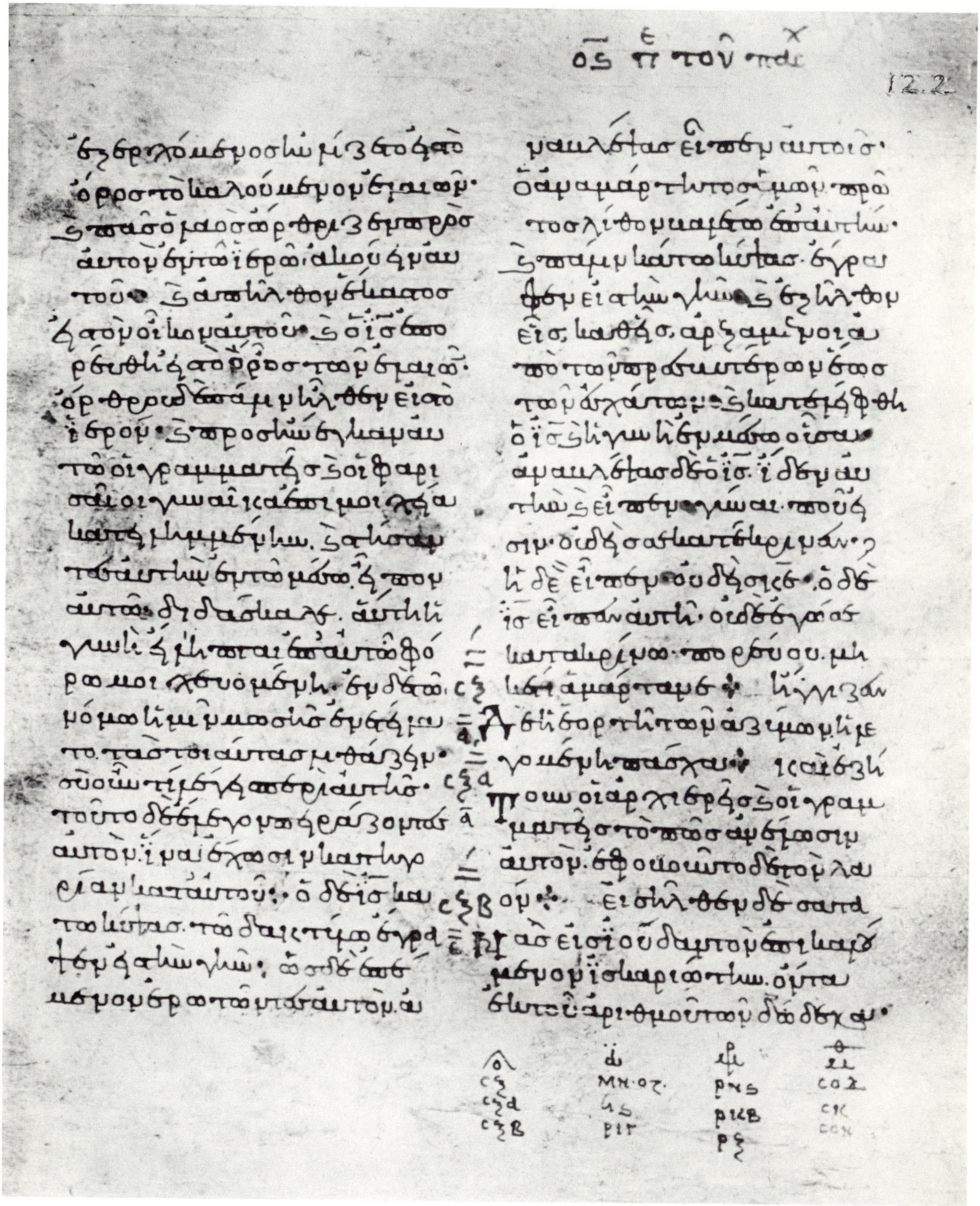

37. Luke 11:2–8. Gregory–Aland 700. xi cent.

LONDON, BRITISH LIBRARY, EGERTON 2610, FOL. 184 VERSO.

Parchment codex, containing the four Gospels, xi century, 5⅞ × 4⅝ inches (14.8 × 11.7 cm.), 297 leaves, one column, 19 lines to a page.

The manuscript was bought by the British Museum at an auction held in London in the year 1882; it was previously in the possession of a German bookseller. Each Gospel is prefixed by a beautifully executed miniature of the Evangelist, and the first letter of each Gospel is a large decorated capital in blue and gold. The numbers and titles of chapters are given in the earlier part of Matthew and Mark and in the first half of Luke, and only nine times in John. Sufficient space was left in the text for the insertion of the words ἀρχή and τέλος to mark the beginning and ending of each lection, but only in Luke and John did the original scribe insert these notations sporadically (in gold). In Matthew and Mark they were added here and there by a second hand. The scribe employs a rather wide variety of compendia and ligatures (see Hoskier, pp. xi–xiii), and is quite erratic in his (mis)use of the *iota* adscript.

The text of MS. 700 exhibits (so Hoskier) 2724 variations from the Textus Receptus (of which 791 are omissions and 353 are additions), and besides has 270 readings that are peculiar to itself. Among unusual readings are the omission of ὁ υἱός μου, Luke 3:22; the substitution of ἐβαπτίσθη for ἐδοξάσθη, John 7:39; ὀνόματι for αἵματι, Luke 22:20; and the replacement of the petition 'Thy kingdom come' in Luke's form (11:2) of the Lord's Prayer with 'Thy holy Spirit come upon us and cleanse us,' ἐλθέτω τὸ πνεῦμά σου τὸ ἅγιον ἐφ' ἡμᾶς καὶ καθαρισάτω ἡμᾶς (see lines 2 and 3 of the Plate). This reading occurs also in MS. 162 (though without ἐφ' ἡμᾶς) and was known to Marcion and/or Tertullian (in place of 'Hallowed be thy name'), to Gregory of Nyssa, and to Maximus Confessor. Although several modern scholars (including Blass, Harnack, Streeter, Leaney) have argued that this petition was original to the Lord's Prayer, it is more likely that the reading is a liturgical adaptation of the Prayer, used when celebrating the rite of baptism or the laying on of hands. The cleansing descent of the Holy Spirit is so definitely a Christian, ecclesiastical concept that one cannot understand why, if it were original in the prayer, it should have been supplanted in the overwhelming majority of the witnesses by a concept originally so much more Jewish in its piety ('Thy kingdom come').

In the left-hand margin of the page shown in the Plate are the Latin[1] abbreviation of the words *Oratio dominica* ('the Lord's Prayer'), the Ammonian section and Eusebian canon numbers identifying the passage opposite as the 124th ($\overline{\rho\kappa\delta}$) in the tenth canon ($\overline{\iota}$), and the correction δώσει replacing δίδωσιν in the text (the letters of which have been expunged by putting dots beneath them), the scribe connecting the two words by means of the siglum /. written near each.

In the upper and the right-hand margins are imprinted the mirror-image of the heading and the Eusebian apparatus from the facing page (fol. 185 recto).

BIBLIOGRAPHY: Herman C. Hoskier, *A Full Account and Collation of the Greek Cursive Codex Evangelium* 604 [=700] . . . (London, 1890); B. M. Metzger, 'The Lord's Prayer,' *Twentieth Century Encyclopedia of Religious Knowledge*, ii (Grand Rapids, 1955), p. 673; Robert Leaney, 'The Lucan Text of the Lord's Prayer,' *Novum Testamentum*, i (1956), pp. 103–11.

[1] Elsewhere in the manuscript one finds occasional Latin marginalia written by a later scribe.

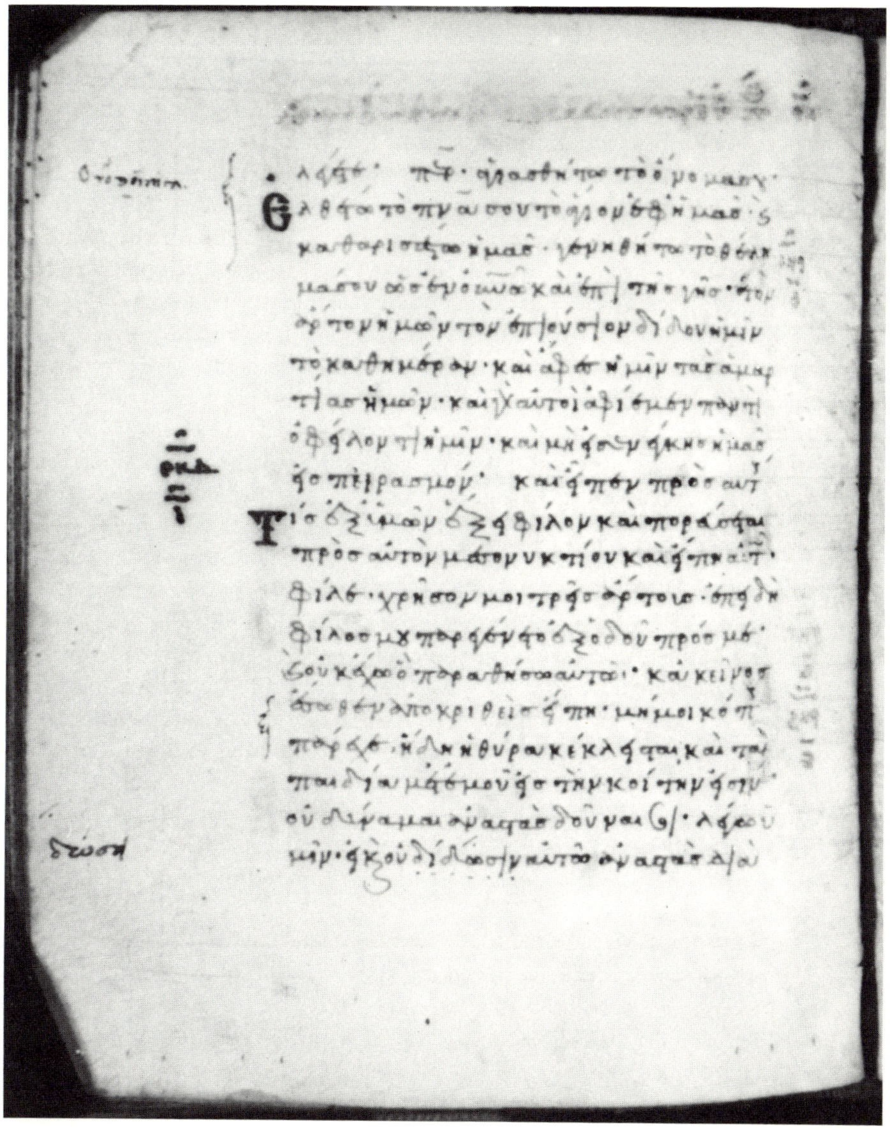

37

38. Matthew 3:10–11; John 1:19–21. Gregory–Aland *l*303. xii cent.

PRINCETON, THEOLOGICAL SEMINARY LIBRARY, 11.21.1900, FOL. 235 RECTO.

Parchment codex, containing a Gospel lectionary, xii century, 12⅜ × 10⅝ inches (31.6 × 27 cm.), 340 leaves, two columns, 23 lines to a column in the synaxarion, 20 in the menologion.

This handsome Greek Gospel lectionary was donated in the fourteenth century by the Presbyter Abul Fatḥ, son of the Presbyter Abul Badr, to the Church of Mar Saba in the diocese of Alexandria. A colophon in Greek and Arabic on fol. 1 verso declares, 'No one has authority from God to take it away under any condition, and whoever transgresses this will be under the wrath of the eternal Word of God, whose power is great. Gregory,[1] Patriarch by the grace of God, wrote this.'

As is mentioned in §29, the Greek Gospel lectionary comprises two parts, the synaxarion and the menologion. The former, beginning with Easter, presents for every day until Pentecost lessons drawn almost entirely from the Gospel according to John. From the Monday after Pentecost to approximately mid-September the lessons for Saturdays and Sundays are from Matthew, and for the other days of the week from Matthew and (from the twelfth week onward) from the first half of Mark. From about mid-September to Lent, the lessons for Saturdays and Sundays are from Luke, and for the other days of the week from Luke and (from the thirteenth week onward) from the second half of Mark. During Lent and Holy Week the lessons, some of them extensive, are provided from one or another of the four Gospels.

The menologion, which follows the civil calendar month by month, beginning with the first of September, is organized in celebration of festivals and saints' days. Except for unanimity as to the thirteen major festivals of the Church year,[2] menologia present many differences among themselves as to choice of Scripture lessons as well as of saints and festivals to be commemorated. Very often when it happens that the Scripture lesson for a particular day in the menologion is the same as a lesson already provided in the synaxarion for a given day, the actual text will not be written again in the menologion, but a rubric will direct the lector to turn to the proper section in the synaxarion.

The page reproduced in the Plate shows a page of the menologion of *l*303 for January. The lesson appointed for January 3, namely Matt. 3:1, 5–11, begins on the previous page; it ends (col. *a*, line 3 from bottom) with the words *πν(εύματ)ι ἁγίῳ*, the concluding words of the verse (*καὶ πυρί*) being absent.[3]

Following the conclusion of the lesson for January 3rd, the last two lines of col. *a* and the first seven lines of col. *b* present several rubrics in red ink (line 7 is in red and gold). With abbreviations expanded they are:

τῇ αὐτῇ ἡμέρᾳ τοῦ ἁγίου μάρτυρος Γορδίου, ζήτει [the text of the lesson appointed for] *σάββατον* $\overline{\gamma}$ *τοῦ Πάσχα.*

τῇ αὐτῇ ἡμέρᾳ τοῦ ἁγίου προφήτου Μαλαχίου, ζήτει [the text of the lesson appointed for] *τῇ* $\overline{\delta}$ *τῆς* $\overline{\iota\alpha}$ *ἑβδομάδος τοῦ Ματθαίου.*

Then follows the lesson appointed for January 4 (the numeral stands in the left-hand margin), which is the day preceding the Festival of Lights (*Προεόρτια τῶν φωτῶν*). The lesson *ἐκ τ(οῦ εὐαγγε-λίου) κατ(ὰ) Ἰω(άννου)* (John 1:19–26) begins with the customary liturgical incipit, *τῷ καιρῷ ἐκείνῳ*,[4] the initial letter of which is written in red and gold.

BIBLIOGRAPHY: B. M. Metzger, 'Studies in a Greek Gospel Lectionary (Greg. 303),' unpublished Ph.D. diss., Princeton University, 1942; idem, 'A Treasure in the Seminary Library,' *Princeton Seminary Bulletin*, xxxvi, no. 4 (March 1943), pp. 14–19. On the earlier history of the manuscript, see Caspar René Gregory, *The Independent*, 15 October 1888, p. 1343, and 24 January 1889, p. 111.

[1] It appears that this Gregory is the Melchite dignitary of that name who was the seventy-fourth Greek Patriarch of Alexandria.

[2] Cf. Morgan Ward Redus, *The Text of the Major Festivals of the Menologion in the Greek Gospel Lectionary* (Chicago, 1936).

[3] They are lacking also in E S V 28, 59, 241, 245, 349, 470, 517, 692, and a few other witnesses.

[4] The scribe uses *iota* adscript for the first two words, but omits it for the third.

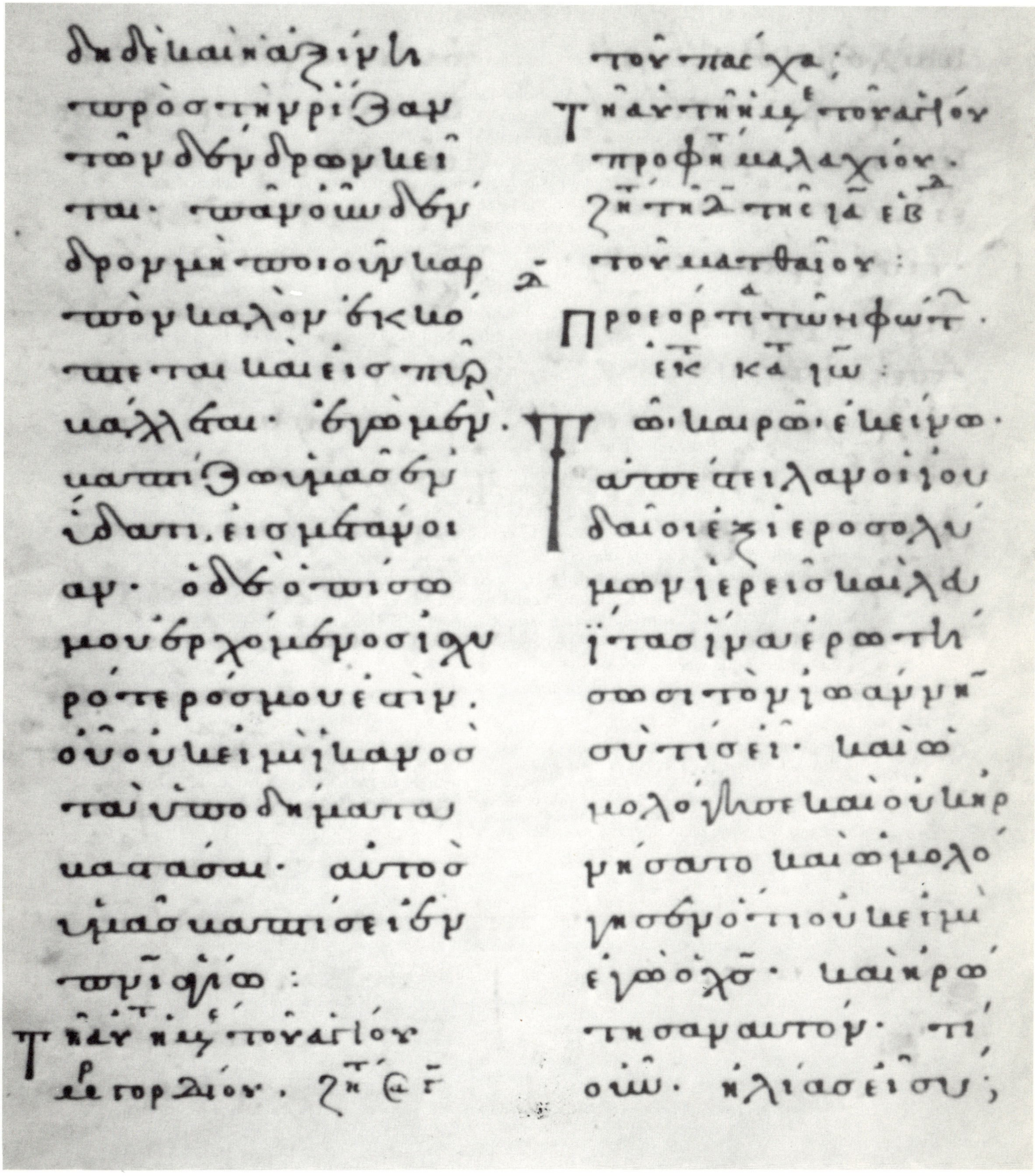

ἤδη δὲ καὶ ἡ ἀξίνη
πρὸς τὴν ῥίζαν
τῶν δένδρων κεῖ
ται· πᾶν οὖν δένδρον
μὴ ποιοῦν καρ
πὸν καλὸν ἐκκό
πτεται καὶ εἰς πῦρ
βάλλεται· ἐγὼ μὲν
βαπτίζω ὑμᾶς ἐν
ὕδατι εἰς μετάνοι
αν· ὁ δὲ ὀπίσω
μου ἐρχόμενος ἰσχυ
ρότερός μού ἐστιν·
οὗ οὐκ εἰμὶ ἱκανὸς
τὰ ὑποδήματα
βαστάσαι· αὐτὸς
ὑμᾶς βαπτίσει ἐν
πν(εύματ)ι ἁγίῳ:
Τῇ παρ(ασκευῇ) ... τοῦ ἁγίου
γρηγορίου. ζη ... ε
τοῦ πάσχα;
Τῇ αὐτῇ ἡμέρᾳ τοῦ ἁγίου
προφήτου μαλαχίου.
ζη τη ... τη ιβ
τοῦ ματθαίου:
Προεόρτια τῶν φώτων.
ἐκ κα ἰω:
Τῷ καιρῷ ἐκείνῳ·
ἀπέστειλαν οἱ ἰου
δαῖοι ἐξ ἱεροσολύ
μων ἱερεῖς καὶ λευ
ΐτας ἵνα ἐρωτή
σωσιν τὸν ἰωάννην
σὺ τίς εἶ· καὶ ὡ
μολόγησε καὶ οὐκ ἠρ
νήσατο καὶ ὡμολό
γησεν ὅτι οὐκ εἰμὶ
ἐγὼ ὁ χ(ριστό)ς· καὶ ἠρώ
τησαν αὐτόν· τί
οὖν· ἠλίας εἶ σύ;

39. Galatians 2:16–20; Colossians 2:13–14. Gregory–Aland *l*809. xii cent.

SINAI, MONASTERY OF ST. CATHERINE, GR. 286, FOL. 141 RECTO.

Parchment codex, containing an Apostolos lectionary, xii century, 11⅝ × 9 inches (29.5 × 22.8 cm.), 286 leaves, two columns, 23 lines to a column.

The structure of the Apostolos lectionary follows that of the Gospel lectionary (see the description of Plate 38), namely the Johannine section from Easter to Pentecost, the Matthean section from Monday after Pentecost to approximately mid-September, the Lukan section from mid-September to the beginning of Lent, and the Lenten and Holy Week section. The Apostolos lessons for each of the sections are usually arranged in the following sequence:

In the Johannine section lessons are chosen from the Acts of the Apostles. Out of a total of 1007 verses in this book, 583 are used at least once, and the remaining 424 verses (largely historical and narrative material) are not used in any lesson.

Of a total of 2767 verses in the New Testament Epistles, 2397 are used at least once, and the remaining 370 are not used in any lesson. It is difficult to ascertain any principle for selection and omission.[1]

The sequence of lessons for the Matthean, Lukan, and Lenten sections runs in a generally consecutive way from Romans to Jude, but there are occasional differences of selection of lessons among Apostolos manuscripts.

Lectionary 809, shown in Plate 39, contains both synaxarion and menologion as well as a concluding list of lessons for various occasions (*ἀναγνώσματα εἰς διαφόρους μνήμας καὶ λειτουργείας*). Written in a flowing yet careful hand, with enlarged initials at the beginning of the lessons, the scribe provides a decorative headpiece at the beginning of the synaxarion (fol. 1 recto) and the menologion (fol. 222 recto). Fol. 286 recto contains a prayer addressed to Christ to relieve the scribe of his troubles: Χ(*ριστ*)*ὲ παράσχου τοῖς ἐμοῖς κόποις χ*... *ἀμήν*.

The Plate shows the conclusion of the lesson for the fourth Sunday of Luke and the beginning of the lesson for Monday of the twenty-second week (*τῇ β̄ τῆς κβ̄ ἑβδομάδου*). The lesson begins, as usual in the Apostolos, with the incipit *ἀδελφοί*. The text of both lessons agrees with that of the Textus Receptus, except that at the beginning of the lesson from Colossians Χ(*ριστό*)*ς* is inserted as the subject of the verb *συνεζωποίησεν*.

The manuscript is furnished with neumes.

BIBLIOGRAPHY: Sakae Kubo, 'The Catholic Epistles in the Greek Lectionary: a Preliminary Investigation,' *Andrews University Seminary Studies*, i (1963), pp. 65–70; Ronald E. Cocroft, *A Study of the Pauline Lessons in the Matthean Section of the Greek Lectionary* (Studies and Documents, vol. xxxii; Salt Lake City, 1968); Klaus Junack, 'Zu den griechischen Lektionaren und ihrer Überlieferung der Katholischen Briefe,' *Die alten Übersetzungen des Neuen Testaments, die Kirchenväterzitate und Lektionare*, ed. K. Aland (Berlin and New York, 1972), pp. 498–591.

[1] Strangely enough, such passages as Heb. 5:7–10 and 7:26–8:6, which present Christ as high priest, are omitted, while 1 Cor. 16:13–24, which contains Paul's personal greetings and remarks to and about specific individuals, is included.

δικαιωθῶμεν ἐκ
πίστεως χυ· καὶ οὐ
κ ἐξ ἔργων νόμου· διό
ὅτι· οὐ δικαιωθήσε
ται ἐξ ἔργων νόμου
πᾶσα σάρξ· εἰ δὲ
ζητοῦντες δικαιω
θῆναι ἐν χω· εὑρέθη
μεν καὶ αὐτοὶ ἁμαρ
τωλοί· ἆρα χς ἁμαρ
τίας διάκονος· μὴ
γένοιτο· εἰ γὰρ ἃ κα
τέλυσα· ταῦτα
πάλιν οἰκοδομῶ
παραβάτην ἐ
μαυτὸν συνιστάνω·
ἐγὼ γὰρ διὰ νόμου·
νόμῳ ἀπέθανον,
ἵνα θεῷ ζήσω· χω
συνεσταύρωμαι· ζῶ
δὲ οὐκέτι ἐγώ· ζῇ δὲ
ἐν ἐμοὶ χς· ὃ δὲ νῦν
ζῶ ἐν σαρκί· ἐν πί

στει ζῶ τῇ τοῦ υἱοῦ
τοῦ θυ τοῦ ἀγαπή
σαντός με· καὶ πα
ραδόντος· ἑαυτὸν
ὑπὲρ ἐμοῦ·

τῇ β´ τῆς κβ´ ἑβδομάδος
πρὸς Κολασσαεῖς·

Ἀδελφοί· χς ὑμᾶς
νεκροὺς ὄντας ἐν
τοῖς παραπτώμα
σι· καὶ τῇ ἀκροβυ
στίᾳ τῆς σαρκὸς ὑ
μῶν· συνεζωοποί
ησεν ὑμᾶς σὺν αὐ
τῷ· χαρισάμενος
ἡμῖν πάντα τὰ
παραπτώματα·
ἐξαλείψας τὸ καθ'
ἡμῶν χειρόγρα
φον· τοῖς δόγμασιν·
ὃ ἦν ὑπεναντίον
ἡμῖν· καὶ αὐτὸ ἦρεν

40. Luke 1:1–6. Gregory–Aland 165. A.D. 1292.

ROME, BIBLIOTECA VATICANA, BARB. GR. 541, FOL. 100 VERSO.

Parchment codex, containing the four Gospels in Greek and Latin, dated A.D. 1292, 12 × 8 inches (30.5 × 20.3 cm.), 215 leaves, two columns, 33–34 lines to a column.

This bilingual manuscript, with Greek in the left-hand column, Latin in the right-hand column, has decorated headpieces and intricate initial letters at the opening of each of the Gospels. The Plate shows the beginning of the Gospel according to Luke, with initial E in Greek, initial Q in Latin. The style of the Greek calligraphy is regarded by Devreesse to be typical of the area of Rhegina in south Italy.

A colophon on fol. 213 recto indicates that the manuscript was written at the town Ullano in Calabria by Romanus, an abbot of the monastery of St. Benedict, which was located in the 'Valley Grata,' the cost having been borne by Paul Mezzabarba, archbishop of Rossanensis [1287–1299/1300], during the reign of Carolus II [king of Sicily, Apulia, and Capua, 1289–1309]: *ἐγράφη ἡ παροῦσα βίβλος· | διὰ σπουδῆς καὶ συνδρομῆς | καὶ ἀναλωμάτων. τοῦ εὐλαβοῦς | ἀρχιεπισκόπου κυροῦ Παύλου τοῦ τὴν σι|ρὰν ἔχοντες· ἀπὸ τῶν Μετξα|βάρβων. πολιτῶν ρ̅ν̅ ἔτους | τρέχοντος ,ς̅[ψ]ω̅ χειρὶ | Ῥωμανοῦ ἱερομονάχου καὶ καθη|γουμένου. μονῆς τοῦ ἁγίου Βενε|δίκτου τοῦ Οὐλλάνου : τῆς Βάλλης | Γράτης : ἰνδικτιῶνος ς̅ : ῥηγεύοντος Κά|ρουλλου* (*sic*) *δευτέρου.*

In the Greek column the scribe occasionally writes one or more letters above the line (e.g. lines 8, 12, 15, 24). In order to keep the Latin text more or less parallel with the Greek, the final letter of a line may be extended to the right (*s* is extended in lines 16, 23, 24). In line 1 of the Latin column the word *quidem*, having been omitted, has been inserted (in abbreviated form) above the line.

BIBLIOGRAPHY: For other manuscripts written in Calabria, see Robert Devreesse, *Les manuscrits grecs de l'Italie méridionale* (Studi e testi, 183; Vatican City, 1955), pp. 37–43; cf. M.-L. Concasty, 'Manuscrits grecs originaires de l'Italie méridionale conservés à Paris,' *Atti dello VIII Congresso Internazionale di studi bizantini, I—Studi Bizantini e Neoellenici*, vii (1953), p. 29, n. 1, and Paul Canart, 'Le problème du style d'écriture dit "en as de pique" dans manuscrits italo-grecs,' *Atti del 4° congresso storico calabrese* (Naples, 1969), pp. 53–69. Concerning the monastery of St. Benedict de Ullano, cf. Pietro P. Rodotà, *Dell'origine, progresso, e stato presente del rito greco in Italia*, iii (Rome, 1763; reprinted Cosenza, 1961), pp. 68–78.

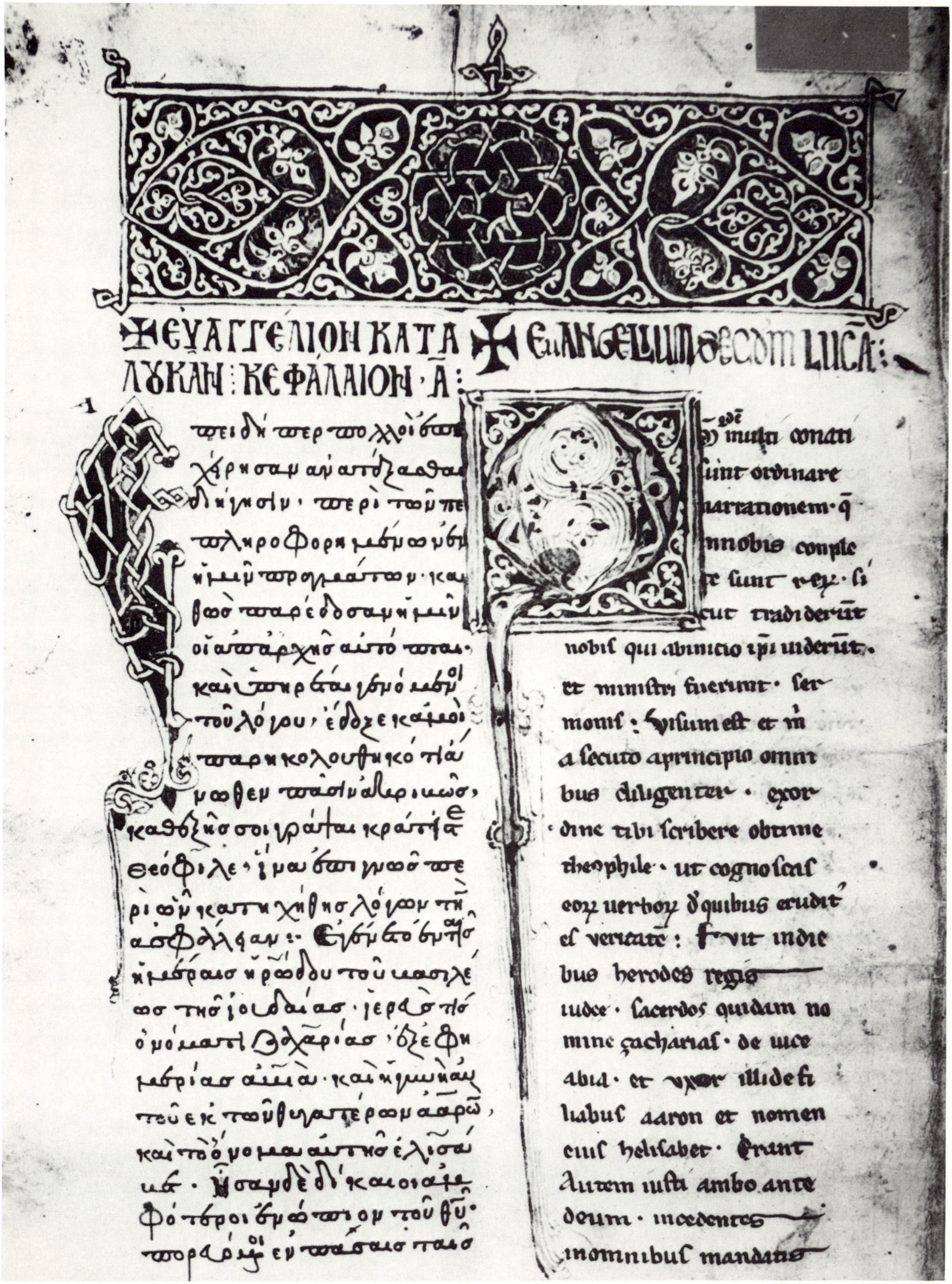
ΕΥΑΓΓΕΛΙΟΝ ΚΑΤΑ ΛΟΥΚΑΝ : ΚΕΦΑΛΑΙΟΝ Α :

EUANGELIUM SECDM LUCA :

1

[Q]uoniam quidem multi conati
sunt ordinare
narrationem q̄
in nobis comple
te sunt rer̄. si
cut tradiderūt
nobis qui abinicio ipsi uiderūt.
et ministri fuerunt. ser
monis : uisum est et m̄
a secuto aprincipio omni
bus diligenter. exor
dine tibi scribere obtime
theophile. ut cognoscas
eorū uerborū d̄quibus erudit̄
es ueritate : Fuit indie
bus herodes regis
iudee. sacerdos quidam no
mine zacharias. de uice
abia. et uxor illi de fi
liabus aaron et nomen
eius helisabet. Erant
Autem iusti ambo ante
deum. incedentes
inomnibus mandatis

41. Hebrews 11:33–38. Gregory–Aland 1922. A.D. 1317/1318.

FLORENCE, BIBLIOTECA LAURENZIANA, MS. PLUT. X, 19, FOL. 251 VERSO.

Parchment codex, containing the Pauline Epistles (with the commentary of Pseudo-Oecumenius), dated A.D. 1317/1318, 9¾ × 7¼ inches (24.7 × 18.5 cm.), 260 leaves, one column, framed by commentary on three sides (in upper, outer vertical, and lower margins).

A colophon in red ink (fol. 259 recto) indicates that the manuscript was written by *Τιμόθεος θύτης τε καὶ* Ναζιρέος (*sic*) ὁ Παραδεισίου ('Timothy, priest and monk, the son of Paradisios').[1]

The Scripture text is written in a careful hand, equipped with accent and breathing marks; the latter, as would be expected from the date, are round. The commentary of Pseudo-Oecumenius is written in smaller script with a good number of abbreviations, and the glosses are keyed by Greek numerals to the appropriate word or phrase in the Scripture text.

Ecclesiastical history knows two important writers named Oecumenius: one, who lived in the first half of the sixth century, was the author of the earliest extant Greek commentary on the Book of Revelation; the other was bishop of Tricca in Thessaly during the tenth century, to whom commentaries on Acts and the Pauline and Catholic Epistles have been ascribed. The comments given in codex 1922 are slightly abbreviated as compared with those printed in Migne, *Patrologia Graeca*, cxix, col. 421 A-C. A transcription of the first lines of the commentary on Heb. 11:33 f. is as follows:

ϛ̄θ̄ Οἱ πατριάρχαι. ὁ Ἡλίας, καὶ ἕτεροι πλείους ὁ Δαυΐδ: ρ̄ ὁ Δανιήλ, ὁ Σαμψών:—ᾱ οἱ ἀμφὶ τὸν Ἀνανίαν καὶ Ἀζαρίας καὶ Μισαήλ:—

β̄ Λέγει μὲν περὶ τῶν ἐπανελθόντων ἀπὸ Βαβυλῶνος: ἀσθενείας τ(ῆς) αἰχμαλωσίας λέγων· λέγει δὲ καὶ περὶ τοῦ Ἐζεκίου:—γ̄ οὐ μόνον, φησίν, ὅτι διὰ τῆς πίστεως, ὑπέστρεψαν, ἀπὸ τῆς ἐν Βαβυλῶνι αἰχμαλωσίας, ἀλλὰ καὶ τὰ πρόσοικα ἔθνη ἐνίκησαν:

δ̄ Ἡ Σωμανῖτις διὰ Ἐλισσαίου, καὶ πρὸ τούτου ἡ Σαραφθία δι' αὐτοῦ Ἡλίου:—

BIBLIOGRAPHY: Karl Staab, *Die Pauluskatenen nach den handschriftlichen Quellen untersucht* (Rome, 1926), p. 110; idem, *Pauluskommentare aus der griechischen Kirche aus Katenenhandschriften gesammelt und herausgegeben* (Münster/Westf., 1933), pp. 423–69; and Josef Schmid, 'Ökumenios der Bischof von Trikka,' *Byzantinisch-neugriechische Jahrbücher*, xiv (1938), pp. 322–30.

[1] For another manuscript written by this scribe, see Vogel-Gardthausen, op. cit. (footnote 149 above), p. 415. For the meaning of Ναζηραῖος as ascetic or monk, see Du Cange, *Glossarium ad Scriptores mediae et infimae Graecitatis*, i (Paris, 1688; reprinted, Graz, 1958), cols. 983 f., and Lampe, *Patristic Greek Lexicon* (Oxford, 1961), p. 896.

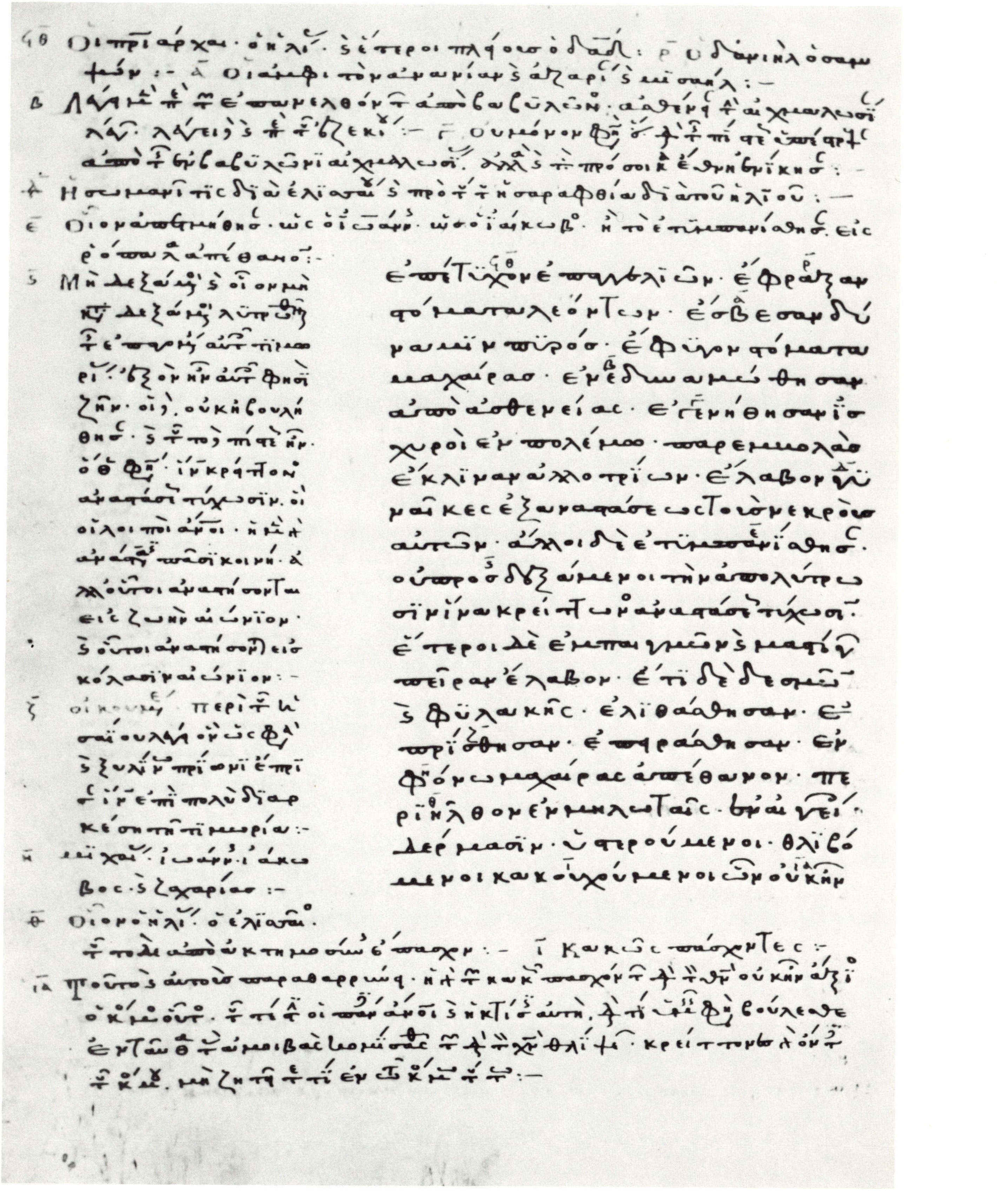

[illegible]

ἐπὶ τῇ χόνε ἐπαγγελιῶν· ἔφραξαν
στόματα λεόντων· ἔσβεσαν δύ-
ναμιν πυρός· ἔφυγον στόματα
μαχαίρας· ἐνεδυναμώθησαν
ἀπὸ ἀσθενείας· ἐγενήθησαν ἰσ-
χυροὶ ἐν πολέμῳ· παρεμβολὰς
ἔκλιναν ἀλλοτρίων· ἔλαβον γυναῖκες ἐξ ἀναστάσεως τοὺς νεκροὺς
αὐτῶν· ἄλλοι δὲ ἐτυμπανίσθησαν·
οὐ προσδεξάμενοι τὴν ἀπολύτρω-
σιν, ἵνα κρείττονος ἀναστάσεως τύχωσιν·
ἕτεροι δὲ ἐμπαιγμῶν καὶ μαστίγων
πεῖραν ἔλαβον· ἔτι δὲ δεσμῶν
καὶ φυλακῆς· ἐλιθάσθησαν· ἐ-
πρίσθησαν· ἐπειράσθησαν· ἐν
φόνῳ μαχαίρας ἀπέθανον· πε-
ριῆλθον ἐν μηλωταῖς· ἐν αἰγείοις
δέρμασιν· ὑστερούμενοι· θλιβό-
μενοι κακουχούμενοι ὧν οὐκ ἦν

[illegible]

42. Revelation 11:7–8 and 9. Gregory–Aland 2060. A.D. 1330/1331.

ROME, BIBLIOTECA VATICANA, GR. 542, FOL. 308 VERSO.

Parchment codex, containing the Book of Revelation (with the homilies of St. John Chrysostum and the commentary of Andrew of Caesarea on that book), dated A.D. 1330/1331, 11 × 8⅜ inches (28 × 21.3 cm.), 369 leaves (text of Revelation and commentary, folios 149–251), one column, 29 lines to a page.

Between about 563 and 614 Archbishop Andrew of Caesarea in Cappadocia wrote a commentary on the Book of Revelation which has some importance in exegetical history. From the standpoint of textual criticism, as was first recognized by Bengel, the commentary is useful in supplying information on one of the two later recensions of the Greek text of Revelation. The uncertainty of several minuscule texts of the Apocalypse is partly due to glosses that have crept into them from adjoining sections of Andrew's commentary.

The scribe of MS. 2060 alternates sections of Scripture text with sections of Andrew's commentary; he indicates the beginning of each section by enlarging the initial letter, extending it into the left-hand margin, and prefixing (in red ink, now much faded) at the end of the preceding line the word *κείμενον* ('text') or *ἑρμν* or *ἑρμηνεία* ('commentary'). In the left-hand margin attention is drawn to the Scripture text by a series of stylized sigla arranged vertically.

In Rev. 11:7 the manuscript, in company with MS. 1 and a few other witnesses, omits the words *καὶ ἀποκτενεῖ αὐτούς*, which are read by most of the other witnesses.

Transcription of Andrew's commentary, lines 12 ff.:

Μετὰ τὸ διαμαρτυράσθαι αὐτούς, φησί, τὴν τῆς (MS. *τὴν*) *ἀπά|της ἀποφυγὴν* (MS.–*γεῖν*) *τὸ θήριον, δηλαδὴ ὁ ἀντίχριστος, | ἐκ τῶν σκοτ(ε)ινῶν καὶ βυθίων χωρίων τῆς γῆς ἐ|ξιών, ἐν οἷς ὁ διάβολος καταδεδίκασται, ἀνε|λεῖ αὐτοὺς κατὰ τὴν θείαν συγχώρησιν καὶ ἄ|ταφα καταλείψει τὰ σώματα ἐν αὐτῇ τῇ Ἱερουσαλήμ, | δηλαδὴ τῇ παλαιᾷ καὶ κατεστραμμένῃ, ἐν ᾗ ὁ | κύριος πέπονθεν. ταύτῃ, ὡς ἔοικεν, καθιστῶν τὰ | βασίλεια κατὰ μίμησιν Δαυΐδ, οὗ υἱὸς Χριστός, ὁ ἀ|ληθινὸς θεὸς ἡμῶν κατὰ σάρκα γεγέννηται, | ἵνα κἂν τούτῳ ἑαυτὸν εἶναι τὸν Χριστὸν πιστώσηται, | πληροῦντα τὸ προφητικὸν λόγιον τὸ φάσκον· | ἀναστήσω τὴν σκηνὴν Δαυΐδ τὴν πεπτωκυῖαν, | καὶ τὰ κατεστραμμένα αὐτῆς ἀνοικοδομήσω, | ὅπερ πλανώμενοι Ἰουδαῖοι εἰς τὴν ἐκείνου πα|ρουσίαν ἐκλαμβάνουσιν:* +

BIBLIOGRAPHY: Andrew of Caesarea's Commentary on the Apocalypse, in Migne, *Patrologia Graeca*, cvi, col. 313; also in Josef Schmid, *Studien zur Geschichte des griechischen Apokalypse-Textes*, i (Münster/W., 1955), pp. 114 f.

καὶ πυρός, καὶ τῆς τῶν στοιχείων μεταποιήσε-
ως, καὶ τῶν ὁμοίων· τὸν δὲ πλάνον παραδειγ-
ματίσοντας, καὶ μηδὲν μή τι ὑπ' ἐκείνου μήτε
ὑφ' ἑτέροις πειθομένοις, ἄχρι τοῦ τῆς οἰκείας
προφητείας πληρώματος :+ κέφ …

Καὶ ὅταν τελέσωσι τὴν μαρτυρίαν αὐτῶν, τὸ θηρίον τὸ ἀναβαῖνον ἐκ τῆς ἀβύσσου, ποιήσει πόλε-
μον μετ' αὐτῶν, καὶ νικήσει αὐτούς· καὶ τὰ πτώματα αὐτῶν, ἐπὶ τῆς πλατείας τῆς πόλεως τῆς
μεγάλης, ἥτις καλεῖται πνευματικῶς Σόδομα καὶ
Αἴγυπτος· ὅπου καὶ ὁ κύριος αὐτῶν ἐσταυρώθη :+ …

Μετὰ τὸ διαμαρτύρασθαι αὐτοῖς φησὶ τὴν τῆς ἀπά-
της ἀποφυγήν, τὸ θηρίον δηλαδὴ ὁ ἀντίχριστος,
ἐκ τῶν σκοτεινῶν καὶ μυχίων χωρίων τῆς γῆς ἐξ-
ιών, ἐν οἷς ὁ διάβολος καταδεδίκασται, ἀναι-
ρεῖ αὐτοὺς κατὰ τὴν θείαν συγχώρησιν· καὶ ἄ-
ταφα καταλείψει τὰ σώματα· ἐν αὐτῇ τῇ Ἱερουσαλὴμ
δηλαδὴ τῇ παλαιᾷ, καὶ κατεστραμμένῃ ἐν ᾗ ὁ
κύριος πέπονθεν· ταύτης ὡς ἔοικεν καθέξων τὰ
βασίλεια, κατὰ μίμησιν δὲ Δαβὶδ οὗ ἐκ σπέρματος Χριστὸς ὁ ἀ-
ληθινὸς Θεὸς ἡμῶν κατὰ σάρκα γεγέννηται·
ἵνα κἀν τούτῳ ἑαυτὸν εἶναι τὸν Χριστὸν πιστώσηται,
πληρῶν τὸ τοῦ προφητικὸν λόγιον τὸ φάσκον·
ἀναστήσω τὴν σκηνὴν Δαβὶδ τὴν πεπτωκυῖαν,
καὶ τὰ κατεστραμμένα αὐτῆς ἀνοικοδομήσω·
ὅπερ παραμένοντες Ἰουδαῖοι, εἰς τὴν ἐκείνου πα-
ρουσίαν ἐκλαμβάνουσιν :+ κέφ …

Καὶ βλέπουσιν ἐκ τῶν λαῶν καὶ φυλῶν καὶ γλωσσῶν
καὶ ἐθνῶν τὰ πτώματα αὐτῶν, ἡμέρας τρεῖς

43. Romans 14:22–23; 16:25–27; 15:1–2. Gregory–Aland 223. xiv cent.

Ann Arbor, University of Michigan, ms. 35, fol. 144 recto.

Parchment codex, containing Acts, the Pauline and the Catholic Epistles, with lacunae, xiv century, 11⅛ × 8⅜ inches (28.2 × 21.3 cm.), 376 leaves, one column, 22–23 lines to a page.

According to K. W. Clark, 'This Ms. is a beautiful piece of bookmaking—one of the finest, and is still in an excellent state of preservation, though three leaves have been lost. It is composed of a fine quality of parchment of ivory tint, is written in an elegant hand throughout with ornamental initials and titles in gold, has been brilliantly illuminated with a headpiece in blue, red, green and gold before every book (II Cor., Eph., Heb. lack their first leaves), and was originally well bound in its present stamped reddish-brown leather over wooden boards.' It was unusual for so much expense and care to be expended on a copy of the Praxapostolos, as compared with the Gospels.

In 1864 the Revd. Reginald H. Barnes, Prebendary of Exeter, acting as agent for the Baroness Burdett-Coutts, bought codex 223, with other manuscripts, from a dealer at Janina in Epirus. It was acquired by the University of Michigan in 1922. While the manuscript was in England one of von Soden's helpers collated it in selected passages in the Pauline Epistles; Clark, who published a collation of the entire manuscript, found 62 errors in 229 readings of von Soden's list.

At the end of Jude a colophon (fol. 367 verso) written in gold reads: κ(ύρι)ε Ἰ(ησο)ῦ Χ(ριστ)ὲ υἱὲ τοῦ θ(εο)ῦ, ἐλέησόν με τὸν πολυαμάρτητον Ἀντώνϊον τάχα καὶ μοναχὸν τὸν μαλακήν.[1] The scribe writes a large and flowing hand, and leaves wide margins. Enlarged initial letters, extending into the left-hand margin, mark new paragraphs. Diaeresis sometimes stands over ι and υ even when they are alone in a syllable. Lectionary equipment is provided (see §29); opposite line 17 in the left-hand margin is ἀρχ(ή), and in the right-hand margin is the notation that Rom. 15:1 ff. is to be read on the fifth σάββατον as well as the lesson appointed for the seventh κυριακή. In the lower margin stands the τίτλος for the 18th κεφάλαιον, beginning at Rom. 15:1, namely περὶ τῆς μιμήσεως τῆς τοῦ Χ(ριστο)ῦ ἀνεξϊκακίας ('Concerning the imitation of the forebearance of Christ').

The doxology, which stands traditionally as Rom. 16:25–27 (so ℵ B C D 81 1739 *al* and the Textus Receptus), occurs after 14:23 in this manuscript (as well as in L Ψ 614 and most Byzantine mss.).[2]

Bibliography: Description and collation in Kenneth W. Clark, *Eight American Praxapostoloi* (Chicago, 1941).

[1] Antonios of Malaka is credited with having written two other manuscripts of the New Testament, Gregory–Aland 1305 and *l*279; see M. Vogel and V. Gardthausen, *Die griechischen Schreiber des Mittelalters und der Renaissance* (Leipzig, 1909; reprinted Hildesheim, 1966), p. 38.

[2] For a succinct discussion of the textual problems concerning the position of the doxology, see B. M. Metzger, *A Textual Commentary on the Greek New Testament* (London, 1971), pp. 533–6; for a fuller discussion, see Harry Gamble, Jr., *The Textual History of the Letter to the Romans* (Grand Rapids, 1977), pp. 129–32.

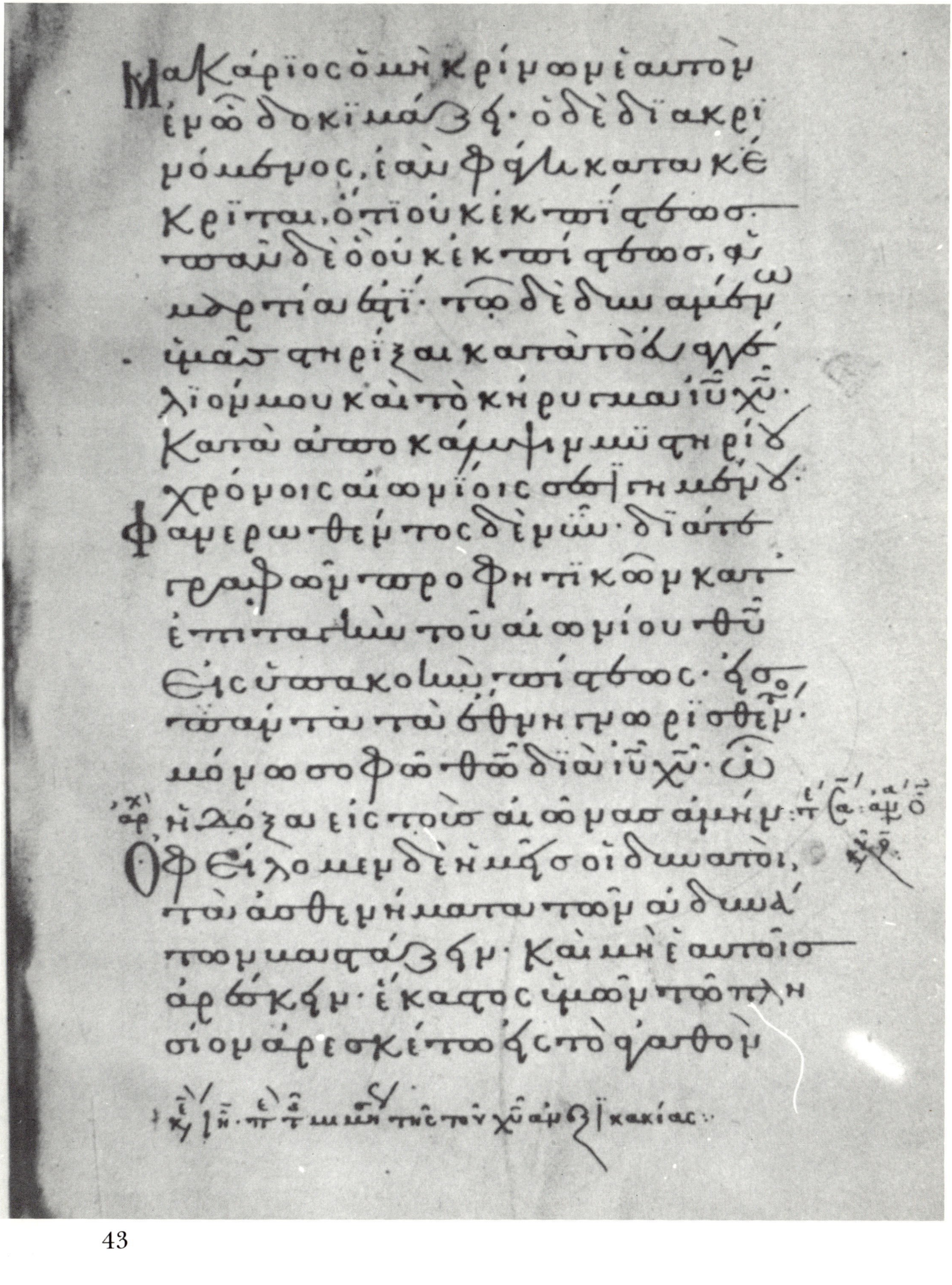
Μακάριος ὁ μὴ κρίνων ἑαυτὸν
ἐν ᾧ δοκιμάζει· ὁ δὲ διακρι-
νόμενος, ἐὰν φάγῃ κατακέ-
κριται, ὅτι οὐκ ἐκ πίστεως·
πᾶν δὲ ὃ οὐκ ἐκ πίστεως, ἁ-
μαρτία ἐστί· τῷ δὲ δυναμένῳ
ὑμᾶς στηρίξαι κατὰ τὸ εὐαγγέ-
λιόν μου καὶ τὸ κήρυγμα ἰυ̅ χυ̅·
κατὰ ἀποκάλυψιν μυστηρίου
χρόνοις αἰωνίοις σεσιγημένου·
φανερωθέντος δὲ νῦν· διά τε
γραφῶν προφητικῶν κατ᾽
ἐπιταγὴν τοῦ αἰωνίου θυ̅
εἰς ὑπακοὴν πίστεως· εἰς
πάντα τὰ ἔθνη γνωρισθέν-
τος μόνῳ σοφῷ θῷ διὰ ἰυ̅ χυ̅· ᾧ
ἡ δόξα εἰς τοὺς αἰῶνας ἀμήν·
Ὀφείλομεν δὲ ἡμεῖς οἱ δυνατοί,
τὰ ἀσθενήματα τῶν ἀδυνά-
των βαστάζειν· καὶ μὴ ἑαυτοῖς
ἀρέσκειν· ἕκαστος ὑμῶν τῷ πλησίον ἀρεσκέτω εἰς τὸ ἀγαθὸν

43

44. I Peter 5:12–14. Gregory–Aland 1022. xiv cent.

BALTIMORE, WALTERS ART GALLERY, MS. 533, FOL. 107 VERSO.

Parchment codex, containing Acts, the Catholic and the Pauline Epistles, xiv century, 9 3/16 × 6 3/4 inches (23.3 × 17.1 cm.), 360 leaves, one column, average of 25 lines to a page.

K. W. Clark describes 1022 as 'an impressive codex, containing as it does twenty-one miniatures, a portrait before each book (two before I Thess.). The miniature before II Cor. has been cut out, while before I Tim. there is space for a miniature on a later supplied leaf replacing the lost Folio 267.' The scribe provides *ὑποθέσεις* for the Catholic and the Pauline Epistles, *κεφάλαια* and *τίτλοι* for the Pastoral Epistles and Hebrews, occasional indications of the number of *στίχοι*, and lectionary notes in the margins. Folios 314–360 contain extensive lection tables by a later hand (xv century?). A corrector has made many corrections throughout the manuscript.

The Plate shows a miniature of the Apostle Peter, with nimbus, holding a closed roll. The text of I Pet. 5:12–14, which agrees with the Textus Receptus, is followed by the subscription *Πέτρου ἐπιστολὴ καθολικὴ, ά· ἐγράφη ἀπὸ Ῥώμης· στίχων σλϛ*.

The hypothesis prefixed to 2 Peter (*ὑπόθεσις τῆς Πέτρου β̄ ἐπιστολῆς*) reads as follows: *'Επειδὴ καὶ ταύτην πάλιν ὁ Πέτρος ἐπιστέλλει τοῖς ἤδη πιστεύσασιν· ἔστι δὲ ἡ ἐπιστολή. ὑπόμνησις τῶν πρώτων· εἰδὼς γὰρ ταχεῖαν ἑαυτοῦ ἔσεσθαι τὴν ἀνάλυσιν τοῦ σώματος· ἐσπούδασε* (final *ν* has been erased) *πάντας ὑπομνῆσαι περὶ ὧν κατηχήθησαν τὴν διδασκαλίαν· καὶ πρῶτον μὲν περὶ τῆς πίστεως ἐξηγεῖται· δεικνὺς ταύ* . . .[1]

BIBLIOGRAPHY: Description and collation in Kenneth W. Clark, *Eight American Praxapostoloi* (Chicago, 1941). For a discussion of the miniatures, see Sirarpie Der Nersessian, 'The Praxapostolos of the Walters Art Gallery,' *Gatherings in Honor of Dorothy E. Miner*, ed. by Ursula E. McCracken et al. (Baltimore, 1974), pp. 39–50.

[1] For the text of the entire hypothesis, see H. von Soden, *Die Schriften des Neuen Testaments in ihrer ältesten erreichbaren Textgestalt*, i (Berlin, 1902), p. 336.

ρῶν· ταύτην εἶναι ἀληθῆ χά
ριν τοῦ θεοῦ, εἰς ἣν ἑστήκατε·
ἀσπάζεται ὑμᾶς ἡ ἐν βαβυ
λῶνι συνεκλεκτή· καὶ μάρκος
ὁ υἱός μου· ἀσπάσασθε ἀλλήλους
ἐν φιλήματι ἀγάπης· εἰρήνη
ὑμῖν πᾶσι τοῖς ἐν χριστῷ ἰησοῦ,
ἀμήν:- πέτρου ἐπιστολὴ καθολικὴ α'
ἐγράφη ἀπὸ ῥώμης· στίχων· σλϛ'

ὑπόθεσις τῆς πέτρου
β' ἐπιστολῆς:-
Ἐπειδὴ καὶ ταύ
την πάλιν ὁ πέτρος
ἐπιστέλλει· τοῖς
ἤδη πιστεύσασι·
ἔστι δὲ ἡ ἐπιστολὴ·
ὑπόμνησις τῶν
πρώτων· εἰδὼς
γὰρ ταχεῖαν ἑαυτοῦ ἔσεσθαι τὴν
ἀνάλυσιν τοῦ σώματος· ἐσπού
δασε πάντας ὑπομνῆσαι περὶ
ὧν κατηχήθησαν τὴν διδασκα
λίαν· καὶ πρῶτον μὲν περὶ τῆς
πίστεως ἐξηγεῖται· δεικνὺς τὰ

45. Luke 2:33–50. Gregory–Aland 69. xv cent.

LEICESTER, TOWN MUSEUM, MUNIMENT ROOM, COD. $\frac{6D32}{1}$, FOL. 39 RECTO.

Parchment and paper codex,[1] containing the New Testament, with lacunae[2] (Gospels, Pauline Epistles [including Hebrews], Acts, Catholic Epistles, and Revelation[3]), xv century, 14⅞ × 10⅝ inches (37.8 × 27 cm.), 213 leaves, one column, 37 and 38 lines to a page.

From a variety of data it appears certain that the name of the scribe of codex 69 was Emmanuel, a Greek originally from Constantinople and then residing in England, who occupied himself in the transcribing of classical and Biblical texts.[4] The manuscript was presented to George Neville, Archbishop of York (1465–72).

At the top of the first page stand the words Ειμι Ιλερμου Χαρκου, then in a later hand 'Thomas Hayne.' William Chark of Cambridge, who probably lived in the reign of Elizabeth I, entered changes of readings in the margins of the manuscript. About the middle of the seventeenth century it was the property of Thomas Hayne of Trussington, who gave the volume to the Leicester Library in 1640.

The scribe of MS. 69 seems to have used a reed rather than a pen, and the style of writing is most peculiar. The smooth and rough breathing marks are often very hard to distinguish, and ε is usually placed in a recumbent position, so much resembling α that it is not always clear which was intended. Scrivener, who made a careful collation of the codex, declares: 'We cannot praise the care of the scribe in copying this MS. Many words occur which are only begun, broken off perhaps after the first syllable, and I have counted the large number of 74 omissions from ὁμοιοτελευτον and the like causes. . . . The acute accent is much used where the grave is commonly written by others. The vowels ι and υ have mostly a single dot over them. . . . This copy is remarkable for always writing ιησους at full length up to John xxi.15, where we meet with ι̅ς̅, and in 41 other places, 19 of which are in the Acts.'[5]

Textually cod. 69 is most remarkable. Although it dates from the fifteenth century, the type of text which it contains has been identified as Caesarean, resembling, in the Gospels, that used by Origen and Eusebius. It belongs to Family 13 (the Ferrar group), and in spite of its date is one of the best of the group. (See also Plate 36.)

The Plate shows the page reduced in size.

BIBLIOGRAPHY: Collation in Frederick Henry [A.] Scrivener, *An Exact Transcript of the Codex Augiensis . . . to which is added a Full Collation of Fifty other Manuscripts . . .* (Cambridge, 1859); William Hugh Ferrar, *A Collation of Four Important Manuscripts of the Gospels . . .*, ed. by T. K. Abbott (Dublin, 1877); J. Rendel Harris, *The Origin of the Leicester Codex of the New Testament* (London, 1887).

1 The codex is written on 91 leaves of parchment and 122 of coarse paper, arranged so that usually two parchment leaves are followed by three paper leaves. The paper is of such poor quality that four of the leaves would bear writing only on one side.

2 The manuscript begins at Matt. 18:15; after Acts 10:45, *πιστοί*, we read in the same line, with no break, *οὐρανόθεν*, 14:17, the intervening material being entirely omitted (probably it was lacking in the archetype); portions of Jude (7–25) and the Apocalypse (19:10–22:21) are lacking.

3 According to Hatch (*Facsimiles and Descriptions*, p. 260), the four Gospels originally stood at the end of the codex. Between Hebrews and the Acts of the Apostles are five pages containing (*a*) an exposition of the Creed and statement of the errors condemned by the seven general Councils, and (*b*) the traditional lives of the Apostles, followed by a description of the limits of the five Patriarchates.

4 Several other manuscripts have been identified as having been written by the same man; see M. R. James, 'The Scribe of the Leicester Codex,' *Journal of Theological Studies*, v (1903–4), pp. 445–7; cf. also Howard L. Gray, 'Greek Visitors to England in 1455–1456,' *Anniversary Essays in Mediaeval History by Students of Charles Homer Haskins* (Boston and New York, 1929), pp. 81–116, esp. 105–8.

5 Frederick Henry [A.] Scrivener, *An Exact Transcript of the Codex Augiensis . . .* (Cambridge, 1859), pp. xliii sq.

λουμένοις περὶ αὐτοῦ· καὶ εὐλόγησεν αὐτοὺς συμε-
ών, καὶ εἶπε πρὸς μαριὰμ τὴν μητέρα αὐτοῦ· ἰδοὺ οὗ-
τος κεῖται εἰς πτῶσιν καὶ ἀνάστασιν πολλῶν ἐν τῷ ἰσλ·
καὶ εἰς σημεῖον ἀντιλεγόμενον· καὶ σοῦ δὲ αὐτῆς τὴν
ψυχὴν διελεύσεται ῥομφαία· ὅπως ἂν ἀποκαλυ-
φθῶσιν ἐκ πολλῶν καρδιῶν διαλογισμοί· καὶ ἦν
ἄννα προφῆτις θυγάτηρ φανουὴλ ἐκ φυλῆς ἀσήρ·
αὕτη προβεβηκυῖα ἐν ἡμέραις πολλαῖς ζήσασα μετὰ
ἀνδρὸς ἔτη ἑπτὰ ἀπὸ τῆς παρθενίας αὐτῆς· καὶ αὐτὴ χήρα ὡς ἐτῶν ὀγδοήκοντα τεσσάρων· ἣ οὐκ ἀφί-
στατο ἀπὸ τοῦ ἱεροῦ· νηστείαις καὶ δεήσεσι λατρεύου-
σα νύκταν καὶ ἡμέραν· καὶ αὐτὴ αὐτῇ τῇ ὥρᾳ,
ἐπιστᾶσα ἀνθωμολογεῖτο τῷ κῶ καὶ ἐλάλει περὶ αὐτοῦ πᾶσι τοῖς προσδεχομένοις λύτρωσιν ἐν ἱερουσα-
λήμ· καὶ ὡς ἐτέλεσαν ἅπαντα κατὰ τὸν νόμον κυ,
ὑπέστρεψαν εἰς τὴν γαλιλαίαν εἰς τὴν πόλιν αὐτῶν
ναζαρέθ· τὸ δὲ παιδίον ηὔξανε καὶ ἐκραταιοῦτο
πνι· πληρούμενον σοφίας καὶ χάρις θυ ἦν ἐπ' αὐτό.
καὶ ἐπορεύοντο οἱ γονεῖς αὐτοῦ κατ' ἔτος εἰς ἱερουσαλὴμ τῇ ἑορτῇ τοῦ πάσχα· καὶ ὅτε ἐγένετο ἐτῶν
δώδεκα ἀναβάντων αὐτῶν εἰς ἱεροσόλυμα κατὰ τὸ
ἔθος τῆς ἑορτῆς καὶ τελειωσάντων τὰς ἡμέρας ἐν
τῷ ὑποστρέφειν αὐτοὺς ὑπέμεινεν ὁ ἰησοῦς ὁ παῖς
ἐν ἱερουσαλήμ, καὶ οὐκ ἔγνω ἰωσὴφ καὶ ἡ μήτηρ
αὐτοῦ· νομίσαντες δὲ αὐτὸν ἐν τῇ συνοδίᾳ εἶναι,
ἦλθον ἡμέρας ὁδόν· καὶ ἀνεζήτουν αὐτὸν ἐν τοῖς
συγγενεῦσιν καὶ τοῖς γνωστοῖς· καὶ μὴ εὑρόντες αὐτὸν ὑπέστρεψαν εἰς ἱερουσαλὴμ ἀναζητοῦντες αὐτόν.
καὶ ἐγένετο μεθ' ἡμέρας τρεῖς, εὗρον αὐτὸν ἐν τῷ
ἱερῷ καθεζόμενον ἐν μέσῳ τῶν διδασκάλων καὶ
ἀκούοντα αὐτῶν· καὶ ἐπερωτῶντα αὐτούς· ἐξί-
σταντο δὲ ἐπὶ τῇ συνέσει καὶ ταῖς ἀποκρίσεσιν αὐτοῦ πάντες οἱ ἀκούοντες αὐτοῦ· καὶ ἰδόντες αὐτὸν
ἐξεπλάγησαν· καὶ πρὸς αὐτὸν ἡ μήτηρ αὐτοῦ εἶπε· τέ-
κνον τί ἐποίησας ἡμῖν οὕτως· ἰδοὺ ὁ πὴρ σου καὶ
ἐγὼ ὀδυνώμενοι ζητοῦμέν σε· καὶ εἶπε πρὸς αὐτούς· τί
ὅτι ἐζητεῖτέ με· οὐκ ᾔδειτε ὅτι ἐν τοῖς τοῦ πρς μου
δεῖ εἶναί με·, καὶ αὐτοὶ οὐ συνῆκαν τὸ ῥῆμα ὃ ἐλάλησεν αὐτοῖς.

Continued from p. 60, Description of Plate 3

BIBLIOGRAPHY: Fragments 105–106 were edited (with facsimile) by W. G. Waddell in the *Journal of Theological Studies*, xl (1944), pp. 158–61; fragments 1–113, by Françoise Dunand, 'Papyrus grecs bibliques (Papyrus F. Inv. 266), Volumina de la Genèse et du Deutéronome (Introduction),' *Recherches d'archéologie, de philologie et d'histoire*, xxvii (Cairo, 1966), and *Études de papyrologie*, ix (Cairo, 1971), pp. 81–150; and Zaki Aly, *Three Rolls of the Early Septuagint: Genesis and Deuteronomy* (Papyrologische Texte und Abhandlungen, 27; Bonn, 1980). For textual analysis of Rahlfs 848, see John W. Wevers in *Catholic Biblical Quarterly*, xxxix (1977), pp. 240–4, and, in greater detail, idem, *The Text History of the Greek Deuteronomy* (Göttingen, 1978), pp. 64–85.

Continued from p. 62, Description of Plate 4

BIBLIOGRAPHY: C. H. Roberts, *An Unpublished Fragment of the Fourth Gospel in the John Rylands Library* (Manchester: The Manchester University Press, 1935); republished, with slight alterations, in the *Bulletin of the John Rylands Library*, xx (1936), pp. 45–55, and again, with bibliography of reviews and opinions expressed by other scholars, in C. H. Roberts, *Catalogue of the Greek and Latin Papyri in the John Rylands Library*, vol. iii (Manchester, 1938), pp. 1–3.

Continued from p. 62, Description of Plate 5

BIBLIOGRAPHY: C. Bradford Welles, 'The Yale Genesis Fragment,' *Yale University Library Gazette*, xxxix (1964), pp. 1–8, with two plates; re-edited in J. F. Oates, A. E. Samuel, C. B. Welles, *Yale Papyri in the Beinecke Rare Book and Manuscript Library*, i (New Haven–Toronto, 1967), pp. 3–8; C. H. Roberts, 'P. Yale 1 and the Early Christian Book,' *Essays in Honor of C. Bradford Welles* (American Studies in Papyrology, 1; New Haven, 1966), pp. 25–28.

BIBLIOGRAPHY

THE following is a selected bibliography of works dealing with various aspects of Greek palaeography. The titles are arranged chronologically under the headings 'General Works,' 'Papyrology,' 'Codicology,' and 'Collections of Facsimiles of Greek Manuscripts.' For other titles, particularly of older works, see §§2 and 3.

GENERAL WORKS

V. GARDTHAUSEN, *Griechische Palaeographie*, 2nd ed.: I. Band, *Das Buchwesen im Altertum und im byzantinischen Mittelalter* (Leipzig, 1911); II. Band: *Die Schrift, Unterschriften und Chronologie im Altertum und im byzantinischen Mittelalter* (Leipzig, 1913), xii+243 pp., viii+516 pp.

E. MAUNDE THOMPSON, *An Introduction to Greek and Latin Palaeography* (Oxford, 1912), xvi+600 pp.

PAUL MAAS, *Griechische Palaeographie*, in Alfred Gercke and Eduard Norden's *Einleitung in der Altertumswissenschaft*, I, 9 (Leipzig, 1924), pp. 69–81.

WILHELM SCHUBART, *Griechische Palaeographie*, in Ivan von Müller, and W. Otto's *Handbuch der Altertumswissenschaft*, I, 4, 1 (Munich, 1925), 184 pp.

ANTONIOS SIGALAS, Ἱστορία τῆς Ἑλληνικῆς Γραφῆς (Thessaloniki, 1934), vii+327 pp.; 2nd ed. (1974), xv+383 pp.

L. GONZAGA DA FONSECA, *Epitome introductionis in palaeographiam Graecam* (*Biblicam*), ed. altera (Rome, 1944), 132 pp.

ROBERT DEVREESSE, *Introduction à l'étude des manuscrits grecs* (Paris, 1954), viii+347 pp.

B. A. VAN GRONINGEN, *Short Manual of Greek Palaeography* (Leiden, 1940; 3rd edition, 1963), 66 pp.+12 plates.

GUGLIELMO CAVALLO, *Ricerche sulla maiuscola biblico* (Florence, 1967), xvi+152 pp.+115 plates.

ELPIDIO MIONI, *Introduzione alla paleografia greca* (Studi bizantini e neogreci [dell'] Università di Padova, 5; Padua, 1973), viii+140 pp.+30 plates.

AURORA LEONE, *L'evoluzione della scrittura nei papiri greci del Vecchio Testamento* (Papyrologica Castroctaviana, Studia et textus, 5; Barcelona, 1975), 50 pp.+7 plates.

La paléographie grecque et byzantine, Paris, 21–25 Octobre 1974 (Colloques internationaux du Centre National de la Recherche scientifique, nr. 559; Paris, 1977).

PAPYROLOGY

F. G. KENYON, *The Palaeography of Greek Papyri* (Oxford, 1899), viii+160 pp.

WILHELM SCHUBART, *Einführung in die Papyruskunde* (Berlin, 1918), 508 pp.

ARISTIDE CALDERINI, *Manuale di papirologie antica Graeca e Romana* (Milan, 1938), 5+196 pp.

A. BATAILLE, *Les papyrus* (Traité d'études byzantines 2; Paris, 1955), 95 pp.+14 plates.

ERIC G. TURNER, *Greek Papyri; an Introduction* (Oxford, 1968), ix+220 pp. Includes a comprehensive listing of the principal editions of papyri.

ORSOLINA MONTEVECCHI, *La Papirologia* (Manuali universitari; I, Per lo studio della scienze dell'antichità; Turin, 1973), xvi+544+184 pp.

KURT ALAND, *Repertorium der griechischen christlichen Papyri*. I, *Biblische Papyri. Altes Testament, Neues Testament, Varia, Apokryphen* (Patristische Texte und Studien, 18; Berlin and New York, 1976), xiv+473 pp.

JOSEPH VAN HAELST, *Catalogue des Papyrus littéraires juifs et chrétiens* (Paris, 1976), xi+424 pp.

CODICOLOGY

C. H. Roberts, 'The Codex,' *Proceedings of the British Academy*, xl (1954), pp. 169–204. A revised edition is in preparation.

A. Dain, *Les manuscrits* (Paris, 1949); nouvelle édition revue (Paris, 1964), 197 pp.

Tönnes Kleberg, *Buchhandel und Verlagswesen in der Antike* (Darmstadt, 1967), xii+121 pp.

T. C. Skeat, 'Early Christian Book-Production: Papyri and Manuscripts,' *The Cambridge History of the Bible*; ii, *The West from the Fathers to the Reformation*, ed. by G. W. H. Lampe (Cambridge, 1969), pp. 54–79.

James M. Robinson, 'On the Codicology of the Nag Hammadi Codices,' *Les textes de Nag Hammadi: Colloque du Centre d'Histoire des Religions (Strasbourg, 23–25 octobre 1974)*, ed. by Jacques-É. Ménard (Leiden, 1975), pp. 15–31.

Eric G. Turner, *The Typology of the Early Codex* (Philadelphia, 1977), xxiii+188 pp.

Léon Gilissen, *Prolégomènes à la codicologie; Recherches sur la construction des cahiers et la mise en page des manuscrits médiévaux* (Ghent, 1977), 252 pp., 63 fig., 97 plates.

Kurt Treu, ed., *Studia Codicologica* (*Texte und Untersuchungen*, Band 124; Berlin, 1977), ix+509 pp.+28 plates.

James M. Robinson, 'The Future of Papyrus Codicology,' *The Future of Coptic Studies*, ed. by Robert McL. Wilson (Leiden, 1979), pp. 23–70.

F. Gastaldelli, 'Orientamenti bibliografici di codicologia e critica testuale,' *Salesianum*, xli (1979), pp. 115–39 [classified list of 326 titles dealing with codicology].

COLLECTIONS OF FACSIMILES OF GREEK MANUSCRIPTS

Ch. Graux and A. Martin, *Fac-similés de manuscrits grecs d'Espagne* (Paris, 1891), vii+127 pp.

Henri Omont, *Fac-similés des manuscrits grecs datés de la Bibliothèque Nationale du IXe au XIVe siècle* (Paris, 1891), xii+24 pp.+100 plates.

Henri Omont, *Fac-similés des plus anciens manuscrits grecs en onciale et en minuscule de la Bibliothèque Nationale du ive au xiie siècle* (Paris, 1892), 18 pp.+50 plates.

Henri Omont, *Très anciens manuscrits grecs bibliques et classiques de la Bibliothèque Nationale . . .* (Paris, 1896), 20 plates.

The Palaeographical Society, *Facsimiles of Manuscripts and Inscriptions . . .*, First Series (London, 1873–1883), 260 plates; Second Series (London, 1884–1894), 205 plates; *Indexes* (1901), 63 pp.

F. G. Kenyon, *Facsimiles of Biblical Manuscripts in the British Museum* (London, 1900), vi pp.+25 plates.

The New Palaeographical Society, *Facsimiles of Ancient Manuscripts . . .*, First Series (London, 1903–1912), 250 plates; *Indexes* (1914), 50 pp.; Second Series (London, 1913–1930), 202 plates; *Indexes* (1932), 43 pp.

Gregorius Cereteli and Sergius Sobolevski, *Exempla codicum Graecorum litteris minusculis scriptorum annorumque notis instructum*, vol. 1, *Codices Mosquenses* (Moscow, 1911), 43 plates; vol. 2, *Codices Petropolitani* (1913), 56 plates.

Pius Franchi de' Cavalieri and Hans Lietzmann, *Specimina codicum Graecorum Vaticanorum* (Bonn, 1910; editio iterata et aucta, Berlin and Leipzig, 1929), xvi pp.+50 plates.

H. J. Vogels, *Çodicum Novi Testamenti Specimina* (Bonn, 1929), 13 pp.+54 plates.

Wm. H. P. Hatch, *The Greek Manuscripts of the New Testament at Mount Sinai* (Paris, 1932), 12 pp.+78 plates.

Wm. H. P. Hatch, *The Greek Manuscripts of the New Testament in Jerusalem* (Paris, 1934), 12 pp.+66 plates.

L. Th. Lefort & J. Cochez, *Palaeografisch album van gedagteekende Grieksche minuskelhandschriften uit de IXe en X^e^ eeuw*, met enkele specimina van handschriften uit de XIe–XVIe eeuw (Louvain, 1934), 100 plates. (New printing with Latin title, 1943.)

KENNETH W. CLARK, *A Descriptive Catalogue of Greek New Testament Manuscripts in America* (Chicago, 1937), xxix+418 pp.+72 plates.

WM. H. P. HATCH, *The Principal Uncial Manuscripts of the New Testament* (Chicago, 1939), xiv+34 pp.+76 plates.

KIRSOPP LAKE and SILVA LAKE, *Dated Greek Minuscule Manuscripts to the Year 1200 A.D.* (Monumenta Palaeographica Vetera, First Series), Parts I–X (Boston, 1934–1939). Index Volume, ed. by Silva Lake (Boston, 1945), xxxv+185 pp. The 757 plates contain approximately 1000 facsimiles of folios from 401 manuscripts in 30 different libraries. The index volume contains indexes in 14 categories (including names of scribes).

WM. H. P. HATCH, *Facsimiles and Descriptions of Minuscule Manuscripts of the New Testament* (Cambridge, Massachusetts, 1951), xii+289 pp.

C. H. ROBERTS, *Greek Literary Hands, 350 B.C.–A.D. 400* (Oxford Palaeographical Handbooks; Oxford, 1955), xix+24 pp.

ALEXANDER TURYN, *Codices graeci Vaticani saeculis XIII et XIV scripti annorumque notis instructi. . . .* (Vatican City, 1964), xvi+206 pp.+205 plates.

M. WITTEK, *Album de paléographie grecque* (Ghent, 1967), 29 pp.+64 plates.

H. FOLLIERI, *Codices graeci Bibliothecæ Vaticanæ selecti temporum locorumque ordine digesti, commentariis et transcriptionibus instructi* (Exempla Scriptuarum . . ., iv; Città del Vaticano, 1969), 111 pp.+70 Tabl.

E. G. TURNER, *Greek Manuscripts of the Ancient World* (Oxford and Princeton, 1971), xiv+132 pp.

ALEXANDER TURYN, *Dated Greek Manuscripts of the Thirteenth and Fourteenth Centuries in the Libraries of Italy*, 2 vols. (Urbana, 1972), 265 plates depicting folios from 137 mss. from 19 libraries.

NIGEL [G.] WILSON, *Mediaeval Greek Bookhands; Examples selected from Greek Manuscripts in Oxford Libraries*, 2 vols. (Cambridge, Massachusetts, 1973), 38 pp.+88 plates.

GARY VIKAN, ed., *Illuminated Greek Manuscripts from American Collections; an Exhibition in Honor of Kurt Weitzmann* (Princeton, 1973), 231 pp., 67 MSS. from twenty collections.

DIETER HARLFINGER, *Specimina griechischer Kopisten der Renaissance*; I, *Griechen des 15. Jahrhunderts* (Berlin, 1974), 35 pp.+78 plates.

ELPIDIO MIONI and MARIAROSA FORMENTIN, *I codici greci in minuscola dei sec. IX e X della Biblioteca Nazionale Marciana* (Padua, 1975), 119 pp.+49 plates.

T. S. PATTIE, *Manuscripts of the Bible* (London, 1979), 36 pp.+18 plates.

RUTH BARBOUR, *Greek Literary Hands, A.D. 400–1600* (Oxford, in press), 72 pp., 110 plates.

ALEXANDER TURYN, *Dated Greek Manuscripts of the Thirteenth and Fourteenth Centuries in the Libraries of Great Britain* (Dumbarton Oaks Studies, vol. xvii; in press).

I. Index of Scripture Passages Shown in the Plates

	Plate
Genesis 14:12–15	5
Genesis 39:9–18	20
Genesis 42:7–19	11
Exodus 28:4–6	2
Deuteronomy 10:6–15	17
Deuteronomy 25:1–3	1
Deuteronomy 31:28–30; 32:1–7	3
Joshua 11:9–16	15
Psalm 27 [28]:6–7	30
Psalm 72 [73]:1–10*a*	27
Isaiah 13:3–10	21
Isaiah 61:1–5	34
Ezekiel 31:8–15	10
Matthew 3:10–11	38
Matthew 8:1–10	31
Matthew 27:3–5	33
Matthew 27:16–23	25
Mark 1:1–6	26
Mark 9:2–29	18
Mark 16:2–11	24
Mark 16:12–17	16
Luke 1:1–6	40
Luke 2:33–50	45
Luke 5:38–6:9	19
Luke 11:2–8	37
Luke 21:37–22:3	36
Luke 22:38–45	29
Luke 24:23–53	14
John 1:19–21	38
John 4:47–5:6	23
[John 7:53–8:11]	36
John 11:31–37	7
John 18:31–34, 37–38	4
John 19:10–16	33
Acts 8:36–38	22
Romans 14:22–23; 15:1–2	43
Romans 16:23	6
Romans 16:25–27	43
1 Corinthians 2:9–3:3	28
Galatians 2:16–20	39
Colossians 2:13–14	39
2 Thessalonians 3:11–18	13
Philemon 10–25	32
Hebrews 1:1–7	6
Hebrews 1:1–2:2	13
Hebrews 11:33–38	41
1 Peter 5:12–14	44
Jude 3–25	35
Revelation 3:19–4:1	12
Revelation 11:7–9	42

II. Index of Manuscripts Arranged According to Their Sigla

I. SIGLA ASSIGNED BY RAHLFS

Codex	*Plate*
G	15
L	20
Q	21
W	17
803	2
814	5
848	3
957	1
962	11
967	10
1098	30
1101	27

II. SIGLA ASSIGNED BY GREGORY AND/OR ALAND

Codex	*Plate*
$\mathfrak{p}^{46}$	6
$\mathfrak{p}^{52}$	4
$\mathfrak{p}^{66}$	7
$\mathfrak{p}^{75}$	9
ℵ	14
A	18
B	13
D	19
E	22
G	28
S	31
W	16
Θ	25
Ψ	24
047	23
0169	12
0212	8
69	45
124	36
165	40
223	43
461	26
623	35
700	37
892	29
1022	44
1739	32
1922	41
2060	42
*l*303	38
*l*562	33
*l*809	39

III. Index of Manuscripts Arranged According to Their Present Location

Plate

Ann Arbor: University of Michigan
MS. Inv. 6238 6
MS. 35 43
Baltimore: Walters Art Gallery
MS. 533 44
Cairo: University Library
MS. P. Fouad Inv. 266 3
Cambridge: University Library
MS. Nn. 2.41 19
Cologny-Geneva: Bibliotheca Bodmeriana
MS. Pap. 2 7
MS. Pap. XIV 9
Dresden: Sächische Landesbibliothek
MS. A 145b 28
Dublin: Chester Beatty Library
MS. Pap. V 11
Florence: Bibliotheca Laurenziana
MS. Plut. X. 19 41
Jerusalem: Palestine Archeological Museum
MS. 7Q1 LXX Ex. 2
Jerusalem: Greek Patriarchal Library
MS. Saba 247 34
Leicester: Town Museum, Muniment Room
MS. $\frac{6D32}{I}$ 45
Leiden: University Library
MS. Voss. Gr. Q8 15
Leningrad: State Public Library
MS. Gr. 219 26
London: British Library
MS. Add. 33277 29
MS. Add. 43725 14
MS. Egerton 2610 37
MS. Royal, I.D.v–viii 18
Manchester: John Rylands Library
MS. P. Ryl. 457 4
MS. P. Ryl. 458 1

Plate

Milan: Bibliotheca Ambrosiana
MS. O 39 Sup 30
Moscow: Historical Museum
MS. cod. 129 27
Mount Athos:
MS. Laura 172 (B′ 52) 24
MS. Laura 184 (B′ 64) 32
New Haven: Yale University, Beinecke Library
MS. P. Yale 1 5
MS. Dura Parch. 24 8
Oxford: Bodleian Library
MS. Laud. 35 22
Princeton: University Library
MS. Scheide Pap. 1 10
MS. Garrett 1 23
Princeton: Theological Seminary Library
MS. Pap. 5 12
MS. 11.21.1900 38
Rome: Biblioteca Vaticana
MS. Gr. 354 31
MS. Gr. 542 42
MS. Gr. 1209 13
MS. Gr. 1650 35
MS. Gr. 2125 21
MS. Gr. 2138 33
MS. Barb. Gr. 541 40
Sinai: Monastery of St. Catherine
MS. Gr. 286 39
Tiflis: Inst. rukop.
MS. Gr. 28 25
Vienna: Nationalbibliothek
MS. Gr. 31 20
MS. Gr. 188 36
Washington: Freer Gallery of Art
MS. 06.274 16
MS. Wash. I 17

IV. Palaeographic Index

abbreviations, 28, 29–31, 52, 106, 124
— chart of, 30
— by combination of letters, 29, 30, 64, 66, 80, 92
— by contraction, 29, 31, 36, 37
— by superposition of letters, 29, 66, 68, 70, 74, 76, 80
— by suspension of letters, 29, 30, 62, 66, 80, 84, 92, 98, 110, 112, 114, 120
accents, 12, 25, 28, 32, 74, 98, 102, 108, 110, 130, 138
— acute, 28, 70
— circumflex, 94
— double, 12, 114
— lack of, 76, 84, 86, 96, 104
alphabet, Armenian, 10
— Coptic, 10
— Cyrillic, 10
— Glagolitic, 10
— Gothic, 10
— Greek, 6–10, 23
— Semitic, 8, 10
amanuensis, 40
Ammonian sections, 42, 74, 86, 98, 106, 110, 120, 122
amulets, 35
Apostolos, 43, 126
apostrophe, 66, 68, 84
Aramaic, 33, 60
aspirates, *see* breathings
asterisk, 38, 80, 94, 98

'Biblical Uncial,' 24, 74, 76, 84, 86
'bilinearity,' 22
bilingual manuscripts, 55, 56, 88–89, 96, 104, 128
books, 14, 15
— order of in NT, 76, 82, 88
book-hand, 22, 24, 25
brackets, 22, 66, 70
breathings, 12, 25, 28, 32, 49, 74, 102, 108, 110, 138
— as guide to date of manuscript, 49
— forms of, 12
— lack of, 76, 86, 96, 104
— rough, 12, 68, 72, 80
— round, 130
— smooth, similar to mark of word division, 31, 84
— square, 28, 64, 98, 106
bone, as writing material, 3
boustrophedon style of writing, 7

'Cadmean letters,' 6
calligraphy, 22, 31 n. 56
cancel-dot, 22, 66, 122
cancel-stroke, 22, 114
canon tables, Eusebian, 42, 120
capital letters, 22, 23, 66, 104, 122
cartonnage, 60
catena, 48
chanting, 44, 116

chapter divisions, 40–43, 74, 96, 118
chi-rho monogram, 31, 84, 118
Christogram, 31, 84, 118
codex, 16, 17
— pocket-sized, 72
— reasons for adoption by Christians, 17
— single quire, 16 n. 30, 64
codicology, 3, 16 n. 29, 142
coins, 3, 34
cola, 39, 88, 96
collation of manuscripts, 52–53
colometry, 38–40, 88–89, 96
colophons, 20, 49, 102, 110, 112, 114, 118, 124, 128, 130, 134
columns, width of, 16
combinations of letters, 26, 27, 30
— as means of abbreviation, 29, 30
— chart of, 27, 30
comma, 32; *and see* punctuation
commentaries, 46, 48
— alternating with text, 132
— marginal, 48, 110, 130
contractions, 29, 31, 36, 37, 84, 102
Coptic uncial, 25, 74, 94
copying of manuscripts, 21–22, 25, 29
coronis, 77
corrections, scribal, 60, 66, 72, 74, 77, 78, 86, 96, 112, 114, 118, 122, 136
— different methods of, 66
— secondary position of, 22; *and see* cancel-dot, cancel-stroke
corrector, 22, 77, 86, 96, 136
critical signs, 78, 132
— asterisk, 38, 80, 94, 98
— brackets, 22, 66, 70
— dots, 38, 80, 102, 110
— expunging dot, 22, 66, 122
— fillers, 66, 70
— hexaplaric, 38, 80, 94, 108
— indicating word-division, 31, 62, 84
— lines in margin marking quotations, 74, 104
— lozenge, 32, 114
— marking spurious passages, 98, 106
— obelus, 38, 80, 98, 112
cruciform text, 98
cursive, 22, 23, 24, 64, 66, 84
— development from uncial, 24
— special form for book production, 24; *and see* minuscule

date of manuscripts, estimating, 49–51, 77–78
dated manuscripts, 110, 118, 126, 130, 132
— earliest minuscule, 102
— uncial, 110
decorated style, 24; *and see* 'Zierstil'
decorations, 74, 104, 114, 116, 122, 126, 128, 134
— zoomorphic, 114; *and see* illumination, ornamentation

deletions, 22, 66, 114, 122
deluxe editions, 15, 44–45
diaeresis, 12–13, 60, 64, 68, 72, 80, 82, 92, 96, 102, 134
— as a single dot, 138
Diatessaron, 66
dictation, 21–22
digamma, 7, 9
diorthotēs, 22; *and see* corrector
diplē, 32
dividers between words, 31, 62, 84
divisions, chapter, 40–42, 74, 96, 118
— paragraph, 32; *and see* paragraph division
— verse, 41–42
documentary hand, 72

elision, 13, 84
'en as de pique,' 28, 128
end fillers, 66
enlarged letters marking paragraphs, 32, 86; *and see* initial letters, enlarged
epigraphy, 3
erasures, 80, 114
Eusebian canons, 42, 74, 76, 78, 86, 98, 106, 110, 120, 122
Euthalian apparatus, 42–43, 118
Evangelarium, 43, 114, 124
expunging dot, 22, 66, 122

'Fettaugenmode,' 28
fillers at end of lines, 66

gematria, 9, 62
glossary, 48
glosses, 46, 47, 48, 88, 112, 130
gold ink, 15, 17, 18, 46, 124, 134
grave accent, 31, 62, 138; *and see* accents
Greek, pronunciation of, 11, 13, 22, 62
guidelines, 15, 66, 102

handwriting, Greek, 22–29
— deliberately archaized, 50
— evolution of as means of dating, 49–50
— non-literary, 72
— styles of, 24–29, 49, 50, 60, 74, 76, 84, 86, 94, 110
headings, chapter, 40–42, 98
— decorative, 15, 126, 128, 134
Hebrew letters, 6, 7, 8, 33, 34, 35, 38, 60, 108
'helps for readers,' 33, 43, 47, 94
hexameter line, as standard of measure, 38–39
Hexapla, 34, 38, 94, 108
— Tetragrammaton in, 35, 94, 108
Hexaplaric signs, 38, 80, 94, 108
hiatus, 13, 70
hypotheses, 43, 136

illuminated manuscripts, 92, 102, 134; *and see* decorations, miniatures, ornamentation
incipits, 44, 106, 114, 124, 126
— collation of, 53
— list of, 53 n. 153

indiction, 49, 110, 118
infralinear writing, 49
initial letters, 15, 74, 114, 124
— decorated, 120, 122, 128, 134
— enlarged, 32, 70, 86, 98, 102, 126, 132, 134
— zoomorphic, 114
ink, 17, 18, 44
— colored, 15, 17, 76, 84, 88, 92, 98, 102, 130, 132
— gold, 15, 17, 18, 46, 124, 134
— multiple colors in one manuscript, 18, 46, 74, 104, 114, 120, 122, 124, 134
— silver, 15, 17, 46, 92
inkstand, 18
interlinear manuscript, 104
iota adscript, 24, 28, 60, 62, 108, 122, 124
— subscript, 28
itacism, 13, 62

kai-compendium, 30, 66, 80, 92, 114, 120
kephalaia, 41, 98, 106, 110, 118, 134, 136

lectionaries, 30, 43–44, 53, 98, 114, 122, 124, 126
— beginning and/or end of lections noted, 43, 98, 106, 112, 134
— equipment or aids, 43, 84, 98, 106, 112, 114, 116, 124, 126, 134, 136
lector, 21, 114
lexica, 46, 47, 48
ligatures, 24, 27, 28, 49, 66, 92, 102, 116 n. 1, 122
— charts of, 27, 30
lozenge, 32, 114

magical formulae, 35
majuscule, 22
— 'Biblical majuscule,' 24, 74, 76, 86
manuscripts, Biblical, determining date of, 49–51
— earliest dated minuscule, 26, 102
— indexes, catalogs, and check-lists of, 4–5, 50, 54
— multi-lingual, 55–56, 88–89, 96, 104, 128
— minuscule, classification into periods, 26, 28, 29
— order of books in, 55, 82, 88
— statistics relating to, 26, 54–56
— transcription of, 20–22
manuscripts, dated, 110, 118, 126, 130, 132
manuscripts, with commentary, 48, 110, 130, 132
margin, extension of letters into, to mark paragraph, 68, 70, 76, 80, 84, 86, 98, 102, 120, 132, 134
marginal notes, 43, 46, 47, 48, 74, 78, 88, 94, 104, 106, 110, 112, 114, 118, 120, 122, 130, 134, 136, 138
marginal signs, *see* critical signs
marks, indicating word-division, 31, 62, 84
menologion, 44, 106, 124, 126
miniatures, 44–46, 92, 102, 122, 136; *and see* illuminated manuscripts
minium, 45
'minuscule bouletée,' 28
minuscule handwriting, 25–29
— letters, 22, 23, 24, 50
— manuscripts, classification into periods, 26, 28–29
musical notation, *see* neumes

neumes, 44, 98, 110, 116, 126
nomina divina, 37
nomina sacra, 36–37, 52, 66, 70, 72, 80, 92, 102
non-literary hands, 22, 72
notation ekphonétique, 44
nu, final, represented by horizontal line, 66, 68, 70, 80
— moveable, 13, 53
numerals, Greek, 7, 9, 53, 62

obelus, 38, 80, 98, 112
Oktoēchos, 44, 108
omission signs, *see* critical signs, deletions
onomasticon, 46, 47–48, 94
order of books in NT, 64, 76, 82, 88
ornamentation, 42, 45, 60, 62, 72, 120, 126, 128, 134; *and see* decorations, illumination, miniatures
— lack of, 74, 76
ostraca, 37, 54 n. 154

palaeography, aims and definition of, 3–4
— modern research tools for, 4–5
palimpsest, 18–19, 34, 108
pandect, 54
paper, 315, 106 n. 1, 138
papyrus, 3, 14, 22, 60, 62, 66, 68, 70, 72
— manufacture of, 14
paragraph division, 32, 82
— by extension into margin, 68, 70, 76, 80, 84, 86, 98, 102, 120, 132, 134
— critical marks indicating, 32, 70
—spaces indicating, 32, 66, 68
Paraklētikē, 44
parchment, 3, 14, 15, 17, 18, 22, 25
— purple, 17, 18, 46, 92
pen, 17, 18, 138
— use of brush or reed instead of, 17, 138
penknife, 18
'Perlschrift,' 28
petuḥot, 70
'Phoencian letters,' 6
'Pipi,' 35, 94, 108
potsherds, 3
Praxapostolos, 134
prickings, 15, 66
printing, 20, 26, 28, 29
prologues, *see* hypotheses, superscriptions, titles
— Euthalian, 43
pronunciation of Greek, *see* Greek, pronunciation of
prophetologion, 43, 116
pumice, 14, 18
punctuation, 31–32, 70, 74, 82, 84, 86, 98, 114
— lack of, 31, 74, 96
— marks, value of, 32
purple manuscripts, 17–18, 46, 92

question mark, 32, 114; *and see* punctuation
Quinta, 38 n. 87, 108
quire, 16
Qumran, 60
— date of papyrus fragments found at, 24 n. 41
— treatment of Tetragrammaton at, 33, 35
quotations, identified in margin, 118
— lines in margin indicating, 74, 104

reading, oral, 31, 31 n. 57; *and see* lector
recto, 15, 16 n. 31, 62, 70
red ink, 15, 17, 76, 84, 88, 98, 102, 124, 130, 132
reed, 17, 138
reference marks, *see* critical signs
roll, 15–16, 34, 60, 66, 136
roundels, 24
rubrics, 15, 98, 102, 106, 108, 124
ruler, 18
ruling, 14–15, 102
— patterns of as guide to identification, 15

scholia, 48, 110, 112
scribes, 18, 20, 21, 31, 32, 36
— more than one in same manuscript, 74, 76–77, 82, 86
— payment of, 39
— posture of, 21 n. 37
— tools of, 18
scriptio continua, 31
scriptorium, 21, 22
'sense-lines,' 39, 40, 88
separation, between words or sentences, 26, 31, 62, 84
Septima, 38 n. 87
Septuagint, 33, 35, 38, 60, 62, 70, 72, 80, 84, 92, 94, 102, 108, 116
serifs, 24, 24 n. 40, 60, 66, 76, 94
setumot, 70
Sexta, 38 n. 87
shorthand, Greek, 31
signs, critical, *see* critical signs
silver ink, 15, 17, 46, 92
Slavonic uncial, 25, 110
sortes sanctorum, 88
spaces, 26
— at end of line, 60, 84
— between words, 64, 66
— indicating paragraph divisions, 32, 66, 68
sponge, 18, 66
spurious passages, marks indicating, 98, 106
staurogram, 31, 84, 118
stichoi, 38–39, 64, 104, 120, 136
stichometry, 38–40
— Syriac, 39
stops, *see* punctuation
styles of handwriting, *see* handwriting, styles of
stylus, 18
subscriptions, 40, 74, 77, 98, 118, 120, 136
superposition of letters, 28, 29, 30, 66, 68, 70, 74, 76, 80
superscriptions, 40, 112, 136
suspension of letters, 29, 30, 62, 66, 80, 84, 92, 98, 110, 112, 114, 120
symbols, 29–31, 52; *and see* critical signs
synaxarion, 44, 106, 124, 126

talismans, 54
Tetragrammaton, 33–35, 60, 108
— in Greek letters, 35, 94, 108
Tetrapla, 38
titles, 40, 41, 74, 98, 114, 118, 120, 122, 134, 138; *and see* colophons, hypotheses, superscriptions, *titloi*
titloi, 41, 98, 106, 110, 118
trilingual manuscripts, 56

ultra-violet lamp, 18, 77
uncial, 10, 25, 29, 60, 66, 68, 72, 82, 84, 86, 88, 92, 96, 102, 104, 110
— 'Biblical,' 24, 74, 84, 86
— Coptic, 25, 74, 94
— handwriting, 24, 25
— letters, 22, 23, 28, 50, 114
— Slavonic, 25, 110

vellum, 14, 15, 74, 76, 86
— purple, 15, 17, 92
verse-division, 41–42
verso, 15, 16 n. 31, 60, 62, 70

wax tablets, 3
'Western' order of Gospels, 82, 88
word-division, ambiguity of in *scriptio continua*, 31
— marks indicating, 31, 62, 84
— rules for, 31
— spaces indicating, 64, 66
writing, direction of, 7
— implements, 18
— materials, types of, 3, 17

'Zierstil,' 24, 60

ἀναγνώστης, 21, 44
ἀρχή, 30, 43, 84, 98, 106, 122, 134
βαρύς, 12
βουστροφηδόν, 7
διορθωτής, 22
ϝοῖδα, 11
Ἰαώ, 35
Καδμήϊα γράμματα, 6
καθαρεύουσα, 11
κανόνες, 42
κεφάλαια, 41, 98, 106, 110, 118, 134, 136
κόμματα, 39
κῶλα, 39, 88, 96
ν ἐφελκυστικόν, 13
ὀκτώηχος, 44, 108
ὀξύς, 12

πανδέκτης, 54
ΠΙΠΙ, 35, 94, 108
πνεύματα, 12
ῥήματα 39, 120
στίγμη μέση, 12
στίγμη τελεία, 32
στίχος, 38, 39, 64, 104, 120, 136
σχόλια, 48
τέλος, 30, 43, 98, 106, 110, 112, 122
τίτλος, 41, 88, 98, 106, 110, 118, 134, 136
ὑπογραφαί, 40
ὑποθέσεις, 43, 136
ὑποστιγμή, 32
Φοινικήϊα γράμματα, 6
☧, 118